TORN
APART

TORN APART

How the Child Welfare System
Destroys Black Families—
and How Abolition Can
Build a Safer World

DOROTHY ROBERTS

BASIC BOOKS
New York

Cover design by Ann Kirchner
Cover images copyright © Gabriel (Gabi) Bucataru/Stocksy.com; © Elnur/Shutterstock.com
Cover copyright © 2022 by Hachette Book Group, Inc.

Basic Books
Hachette Book Group
1290 Avenue of the Americas, New York, NY 10104
www.basicbooks.com

Printed in the United States of America
First Edition: April 2022

Published by Basic Books, an imprint of Perseus Books, LLC, a subsidiary of Hachette Book Group, Inc. The Basic Books name and logo is a trademark of the Hachette Book Group.

The Hachette Speakers Bureau provides a wide range of authors for speaking events. To find out more, go to www.hachettespeakersbureau.com or call (866) 376-6591.

The publisher is not responsible for websites (or their content) that are not owned by the publisher.

Print book interior design by Linda Mark.

Library of Congress Cataloging-in-Publication Data
Names: Roberts, Dorothy E., 1956– author.
Title: Torn apart : how the child welfare system destroys black families—and how abolition can build a safer world / Dorothy Roberts.
Description: First edition. | New York : Basic Books, 2022. | Includes bibliographical references and index.
Identifiers: LCCN 2021036512 | ISBN 9781541675445 (hardcover) | ISBN 9781541675452 (ebook)
Subjects: LCSH: Child welfare—Government policy—United States. | African American families—Government policy. | African American families—Social conditions. | Racism in social services—United States. | Social work with African American children.
Classification: LCC HV741 .R6225 2022 | DDC 362.70973—dc23/eng/20211202

LC record available at https://lccn.loc.gov/2021036512

ISBNs: 9781541675445 (hardcover), 9781541675452 (ebook)

LSC-C

Printing 1, 2022

For my granddaughters, Akari and Josephine

Contents

PROLOGUE

SHATTERED BONDS

My book *Shattered Bonds: The Color of Child Welfare*, published in 2001, documented the racial realities of the child welfare system in America. At the time, more than a half million children had been taken from their parents and were in foster care. Black families were the most likely of any group to be torn apart. Black children made up nearly half of the US foster care population, although they constituted less than one-fifth of the nation's children. That made them four times as likely to be in foster care as white children. Nearly all the children in Chicago's foster care system were Black. The racial imbalance in New York City's foster care population was also mind-boggling: out of forty-two thousand children in the system at the end of 1997, only thirteen hundred were white, though a majority of the city's children were white. That year, one out of ten children in central Harlem had been placed in foster care.[1] Today, stark racial disparities continue to mark foster care in Chicago, New York, and other cities.

I was floored by these astonishing statistics when I first encountered them in the 1990s while working on my first book, *Killing the Black Body*. I had been researching the arrests of numerous Black mothers across the country for being pregnant and using crack cocaine. Racist myths about them giving birth to so-called crack babies, described as irreparably damaged, bereft of social consciousness, and destined to delinquency, had turned a public health issue into a crime. I saw the prosecutions as part of a long legacy of oppressive policies, originating in slavery, that devalued Black women and denied their reproductive freedom. As I focused on the criminal punishment of Black women's childbearing, I discovered a far more widespread repression of Black mothers for prenatal drug use: the forcible removal of their newborns from their custody.

The war on crack cocaine in Black communities in the 1980s and 1990s included testing Black pregnant women and their babies for drugs and reporting them to child welfare authorities at high rates. The government's main source of information about prenatal drug use was hospitals' reporting of positive toxicologies to law enforcement or child welfare agencies. This testing was performed almost exclusively by public hospitals that served poor communities of color. One study published in the prestigious *New England Journal of Medicine* in 1990 examined the results of toxicological tests on pregnant women who received prenatal care in public health clinics and in private obstetrical offices in Pinellas County, Florida. The researchers found that, despite similar rates of positive test results, Black women were almost ten times more likely than white women to be reported to government agencies. Neonatal wards in urban hospitals were filling with Black babies who couldn't go home, labeled by the press as "boarder babies"—"taking up space that could be used for treating sick children," the *Los Angeles Times* reported in July 1989. News stories typically blamed their "crack-addicted" mothers for abandoning them, failing to mention that most of the babies languishing in hospitals had been taken from their mothers at birth.[2]

Investigating the racial disparities in reporting newborns for drug exposure and separating them from their mothers led me to the broader child welfare system, which I argue in this book is more accurately described as the family-policing system. Its racial makeup immediately aroused my suspicion. If this system were truly devoted to protecting children and promoting their welfare, why weren't the vast majority of its clients white? The United States has consistently reserved its best resources for white people; Black people have had to fight tooth and nail to gain access to services meant for whites only. Conversely, the institutions where government has confined Black people, like segregated schools, housing, and prisons, have been substandard. Why would this state system that takes children from their parents be any different?

What's more, America has never viewed Black children as innocent victims in need of protection. White Americans literally see Black children as older than they are. In the criminal punishment system, Black children are far more likely than white children to be charged as adults, caged in adult prisons, and held in solitary confinement. Black girls and boys are even kicked out of preschool at higher rates. The police shooting of twelve-year-old Tamir Rice while he played in a park, the confinement of six-year-old Nadia King in a mental health facility for throwing a tantrum in kindergarten, and the suicide of Kalief Browder after he spent years in solitary confinement on Rikers Island for allegedly snatching a backpack exemplify the violence the US state inflicts on Black children. "Kids were being sent away simply for being alive in a place where war had been declared against us," writes Black Lives Matter cofounder Patrisse Cullors. The claim that the United States runs a system for Black families that is immune from this vicious posture against Black children and operates instead out of concern for them seemed patently absurd. The fact that the family-policing system so disproportionately enmeshes Black families was the biggest clue that its aim wasn't child welfare.[3]

Despite my training as a lawyer and my devotion to social justice activism, foster care's racial dimension had escaped my attention. But all the people involved in this racial caste system—the administrators, social workers, therapists, lawyers, and judges, as well as the families policed by it—knew full well its discriminatory nature. Its racial divide was obvious to me as soon as I started observing child welfare proceedings in Chicago. As I later wrote in *Shattered Bonds*:

Spend a day at dependency court in any major city and you will see the unmistakable color of the child welfare system. Dependency court is where judges decide the fate of children who have been taken into state custody because their parents are charged with abusing or neglecting them. Nearly every family in these urban courts is Black. If you came with no preconceptions about the purpose of the child welfare system, you would have to conclude that it is an institution designed to monitor, regulate, and punish poor Black families.[4]

When I looked into what seemed to me a grave racial injustice, I discovered that no book had been published on the topic since *Children of the Storm: Black Children and American Child Welfare*, by sociologists Andrew Billingsley and Jeanne M. Giovannoni, in 1972. The authors traced the history of the government's discriminatory treatment of African American children, who were virtually excluded from openly segregated child welfare services until World War II. By the time I became acutely aware of the system in the 1990s, the political and demographic landscape of child welfare had shifted dramatically. As Black children began to fill the government caseloads in the 1960s, public agencies pivoted sharply from providing services to children in their homes to taking children from their parents. The total size of the foster care population and the share of Black children skyrocketed simultaneously. The number of children in foster care more than doubled in less than fifteen years, from 276,000 in 1985 to 568,000 in 1999, along with an exponential increase in federal funding for foster care. Propelling the spike was the massive removal of Black children from their homes.[5]

It would be a mistake to conclude that the increase in the foster care population was a response to the needs of Black children. The removal of Black children at four times the rate of white children could not be justified by any matching discrepancy in rates of child abuse and neglect. A rigorous 2006 study found that the spike in foster care caseloads was driven by increases in female incarceration and decreases in welfare benefits. More important, the skyrocketing foster care population was the result of a political decision to turn to child removal as the primary way of addressing the needs of Black families, who were most devastated by the state's concurrent crime-control and welfare-restricting agendas. The racial politics of the 1980s and 1990s, which entrenched Black subordination through policies of mass incarceration and welfare restructuring, were also responsible for reinforcing the equally oppressive, but less noticed, system that had caught my attention—the family-policing system. The punitive approach that characterized criminal law enforcement, public assistance, and child welfare policies then continues to drive violent state containment of Black communities now.[6]

JORNELL

Soon after I began my own research, while teaching law in Chicago, I met a Black mother named Jornell who was fighting to be reunited with her two-year-old son, David. A chubby woman with an effervescent personality, Jornell was eager to tell me how she became entangled in the city's child protection net. When Jornell became pregnant, she was living in public housing on Social Security benefits and was suffering from diabetes and problems with drugs and alcohol. She was relieved when she saw a flyer for a program called Healthy F.I.T., for Healthy Family Intervention Team, based at the hospital where she received prenatal care. Healthy F.I.T. "provides drug and/or alcohol assessment, treatment, and case management services for pregnant or newly delivered women receiving care within the Sinai Health System," the flyer promised. Jornell eagerly signed up. "I felt that I had a right to heal," Jornell told me. "I didn't want the drugs, I didn't want the alcohol, I didn't want to be mentally ill anymore."[7]

Because she was participating in Healthy F.I.T., Jornell was known to the hospital social workers even before David was born, in January 1998. They put the newborn on "social hold" until they could inspect Jornell's living arrangements. Jornell wasn't allowed to bring David home until four days after she was released. Then, when David was one month old, Jornell made a fateful mistake. She had taken David to the hospital emergency room several times when he had recurring digestive problems. One time, while he was being treated at the hospital, she gave the baby an enema. "The nurses were busy with other children and weren't taking David's illness seriously," Jornell explained. At the time, she thought she was following the advice of a doctor who had seen the baby earlier. She later acknowledged that her judgment might have been clouded by the stress of a difficult pregnancy and delivery, complicated by her diabetes.

Alarmed by Jornell's interference with David's medical care, the hospital staff called the child abuse hotline. A caseworker with the Department of Children and Family Services, known as DCFS, determined that the report was "indicated"—there was credible evidence that David was at risk of harm—and took custody of the baby. He was placed in a stranger's home with four other foster children. A month later, an internal review team overturned the caseworker's finding of potential abuse. The decision reported that, according to a social worker who interviewed Jornell, "natural mother thinks very clearly and decisively, would not harm a child and is capable of caring for the child." It also stated that a psychiatrist who had been treating Jornell disclosed that Jornell had had drug and alcohol problems in the past, but had not used either for more than a year. "Natural mother is committed to being clean," the psychiatrist reported. "In professional opinion NM is capable of parenting baby and has been consistent in interest of baby's needs over her own during pregnancy." Tests performed on David when he was born showed he had not been exposed to drugs.

But DCFS did not return David. Instead, it filed a new report alleging that the baby would be at risk of harm if released to his mother because of her history of substance abuse and possible mental illness. It issued a list of steps Jornell would have to take to be rehabilitated enough for reunification: enroll in a drug treatment program, submit monthly urine samples for drug testing, attend Alcoholics Anonymous meetings, see a parenting coach once a week, undergo a series of psychological evaluations, meet with a psychotherapist regularly, and make scheduled visits with David under a social worker's supervision. Then she would be evaluated by a parenting assessment team, composed of a psychiatrist, psychologist, child development specialist, and social worker. If she completed all the prescribed tasks successfully and passed the team's assessment, she could have David back.

Determined to be reunited with her baby, Jornell complied with every single requirement. But the parenting assessment team kept finding reasons to recommend against reunification. In its first report, in January 1999, the team found that Jornell displayed no symptoms of mental illness, was constructively using all the services offered to her, and had remained substance free for more than a year. During supervised visits, she showed a caring and responsible attitude toward David. Nevertheless, the team was concerned that Jornell's "elevated mood and accelerated speech" might indicate a "subtle" mental disorder. It felt that her support network was too small. It didn't trust her recovery—despite her successful completion of an intensive outpatient drug treatment program *twice*. It recommended that she attend an additional rehabilitation program for relapse prevention. The team would reassess her case at the end of the year.

In the meantime, Jornell began to see a Black clinical psychiatrist in her neighborhood who understood her better than the one prescribed by DCFS. The new psychiatrist prepared several reports attesting to Jornell's ability to care for David. But DCFS authorities didn't appreciate Jornell's attempt to direct her own treatment. When the parenting assessment team issued a follow-up report in December 1999, it chastised Jornell for choosing her own therapist. The team interpreted her impatience with the agency's delays in reuniting her with her son as a failure to take full responsibility for her own parenting deficits. It recommended that the agency refer her to the "correct service providers" for more evaluations and treatment. "I followed all their recommendations. I went into long-term treatment. I did everything I was supposed to do—for myself, before the intervention," Jornell told me. "The intervention was supposed to assist me to be a family. But this is the worst entanglement anybody can become involved in."

Jornell's frustrating experience with DCFS inspired her to organize a small group of Black mothers whose children had been taken by the agency. They called themselves Operation MOSES, for Mothers Organizing Systems for Equal Services, and exemplified collectives of Black mothers springing up across the nation that were dedicated to resisting the child welfare system's destruction of their families. "I live for this now. I have no other purpose," Jornell told me the first time we spoke. "My life is an ongoing battle to hold on to my child."

I first met with Operation MOSES on a summer evening in 2000 at St. Stephen's Church in Englewood, one of Chicago's poorest, most segregated Black neighborhoods. After walking down the steps to the church basement, I found a half dozen Black women sitting around a table. The women were strategizing about a citywide campaign to call attention to the crisis of Black children being snatched from their homes. They greeted me warmly, grateful to have the ear of an empathetic law professor. I was noticeably pregnant with my fourth child, who was due in September, and we instantly bonded as Black mothers concerned for the well-being of our children. At one end of the table was an expanding file stuffed with court papers, newspaper clippings, and letters. Jornell sat me at the other end so I could face everyone. Each woman told me about her battle with the family-policing authorities to get her children back.

By the time I met with Operation MOSES, I'd conducted several years of research on the family-policing system. I recognized the stories I heard in the church basement as typical of hundreds of thousands of Black mothers in Chicago and cities across the nation. Most of the mothers were raising their children as best they could and needed help with meeting their material needs. They were targeted for state intrusion, not because their parenting was egregiously lacking or harmful, but because their bonds with their children weren't valued enough. Their children were taken not only because biased caseworkers discriminated against them, but also because the family-policing system was designed to regulate rather than support them.

BECOMING AN ABOLITIONIST

In my introduction to *Shattered Bonds*, I stated that we should "finally abolish" America's destructive child welfare system. In this book, I renew my call to abolish family policing. This time, however, I argue for completely replacing it, not with another reformed state system, but with a radically reimagined way of caring for families and keeping children safe.

Three things happened after the publication of *Shattered Bonds* that solidified my abolitionist stance. First, over the last two decades, I've participated in numerous reform efforts to improve foster care, address its racial disparities, and reduce its population. I served for nine years on a task force to implement the settlement agreement in a class action lawsuit brought in 1998 by children's rights advocates against the Department of Social and Health Services (DSHS) in Washington State, *Braam v. State of Washington*. The department's treatment of children in foster care was so horrendous that the lawyers claimed it violated the state constitution. The named plaintiff, Jessica Braam, had been tossed among foster homes more than thirty times.[8]

In 2004, after six years of litigation, the children's attorneys reached an agreement with DSHS to resolve the lawsuit by handing the problems over to a panel of five mutually agreed upon national experts. I accepted an invitation from the children's attorneys to be one of their choices. The Braam Oversight Panel worked with the DSHS Children's Administration and the children's attorneys to develop a complicated plan with outcomes, benchmarks, and action steps to improve health care for foster children, lower child protection worker caseloads, enhance foster parent training, and decrease the number of children who ran away from foster care. For nearly a decade we monitored the state's progress in performing the action steps, meeting the benchmarks, and achieving the outcomes. After dozens of meetings with administrators and attorneys at a hotel across from the SeaTac airport, we calculated some progress on some of the measures. But we were unable to fix the long list of deficiencies that harmed children placed in the state's custody.

I've lost count of the trainings of caseworkers, administrators, lawyers, judges, and court volunteers I've conducted in the last twenty years on confronting racial disparities and biases in child welfare decision making. I wrote articles for scholarly journals and reports for foundations, organizations, and think tanks on policies that destroyed families, especially Black families, and made recommendations for re-ducing the casualties. I helped to make "racial disproportionality" a new buzzword for a problem in child welfare practice. No doubt some of the reforms I participated in helped raise awareness of the racism and harm in America's child welfare system. None rendered a signifi-cant blow to the system's fundamental design.

Second, in the last twenty years, the prison abolition movement emerged and came to occupy an increasingly prominent place in the popular consciousness. Some activists mark its launch at an interna-tional conference and strategy session, Critical Resistance: Beyond the Prison Industrial Complex, held at the University of California, Berke-ley, in September 1998. Formed in 1997, the Critical Resistance or-ganizing collective gathered more than thirty-five hundred activists, former prisoners, lawyers, and scholars over three days "to address the alarming growth of the prison system, popularize the idea of the 'prison industrial complex' and make 'abolition' a practical theory of change."[9]

Critical Resistance founders developed the concept of the prison-industrial complex to name the expanding apparatus of surveillance, policing, and incarceration the state increasingly employs to solve problems caused by social inequality, stifle political resistance by op-pressed communities, and serve the interests of corporations that profit from prisons and police forces. Professor Dylan Rodríguez, a founding member of Critical Resistance, lyrically describes abolition as "a prac-tice, an analytical method, a present-tense visioning, an infrastructure in the making, a creative project, a performance, a counterwar, an ideo-logical struggle, a pedagogy and curriculum, an alleged impossibility that is furtively present." Abolitionists believe we can imagine and build a more humane and democratic society that no longer relies on caging people to meet human needs and solve social problems.[10]

Third, organizing by parents subjected to the family-policing system grew dramatically, with Black mothers at the forefront. Back in 1999, Operation MOSES struggled to offer mutual support to its members as each one fought an uphill battle against a seemingly immovable behe-moth. In the two decades since, parent-led organizations have emerged across the country and have begun networking with each other. Youth who were formerly in foster care are increasingly leading and participating in efforts to end family policing. Coupled with the rise of parent groups was the development of family defense: lawyers dedicated to representing parents in family-policing proceedings. I joined the inaugural advisory board of the Family Defense Center in Chicago, founded in 2005 by Diane Redleaf, a pioneer in representing parents in child welfare proceedings.

I have also served for more than twenty years on the board of the National Coalition for Child Protection Reform, whose mission is to shift public policy away from child removal and toward keeping more families together, including by educating journalists about the harms of family policing. Our work with parent organizers, along with reporting by alternative media outlets like *Rise Magazine*, which publishes the writings of system-impacted parents, is making a difference in the media. There has been an exponential increase in news stories about the injustices inflicted by child protective services (CPS), even in mainstream outlets, like the *New York Times* 2017 story "Foster Care as Punishment: The New Reality of 'Jane Crow.'"

As I write these words, I have seen in the past few years more support for dismantling the family-policing system than in all the prior years combined. Many activists have credited *Shattered Bonds* with inspiring them—the seeds I planted after meeting with Operation MOSES were beginning to sprout two decades later. I could not have predicted when I met Jornell and her ragtag band of Black mothers in a church basement that rebellious women like them would be at the forefront of a burgeoning movement to end family policing once and for all.[11]

From my vantage point at the intersection of these developments— a multitude of failed initiatives to fix the child protection system, a flourishing prison abolition movement, and nascent organizing to end family policing and to radically reimagine child welfare—I came to envision more clearly an abolitionist framework to contest family policing, one that integrates our understanding of police and prisons with the state's surveillance, control, and demolition of Black families. The only way to stop the destruction caused by family policing is to stop policing families.

A BENEVOLENT TERROR

HOG-TIED

On a summer day in 2017, a Black family was enjoying a picnic in a park in Aurora, Colorado. Among the dozen or so relatives who gathered there was Vanessa Peoples, a twenty-five-year-old nursing student, and her two sons, Malik and Talib, ages two and four. Vanessa was undergoing treatment for leukemia. She also suffered from asthma and was prone to seizures, and her illnesses had turned her naturally lanky frame rail thin. Vanessa, the boys, and Vanessa's husband lived with Vanessa's mother, Patricia Russell, in a modest, single-story brick house on a tree-lined street on Delmar Parkway in Northwest Aurora. All the adults pitched in to care for the rambunctious little boys. That day was supposed to be a relaxing retreat from Vanessa's exhausting schedule of classes, cancer, and caregiving. Had Vanessa known that the outing would lead to the most terrifying experience of her life, she would have stayed at home.[1]

Vanessa had asked one of her cousins to keep an eye on the toddler, Malik, while she played with his older brother, Talib. The cousin decided to leave the park without telling Vanessa, and as the cousin walked toward her car, Malik traipsed behind her. Vanessa grabbed

Talib to run after them. Before Vanessa could reach them, a woman who happened to be passing by snatched up Malik. Vanessa could see her talking on her cell phone as Vanessa approached. "Ma'am, that's my son," Vanessa told the stranger holding her child when she caught up to them, only a minute later. But the woman refused to let him go. She had called 911 to report Malik as being unattended. Vanessa was in no shape to physically pull Malik from the woman's arms, so she waited for the police to intervene. But when an officer arrived, he questioned Vanessa and demanded proof that she was Malik's mother. The officer finally let Vanessa take Malik back when relatives gathered around to vouch for her. As the officer was leaving, he handed Vanessa a ticket for child neglect.[2]

A month later, on the morning of July 13, 2017, Vanessa had just given Malik and Talib their baths and was cleaning up in the basement. They were alone in the house: Vanessa's husband was at his job as an apprentice electrician, and Patricia had just left to check on her fiancé, who had broken his foot. Vanessa didn't hear when a white caseworker from the Adams County Social Services Department, accompanied by a Black female trainee, unexpectedly knocked on the front door. When the police officer cited Vanessa for child neglect at the family picnic, she became the subject of a government child welfare investigation. Local child protection offices routinely dispatch staff to make surprise visits to the homes of children who come to their attention through anonymous calls to the child abuse hotline, allegations made by mandated reporters, such as teachers, doctors, and day care workers, or charges brought by police officers.

The caseworker noticed Malik, still undressed, peering out an open first-floor window. Worried that no one had come to the door, she called the Aurora Police Department for assistance. Two male officers arrived first, soon followed by a female officer. The caseworker pointed to Malik, who was still standing at the window. "My guess is he's fairly neglected," the caseworker told them. When they discovered the front door unlocked, the officers entered the house, without a warrant or permission. "Aurora Police! Anybody here?" one of them shouted. As the officers proceeded down the basement stairs, guns drawn, they confronted Vanessa at the bottom, wearing blue pajama pants and a pink Betty Boop top. Vanessa explained that she didn't hear the caseworker knocking while she was in the basement because she was hard of hearing in one ear. "The children are fine," Vanessa told them, indicating they could leave now that they knew she was in the house.

The three officers and the two caseworkers hovered around Vanessa and her children at the front of the house, unwilling to leave her alone without interrogation. Vanessa stood at the open front door, Talib and Malik at her side; the other three women—the police officer and the two caseworkers—stood on the front steps facing her; the male officers were positioned behind her in the living room. When Vanessa objected to their continued presence, they began to berate her about the danger she created for Malik. "So you don't think it's concerning when someone sees a child hanging out and no one is answering the door?" An officer posed the question as an accusation. "A child hanging out the window and you're not answering the door, you don't think that's a problem?"

Vanessa was growing more and more frustrated by the inquisition. She called Patricia on her cell phone to tell her that police officers and caseworkers were at the house. "Mom, can you get here because they're really pissing me off," she said in front of the five government agents. Two of the officers then engaged Vanessa in an increasingly combative colloquy:

"And we're supposed to know if you were maybe sick or injured or had maybe a stroke?"

"I *am* sick. Do you guys think by being here you're helping the situation at all?" Vanessa replied.

"You've got to be kidding me," one officer sighed.

"Ma'am, if you're sick, then you need to figure out a way to get your kids taken care of," the other officer chimed in.

"Excuse me. I have a way to get my kids taken care of. And I don't need you in my house."

Vanessa turned to the caseworkers. "And I don't need you all here either."

The caseworker in charge tried to interject a more empathetic tone. "I understand. So, ma'am—"

Vanessa cut her off. "No, you don't understand, or you wouldn't be here. Point blank. Period."

While Vanessa continued to argue, the third officer began to walk around the house, recording the condition of each room with his body camera. As he scanned the kitchen, he opened the refrigerator and cabinets to record their contents.

A couple of minutes later, Patricia arrived in a huff, demanding that the intruders leave as she swept into the living room past everyone gathered at the front door. "I don't need you guys in our lives like that. Please leave," she yelled. "They're well taken care of. They're just two little boys. You see they're fine. If there's nothing else, please leave my home. Stay out of our lives."

Despite the protestations, none of the state agents budged. They seemed to assume they had complete authority to stay in the home uninvited, to interrogate Vanessa and Patricia, and to inspect every corner of the house—without ever suggesting the women had any right to object, to remain silent, or to obtain legal counsel. No one cared what Vanessa and Patricia thought would help them provide for Malik and Talib. Nor did they consider why the women didn't find the imposing squad of armed officers supportive. To the contrary, the police and caseworkers treated the women's defiance as evidence of their danger to the children. "From the onset, Vanessa was very confrontational and uncooperative. . . . She CLEARLY did not care and continued her confrontational demeanor," one officer would later report. "The disdain both Vanessa and Patricia had for the police and Social Services was quite evident."

Patricia pulled Talib and Malik from their mother's side and took them to their bedroom to get them dressed. A male officer followed close behind. "You don't need to follow me," Patricia told him. But he insisted she wasn't allowed to be in the room alone with her grandsons. When Patricia tried to close the bedroom door to get underwear for the boys from a dresser, she and the officer waged a tug of war until he pushed the door open and entered the room.

Meanwhile, in the living room, Vanessa began shouting, "It's my house, my kids; that's my mom!" As she headed to join her mother and children in the bedroom, she was blocked by yet a fourth officer, who had arrived as backup and was standing guard in the narrow hallway. He thrust out his hand to stop her. "Stand back, stand back, stand back, stand back!" he commanded. Vanessa tried to assert her right to see her children: "No, I don't have to stand back."

At that moment, the officer lunged at Vanessa and violently pushed her face down into a large beanbag on the living room floor. The female officer and a fifth officer now on the scene leapt to assist him, all three pinning down the distraught, skinny woman as she flailed beneath them. Vanessa's arms were yanked behind her back while her wrists were cuffed together and her head and shoulders held down. The officer who had confronted Patricia guarded her and the children in the bedroom. Two more officers arrived and entered the bedroom while Patricia frantically tried to console her grandsons, bringing the count to seven uniformed police officers in the family's home.

"Mom! Mom! . . . Help! Help! . . . I'm not doing nothing! . . . You're breaking my arm!" Vanessa shrieked from the living room.

"No one's breaking your arm," one of the officers responded. "Probably popped out of socket."

Working in unison, the three officers restrained Vanessa with hobbles—a set of hand and ankle cuffs that shackled her wrists behind her back and chained them to her shackled legs. Then they carted her to a police car, her body contorted by the hobbles, her stomach and face toward the ground.

"You know how you tie a pig upside down and his feet are hanging from the stick?" Vanessa would recall. "That's how they carried me."

The pain was excruciating. "Let me go, let me go. I got asthma. I can't breathe," Vanessa cried over and over. While Vanessa lay across the back seat of the patrol car, the officers' supervisor, a sergeant, pulled up, police vehicles now lining the block, their lights flashing. She told the officers to put Vanessa on the grass, loosen the chain wrapped too tightly around her waist, and call paramedics. Vanessa remained restrained on the lawn until the ambulance arrived. She had been hog-tied for thirty agonizing minutes.

As the paramedics carried Vanessa, handcuffed and strapped to a stretcher, some of the officers milled around outside discussing next steps. "What are we doing with grandma?" one asked. "Grandma's just staying in the bedroom for the moment," the sergeant replied. "My thing is, if their supervisor wants the kids to go with grandma, let's arrest grandma," the officer said, pointing to the caseworkers. "Cuz I'm tired of that."

"Well, find out what they want to do. We haven't lost standing inside yet," the sergeant said, as if referring to a military occupation.

The sergeant stayed behind to do a thorough inspection of the house while one of the officers followed closely to take photographs. "You want to make sure they have food," the sergeant instructed the officer. "Are they all potty trained? Maybe look at the bathroom. Make sure there are no dangers in the bathroom."

After moving down to the basement, the officer noticed a stand with bottles of alcohol in the corner of a living room and took several photos of it. In an adjacent bedroom, the sergeant motioned him to come closer and pointed to a corner. "The bottle of whiskey or whatever it is." The officer snapped a photo of it.

At one point, Patricia led the officers and caseworkers to the large, fenced-in backyard with lawn furniture and a yellow plastic gym for young children. "Go out there," she directed them. "I want you to take a good look. I want you guys to see. That these kids don't suffer for nothing. This is how much I got love for my family."

One of the officers rode in the back of the ambulance as it transported Vanessa to the hospital. There, Vanessa learned that the police had dislocated her shoulder when they yanked her arm back to hobble her. She was cuffed to the bed while the hospital staff put her shoulder back in place. Within hours, she was given a sling, a bag of ice, and ibuprofen and hauled off to the Aurora municipal jail. Patricia bailed her out that night.

The police charged Vanessa with a new count of child abuse and obstructing a police officer. Although the sergeant's offense report stated that "the house was in fair condition with food," another officer wrote, "while clearing the house I noticed it to be very dirty, with no food in the refrigerator, and very little food in the pantry." Neither officer mentioned the backyard fitted with the gym that Patricia had shown them so proudly. Nor did they seem to care about the loving relationship Malik and Talib had with their mother and grandmother.

On the advice of her public defender, Vanessa took a deal from the prosecutor: she pled guilty to reckless endangerment of a child to avoid prison and was sentenced to one year of probation. Before the incident at the park, Vanessa had never been in trouble with the law. Now she had a record as a child abuser. Later, represented by a civil rights attorney from Denver, Vanessa sued the Aurora Police Department for their use of excessive force and agreed to a modest monetary settlement. None of the officers who brutalized her were ever disciplined.

This was par for the course for the Aurora police. Between 2003 and 2017, the city paid over $4.6 million to settle more than a dozen legal claims involving unarmed Black and Latinx men and women who had been assaulted or killed by officers, as well as that of a twelve-year-old girl whose shoulder was fractured when officers choked her and threw her to the ground following a dispute with her mother over a parking spot. In every case of racialized violence, the officers were cleared of wrongdoing and never held accountable.[3]

Two years after Vanessa's arrest, on the night of August 24, 2019, three Aurora police officers approached Elijah McClain, a slight twenty-three-year-old Black man who worked as a massage therapist, as he walked home from a quick stop at a nearby convenience store to buy iced tea for his brother. The police said someone had called 911 and reported Elijah as looking "sketchy." Though Elijah was unarmed and doing nothing illegal, the officers tackled him to the ground and put him in a carotid hold, incapacitating him by applying pressure to the side of his neck to cut off blood to his brain. When paramedics arrived, they injected Elijah with the powerful sedative ketamine. Elijah had a massive heart attack on the way to the hospital and died six days later.[4]

The killing of Elijah McClain illustrates how encounters with police officers on public streets put unarmed Black people at alarming risk of injury or death. A 2018 study found that "1 in 1,000 Black men can expect to die of police violence over the course of their lifetime if present rates hold." Taking Aurora police officers along on home inspections, as happened in Vanessa's case, increases the potential for violent encounters with the city's Black residents, especially Black mothers.[5]

The plea deal and settlement Vanessa entered into didn't end her ordeal. Vanessa may have resolved her criminal case, but the young mother was now ensnared in another form of government oversight—the family-policing system. The state's intrusion into her home began with an allegation of child neglect for letting her toddler stray at the park. The officers terrorized her, her mother, and her children in the name of child protection. After that, Vanessa's parenting remained under scrutiny by child welfare authorities. The caseworker returned the day after the arrest and told Vanessa she would have to permit more random visits from social services and complete parenting classes prescribed by the agency. For thirty days, two caseworkers came twice a week to Vanessa's house to watch her interact with Malik and Talib.

Vanessa complied with every agency requirement and was released from probation several months early. But her arrest and record of child abuse continued to devastate her family. For one thing, the trauma of seeing their mother arrested had lasting effects on Malik and Talib. "I had to watch my children suffer. My children were having nightmares," Vanessa told me when I reached her by phone in November 2020 after reading a magazine article about her case. "Whenever they see a police officer they ask me, 'Mom, are they coming to take you away from us?'" Vanessa still hadn't recovered from the terrifying incident either. "Anytime I leave the house, I'm looking over my shoulder," she said. "Every time I see the police, I clutch. I'm petrified."

In addition, being branded a child abuser had collateral consequences for Vanessa's livelihood. The imposed schedule of court dates, parenting classes, and caseworker visits meant she had to take time off from nursing school, forcing her to postpone her plans for graduation. She was fired from her job at a temporary agency when her boss found out about the child endangerment charges. Her listing on the state's child abuse registry significantly restricts her prospects for employment, barring her from working in day care centers, schools, and health care facilities. She also lost a chance to rent a three-bedroom townhouse. "They were getting ready to hand me the keys, then they said my application was rejected," Vanessa recounted. "When I called the office, a man told me, 'We're not going to take a chance on a child abuse charge.'"

"People judge me. I'm hurt. I'm financially in a hole. It's hard. It's a living nightmare," Vanessa went on, her voice cracking. "Now I can't even provide for my children."

A failure to comply with the child protection requirements could have resulted in a far worse punishment than jail time for violating probation. It could mean child welfare authorities taking Malik and Talib and putting them in foster care with strangers. In 2017, the year Vanessa was arrested, more than five thousand children entered foster care in Colorado. Black children had the highest risk of being taken from their parents. Less than 6 percent of children in Colorado were Black, but Black children made up more than 12 percent of the state's foster care population. This disparity mirrors national statistics: that same year, Black children were more than 25 percent of the foster care population despite making up only 15 percent of the general population. Vanessa's momentary maternal lapse in the park had set in motion the gears of a giant state machine with the power to destroy her family.[6]

—

EVERY YEAR, GOVERNMENT AGENTS INVADE THE HOMES OF HUN-dreds of thousands of families in poor and low-income communities, without a warrant or any other kind of judicial authorization, in the name of protecting the children who live there. In 2018 alone, 3.5 million children were involved in an investigation by child protective services (CPS). Black families are disproportionately subjected to state intrusion. Caseworkers and police officers inspect the premises for what in their opinion constitutes a risk to the children. Based on state child neglect laws, the investigators interpret conditions of poverty—lack of food, insecure housing, inadequate medical care—as evidence of parental unfitness. They also perceive the homes in Black communities as more hazardous for children, even when the alleged parental infraction—like allowing a toddler to momentarily stray away, or having bottles of alcohol in the house—happens in white affluent homes, too.[7]

The parents under investigation rarely know their legal rights and aren't informed of them. Asserting their rights is usually futile—or may garner a violent reprimand, as Vanessa painfully discovered. Caseworkers subject family members to humiliating questioning. They interrogate children separately and pressure them to make statements against their relatives. During these interrogations, caseworkers inspect children for evidence, sometimes strip searching them. Most Black children in America, like Malik and Talib, will undergo a CPS investigation at some point in their childhoods. This surveillance constitutes the stop-and-frisk of Black families that falls off the radar of public protest.[8]

Like the charges leveled against Vanessa, most allegations prompting a child welfare investigation are for neglect. The vast majority of the families subjected to investigation have low incomes or are living in poverty and could use help meeting their material needs. But the government agents who investigate them don't offer the resources struggling families need. Instead, they brandish a terrifying weapon against them—the threat of taking their children away. Every year, state child protection agencies make good on their threat and remove about 500,000 children from their homes. Officially, these agencies seize about 250,000 children annually. And it's estmated that they take another 250,000 children through informal coerced arrangements that never make it into official statistics. More than one in ten Black children in America will be forcibly separated from their parents and placed in foster care by the time they reach age eighteen.[9]

Parents accused of child maltreatment are intensively monitored by child welfare agencies and compelled to follow their commands. In order to keep their children at home or to be reunited with those who are seized, parents are typically required to perform a list of back-breaking tasks, made all the more overwhelming by the problems the families faced in the first place. Parents surviving on low-wage jobs or public assistance, who may have a drug or mental health problem and no car or secure shelter, are directed to juggle a dizzying array of parent trainings, substance abuse treatments, and psychological counseling sessions on top of scheduled visits with their children (who may be spread among multiple placements), all while finding and maintaining adequate employment and housing to support their families. Failure to comply with every order risks a judge permanently severing their legal ties to their children. Termination of parental rights, as this permanent dissolution is called, ends a parent's physical custody as well as the right to ever communicate with or regain custody of the child. It is the death penalty of the family-policing system—the ultimate punishment the family court can impose. The United States extinguishes the legal rights of more parents than any other nation on Earth. As with every aspect of the child welfare system, Black and Native children suffer the most—they are more than twice as likely as white children to experience the termination of both parents' rights. In some states, the legal demolition of family ties has risen dramatically in the last two decades, spurred by federal law's acceleration of termination proceedings. Terminations in Minnesota, which removes Black and Native children at exceptionally high rates, increased by 80 percent from 2010 to 2019.[10]

Child welfare authorities wield these powers to supervise, reassemble, and destroy families with stunningly little judicial constraint or public scrutiny. Such extreme state intrusion in homes violates well-established principles of US constitutional law that protect us from tyrannical government rule. Such traumatic assaults on people's most cherished relationships, targeted against vulnerable populations, constitutes torture under international declarations. Such a powerful mechanism for reinforcing racial capitalism—the US system of wealth accumulation grounded in racist hierarchy and ideology—parallels the function of police and prisons. Recent foster care rates for US children, at 576 per 100,000, are about the same as incarceration rates for US adults, at 582 per 100,000. The child welfare system has unparalleled powers to terrorize entire communities, shape national policies, and reinforce our unequal social order. Yet most Americans have never thought of this form of state violence imposed on oppressed communities as a political injustice. To the contrary, they have been led to believe that the government is saving these communities' children. The state violence inflicted in the name of child protection is a benevolent terror.[11]

The facade of benevolence makes most Americans complacent about a colossal government apparatus that spends billions of dollars annually on surveilling families, breaking them apart, and thrusting children into a foster care system known to cause devastating harms. Even when President Trump's cruel policy of separating migrant children from their parents at the Mexican border drew national condemnation, hardly anyone connected it to the far more widespread family separation that takes place every day in Black neighborhoods. Besides hiding the trauma inflicted on families, the state's fictitious compassion serves a crucial political purpose. This nation's terroristic approach to protecting children blames the most marginalized parents for the impact of race, class, and gender inequalities on their children, obscuring those unequal structures and the need to dismantle them.

We should stop calling this brutal regime by its benevolent titles— child *welfare* system, child *protective* services, foster *care*. The mission of CPS agencies is not to care for children or protect their welfare. Rather, they respond inadequately and inhumanely to the effects of our society's abysmal failure to care *enough* about children's welfare. Far from promoting the well-being of children, the state weaponizes children as a way to threaten families, to scapegoat parents for societal harms to their children, and to buttress the racist, patriarchal, and capitalist status quo. "Policing" is the word that captures best what the system does to America's most disenfranchised families. It subjects them to surveillance, coercion, and punishment. It is a family-policing system.

———

IN THE SUMMER OF 2020, SPARKED BY THE MURDER OF GEORGE Floyd by Minneapolis police, people gathered in unprecedented numbers around the nation and the world to protest police violence against Black people. The uprisings brought new attention to abolition as a political vision and organizing strategy. More and more Americans are recognizing that police killings of Black people are so pervasive that they can no longer be considered aberrations. Rather, police violence stems from the very function of policing to enforce an unjust racial order. From its origins in slave patrols, policing has served as a violent arm of the racial capitalist state by protecting the interests of white elites and controlling Black and other marginalized communities through everyday physical intimidation and arrests.

Policing, therefore, cannot be fixed by more failed reforms; it must be abolished.

The most prominent demand emerging from the protests was to defund the police and reallocate the money to provide health care, education, jobs with living wages, and affordable housing. Defunding police is part of a broader struggle to abolish the prison-industrial complex, including jails, prisons, detention centers, and other carceral practices, while building a radically different society that has no need for them. As abolitionist organizer Mariame Kaba wrote in a June 12, 2020, *New York Times* op-ed, "The surest way of reducing police violence is to reduce the power of the police, by cutting budgets and the number of officers." In moving toward abolition, then, it is critical to support reforms only if they reduce—and do not increase—police funding, tools, and power.[12]

As I witnessed the protests, I became increasingly concerned that family policing was absent from most demands to defund the police. Some activists even recommended transferring money, resources, and authority from police departments to health and human services agencies that handle child protection. These proposals ignored how the family-policing system surveils and represses Black and other marginalized communities in ways similar to the law enforcement systems condemned by the protesters. The child welfare system must be seen as part of what I call the foster-industrial complex—and, like the prison-industrial complex, it's a multibillion-dollar government apparatus that regulates millions of vulnerable families through intrusive investigations, monitoring, and forcible removal of children from their homes to be placed in foster care, group homes, and "therapeutic" detention facilities that resemble prisons.

Diverting money and power to child protection agencies would result in even more state intrusion in Black communities. Linking 911 to the child abuse hotline would increase disruptive child maltreatment allegations and investigations. Even well-meaning recommendations to deploy social workers to conduct "wellness checks" in homes would likely result in increased maltreatment reports, expanding the state's monitoring and separation of families. Residents of Black neighborhoods live in fear of CPS agents entering their homes, interrogating them, and taking their children as much as they fear police stopping them in the streets, harassing them, and taking them to jail.

Rather than divesting one oppressive system to invest in another, we should work toward abolishing all carceral institutions and creating radically different ways of meeting human needs and solving social problems. Prison abolitionists should support defunding the family-policing system and be careful not to enrich it more with funds divested from the police.

The failure to include family policing in abolitionist demands isn't surprising. In addition to being fooled by its benevolent guise, many politically astute people don't even see the child welfare system as a significant part of the state. Sociologists, political scientists, economists, and legal scholars have barely interrogated the role of family policing in perpetuating structural inequalities, containing resistance by subordinated communities, and upholding a political elite. Compared to the robust literature on the social and political implications of mass incarceration, analysis of the impact of mass child removal falls pitifully short. While big government assistance programs such as Social Security, Medicaid, food stamps, and Temporary Assistance to Needy Children (TANF) are widely studied to understand their effects on economic and physical well-being, the effects of the multibillion-dollar foster care industry get relatively scant examination.

Why have social scientists largely overlooked this powerful system that determines the outcomes of so many children, reassembles so many families, and structures so much social policy? Like the broader public, researchers may mistakenly view family policing as a benign social service with no political impact worthy of study. I suspect, as well, that the family-policing system garners less serious attention because it involves primarily stigmatized mothers and their children. Yet the state's violence against these mothers implements and rationalizes policies that hold in place America's fundamentally unjust political order.

In this book, I tear off the benevolent veneer of family policing to reveal its political reality. Family policing, like criminal law enforcement and prisons, is designed to serve the US racial capitalist power structure, governed by profit, wealth accumulation, and market competition for the benefit of a wealthy white elite, by regulating and disrupting the most disenfranchised populations in place of meeting human needs. Family policing targets Black families in particular and relies on racist beliefs about Black family dysfunction to justify its terror. It is deeply entangled with cops, criminal courts, and prisons, forming an integrated arm of the US carceral regime. Regulating and destroying Black families—in addition to Latinx, Indigenous, and other impoverished families—in the name of child protection has been essential to the "ongoing white supremacist nation building project," to quote Mariame Kaba, as much as prisons and police. Like the prison system, the family-policing system frays social bonds and strains the ability of community members to resist oppression and organize politically. In our protests against anti-Black state violence, we should amplify the voices of parents who fight every day for their families in the halls of family court and in their communities.[13]

—

SINCE I WROTE *SHATTERED BONDS*, "RACIAL DISPROPORTIONALITY" has become a buzzword in child welfare research and policy making. State child welfare departments and nonprofit organizations alike have launched projects across the nation to reduce the foster care population, along with its racial disparities. Despite numerous reforms, the family-policing system has not changed its punitive ideology or racist impact. Given its foundational logic, which is centered on threatening politically marginalized families with child removal, the system has absorbed efforts to mitigate its flaws and has continued reproducing its benevolent terror. The family-policing system can't be fixed. It must be abolished. We need instead a paradigm shift in the state's relationship to families—a complete end to family policing by dismantling the current system and reimagining the very meaning of child welfare.

I realize abolishing the machinery the government currently relies on to keep children safe will seem outlandish and dangerous to many readers. So I begin Part I of this book, "Terror," by showing how the child protection agencies assumed to be helpful are actually destructive. Black families are policed the most not only because they are more likely to live in poverty but also because their regulation is essential to upholding a racist power structure. Family policing has a racial geography. Like policing, prisons, and redlining, the state's benevolent terror is concentrated in segregated Black neighborhoods, where it can contain the residents surviving and resisting the fallout from deliberate disinvestment.

Part II, "Design," explains why. The family-policing system terrorizes Black families because that's what it is designed to do. By tracing the history of family policing to the sale of enslaved African family members, the apprenticeship of emancipated Black children to former enslavers, the systematic transfer of Native children to boarding schools, and the servitude of impoverished European immigrant children, I show that today's system is rooted in white supremacist, capitalist, and patriarchal logics. Family policing, though taking various historical forms, has always served to subjugate the most politically marginalized groups and to maintain an unjust political structure in the name of saving children. Today, family policing continues to obscure its repressive political role by casting its work as rescuing individual children from pathological parents. The system is backed by huge financial investments in—yet little legal constraint on—its prowess.

Part III, "The Carceral Web," delves into the symbiotic relationship between family policing and criminal law enforcement. I lay out the multiple ways the child welfare system fits into a cohesive carceral apparatus that includes police and prisons. As the brutal arrest of Vanessa Peoples shows, police officers, criminal courts, and jails work hand in hand with their seemingly benign counterparts in the family-policing system. Warrantless home investigations, monitoring of families by state agents, civilians deputized to report on parents, seizure of children followed by placing them in foster care, prosecution of parents accused of maltreatment, and permanent severing of family ties for failing to comply with agency dictates—all reflect a carceral logic with parallels in the criminal punishment system. State CPS authorities increasingly use modern surveillance technologies and coordinate with law enforcement agencies to manage regulated populations more efficiently. Family policing is not just similar to the parts of the carceral regime abolitionists are working to tear down. Family policing is *part of* the carceral regime.

I also demonstrate that the child welfare system is *structured* to cause devastating injuries to the children it separates from their families. Because its fundamental design is violent and unjust, family policing produces damaging outcomes for the children it ensnares. On top of inflicting the trauma of separating children from their loved ones, state agencies fail to ensure that the children in their custody receive the care they need, and subject many of them to sexual and physical abuse. The system is set up to interfere with their emotional and physical health, their education, and their social relationships. It forces many of them into poverty, homelessness, and prisons. It drives many of them to suicide. There is a thin line between the state's treatment of Black children in foster care and its treatment of those in juvenile detention. Foster care criminalizes Black children. The family-policing system should be judged against the best our society could offer children and their families. By any ethical measure, it fails abysmally.

Many will still ask, "But how will we protect children from abuse without child protection services?" Abolishing family policing does not mean ignoring children suffering from deprivation and violence. To the contrary, abolition means imagining ways of meeting families' needs and preventing family violence that do not inflict the damage caused by tearing families apart. Family policing is a barrier to galvanizing the radical change and revolutionary care required to keep children safe and thriving. Ending it is the best way—the only way—to ensure the well-being of children and their families.

In Part IV, "Abolition," I conclude by describing a small but dynamic movement to abolish the family-policing system and radically transform child welfare. Ignited by Black mothers who have been separated from their children, this burgeoning movement rests on a long tradition of resistance against state destruction of families and includes former foster youth, social justice activists, legal services providers, nonprofit organizations, and scholars. Our goal is not only to dismantle the current system, but also to imagine and create better ways of caring for children, meeting families' needs, and preventing domestic violence. Like demands to defund police, abolishing family policing includes diverting the billions of dollars spent on regulating and breaking up families to cash assistance, health care, housing, and other material supports provided directly and noncoercively to parents and other family caregivers, as well as to community care networks that are disconnected from state surveillance.

The abolitionist mission to liberate Black people from captivity must include freeing family caregivers from state supervision and children from foster care. Ultimately, movements to dismantle different parts of the carceral state are working toward the same world—a world where all children are safe and cared for without the need for police, prisons, and family separation. A more expansive understanding of policing and abolition that contests the state's benevolent terror is essential to collectively building a new society that supports rather than destroys families and communities. This book is dedicated to that abolitionist vision.

PART I
TERROR

ONE

DESTROYING BLACK FAMILIES

THE BEHEMOTH

The sun had just begun to rise over Manhattan on an August morning in 2013. Angeline Montauban was whispering into the phone as she crouched in the bathroom of her apartment. As her partner and their two-year-old son slept, she had tiptoed there to call Safe Horizon, a domestic abuse hotline she had seen advertised in subway stations. She had decided it was time to stop the violence she was experiencing at the hands of her partner, and she hoped Safe Horizon could provide counseling or help her relocate with her son. At first, the social worker who answered her call listened sympathetically to Montauban's story. But once Montauban mentioned the couple had a little boy, the voice on the other end turned harsh and began collecting information about the family's whereabouts.[1]

That very afternoon, a caseworker with the city's Administration for Children's Services (ACS) arrived at Montauban's apartment, explaining that she was there to investigate a report of child maltreatment. At first Montauban was confused; she and her partner took excellent care of their son and had never abused him. Then she realized the social worker at Safe Horizon had contacted child protection authorities based on Montauban's call for help. "The minute she knocked on my door, she was building a case against me," Montauban would recall about the ACS worker. The caseworker inspected her son's body, as well as the entire apartment, finding no evidence of harm to the boy. Yet she told Montauban that her family was under ACS supervision for the next sixty days. Twice a month a caseworker would make an unannounced visit to inspect their home, looking for evidence that might warrant removing her son and putting him in foster care. Within a few weeks, Montauban obtained an order of protection for herself against her partner, and he moved out of their apartment. But the visits and order didn't satisfy ACS. In a family court hearing, ACS insisted that Montauban file for an order of protection for her son against his father as well. Montauban disagreed, explaining to the judge she wanted her son to maintain a relationship with his father, who had never hurt him.

A few days later, Montauban's partner took their son to family court for an appointment. ACS instructed him to leave the boy at a day care center on the first floor of the court building. It was a setup: ACS had filed a petition to apprehend Montauban's son on the grounds that he was neglected because Montauban allegedly had allowed him to witness domestic violence and declined to file an order of protection against his father. That evening, the caseworker called Montauban to inform her that ACS had snatched her son from the family court day care center. Her toddler was in foster care—in the custody of strangers in the Bronx.

Instead of working toward reunifying Montauban with her son, ACS moved him to several foster homes, promised the foster caretakers he would be free for adoption, and retaliated against Montauban when she expressed concerns by suspending her visits with him. When Montauban faced termination of her parental rights, it was her son's insistence on being reunited with her that preserved their legal bond. It took Montauban five years to retrieve her son from what she calls the "labyrinth" of family policing.

Many Americans believe that the child welfare system consists of teams of well-meaning social workers who investigate disturbing reports of child abuse and rescue children from monstrous parents who are injuring them or from incompetent parents who are incapable of keeping them safe. News stories tend to feature the most egregious incidents of children who were tortured in their homes and the caseworkers who saved them or—more often—failed to prevent their deaths. The general public has little idea about the true size, scope, and prowess of the family-policing regime. If anything, many are left with the impression that overwhelmed caseworkers need more time and money to find and salvage children from domestic destruction.

In this chapter, I will describe how America's family-policing system actually works. Angeline Montauban's devastating experience with ACS is typical. Far from functioning as a helpful service provider, the child welfare system operates as a destructive behemoth. Child protection authorities wield one of the most terrifying powers a government can exercise: the power to forcibly remove children from their homes and permanently separate them from their families. The state deploys this disruptive force disproportionately on Black families. Black families are at high risk—far higher than white families—of being reported, investigated, torn apart, and demolished. In cities across the nation, CPS surveillance is concentrated in impoverished Black neighborhoods, where all the residents are collectively ruled and terrified by the agencies' threatening presence. As we will see, most Black children in America will experience at some point in their young lives the intrusion of CPS agents in their homes.

With the threat of child removal at its core, the child welfare system regulates massive numbers of families. In 2019 alone, CPS agencies received referrals of nearly 8 million children suspected to be victims of abuse or neglect. Intake workers screened out more than half the reports as inappropriate for CPS involvement and sent the remaining allegations (regarding 3.5 million children) to CPS field offices for investigation or an alternative response. Most initial CPS investigations determined that the triggering allegations were "unsubstantiated"—there was insufficient evidence to indicate the allegations were true. CPS investigators find abuse or neglect only in one-sixth of screened-in referrals.[2]

The screening process still leaves hundreds of thousands of families subject to state intervention each year. Even after CPS investigators closed the unsubstantiated cases, they identified 656,000 children as victims of abuse and neglect in 2019. The families of these children are put through an indefinite period of intensive scrutiny and control by CPS workers and judges who have the power to keep children apart from their parents for years on end and ultimately to sever their family ties forever. Every year state agents forcibly take some 250,000 children from their parents and put them in the formal foster care system. At the same time, CPS agencies informally separate an estimated 250,000 more children from their parents based on so-called safety plans, arrangements parents are pressured to agree to in lieu of a formal court proceeding. That is a total of half a million children taken from parents' physical custody annually as a result of CPS involvement. This is no benign social service program.[3]

THE COLOR OF FAMILY POLICING

Despite its wide net, the family-policing system doesn't universally put all families at risk of entanglement. To the contrary, the government targets specific groups for intervention. Black and Indigenous families are the most likely to be disrupted by child welfare authorities. Although the rates of white family involvement are lower, white children from very impoverished areas, such as rural Appalachia, also experience extreme amounts of state involvement. Family policing is most intense in communities that exist at the intersection of structural racism and poverty.[4]

Not much has changed since I observed child welfare proceedings in Chicago in the 1990s and saw nothing but Black mothers appearing before the judge. In 2011, although only about a quarter of children in Chicago's Cook County were Black, they made up more than three-quarters of the foster care population. Nicole Rousseau, a Black sociologist at Kent State University, experienced a similar racial dynamic in her prior job as a social worker serving hundreds of children in two states, three major cities, and numerous suburbs. During this period, Professor Rousseau encountered only three white families—and they "were the most extreme cases that anyone in any of the facilities had ever witnessed." Rousseau notes that the Black families who constituted virtually all of her cases looked very different: "I never ever once had a case against a Black family that did not involve drugs and poverty." Rousseau's observations reflect the child welfare system's racial reality: although there are many white families under CPS supervision, authorities are much more likely to intervene in Black families and to look for less justification to do so. As a whole, white families don't experience the intensity of policing that CPS concentrates on Black communities.[5]

The number of children in the United States who are involved in child welfare investigations is staggering. A team of leading social work researchers recently counted for the first time the chances that children will be investigated by CPS for child maltreatment over the course of their lifetimes. Their pathbreaking study, published in 2017, estimated that more than a third of all children (37.4 percent) experience a CPS investigation at least once by their eighteenth birthday. The figure for Black children is even more astounding: more than half of Black children (53 percent) are subjected to a CPS investigation at some point during their childhoods—almost twice the lifetime prevalence for white children (28.2 percent). A 2021 study that focused on data from America's largest counties revealed even higher rates of investigation in some urban areas. For example, the study estimated that 72 percent of Black children in Los Angeles County will endure a CPS investigation during the course of their childhoods. In none of the big cities surveyed did the percentage of Black children subjected to investigation fall below 40 percent. We shouldn't minimize the significance of undergoing an investigation by itself, regardless of the outcome. Even when charges are dropped, the children and parents can feel the traumatizing effects—the children interrogated and possibly strip searched by strangers, the parents humiliated and marked as suspects, everyone terrified of what might come next.[6]

Whether you view this large number of CPS investigations as evidence of excessive child maltreatment or evidence of excessive state intrusion, it indicates that America is doing a poor job of promoting children's welfare. The extent of state intervention in Black children's lives is particularly disturbing. We can only imagine the impact of subjecting half of Black children to investigation on their sense of security, their relationship with their parents, and their view of the government.

More disruptive still is the forced family separation that often follows CPS investigations. In 2018, the national foster care population stood at 435,225. That figure represents the number of children who were already in foster care on the first day of the fiscal year. If we add those who entered foster care over the course of 2018, the number jumps to 700,000 children who were taken from their parents and kept in foster care at some point during the year. Black children remain grossly overrepresented in the national foster care population: although Black children were only 14 percent of children in the United States in 2019, they made up 23 percent of children in foster care.[7]

While Black children are removed from their homes at higher rates in every state, some states have especially egregious disparities. In Wisconsin, white children are 71 percent of the child population, but 46 percent of the foster care population, while Black children, who are only 9 percent of the child population, represent 30 percent of the children in foster care. Black children and white children each make up 20 percent of California's foster care population, but Black children are only 5 percent of the state's child population, compared to white children's 26 percent share. In New York as well, Black children and white children have diametrically opposed chances of being taken from their families. White children are very underrepresented in foster care (48 percent of child population versus 23 percent of foster care population), while Black children are very overrepresented in the system (15 percent of child population versus 44 percent of foster care population).

More telling are recent data indicating children's chances of landing in foster care at some point while growing up. About 15 percent of Indigenous children and 11 percent of Black children can expect to enter foster care before their eighteenth birthday. The rate for white children, one in twenty, is substantially lower, but still a troubling figure for government-imposed family separation.[8]

Latinx families are "underrepresented" in national foster care statistics compared to their population size. According to federal statistics, children who fell in the category "Hispanic (of any race)" were 26 percent of the total child population in 2019 and 21 percent of children in foster care. Yet a 2018 study found that placement of Latinx children varied greatly across locations, and these children were overrepresented in the system in twenty states. As Latinx families increasingly have become targets of surveillance by US Immigration and Customs Enforcement (ICE) and of anti-immigrant vitriol, they have experienced intensified intervention by CPS authorities in some parts of the country. Overall, Black, Brown, and Indigenous children are the most likely to be separated from their parents, and nonwhite children make up more than half of America's foster care population.[9]

THE RESEARCH BATTLE

There is no question that Black children are overrepresented in CPS statistics; they comprise a percentage of the foster care population that is nearly double their share of the overall population. Federal data plainly show that Black children are more likely than white children to be reported for maltreatment, to have allegations of their maltreatment investigated, and to be placed in foster care. Once taken from their homes, they and their families receive inferior services, including family preservation support, financial aid, housing, and child care. Black children are shuffled to more placements and stay in foster care longer. They are less likely to ever return to their parents and more likely to have their parents' rights terminated.[10]

The data showing stark racial disparities in every aspect of the child welfare system are undeniable. What is controversial among child welfare experts is whether or not these statistical disparities constitute racial discrimination.

Since the 1990s, child welfare researchers have tried to determine the role of race in child welfare decision making. Are Black children investigated and removed from their homes at higher rates because of their race or because of other factors that make them more vulnerable to CPS intervention? Does poverty rather than race explain Black children's overrepresentation in the system? Does the extra risk of CPS involvement experienced by Black families result from racial bias in decision making? For thirty years, the National Incidence Study, the federal government's periodic survey of child abuse and neglect, seemed to some experts to settle the question. The first three studies, published in 1981, 1988, and 1996, revealed no statistically significant differences in child maltreatment rates between Black and white homes. In fact, NIS-3 found that, after controlling for socioeconomic status, Black children were less likely to be maltreated than white children. Some child welfare critics pointed to the discrepancy between Black families' lower rates of maltreatment and higher rates of system involvement as compelling evidence that the system was racially biased.

Other researchers took the opposite view. A group of prominent child welfare scholars have contended for just as long that the racial disparities in investigations and foster care are based on justifiable reasons for CPS to intervene in Black families. They challenged the NIS findings as distorted by methodological lapses and claimed that dysfunction in Black families and disorder in their neighborhoods were evidence of Black children's greater deprivations. This group of child welfare researchers were disparity defenders: they argued that the statistics don't mean Black children are overrepresented in the child welfare system; they simply reflect Black children's greater need for child welfare services.[11]

One of the most prominent disparity defenders is Elizabeth Bartholet, a former professor at Harvard Law School who directed its Child Advocacy Program. For over two decades, she has unabashedly advocated for intensified removal of Black children from their families. In *Nobody's Children: Abuse and Neglect, Foster Drift, and the Adoption Alternative*, published in 1999, she called for removing barriers to state intervention in Black families and for escalating termination of parental rights so more Black children could be adopted into white homes. "Keeping them in their families and their kinship and racial groups when they won't get decent care in those situations may alleviate guilt,"

Bartholet wrote, "but it isn't going to do anything to promote racial and social justice. It isn't going to help groups who are at the bottom of the socioeconomic ladder to climb that ladder. It is simply going to victimize a new generation." Bartholet had argued previously that Black children benefited from transracial adoption because "whites are in the best position to teach black children how to maneuver in the white worlds of power and privilege." Bartholet's staunch advocacy stamped with Harvard's prestige helped garner support for federal legislation in the 1990s that facilitated termination of Black parents' rights and transracial adoption of Black children in foster care.[12]

The debate intensified in 2010 when the fourth NIS reported for the first time that Black children were more likely than white children to be victims of physical abuse, neglect, and endangerment (circumstances that put children in danger of being harmed). The disparity defenders immediately latched on to NIS-4 as a "gotcha" moment. Professor Bartholet had primed the pump in a 2009 law review article, "The Racial Disproportionality Movement in Child Welfare: False Facts and Dangerous Directions," which vehemently opposed the "powerful coalition" that had made the disproportionate involvement of Black children in foster care "the central issue in child welfare today." Calling me "a major Movement figure," she mischaracterized the arguments I had made in *Shattered Bonds* and that had guided early organizing against racism in the child welfare system. She claimed that "their goal is to achieve what they term racial equity—the removal of black and white children to foster care at rates equal to their general population percentages" based on evidence that "relied overwhelmingly on one source . . . the National Incidence Studies (NIS)."

Bartholet was wrong on both counts. My vision of racial justice was ending child removal, not equalizing it, and it didn't depend on NIS analyses of maltreatment. The earlier NIS studies were a minor part of the compelling evidence documenting the system's discrimination against Black families. Yet Bartholet had set up a straw man that she and her colleagues could easily knock down when NIS-4 was published. The disparity defenders downplayed racism in the child welfare system by reducing it to a problem of racially disparate statistics rather than a problem of state repression of Black communities. Casting themselves as liberal do-gooders, they rationalized the racial disparities as benefiting Black children, constructing a Machiavellian obstacle to the growing campaign to end the state's destruction of Black families.[13]

The disparity defenders argued that NIS-4 proved what they had suspected all along: Black children are actually victimized more by parental maltreatment, so greater CPS involvement in their lives is therefore warranted. They claimed that NIS-4 definitively shut down concerns about racism in the child welfare system. "Reducing Black/White disproportionality should not be a general policy goal," Brett Drake, a professor at Washington University in St. Louis, stated as the first recommendation in his response to NIS-4. "CPS has already achieved congruency between Black/White disproportionality *in the occurrence of CPS investigations* and Black/White disproportionality *in the need for CPS investigations*. Any implicit suggestions that disproportionality in child welfare is necessarily a problem should be radically changed."[14]

A special report on foster care in Los Angeles published in March 2013 by the local newspaper *Whittier Daily News* began by disclosing that Black children were 8 percent of Los Angeles County's general child population, but comprised 29 percent of its foster care caseload. Then, citing NIS-4, it rehearsed the argument that the stark statistics should cause no concern. The story took aim at *Shattered Bonds*, describing me as "one of a host of child welfare experts who during most of the 2000s believed that institutional racism was the leading cause of the high numbers of black children in foster care, an argument that has lost steam in the last few years in the face of new data." The conclusion that the movement against racism in the child welfare system was quenched by the NIS-4 statistics lent misplaced credence to the study and gravely misconceived the movement's claims, objectives, and future. The new data did not excuse the persistent destruction of Black families or assuage advocacy against it. Nevertheless, inflating the accuracy and significance of racial differences in maltreatment figures has proven to be a persistent distraction from tackling the harm family policing inflicts on Black children, families, and communities. Moreover, the disparity defenders completely ignored that NIS-4 found a significant decline in child maltreatment between 1993 and 2005, countering their calls for escalating child removals.[15]

Unsurprisingly, Professor Bartholet led the backlash by organizing an invitation-only conference titled Race and Child Welfare: Disproportionality, Disparity, Discrimination: Re-Assessing the Facts, Re-Thinking the Policy Options, which took place at Harvard Law School in January 2011. Surprisingly, she asked me to give the opening remarks. In my talk, I urged the audience to think about the racial statistics that would be presented by panelists the following day as a "political question, which is how does child welfare policy in the United States historically as well as today reflect and reinforce the disadvantaged status of African American families." When the conference resumed the next morning, Bartholet introduced the first panel, titled Removal Rates: Official v. Actual Maltreatment Incidence, as a refutation of my talk the prior evening. "The evidence is strongly to the contrary of what Dorothy Roberts claimed with respect to over-intervention," she declared. I had a sinking feeling I had been set up. My hunch was confirmed when speaker after speaker made the case that Black children were in danger from their families and communities and had to be saved by child protection authorities.[16]

Throughout the day, white scholars, administrators, and judges proclaimed the need for CPS to intensify its intrusion in Black families. A young white woman who had formerly been in foster care and had recently graduated from college was invited to serve as the representative of Black children in the system. She implored the audience to rescue her "brothers and sisters still in foster care" from their inadequate families and dangerous neighborhoods. On the final panel, Cindy Lederman, a white juvenile court judge in Miami, defended increasing foster care placements as an "unfortunate necessity." "If the choice is that or being maltreated, what choice do we have?" she asked rhetorically. Cassie Statuto Bevan, a former Republican congressional staffer, scoffed at concerns about racism. "We have been putting every ism before the child," she said. "I choose the child over the race claims." She delivered one of the most egregious white savior appeals of the day: "This conference is about African American children. . . . These are my kids, too."

I left the conference physically sickened by the white benevolence that permeated the atmosphere. The sympathy for Black children expressed by many of the white speakers depended on Black children "belonging" to them. I heard all too clearly in their presentations the false compassion that rationalizes terror toward Black families in the name of protecting their children from harm. As I show throughout this book, this white benevolence—on the part of liberals and conservatives alike—is pervasive in child welfare practice and policy. It is an especially pernicious form of benevolence, for it requires stripping Black families of their integrity in favor of white supervision of their children.

REFRAMING THE QUESTIONS

None of the NIS reports can resolve the question of racism in family policing. To begin with, the NIS is not capable of definitively determining which children are at greatest risk of maltreatment. No study can. "Generally, it is understood that a comprehensive measurement of incidence or prevalence of child maltreatment is not possible because maltreatment is most often not observed except by the perpetrator and victim," a group of leading researchers explained in a 2011 report. All the varying methods researchers use to measure child maltreatment have limitations and often result in inconclusive or even conflicting findings. Indeed, many of the same researchers who now rely on NIS-4 to support their dismissal of racism in child welfare rejected the prior NIS reports as methodologically unreliable.[17]

A major problem is that detecting abuse and neglect is always subject to bias on the part of those who report it. The NIS is supposed to measure *actual* occurrences of child abuse and neglect, in addition to official cases substantiated by child welfare workers. This is why the NIS has been held up as a way to test whether there is racial bias in the system. But the NIS measures *reported* child maltreatment based on a survey of professionals called sentinels, such as doctors, teachers, police officers, and social service staff, who regularly encounter children in the course of their jobs. Black families are more likely to come in contact with sentinels in public agencies, and these sentinels are just as likely as anyone else to be influenced by negative stereotypes and prejudices against Black families. Moreover, the NIS definitions of maltreatment are broad and vague, allowing for wide interpretation. They include a sentinel's guess that a child is at risk of experiencing harm in the future. Many Americans readily acknowledge that police officers routinely decide whether to stop and frisk a pedestrian or pull over a driver in racially biased ways. Why would we expect them to be any less biased in the way they interpret how Black parents are treating their children?[18]

What's more, comparing either maltreatment or CPS involvement rates using a variety of intersecting demographic factors, such as race, income, education, and family structure—what researchers call "multivariate" analyses—can be approached from multiple angles. Researchers have reached opposing results depending on which specific variables they choose to examine and control for in their study designs. Because of this complexity of interacting factors, the NIS-4 authors advised that the data should be "interpreted with caution"—a warning the disparity defenders failed to heed. The extensive data generated from attempts to pinpoint the sources of racial disparities haven't brought us any closer to ending them. These confused statistical analyses of biased data have obscured more than clarified the significance of targeting Black families for state surveillance and disruption.[19]

The central problem with the disproportionality research isn't its conflicting or weak methodologies; the problem is that the studies are driven by the wrong questions. Researchers typically determine whether or not race matters by controlling for every other factor that might affect maltreatment rates or CPS involvement—trying to isolate what one research team called a "racial residual." Many are hell-bent on showing there is no racial residual at all or explaining it as a problem with Black families rather than a problem with racism.[20]

It makes no sense to ask to what extent race alone, isolated from other contributing factors, determines either maltreatment or the state's response to it. Being Black in America is systematically tied to poverty, segregated and insecure housing, restricted access to public benefits, and greater exposure to state violence. Racism "has given the Black child a history, a situation, and a set of problems that are qualitatively different from those of the white child," Andrew Billingsley and Jeanne Giovannoni presciently wrote in *Children of the Storm* a half century ago. "In a narrower context, American racism has placed Black children in an especially disadvantaged position in relation to American institutions, including the institution of child welfare." Although the authors made that observation about a time when child welfare agencies were more likely to ignore Black families than to destroy them, their clarity about the role of racism in child welfare policy applies in either case.[21]

Some disparity defenders respond that the institution of child welfare is a racially neutral way of dealing with the set of problems Black families experience as a consequence of societal discrimination. They twist Black children's social disadvantages into an excuse for stepped-up family policing in Black communities. "We are concerned about any CWS [child welfare system] redesign that ignores the need for vigorous CPS," a group of researchers wrote in 2020, because "Black children have a heavy historic burden of racism to carry." This view makes the mistake of seeing the "heavy burden of racism" as the root of child maltreatment instead of the root of state intrusion in Black families. The historic burden Black children have borne includes the way the US state chooses to solve the problems it creates for Black people—by destroying their families instead of ending the structural inequities that produced the problems in the first place.[22]

It isn't enough to argue that Black children are in greater need of help. We should be asking why the government addresses their needs in such a violent way. Even if Black children require more services, why is the main "service" being provided the forced breakup of their families? Regardless of the causal variables identified, government authorities assume that maltreatment of Black children results from pathologies intrinsic to their homes and that helping them requires dislocating them from their families. The disparity defenders take little account of the harm inflicted by the violent solution they propose. At the conference Professor Bartholet organized, speakers enthusiastically presented data to support the need to take Black children from their families. Not once did those speakers count the trauma Black children experience from family separation.

TWO

"THEY SEPARATE CHILDREN AT THE HARLEM BORDER, TOO"

THE TRAUMA OF FAMILY SEPARATION

Although child removal is the fulcrum of US child welfare policy, its traumatizing impact on families didn't receive widespread public attention until 2018, when the Trump administration launched a policy of systematically separating asylum-seeking children from their parents at the Mexican border to deter future migration to the United States. The revelations of children taken from their parents, crowded in detention camps, and dispersed to foster homes sparked immediate outrage. Especially compelling were photographs and videos of ICE agents tearing shrieking children from their parents' arms. Soon the media, foundations, and professional associations circulated scientific studies documenting the terrible psychological damage inflicted on the children when forcibly ripped from their parents. In May 2018, the American Academy of Pediatrics issued a press release warning that the "toxic stress" children experience when separated from their parents "can cause irreparable harm, disrupting a child's brain architecture," potentially leading to "lifelong consequences for children." A month later, more than thirteen thousand mental health professionals chastised the president for ignoring this scientific evidence of devastating harm. "To pretend that separated children do not grow up with the shrapnel of this traumatic experience embedded in their minds is to disregard everything we know about child development, the brain, and trauma," their petition stated.[1]

The *Washington Post* reviewed the psychological research in a June 2018 story, "What Separation from Parents Does to Children," issuing one of the most dramatic descriptions of what happens to children when forcibly taken from their parents: "Their heart rate goes up. Their body releases a flood of stress hormones such as cortisol and adrenaline. Those stress hormones can start killing off dendrites—the little branches in brain cells that transmit messages. In time, the stress can start killing off neurons and—especially in young children—wreaking dramatic and long-term damage, both psychologically and to the physical structure of the brain."

"The effect is catastrophic," Charles Nelson, a pediatrics professor at Harvard Medical School, was quoted as saying. "There's so much research on this that if people paid attention at all to the science, they would never do this."[2]

Media reports of migrant children's reunions with their parents shone additional light on the negative impact of separation. Once back with their parents, children who had been forcibly taken at the border showed signs of fear and anxiety, refusing to take a bath, travel to school, or fall asleep without a parent close by. Human rights experts declared that the suffering inflicted on families by the policy was so egregious as to constitute a crime against humanity under international law. According to international conventions, the grievous harm caused by state-imposed family separation can even constitute torture.[3]

In December 2020, a group of New York City activists put up a sign at the 125th Street subway station that read, "They separate children at the border of Harlem too." The US practice of targeting Black communities for child removal should similarly sound an alarm. But it has the opposite effect: the public all but ignores the trauma experienced by these families torn apart by CPS agencies on a daily basis. There is a noticeable discrepancy between the condemnation rightfully directed at the Trump administration's family separation policy and the relative silence regarding the breakup of families that occurs every day in America's Black neighborhoods. In fact, local CPS agents take as many children from their parents every week as were separated under the entire Trump "zero tolerance" policy.[4]

Just like the immigrant children who garnered the public's sympathy, children in foster care typically have close and loving relationships with their parents and suffer inconsolably when separated from them. Yet psychologists who issued press releases and signed petitions in opposition to Trump's policy haven't collectively condemned the US family-policing system that inflicts the same trauma. Indeed, CPS relies heavily on psychologists, counselors, and therapists to manage the families involved in the domestic child welfare system and to testify in favor of keeping families apart.

It should not require a mountain of scientific research to demonstrate the anguish caused by forcibly taking children from their homes. We hardly need a psychological study to understand that ripping children from the familiar people in their lives and thrusting them into the care of unfamiliar ones is traumatizing. CPS workers snatch children from their beds in the middle of the night, babies from maternity wards, toddlers from playgrounds, and children off school buses. In cases where CPS workers take children from school without warning, their parents often spend agonizing hours without any idea what happened to their children and without having a chance to give them any calming assurance or explanation.

Pause to think what it means to split children from their parents and other loved ones to place them in the hands of strangers. From a political perspective, removing children from their homes is one of the most severe exercises of government power. From a child's perspective, it is terrifying. The very act of being pried away from parents is by itself damaging—"a significant turning point . . . that many children will relive over and over again in their minds," writes Dr. Monique Mitchell, an expert on foster children's feelings of loss at the Dougy Center for Grieving Children and Families in Portland, Oregon. Dr. Mitchell finds that the foster children she counsels mourn the estrangement from their parents, sometimes as much as if their parents had died. Even when foster children maintain contact with their parents through court-mandated visitation, the most important relationships in their lives have been profoundly unsettled. Many children experience serious consequences of grieving—"guilt, post-traumatic stress disorder, isolation, substance abuse, anxiety, low self-esteem, and despair."[5]

When children are seized from helpless parents by more powerful government agents, it creates a sense of vulnerability and betrayal in children, who rely on their parents to keep them safe. It is doubly traumatic to be plunked without warning or preparation into the care of strange adults. As one might imagine, this is a confusing situation for children, not understanding why they are living in someone else's home, where they belong, and what will happen to them in the future. Several studies of foster children have documented this extremely distressing state of mind, what Dr. Mitchell calls "ambiguous loss." Children undergo the stress of destabilization even if well cared for in the kindest of foster homes, let alone when dominated by uncaring or abusive foster caretakers, undergoing multiple placements, or spending long periods of time in institutional care. Children are separated not only from parents, but also from their siblings and friends, as well as from their neighborhoods and schools. This disruption can cause serious setbacks in their social lives, education, and health care.[6]

One child expressed it this way: "Foster care is just sick! . . . You get taken away from your parents. It ruins your life! Your heart is totally destroyed, and the only thing that is left working in your body is your brain. . . . That is why I want out of this foster care right now."[7]

Even less attention has been paid to the suffering parents experience when the state takes away their children. Not only do they lose the joy of their children's company, but they are wracked with worry about how their children are faring. Their children are in someone else's care, and they have no way to protect them or comfort them. Parents, too, feel intense grief, fear, and despair. A study of the mothers who survived abuse only to have their children taken by CPS recorded heart-wrenching confusion about their identity as mothers and distress from not being able to safeguard their children. One of the distraught mothers captured the profound madness evoked by losing one's child:

> I went insane. I broke down, nearly died. I couldn't stay in my house. I couldn't be around their clothes. . . . I found myself just wandering around looking for them. Even though, you know, they are not there. It's just—it's traumatizing. It's awful. [sobbing] . . . It's as if the three of them died. One day just died. That's the grief that I went through. That's the pain that I went through. But meanwhile they didn't [die]. Somebody's got them. Somebody's keeping them from me. . . . It was too much.[8]

Parents suffering these serious effects of losing their children are expected to pull their lives together while meeting pointless agency requirements that often throw more of a barrier in their way. They may lose what inadequate housing, income, and social supports they had before CPS got involved, while adding the stigma of being accused of bad parenting and child abuse. As a number of organizations noted in a recent report to the United Nations Special Rapporteur on Violence Against Women, these consequences "compound societal disadvantages already faced by these mothers prior to removal of their children," only to intensify the "barriers to rebuilding their lives and families."[9]

Court proceedings weighing the costs and benefits of separating children from their parents seldom pay attention to the harm inflicted by the removal itself. States vary widely on the legal standard for emergency removal of children. Some states permit CPS or police officers to remove a child without a court order solely on suspicion that the child is a victim of abuse or neglect, while others require evidence that the child is in imminent danger of serious harm. Federal law requires, as well, that CPS has made "reasonable efforts" to prevent children from entering foster care. In any case, the governing statutes in most states require judges to determine only if there is sufficient risk of harm *caused by the parents* and if CPS made reasonable efforts to avoid removal. As Shanti Trivedi, a clinical fellow at University of Baltimore School of Law, points out, "The majority of jurisdictions *do not* require that courts consider the harm of removal when answering those questions." New York and the District of Columbia are the sole jurisdictions that explicitly require by law that courts consider the harm of removal. Although some states' statutory schemes would permit parents to introduce harm-of-removal evidence (for example, to determine whether removal would be in the child's best interests), judges are under no obligation to consider it. It is as if the intimate relationships between investigated parents and children count for nothing.[10]

Addressing harms that children experience in their homes is no excuse to minimize the pain inflicted by tearing them away—never mind for now the additional damage inflicted by the foster care system itself. If we were seriously to count the harm caused by forcibly taking children from their parents, we would find that in most cases it far outweighs any harm to children the agencies claim to avoid. US child welfare policy, with its long-standing reliance on removing children, has never tried a less violent way of meeting vulnerable children's needs.

THE RACIAL GEOGRAPHY OF CHILD WELFARE

In addition to the trauma inflicted on individual children and their families, family separation also causes widespread damage to entire Black communities. Forced child removal has a racial geography. In cities across the country, child protection cases tend to be concentrated primarily in Black neighborhoods. The racial disparities in the numbers of children investigated and placed in foster care in a given year reveal only a slice of the system's impact on Black families. To grasp its full force, we would have to take into account the damaging effects on all residents who live in Black neighborhoods that are heavily policed by CPS agents. We should regard the overrepresentation of Black children in the CPS caseloads as massive state surveillance and disruption of entire neighborhoods. Because white children are very unlikely to experience these levels of state intrusion in their neighborhoods, the child welfare system means something very different for them.

As we have seen, studies of racial disproportionality report racial differences in the involvement of children in the child welfare system.

But researchers cannot understand the effects of concentrated child welfare agency involvement on relationships at the neighborhood level by aggregating individual child welfare data. In his 1987 classic *The Truly Disadvantaged*, sociologist William Julius Wilson pioneered research on the social effects of neighborhood characteristics. He argued that the deindustrialization of inner cities resulted in the extreme concentration of poverty and unemployment in African American neighborhoods. Residents of these neighborhoods, he claimed, experienced "concentration effects" that imposed burdens on them above and beyond those caused by their individual and family characteristics. Since then, numerous researchers have theorized and measured how the concentration of social and economic disadvantage in urban neighborhoods affects residents, including how neighborhood social composition and processes influence the well-being of children and adolescents. These neighborhood-oriented approaches to child welfare, however, overlook the role the child welfare system plays in mediating the effects of concentrated poverty on the well-being of children and other residents.

Social scientists have done a better job using sociological theories about neighborhoods to study the community-level impact of high incarceration rates in Black neighborhoods. Black communities have suffered the brunt of the staggering buildup of the prison population over the past fifty years. Research in several cities reveals that the exit and reentry of incarcerated adults, like that of children in foster care, is geographically concentrated in the poorest Black neighborhoods. A host of empirical studies conducted in the last two decades has found that incarceration has become a systematic aspect of neighborhood residents' family affairs, economic prospects, political engagement, social norms, and childhood expectations for the future.[11]

The mounting evidence of neighborhood-wide devastation caused by mass imprisonment suggested to me that the concentration of child welfare agency involvement in the very same Black neighborhoods also had widespread repercussions. In 2005, when I could find no research looking into this neighborhood dynamic, I conducted my own small case study in Woodlawn, a Black neighborhood on the South Side of

Chicago. It confirmed community-wide consequences of intense child welfare surveillance in the neighborhood. Woodlawn is not only one of Chicago's most segregated neighborhoods; it is also one of Chicago's poorest. Black families in America are likely to live in predominantly Black neighborhoods where there is a high level of poverty. Even poor white families are unlikely to experience such geographically concentrated poverty.[12]

Woodlawn also had one of the highest rates of foster care placement in Chicago. Most of the city's child protection cases were clustered in a few zip code areas, which, like Woodlawn, had Black residents almost exclusively. The vast majority of Chicago neighborhoods experienced less than half of Woodlawn's foster care rate. In no white neighborhood in Chicago were children placed in foster care at a level even approaching that of Woodlawn and the other Black neighborhoods. While most Black children living in Woodlawn have been touched by the presence of CPS in their neighborhood, there are no children living in Chicago's predominantly white neighborhoods who experience the same intensity of family policing.[13]

A 2019 analysis of Connecticut data by sociologist Kelley Fong revealed a similar pattern. She calculated that, although 10 percent of children in neighborhoods that are over 75 percent white will be reported to CPS by age five, this rate rises to 17 percent in neighborhoods that are 50–75 percent white, and to 27 percent in neighborhoods that are under 50 percent white. Neighborhood poverty rates (the proportion of residents who fall under the poverty line) also made a difference. The risk of being reported for children living in low-poverty neighborhoods doubled for children in moderate-poverty neighborhoods and tripled for children in high-poverty neighborhoods. "The considerable disparities in the prevalence of CPS contact by neighborhood highlight CPS contact as a feature of neighborhoods," Fong concluded. The degree of CPS contact is especially acute for families in predominantly Black neighborhoods where poverty is prevalent.

This racial geography creates a uniquely intense relationship between Black families and the child welfare authorities who police them. As a social worker in New York City remarked when a white woman asked her, "What's ACS?," "There's one group of people walking around not knowing that ACS exists, and there's another group of people walking around living in fear of ACS."[14]

The targeting of Black neighborhoods for state intervention is not an accidental consequence of the racial gap in poverty. During the Great Migration, when millions of Black people arrived in northern cities as refugees from white terror in the South, they were trapped in segregated ghettoes like Chicago's "Black Belt" by violent white gangs and restrictive real estate covenants. As Richard Rothstein documents in *The Color of Law: A Forgotten History of How Our Government Segregated America*, the confinement of Black people to segregated areas was reinforced by housing and law enforcement policies implemented by federal, state, and local governments. Black residents of these disinvested neighborhoods were not only excluded from beneficial government programs but also exploited by the private sector in the 1970s when they sought to become homeowners, a discriminatory mechanism Keeanga-Yamahtta Taylor terms "predatory inclusion" in *Race for Profit: How Banks and the Real Estate Industry Undermined Black Homeownership*.[15]

Today, redevelopment and gentrification that strip cities of affordable housing have pushed Black families into more restricted and insecure living conditions. Take San Francisco. As the cost of housing started to skyrocket in the 1980s, San Francisco's Black population began to plummet, falling from 13 percent of the population in the 1970s to 5.5 percent in 2015. San Francisco has experienced the fastest-declining Black population of any US city. Despite their shrinking share of the city's residents, half the children in foster care are Black. Most Black San Franciscans live in a tiny portion of the city, including a public housing project, where CPS targets its operation. The main function of the child welfare system in San Francisco is to patrol the borders between the neighborhoods of white residents who can afford the city's high housing prices and the segregated zone where most of the Black residents have been crammed.[16]

When I launched my study in Woodlawn, I wanted to understand the impact on the entire neighborhood of such intense child welfare agency presence in cities like Chicago, New York, and San Francisco.

Over the course of the summer, I interviewed twenty-five Black women who lived in Woodlawn about their experiences with the Department of Children and Family Services (DCFS). The director of a child care center located in a Woodlawn housing project allowed me to put up a flier seeking women who were interested in participating in my study. She even gave me a desk in one of the rooms where I could interview women at the end of the day when they came to pick up their children. Many of the women were residents of the housing project, and half of my interviews took place there. The women also referred their friends and neighbors to me, and I interviewed additional residents at their homes and at a local McDonald's restaurant. Most of the women, ages twenty-four to fifty-six, had some personal experience with DCFS—as foster children, kin caregivers, or friends or relatives of those involved in foster care. Although none of the participants said they had been investigated by CPS, it was possible some were ashamed to tell me that they had been.

The women I interviewed were aware of intense involvement by DCFS with families in their neighborhood. Most estimated the number of Woodlawn families under DCFS supervision to be at least half:

"Over half of the community, I would say. Yeah, it's a lot."

"My God, probably thousands."

"I'm gonna say 90 percent."

"It's common because people always getting their children taken away. So, yeah, it's common."

"From 60th to 67th, State to Stoney Island, even with it being 150 cases just in that little vicinity, 150 apartments or families or whatever, or everybody in the whole three-flat."

"I think everyone in Woodlawn knows someone in the system."

The women understood the function of DCFS to center on removing children from their homes and placing them in foster care. Tiara, a twenty-four-year-old whose friend was investigated by DCFS, stated, "I try not to know what the initials stand for, but I do know that in this neighborhood, to me, DCFS is the people that take your kids if you are not taking care of them correctly." Christina, also twenty-four years old, who had a friend investigated by DCFS, agreed: "It just seems like they're all about taking the child out of the home. You know, I've never really known of a situation where if someone told on the family and they let the child stay and deal with the problem."[17]

It was hard for the women to see DCFS as a benevolent service provider as long as it wielded the threat of taking children. Michelle, thirty-four, had served as a kinship foster parent for her nephew for a year when his mother (her sister) had to leave town and his father was incarcerated. She felt that many residents were reluctant to solicit help from DCFS because of its reputation for child snatching. "I think that everybody fears that 'I don't want to lose my children,'" she told me. "I wouldn't wish DCFS on anybody." Tamisha, who was also thirty-four, became familiar with DCFS when her friend was investigated. She confided that she had another friend with a substance abuse problem but would never contact DCFS to seek help for her. "She do have three younger kids, and I think she needs some help for them, so I've been trying to talk to her, letting her know maybe you need to go in a rehab place and have one of your family members take your kids or something," she said. "But personally, me just picking up the phone, calling DCFS, I couldn't do it. It would be on my conscience knowing that I made this phone call and this girl probably never see her kids."

The women all identified profound consequences of the high level of agency involvement in Woodlawn on both family and neighborhood relationships. Many noted that children who have been placed in foster care lose respect for their parents because their parents do not have custody of them. This lack of respect often continues when children are reunited with their families. Aisha, twenty-four years old, told me DCFS ruined the relationship between her aunt and her twenty-year-old cousin who spent time in foster care. "Well, she's staying with her mother now, but she still get checks and stuff from DCFS," Aisha said. "Like the respect—being away from your mother like that, if you haven't been put in a good home, the respect that you have for that person who birthed you is little. It's very, very little." Aisha gave another example of a neighborhood family, whose eight-year-old son was separated from his mother and had grown "rebellious": "Her little boy is like, 'What can you tell me? I'm not even in your household. What can you possibly tell me?' He had a little bit more respect because he was staying under her roof, but now he has very little respect for his mother because he is not there with her. And he feel like she don't have any say-so."

Aisha also believed that the family separation that ravaged her neighborhood hurt the children. "The child's gotta go through all this ridicule, being tossed about, your mother is nothing, your family is nothing, you been taken away. And it kinda makes the child feel like un-wanted," she told me. "And that why we have a lot of men and women growing up today very rebellious and very hurt and doing a lot of things out of their hurt because of the suffering and ridicule that they dealt with as a child. They don't have any sense of security."

Like Aisha, most of the women described the instability, discon-nection, and uncertainty experienced by children placed in foster care. "Really, you splitting the family up," Lauren, twenty-six, whose father's stepdaughter was placed in foster care, observed. "The kids, they need to be with their moms. If that's the only thing they know, then they go somewhere else and they ain't gonna be right. If they used to one envi-ronment and you put them somewhere else and they go place to place to place to place, it's a big impact."

I had anticipated that family separation would have damaging con-sequences for children's relationships with their families. But I had no idea about its power to poison relationships between neighbors. Many of the women recounted stories about residents calling DCFS to report their neighbors for child maltreatment, destroying a sense of trust among them. As one put it, "DCFS disrupts the community. . . . I would say it's a trust thing." Anita, a case manager for a private child welfare agency, chuckled when she described the intensity of neigh-bors reporting neighbors. "I think my friends, family, and neighbors call more than I do," she told me. "Sometimes I think they have DCFS on speed dial like it's an answer, a one-and-only answer. Even though they will say they think DCFS is overly involved, they will be the first to call. It doesn't really make sense, but they do."

As a result, residents must look over their shoulders for fear that a neighbor is noting a parental misstep or that an observant stranger is a DCFS caseworker. "If somebody calling DCFS on you and they come knocking at your door and you wondering why they at your door and you wondering who called them, then that's a problem. That's a big problem," twenty-seven-year-old Cassie warned, as if we were in a spy movie. "That's why you got to watch what you do and what you say, 'cause you don't know who you could be talking to. She could be DCFS, writing down stuff, taking notes, all of that, and you don't know who she is. So you have to be careful. You have to be very careful."

Heightening the sense of suspicion among neighbors was the common perception that residents were falsely accusing others of child abuse in order to seek retribution against them.

"I think friends and neighbors would call out of spite or revenge, but I don't see people calling for any other reason."

"If you did something wrong in the past and now you're trying to turn your life around and it could be somebody saying you did it [maltreated your child] just to get back at you."

"My cousin had her children put in the DCFS out of jealousy because a friend called the DCFS on her."

"I think, personally, that people are using DCFS as revenge now. They're revenging. You can argue with somebody. They call DCFS on you."

Deploying DCFS as a common means of recrimination is a troubling sign of the agency's entrenchment in neighborhood culture. Intensive state surveillance damages neighborhood relationships not only by creating distrust among neighbors but also by encouraging a destructive alternative to productive mechanisms for resolving neighborhood conflicts. I also heard stories about landlords, drug dealers, and abusive partners who threatened to report mothers to DCFS as a form of coercion, or falsely accused mothers of child maltreatment to punish them for disobedience.

Several of the women I interviewed described DCFS as a form of slavery or prison and placed it in a broader context of coercive neighborhood regulation. Early in the interview, Whitney, a twenty-three-year-old who had been in foster care as a child, described DCFS as "jail for kids, basically." Later she characterized the housing project where she lived in the same terms: "This is a hazard to people's lives. I'm serious. They have a camera now, a police camera, and it's just like I'm in jail, girl. I am." Others explicitly tied the detrimental effects of foster care on individual children to the interests of the broader community—and called for community action. "Like, okay, we was all riled for them to take this child from this person, but for you to take him and then put him into a foster home and they getting mistreated, then the community got to get back together and try to fight to get the child back," Tamisha remarked.

Aisha, who had passionately described the harms to children and families, also described in especially powerful terms the impact of family disruption on the neighborhood's civic life. "When you are taken away from your family, that is a form of separation, and they learn from that, growing up to be separated. It's not really set in them to be united, or to be one, or to come together to do anything," she told me. "We can never come together to do anything over here. It definitely has an effect on the community because bringing separation like that, I don't know what it does, but we can't as a people and as a community come together."

At the end of the interview, I asked each woman whether DCFS was too involved in Woodlawn, not involved enough, or involved just the right amount. Given their descriptions of family and community intrusion, I expected the residents to report that DCFS was too involved in their neighborhood. The most surprising discovery I made during my time in Woodlawn was that most of the women I interviewed stated that DCFS should be *more* involved. Although they criticized the agency's injury to neighborhood relationships, most nevertheless expressed a desire for continued or greater DCFS involvement in Woodlawn to meet the material needs of its struggling families.

Any positive comments about DCFS typically concerned its financial support for mothers, kinship caregivers, or foster children, not its protection of children from abuse and neglect. Twenty-seven-year-old Angela, who had been in foster care, explained that DCFS "does help them out with their, you know, financial-wise, pay bills and stuff like that. They help them out. . . . They do give them money for keeping the kids too," she added, referring to kin foster caregivers. Tamisha praised the support DCFS offered when her teenage friend's baby was hospitalized for radiator burns. "DCFS did tell her, if you find your own apartment, we'll pay your first month rent, your first month security. So that's a good thing. I think they paying her rent up until she get twenty-one; she's eighteen now. So it's a good advantage."

But not everyone thought financial assistance from DCFS was worth its cost to the neighborhood. As one woman told me, "I personally don't think they are helping anyone with the exception of money. I just would not go to DCFS for help. There are more better ways we can help in our community, and not just Woodlawn." The child welfare system exacts an onerous price for its support of neighborhood families: it requires parents to relinquish custody of their children in exchange for state support needed to care for them. If community disruption is the price residents must pay for desperately needed financial assistance, then most residents I spoke with were reluctantly willing to pay it. But they did not uncritically accept the terms of DCFS involvement. They made it clear that they wanted more financial support without ravaging family and neighborhood relationships, and they criticized the required linkage of resources families needed with investigation and child removal.

Many residents condemned the agency's narrow role rooted in investigating families rather than supporting them. Michelle, who cared for her nephew for a year, referred to the advertisement for the child abuse hotline, observing:

It just says abuse. If you being abused, this is the number you call. This is the only way you gonna get help. It doesn't say if I'm in need of counseling, or if I'm in need of my children don't have shoes, if I just can't provide groceries even though I may have seven kids but I only get a hundred something dollars in food stamps and my work check only goes to bills. I can't feed eight of us all off a-hundred-something-dollar food stamps. So I'm saying, they don't know that

DCFS can help them in a positive way. They [DCFS] only do negative things. They only take my children away. I think that is the big issue. I don't want to lose my children, so I'm not going to call DCFS for help because I only see them take away children.[18]

Although the residents recognized the corrosive effects of DCFS on their community, most also acknowledged their community's reliance on the agency to meet its needs. Having stripped Woodlawn, like many other Black neighborhoods, of social programs, affordable housing, and guaranteed public assistance, the government uses the punitive system of foster care to deal with struggling families. Black mothers are left in the bind of resenting DCFS surveillance yet wanting the agency's continued presence as one of the few remaining sources of public aid. Racial capitalism's destructive formula of "child protection" makes family assistance hinge on state custody of children. The child welfare system's racial geography concentrates this hellish bargain in Black communities.

THREE

PROFESSIONAL KIDNAPPERS

SNATCHING CHILDREN

It was an ordinary summer day in 2020 at the Prescott office of the Arizona Department of Child Safety. Eight women who worked there left their desks to gather in the parking lot. They lined up shoulder to shoulder in front of the parked cars to pose for a group photo. The lower halves of their faces were covered by masks—at the time, a common protection against the coronavirus that was raging across the nation. At one end, a young blonde woman displayed her work badge dangling from the top of her blue jeans. All the women wore matching bright-pink T-shirts. Four of them faced the camera to show the message on the front, written in prominent white letters:

Professional KIDNAPPER.

The other four women turned away from the camera so the message on the back of their T-shirts was in view:

DO YOU KNOW WHERE YOUR children ARE?

The women were "DCS specialists" in the office's investigative unit, hired to look into allegations of child abuse and neglect that the office received from mandated reporters, relatives and neighbors, and anonymous calls to the hotline. They had designed the pink T-shirts as "an inside joke" about criticism lodged against DCS, one of the women explained. According to a story later published in the *Arizona Republic* about the incident, "the agency's detractors have long raised concerns that it removes children from families too easily, and is biased against parents, with some going so far as to accuse it of kidnapping."[1]

"Kidnappers" was a term I had heard Jornell and many other Black mothers call the family-policing agents who took their children. These mothers viewed caseworkers more as law enforcement officers than as social service providers. They had learned the hard way that the job of CPS investigators is not to help parents take care of their children, but rather to find evidence that can be used against parents to take their children away. For most of the families CPS investigates, their stresses stem from economic insecurity, and CPS offers nothing to solve that, often making their circumstances worse. This is why Vanessa protested the appearance of two caseworkers and three police officers at her doorstep so vehemently, why she asked them, "Do you guys think by being here you're helping the situation at all?"

The photo of the CPS investigators spread quickly, first by text messages and emails among the agency's staff, then nationally via social media. On June 19, 2020, all eight women who appeared in the photo received letters from DCS director Mike Faust notifying them that they were terminated immediately. The Prescott office had a reputation for outrageous conduct. Christina Sanders, a former DCS unit supervisor, told the *Arizona Republic* that the staff dismissals put a "long overdue" stop to "a long-standing practice of bullying and entitlement. . . . They think they're so untouchable," she said. Sanders noted that she herself had been fired a year earlier when she refused to put a little boy in a group home in Phoenix because she thought the placement was inappropriate.

Certainly, the indiscreet stunt crossed the bounds of appropriate office decorum. But the fired women might be credited for being candid about their occupation. The reason the stunt seemed funny to all eight caseworkers was that it contained a kernel of reality. As the saying goes, "Behind every joke there is some truth." Like bounty hunters, they were hired by DCS to enter the homes of accused parents and leave with their children. In 2018, Arizona DCS took about 9,000 children from their parents and farmed them out to substitute homes and institutions. The state's foster care population comprised 13,360 children that year. Black children were the most likely of any group to be separated from their parents. Although they made up only 6 percent of the state's children, they were 12.7 percent of the children in foster care. The Prescott office reflects how family policing generally operates: it gives CPS agents virtually unfettered power to threaten parents and seize their children.[2]

Not all CPS workers treat their jobs in such cavalier fashion. Most people employed by child protection agencies probably start their careers with a commendable desire to improve children's welfare. But they soon find that they are expected to protect children by looking solely for parental pathologies, and the only tools they're given to fix them rely on threatening to take the children away. They are discouraged from analyzing the social structures that harm the children who are brought to their attention. They are denied the material resources that might help the parents navigate the barriers those structures create for their families. "I know I'm supposed to be a miracle worker, but sometimes there's nothing we can do," lamented an investigator in Connecticut who was interviewed by sociologist Kelley Fong. Another worker, who'd been called to investigate a family's housing situation, wondered aloud, "What am I supposed to really do? I don't see the kids being neglected." The caseworker told Fong that she wanted to help the family, but CPS did not provide ongoing rental assistance. "The sad part is there's nothing we can do in the sense that we don't have housing," she said. Left with "nothing we can do" to help families, CPS workers resort to the tools they have at their disposal: forcing parents to undergo intrusive supervision, taking children from their homes, and petitioning to permanently sever family relationships. The family-policing system produces professional kidnappers because that's the nature of the role it assigns to its workers, regardless of their good intentions.[3]

Caseworkers have enormous discretion to determine subjectively if there is any credible evidence of maltreatment, and to make the initial decision whether to let children they believe are at risk stay home or to take them from their parents. This wide latitude accorded CPS agents by law is an invitation to decide cases based on a double standard that treats the conditions of poverty as if it were child neglect and Black parents as if they were natural child abusers.

CONFUSING NEED WITH NEGLECT

The family-policing system justifies its blatant targeting of poor and low-income families by equating poverty with child neglect. The vast majority of children taken by CPS from their parents are alleged to have been neglected. Only 16 percent of children enter foster care because they were physically or sexually abused. Child maltreatment is defined so as to detect deficits on the part of poor parents and to ignore middle-class and wealthy parents' failings. "Inadequacy of income, more than any other factor, constitutes the reason that children are removed," social work scholar Duncan Lindsey concluded in his 1994 classic, *The Welfare of Children*. The state punishes families because they are poor, not because they are dangerous.[4]

The conflation of poverty and neglect is written directly into state statutes that define child maltreatment. Many states broadly permit intervention into families whenever parents fall short of supplying "the proper or necessary support for a child's well-being." A 2020 fifty-state survey of neglect statutes found that most "are very open-ended, allowing child protective investigators and their supervisors to declare a child neglected based on their own unbounded opinions as to what is 'proper' or 'necessary care.'" Others define child neglect as "the failure to provide adequate nurturance, food, clothing, shelter, sanitation, and education," or a similar list of material resources. Neglect can mean living in dilapidated or overcrowded housing, missing school, wearing dirty clothes, going hungry, or being left at home alone. In any case, the definitions are vague enough to give caseworkers ample discretion to decide when living conditions amount to neglect. Very rarely do parents deliberately withhold needed resources from their children. Typically, they simply can't afford them.[5]

Insecure housing, one of the leading reasons parents are accused of child neglect, provides a vivid illustration of how CPS confuses poverty with neglect. Children are routinely apprehended and kept in foster care because their parents are unable to find decent shelter. As a result of America's deep income inequality, predatory banking and real estate policies, residential segregation, and dearth of affordable housing, many families live in crowded or decaying homes that CPS workers consider unfit for children. Many families in which a parent becomes ill, loses a job, or gets a notice that the rent is going up are left homeless. In 2016, sociologist Matthew Desmond calculated that more than two million Americans were evicted from their homes every year. "Today, the majority of poor renting families in America spend over half of their income on housing, and at least one in four dedicates over 70 percent to paying the rent and keeping the lights on," explained Desmond in *Evicted*. "These days, there are Sheriff squads whose full-time job is to carry out eviction and foreclosure orders." In 2020, during the economic crisis triggered by the COVID pandemic, experts estimated that thirty million to forty million Americans faced eviction, with Black and Latinx residents hit the hardest.[6]

When CPS investigators find a family living in a hazardous apartment or homeless shelter, they typically have only one way to address the situation: take the children from their parents and place them elsewhere. The workers don't have the means to provide secure housing for the family, to direct the landlord to fix up the property, or to require the city to guarantee adequate shelter. Once when I took my law students to family court in Chicago, we observed a judge approve DCFS's request to keep a Black mother's children in foster care because the family's apartment was infested with mice and cockroaches. After the hearing ended, the judge let my students question him about the proceedings they had witnessed. One of my students asked the judge why he prolonged the children's separation from the mother instead of ordering the landlord to provide a habitable property. The judge replied that only the housing court had jurisdiction over the landlord; all he could do as a family court judge with jurisdiction over the children was to keep them out of the unsanitary apartment.

Vivek Sankaran, a clinical professor at University of Michigan Law School, similarly recounts how one of his clients, a mother trying to regain custody of her children, informed his students that she had been rendered homeless. The students tried to reach the caseworker by phone and email in an effort to resolve the crisis so the children could be reunited with their mother. "About a week later, they finally received a short message with a list of other community agencies that might be able to assist with housing, which my students had discovered days prior through a simple Google search," Sankaran recalls. "The caseworker ended the email indicating that there was nothing else she could do to help with housing." It is no wonder that the ten neighborhoods with the highest number of CPS cases in New York City are the ones with the greatest income-to-rent disparities in the city. The National Coalition for Child Protection Reform reports that one-third of children in foster care could have remained safely at home if their parents had adequate housing.[7]

In fact, CPS can make the family's housing situation worse when parents lose their space in a family shelter after caseworkers take away the children, making reunification even harder. Elizabeth Brico, a parent activist, uses the term "agency-induced homelessness" to describe the scenario wherein the family-policing system not only punishes families who are unhoused but also deprives parents of housing by separating them from their children. In April 2018, when Brico was falsely accused of abandoning her daughters, ages two and four, a magistrate gave custody of the girls to Brico's in-laws, with whom they had been staying. Noting that Brico had a history of engaging in methadone treatment, the magistrate simultaneously barred her from being in the home with the girls from eight p.m. to nine a.m. "I had just moved to Florida from Seattle and had nowhere else to stay," Brico recalls. "The magistrate made me homeless." That evening, her father-in-law dropped her off at "a shabby Motel 6 across town," and CPS never helped her with housing. Two years later, after Brico was able to get an apartment with a room for her daughters and tried her best to complete the haphazard services CPS mandated, the state of Florida terminated her parental rights and let her in-laws adopt the girls. "In the papers, they cited my 'small' apartment—the one they never saw—as part of the reason, instead of viewing my independent climb from homelessness as an asset," Brico writes.[8]

It is supposed to violate America's espoused values to punish people for being poor. Some states include an economic exemption in their child neglect statutes, charging parents for failing to provide for a child's material needs only if they are "financially able." In 2019, US Representative Gwen Moore, a Democrat from Wisconsin, introduced the Poverty Is Not Child Neglect Act, H.R. 2535, which requires the federal Department of Health and Human Services to ensure that grants given to state child welfare systems are not used to separate children from their parents because of poverty. But poverty usually has the opposite effect. Rather than operating as a defense against a neglect charge, poverty works as an enhancement of parental culpability. Many of the indicators child welfare agencies use to assess whether a child is at risk for maltreatment are actually conditions of poverty. Recall how the police inspected the refrigerator and kitchen cabinets when they entered Vanessa's home. Even children who have never been abused and who are in no immediate danger from their parents may be removed from their homes based on these indicators of poverty. In essence, the family's lack of material resources is presumed to place children at risk of future parental maltreatment.

In my conversations with Black mothers, I discovered a pattern of the state legitimizing these mothers' long-term involvement in the family-policing system, even when they were drawn into that system based on illegitimate pretexts. Their children were initially removed for reasons directly related to their financial situation, ostensibly to protect the children from harm. Once under agency control, the mothers were subjected to intense scrutiny that included mandatory parenting classes, supervised visits with their children, and a battery of psychological evaluations. Any failure to attend a required class, inappropriate interaction with their children, or diagnosis of mental distress became grounds to extend their children's time in foster care. It was a self-fulfilling prophecy: the families' poverty itself made caseworkers suspicious of some vague danger to the children, then the intensive surveillance inevitably turned up proof to substantiate those suspicions. State authorities could find fault with any parent subjected to such thorough inspection.

WHO'S A NEGLECTFUL PARENT?

So far, I have discussed how CPS holds parents accountable for the harms to children caused by poverty by calling those harms "child neglect." By conflating poverty and neglect, family policing targets poor and low-income families by penalizing the kinds of deprivation their children are more likely to experience, like inadequate food, housing, and medical care. But the family-policing system conflates poverty and neglect in another, even more sinister way. It accuses poor parents of neglecting their children for the exact same behavior that is considered perfectly acceptable if wealthier parents engage in it. A whole host of common circumstances can trigger an investigation of poor parents that would appear completely innocent if the parents were affluent.

After an exhausting day in 2010, Maisha Joefield, a Black single mother in Brooklyn, put her five-year-old daughter, Deja, to bed and relaxed into a warm bath with her headphones on. When she came out of the bathroom, she discovered that Deja had vanished from the apartment. Deja had headed across the street to Joefield's grandmother's house. A passerby alerted the police. Officers charged Joefield with child endangerment, and CPS put Deja in foster care for four days. Her name placed on the state child abuse registry, Joefield, a former day care worker, was barred from working with children. Deja began to do worse at her charter school.[9]

"In another community, your kid's found outside looking for you because you're in the bathtub, it's 'Oh, my God'—a story to tell later," observed Scott Hechinger, a lawyer at Brooklyn Defender Services. "In a poor community, it's called endangering the welfare of your child." One of Vivek Sankaran's clients was a Black mother who left her thirteen-year-old in charge of eight- and six-year-old siblings while she ran an errand. "In suburban America, we call this babysitting," Sankaran notes. "In a predominantly Black, public housing complex in Washington, D.C., this constituted neglect." Vanessa was originally accused of child endangerment for letting her toddler momentarily stray at a park—a charge that later resulted in a disastrous visit to her home by caseworkers and police officers. Some low-income mothers leave children at home by themselves because they have to go to work and can't afford child care.[10]

Meanwhile, middle-class white mothers are joining a free-range-kids movement that seeks to end helicopter-parenting norms in favor of letting children have more independence—including spending time outdoors on their own. The movement's chief spokesperson, Lenore Skenazy, who penned the 2009 book *Free-Range Kids: How to Raise Safe, Self-Reliant Children (Without Going Nuts with Worry)*, has enjoyed a platform on major TV networks and popular celebrity podcasts. She first gained notoriety with her op-ed in the *New York Sun*, "Why I Let My 9-Year-Old Ride the Subway Alone," recounting how she dropped her son at the Lexington Avenue subway in New York City with "a subway map, a MetroCard, and a $20 bill, and several quarters, just in case he had to make a call." Skenazy reports that, although her son arrived home safely, "ecstatic with independence," many of her friends were aghast at her neglectful parenting. Yet Skenazy, at little risk of being investigated by CPS, went on to cofound Let Grow, a nonprofit that offers parents and educators "the tools and confidence to raise independent kids."[11]

Let Grow has also advocated for narrowing vague child neglect and endangerment laws that regulate when children can be left alone without adult supervision, which are applied primarily to less privileged mothers and could potentially pose a problem for free-range parenting. In 2018, Utah enacted the nation's first "free-range parenting" law, amending the definition of neglect to allow children to engage by themselves in a list of specified "independent activities," including traveling to and from school or nearby recreational facilities by walking or bicycling. But the legislators added an important condition: these independent activities don't count as neglect only if the child is one "whose basic needs are met," seeming to allow exclusion of poor parents from the law's reprieve. Let Grow opposed the poverty exclusion. Its model bill for legislative reform of neglect laws contains no such limitation, and less restrictive proposals to permit free-range parenting have been introduced in several other states.[12]

My point isn't to criticize Let Grow's needed challenge to vague and expansive neglect laws. Let Grow can be an ally in the movement to end family policing. Still, Skenazy and her white middle-class followers have far greater freedom to let their children roam independently without fear of losing them to foster care—not because they care more for their children, but because their race and class largely exempt them from CPS scrutiny.

To some extent, the distinction between families can stem from a real disparity in risks to children. Neglect statutes blame parents for the harmful effects that poverty really can have on their children. Studies have consistently found that family income is the strongest predictor of child maltreatment. The NIS has always reported that the incidence of child maltreatment is highest in the most economically desperate families. As I've discussed, these findings are subject both to reporter bias and to the conflation of neglect with poverty, so they must be viewed with caution. Still, although child abuse occurs in families across income levels, severe violence against children is more likely to occur in households with annual incomes below the poverty line. It should not be surprising that families living in extreme poverty experience greater stress and have fewer outlets than those with higher incomes.

Moreover, poor and low-income parents have fewer resources to avoid the harmful effects of their risky decisions. Poor parents can't afford to pay others to care for their children when they are unable to because they have to go to work, they have competing family obligations, or they are depressed. Nor can they afford to pay professionals to cover up or mitigate their mistakes. Affluent substance-abusing parents, for example, can check themselves into a private residential drug treatment program and hire a nanny or pay for boarding school to care for their children during their absence. CPS never has to be the wiser.

Wealth insulates children from many of the potentially harmful consequences of having irresponsible parents. Poverty, on the other hand, effectively raises the standard of care the government requires parents to meet.

Poor and low-income families are more likely to come in contact with professionals who are mandated to report child maltreatment. Receiving social services, relying on welfare benefits, living in public housing, and using public clinics all subject parents to an extra layer of surveillance by government workers who are quick to call a hotline or 911 when they suspect maltreatment or a family's need for services. Wealthy parents avoid the home inspections, drug testing, and psychological evaluations that the government imposes on poor and low-income parents.

The COVID-19 pandemic threw this double standard into sharp relief. On October 3, 2020, in its Sunday Styles section, the *New York Times* ran a story titled "Parents' Little Helpers," followed by the message "Weary of raising children in the pandemic, moms and dads are hitting the pot and booze."

> 7:51 p.m.: It's exactly 125 days tomorrow. I am pretg drink [*sic*].
>
> 7:52 p.m.: Drunk
>
> 7:52 p.m.: I can tell.[13]

Its author, journalist Jessica Grose, began with that snippet from her WhatsApp message group composed of fellow mothers of small children living across the United States and Canada. Grose devoted an entire article to describing "a wave of inebriation" that crashes across the continent when children are asleep, as parents indulge in large quantities of marijuana and alcohol to relieve the stress of being locked in with the kids all day. When I read the article, I immediately wanted to tack on the caveat "For white middle-class mothers only." Such conduct by less privileged mothers could literally be the basis for CPS charging them with child endangerment and taking their children.

Also during the COVID-19 pandemic, attorney Emma Ketteringham kept two folders on her desk at the Bronx Defenders. One folder contained commentaries with titles like "Pot-smoking Mamas"

and "Pot for Parents," written by well-to-do parents espousing marijuana use as a way to relieve stress and inspire creative parenting. The
other folder was full of court documents charging low-income Black
and Brown parents in the Bronx with child neglect, wholly or in part
for smoking marijuana. When it comes to her clients in the Bronx,
the child welfare department "uses marijuana use as a proxy for poor
parenting," Ketteringham writes. Affluent white parents can blithely
promote drinking alcohol or smoking marijuana to enhance their caregiving because they have no fear that the state will intrude in their
homes and take their children.[14]

I've found that white professionals are far more comfortable acknowledging the harms that poverty inflicts on other people's children
than they are acknowledging the challenges of their own parenting.
But privileged families are not devoid of parental struggles. Those
struggles are often disclosed, for example, in memoirs by wealthy white
authors. When reading them, I have been struck by the problems that
occured behind closed doors—problems that were often what motivated the authors to write the books. As I was completing the writing
of this book, in 2020, I read *Notes on a Silencing: A Memoir*, Lacy Crawford's account of her sexual assault at a prestigious boarding school
by two male students when she was only fourteen years old, and the
school's conspiracy to cover it up. Her memoir provides a window not
only into the school's misogynistic culture, but also into the mental health issues some of the students were experiencing at home. "A
brilliant ballet dancer would get thinner and thinner until one day we
learned she'd gone home on a health leave, and then, on the walk to
the Schoolhouse from Chapel, her hallmates would reveal the details,"
Crawford wrote. "A suicide attempt with pills, usually—she'd swallow
everything she could get her hands on, prescribed and unprescribed,
and wait to be found."[15]

In these memoirs, teachers, doctors, and therapists are well aware
of the problems the families are grappling with. These are the types
of mandated reporters who, in other circumstances, turn Black mothers over to CPS in droves because of the families' medical and mental
health needs. But in the situations recorded in these memoirs, the same

professionals provide private care that the parents can afford, without any thought of CPS intervention. The possibility that the state would meddle in these elite families' affairs is unthinkable. It is equally unthinkable that the state routinely rips children from the arms of their mothers in poor Black neighborhoods because it cares more about protecting Black children than it does about safeguarding the wealthy white children portrayed in these memoirs. Family policing isn't designed to protect either group of children—the privileged or the disadvantaged. It is designed to maintain the wedge between them.

EVIDENCE OF RACIAL BIAS

Given the vague definitions of child maltreatment and the discretion given to people who report, investigate, and respond to abuse and neglect allegations, it should come as no surprise that studies have discovered bias against Black families at every stage of decision making. Anti-Black discrimination is well documented in every other public system and private institution. Black Americans receive inferior medical care even when they have health insurance, are denied loans and steered into risky financial instruments, get turned away from employment opportunities, and are targeted for harassment and arrest by police officers. The professionals making subjective child welfare determinations are also influenced by negative assumptions about Black families. Racial bias isn't what makes the child welfare system a racist institution, but it facilitates the system's targeting of Black communities for intervention.

A number of studies have revealed that clinicians are more likely to evaluate for, diagnose, and report child abuse in Black infants and toddlers than white children who arrive at the hospital with similar serious injuries. A leading study demonstrating racially biased child abuse evaluations was published in the *Journal of the American Medical Association* in 2002. The researchers examined the records in a Philadelphia hospital database of all children under three years admitted between 1994 and 2000 for treatment of an acute skull or long-bone fracture, and compared a blind review of the records to the decisions hospital staff made. The researchers discovered that in cases where the external reviewer determined the injuries were accidental, Black children were far more likely than white children to have been referred for skeletal surveys to detect fractures and to be reported to CPS for suspected child abuse.[16]

These findings were reinforced by a 2010 study that dug deeper into racial differences in evaluations and diagnoses of suspected abuse in infants admitted to thirty-nine pediatric hospitals from 2004 to 2008 for traumatic brain injury. The study found that, although doctors ordered more skeletal surveys for Black infants, abuse was more likely to be diagnosed in the fewer white infants who were screened. "In fact, the highest proportion of children who received the diagnosis of abuse once a skeletal survey was obtained was among the children who were white," the researchers concluded. This finding is reminiscent of analyses of racial profiling by police officers. Cops stop Black pedestrians and drivers at far higher rates than their white counterparts. But the "hit rate" for finding guns, drugs, and other contraband is far higher for the white people they stop and search. In both cases, the racist assumptions of doctors and police officers similarly lead to inaccurate predictions of harm. A 2020 study by Dr. Modupeola Diyaolu, a pediatric surgeon at Stanford, found similar results when it came to physician reporting of suspected child abuse. Her analysis of 4,288 reports to the National Trauma Data Bank between 2010 and 2014 discovered that although Black children were disproportionately reported, their injuries were significantly less serious and deadly than those of white children. "Physicians are unconsciously or consciously more likely to assume child abuse in Black children, even though their injuries are less severe," Dr. Diyaolu told *MedPage Today*.[17]

These studies suggest that doctors employ a lower threshold for suspicion and reporting of child abuse in Black children than white children. It is also likely that doctors are diagnosing risk of abuse based on their sense of children's overall social situation and not only the "physical, laboratory or radiologic" aspects of the evaluation. At a Philadelphia City Council hearing in 2019, a doctor testified that she reported child abuse based on her "gut feelings." A doctor once conceded after a talk I gave in Chicago that most of the families he reported to DCFS were Black, but that he could tell based on the parents' behavior that the children weren't safe going home. Physicians' gut feelings about Black families are easily influenced by racist stereotypes and unfounded assumptions that can determine whether an injured child goes home from the hospital or gets thrown into foster care.[18]

The authors of all these child abuse studies speculated that the racial differences they found in clinical evaluations meant that white children are being underdiagnosed for abusive head trauma. But surely this isn't because doctors care more about Black children. To the contrary, Black children generally get inferior care in hospitals. For example, Black children taken to emergency rooms suffering from appendicitis are less likely to receive opioid pain treatment and more likely to experience delays in surgery. Moreover, the studies suggest that physicians are more likely to *misdiagnose* accidental injuries as child abuse in the case of Black children. In either case, doctors' greater willingness to report Black parents as suspected child abusers helps to fuel the unjust destruction of Black families.[19]

Imani Worthy, a Black mother who now works as a parent organizer at *Rise Magazine*, noted this discrepancy when she testified before the New York City Council in October 2020. She recalled reading a news article in April 2019 about a white actress, Jenny Mollen, who dropped her five-year-old son on his head, fracturing his skull and landing him in intensive care. Mollen is known for her role on the television show *Angel* and her marriage to the actor Jason Biggs, who starred in the popular movie *American Pie*. The article quoted Mollen describing her worry about her son and gratitude to the Manhattan hospital staff who treated him. Mollen called the experience "a mother's worst nightmare."

"I felt some kind of way, though, as I read this article because my nightmare as a mother was double fold," Worthy said. "When my son was injured, I became an alleged child abuser." She continued:

> I didn't have time to focus on the devastation of my child's injuries. I was too worried about losing him. I was worried that at just six

months he would go off to be raised by another family, separated from me for something that was unintentional.

To this day, I wonder if ACS ever knocked on Jenny Mollen's door. Did they go to the hospital and interrogate her during her emotional turmoil? She had an opportunity to write about her woes in a newspaper. She was able to use her voice. She probably received so much sympathy. I did not.[20]

Looking into the incident, I discovered a raft of media reporting on Mollen's Instagram post about the "traumatic weekend." The NBC News story displays a message from the blonde actress above a large photo of her smiling demurely. "My heart goes out to all parents who have or will ever find themselves in this kind of position," she wrote. "You are not alone." *People* magazine ran a story about the outpouring of support Mollen received from her fans and other "celebs," copying tweets with an abundance of heart emojis that expressed sympathy for the family, telling Mollen to "stay strong" and praising her "good work." Mollen's friend Stacey Bendet remarked that the incident made Mollen's son "officially an nyc kid!": "it's like a rite of passage." In a video accompanying its report, *Entertainment Tonight* noted that "Jason and Jenny haven't shied away from talking about the less than glam side of having kids." "We're a disaster," Mollen said. "A hot mess," Biggs chimed in.[21]

Worthy highlights that Mollen had the privilege of relying on hospital staff to treat her son's accidental injury without accusation, and on the media to report on her angst with compassion. Affluent parents can turn to empathetic professionals to help them care for their children and solve their families' problems without fear of being investigated, blamed, and punished. Worthy's insight is an important complement to the crises recounted in wealthy white people's memoirs. The problem with the family-policing system isn't how much maltreatment goes callously untreated in elite families; it is how crises in less privileged families are treated cruelly as blameworthy parental failures. America does have some inkling of how to care for children without resorting to benevolent terror. But that type of care is reserved only for parents who are preordained by their social status as worthy and who can afford it.

Studies also confirm that caseworkers make racially biased decisions about their investigations of reported abuse and neglect. With Black children five to six times more likely to be involved in Minnesota's child welfare system than their share of the child population, the state has one of the nation's highest racial disproportionality rates. In fact, in April 2018 Black parents filed a federal civil rights lawsuit accusing the state of racial discrimination in its enforcement of the child protection laws. The Minnesota African American Family Preservation Act, which seeks to "prevent any unnecessary removal of African American children," has been pending in the state legislature since 2019. In an especially intriguing 2012 study, researchers used an experimental method to test the "racialized perceptions" of hundreds of child welfare workers across Minnesota. The experiment consisted of sending caseworkers in eighty-two counties an online exercise within a regularly scheduled training session. The exercise involved vignettes describing a messy home environment, accompanied with photos of disheveled bedrooms that randomly varied whether a baby sitting by itself on a bed was Black or white, or whether there was no baby in the photo. The researchers obtained photos from actual case files and digitally superimposed either a white baby or a Black baby.[22]

The experiment was based on prior interviews with child welfare workers to determine what they considered to constitute neglect. The interviews uncovered a concept the researchers called the "messy house" phenomenon. The respondents uniformly indicated that they could visualize neglect in a "filthy, messy, disorderly living environment," one they "know when they see it." The problem was that the caseworkers "saw" neglect through a racist lens. When the researchers tabulated the results of the online exercise, they discovered that the caseworkers were significantly more likely to agree that the vignette accompanied by a photo with a Black baby depicted a situation that met the state's definition of—and their subjective test for—neglect.

The Minnesota study also calculated that caseworkers' racialized perceptions of neglect were statistically related to the disproportionate rates of substantiating child neglect allegations against Black parents. These findings reinforced what researchers had discovered in two prior studies, published in 2008 and 2011, using statewide data from Texas. The studies found that, even after controlling for poverty and other risk factors, Black children were more likely than white children to have substantiated cases and to be removed from their homes. Similar to the analyses revealing doctors' lower threshold for evaluating and reporting Black children for abusive head trauma, the Texas studies showed that it takes less risk of harm for caseworkers to tear Black children from their families. A 2009 survey of child welfare case files in Michigan discovered that CPS workers frequently described Black parents as "hostile," "aggressive," "loud," and "cognitively delayed" and assumed they had drug abuse problems without any justification for these portrayals. The report summed up the racist attitudes that grease the foster care machine: "The belief that African American children are better off away from their families and communities was seen in explicit statements by key policy makers and service providers. It was also reflected in choices made by DHS." Taken together, numerous studies establish that racist beliefs about Black families subject them to greater suspicion and intervention than white families.[23]

The biased definitions of abuse and neglect and the racist ways child welfare professionals apply them should frame our interpretation of the child maltreatment statistics. By the time they reach eighteen years of age, one in eight US children will have a state-confirmed maltreatment report. The figure for Black children—one in five—is the highest for any racial group. "Black children are about as likely to have a confirmed report of maltreatment during childhood as they are to complete college," noted the analysts who calculated these statistics. That comparison takes on a different meaning when we take into account how racism shapes the entire process that produces confirmed maltreatment reports.[24]

When my youngest child was in kindergarten at a public elementary school in Evanston, Illinois, my first meeting with his teacher was tense. She immediately told me in a stern voice that my son had been absent for too many school days without a medical excuse. She was especially upset that he hadn't participated in the class exercise commemorating Thanksgiving. "All the other children made Indian headbands out of paper and feathers," she chastised me. When his classmates were engaged in this questionable activity, my son and I were traveling in England, where I had been invited to give a talk at University of Kent. My daughter was in London at the time, where she spent her college junior year, and this was a fortuitous chance for her little brother to see her and taste life in a foreign country. Before I could respond, the teacher gave me a strict warning: "If your son continues to miss school, I'm going to call a truancy officer to visit your home." The teacher's condescending approach convinced me that she viewed me as an irresponsible Black mother who didn't appreciate the value of education and needed her intervention to raise my son properly.

Several months later, the teacher assigned the students to make little books out of construction paper with pictures of their favorite activities. My son crafted a mini travelogue with photos of our trips when he had accompanied me to overseas universities for lectures and conferences. When I had a second meeting with the teacher, her attitude had changed completely. She was delighted that my son was so experienced in international travel and pleased with his project displaying these adventures. There was no mention of calling the truancy officer. I felt sure she had looked up my background and discovered I was a university professor—I had transformed into an acceptable Black mother who didn't need to be told how to parent her child.

My profession had protected me from a report for truancy that easily could have escalated to a CPS investigation and my entanglement in the family-policing system. My profession also gave my son the possibility of traveling the globe with me. What if he were missing school because we had been evicted or I was suffering from severe depression and couldn't afford appropriate treatment? The teacher's call triggering CPS involvement would not have provided the resources we needed. Indeed, putting my son in foster care would probably have disrupted his education even more.

The inequities in who is targeted by family policing do not mean that privileged families should be policed more. For one thing, the children from elite white homes have no place in a damaging system designed to regulate disenfranchised families. Their parents are too powerful to be subjected to intrusive investigations, traumatic child taking, and disastrous foster care. Rather, all families should have the resources wealthy families have to support their caregiving and to address their problems. Most families are harmed to varying degrees by a child welfare system that relies on market-supplied services for the socially privileged and terror for the socially disadvantaged.

PART II
DESIGN

FOUR

ROTTEN AT THE ROOT

MODERN SLAVERY

In his autobiography, Malcolm X recalled "the nightmare" that happened to his family when the welfare people began to pry into his home in East Lansing, Michigan. In 1931, when Malcolm was six years old, his father, Reverend Earl Little, died. The official story was that the Baptist preacher was run over accidentally by the back wheel of a streetcar, severing his leg and crushing his abdomen. But rumors circulated that he was beaten by white vigilantes and dragged to the tracks to be killed. Reverend Little had been an outspoken organizer for Marcus Garvey's radical back-to-Africa movement, angering the town's white residents.[1]

Malcolm's mother, Louise Little, was left to care for eight children on her own. Unable to keep a job on account of her race and her deceased husband's reputation as a troublemaker, she was eventually forced to rely on government welfare checks to feed the family. That gave workers from the welfare department license to come around regularly to inspect the house and interrogate Malcolm, his mother, and his siblings "in a way that had about it the feeling—at least for me—that

we were not people. In their eyesight we were just *things*, that was all."
The welfare people's aim wasn't to help the family; it was to destroy it.

One ploy the welfare people used was to undermine Mrs. Little's authority over her children and sow discord within the family. The workers "began insisting on drawing us older children aside, one at a time, out on the porch or somewhere, and asking us questions, or telling us things—against our mother and against each other. They began to plant the seeds of division in our minds." Another tactic was to assault Mrs. Little's spirit in front of the children to send the message that the state agents were in control.

"They were vicious as vultures. They had no feelings, understanding, compassion, or respect for my mother. They told us 'she's crazy for refusing food.' Right then was when our home, our unity, began to disintegrate. We were having a hard time, and I wasn't helping. But we could have made it, we could have stayed together."

Mrs. Little was a proud woman who resisted the workers' interference in her family's life:

> She would talk back sharply to the state Welfare people, telling them she was a grown woman, able to raise her children, that it wasn't necessary for them to keep coming around so much, meddling in our lives. And they didn't like that.
>
> But the monthly Welfare check was their pass. They acted as if they owned us, as if we were their private property. As much as my mother would have liked to, she couldn't keep them out.

The welfare workers set their sights on removing Malcolm and his seven siblings from their mother's custody. "I think they felt that getting children in foster homes was a legitimate part of their function, and the result would be less troublesome, however they went about it."

The workers finally got their way. When their incursions drove Louise Little spiraling toward a psychological breakdown, they orchestrated her involuntary commitment to the state mental hospital at Kalamazoo based on examinations by a court-appointed doctor. Malcolm and his younger siblings were scattered to foster homes.

"A Judge McClellan in Lansing had authority over me and all of my brothers and sisters. We were 'state children,' court wards; he had the full say-so over us. A white man in charge of a black man's children! Nothing but legal, modern slavery—however kindly intentioned."

In hindsight, the politically astute Malcolm X recognized the parallels between the modern child welfare system and slavery. He cut through the phony benevolence of the coordinated systems that tore apart his family to expose them as instruments of state control and racial oppression. "I truly believe that if ever a state social agency destroyed a family, it destroyed ours. We wanted and tried to stay together. Our home didn't have to be destroyed. But the Welfare, the courts, and their doctor, gave us the one-two-three punch. And ours was not the only case of this kind," he concluded.

What ties together the families involved in the child welfare system is that they are disenfranchised by some aspect of political inequality—whether race, gender, class, disability, or immigration status—and typically embody an intersection of these subordinated positions. Black mothers raising children in segregated neighborhoods on starvation wages; parents who are jobless, incarcerated, or unhoused; mothers surviving domestic violence; members of dispossessed Native tribes restricted to depleted reservations; white families living in rural poverty; immigrants from Central America under ICE surveillance; parents and children with a disability, mental illness, or drug problem. The child welfare caseloads are filled with people like these from marginalized groups. The chances of affluent white parents getting on the CPS radar are relatively minuscule. The rare cases of their children being removed from the home are either extremely egregious or considered erroneous.

Family destruction has historically functioned as a chief instrument of group oppression in the United States. The family is a critical social institution that serves as a caring shield around its members to protect them from the totalitarian dictates of government officials. Families pass on the cultural norms, moral values, and political commitments of groups within a society. Families prepare children for participating in the economic, political, and social life of the various communities they will be part of as adults. "Stripping people of their children attempts to deny them the opportunity to participate in the progression of generations into the future," writes gender studies scholar Laura Briggs, "to interrupt the passing down of languages, ways of being, forms of knowledge, foods, and cultures." Rupturing families within a group is a means of repressing the entire group. If we stopped pretending that family policing is a form of government benevolence, we would recognize these demographics as a sign of state terror.[2]

Hillary Clinton got US history terribly wrong when she tweeted in response to the Trump administration's family separation policy, "There's nothing American about tearing families apart." Since its inception, the United States has wielded child removal to terrorize, control, and disintegrate racialized populations: enslaved African families, emancipated Black children held captive as apprentices by their former enslavers, Indigenous children kidnapped and confined to boarding schools under a federal campaign of tribal decimation, and European immigrant children swept up from urban slums by elite charities and put to work on distant farms. Today's child welfare machine, which systematically demolishes Black families, can trace its roots directly back to these practices designed to uphold racial capitalism over the course of US history. Family policing continues to take children hostage in order to wield control over communities that are ravaged by economic exploitation, disinvestment, and state violence. Child protection authorities still justify their terror by claiming to defend children from harms created by structural inequities but falsely attributed to parental pathologies. In this chapter, I move from demonstrating that the family-policing system targets and devastates Black communities to examining the role racism has historically played in crafting and perpetuating this nation's destructive approach to child welfare.[3]

THE AUCTION BLOCK

When Josiah Henson was five or six years old, his family was splintered on an auction block in Charles County, Maryland. He was born into slavery in 1789, on a Port Tobacco farm owned by Francis Newman. His mother was enslaved by a nearby doctor named Josiah McPherson, who hired her to Newman, to whom young Josiah's father belonged. Josiah remembered the day his father was whipped with one hundred lashes to his bare back for striking an overseer who was attempting to rape Josiah's mother. His father's ear was nailed to the whipping post and then severed as additional punishment for his offense. Soon after, Newman sold Josiah's father to enslavers in Alabama and returned the rest of Josiah's family to Dr. McPherson. Josiah's mother and her six children were able to live together for several years until the night a drunken Dr. McPherson fell from his horse and drowned in a stream. Josiah's family was put up for purchase at a slave auction so the proceeds could be distributed to Dr. McPherson's heirs.[4]

In *Story of His Own Life*, published in 1858, with a preface penned by famed abolitionist Harriet Beecher Stowe, Josiah Henson recalled the panic elicited by the auction's announcement: "the knowledge that all ties of the past are to be sundered; the frantic terror at the idea of being sent 'down south;' the almost certainty that one member of a family will be torn from another; the anxious scanning of purchasers' faces; the agony at parting, often forever, with husband, wife, child." He remembered standing on the auction block, his family huddled with other Black people up for sale, as a crowd of white prospectors surrounded them, examining their muscles, teeth, and agility:

> My brothers and sisters were bid off first, and one by one, while my mother, paralyzed with grief, held me by the hand. Her turn came, and then she was bought by Isaac Riley of Montgomery county. Then I was offered to the assembled purchasers.
>
> My mother, half distracted with the thought of parting forever from all her children, pushed through the crowd, while the bidding for me was going on, to the spot where Riley was standing. She fell at his feet, and clung to his knees, entreating him in tones that a mother only could command, to buy her *baby* as well as herself, and spare to her one, at least, of her little ones.

Riley disengaged himself from Josiah's mother with "violent blows and kicks," crushing the woman's desperate attempt to keep her baby.

She was forced to leave with her new enslaver without knowing the fate of any of her children. Josiah was sold to another planter in Montgomery County, but he became so ill that his new owner persuaded Riley to purchase him so he could be reunited with his mother. Josiah grew up to be supervisor of Riley's farm and, in 1830, escaped to freedom in Canada with his wife and children.[5]

Although most histories of the US child welfare system start with the charitable organizations founded in the 1800s to rescue poor white children, we can trace its origins back to slavery's control over Black families like Josiah Henson's. Enslavers had the legal right to own not only Black adults but also their offspring, and their property claim was automatic and immediate. In 1662, the Virginia House of Burgesses—the first elected legislature in the colonies—passed a law providing that children born to Black women had the status of their mothers, and therefore could be enslaved, even if the fathers were white. This rule, soon adopted by the other colonies, allowed white men to profit from their sexual assaults on Black women and cast Black women as the reproducers of their children's subjugated status. In fact, the law granted to enslavers a future interest in Black women's potential offspring. Enslaved parents had no legal claim to their children.

One of the most awful atrocities inflicted by the slavery regime was the physical separation of enslaved parents from their children. Slaveholders could dismember Black families at will whenever doing so became economically expedient. For four hundred years, most Black children in America belonged to enslavers who had absolute discretion to sell or give them away apart from their parents. A nineteenth-century South Carolina court noted, for example, that planters could sell children away from their mothers no matter how young, because "the young of slaves . . . stand on the same footing as other animals." Only Louisiana and, in 1852, Alabama enacted laws that placed any restrictions at all on the ages at which children could be sold separately from their mothers. According to historian Heather Andrea Williams, "Approximately one third of enslaved children in the Upper South experienced family separation in one of three possible scenarios: sale away from parents, sale with mother away from father, or sale of mother or father away from child." As Josiah Henson described, the auction block was often the site where families were cruelly torn apart, with parents and children sold to different buyers.[6]

A slaveholder might decide to sell a mother, a father, or their children to pay off a debt or to punish perceived disobedience. Black people were devised in wills, wagered at horse races, and awarded in lawsuits. Bonded families were disbanded when the heirs of an estate decided not to continue the patriarch's business. Family unity could also be shattered when young children were hired or apprenticed out to work on another plantation, sometimes for as long as a decade. Enslaved women's loved ones routinely "got rented out, loaned out, bought up, brought back, stored up, mortgaged, won, stolen or seized," Toni Morrison wrote in *Beloved*. "Nobody stop playing checkers just because the pieces included [their] children."[7]

Mothers often learned the heartbreaking news only when a new owner or his emissary appeared to take their children away. Thomas H. Jones remembered the day a Black man named Abraham showed up to transport him to a new owner who lived forty-five miles from the plantation Thomas lived on with his mother. "Mother wept bitterly and in the midst of her loud sobbings, cried out in broken words, 'I can't save you Tommy; master has sold you and you must go.' She threw her arms around me, and while the hot tears fell on my face, she strained me to her heart. There she held me, sobbing and mourning, till the brutal Abraham came in, snatched me away, hurried me out of the house where I was born, my only home, and tore me away from the dear mother who loved me as no other friend could do." When his mother ran after them, pleading to spend another moment with her child, Abraham struck her with his cowhide and ordered her to return to the house.[8]

The most memorable scene for me in the movie *Twelve Years a Slave* is when white enslavers burst into a plantation house to seize children who have been sold away from their enslaved mother. The mother, crying hysterically, begs the white man who considers the family his property not to separate them. The white mistress of the house tells everyone not to worry—the mother will forget all about her children in a matter of days. Part of the rationale white people constructed for the horrors of slavery was the belief that Black people lacked the capacity to feel emotional pain. "Their griefs are transient," Thomas Jefferson wrote in his 1785 treatise *Notes on the State of Virginia*. "Those numberless afflictions, which render it doubtful whether Heaven has given life to us in mercy or in wrath, are less felt, and sooner forgotten with them." Seventy years later, Georgia legal scholar R. R. Cobb deployed this reasoning to erase the grief Black parents experienced when their children were ripped from them. "The dance will allay his most poignant grief, and a few days blot out the memory of his most bitter bereavement," Cobb argued. "His natural affection is not strong, and consequently he is cruel to his own offspring, and suffers little by separation from them." Watching *Twelve Years a Slave*, I saw in the white mistress's cavalier stance the same disregard by CPS workers, judges, and researchers for the unbearable pain that child removal inflicts on Black parents and children today.[9]

Because it was in slaveholders' economic interest to maintain some family stability in order to maximize production, young children were not frequently sold off from their mothers. Instead, enslavers used children as hostages to prevent bonded women from running away or to lure escaped women back to plantations. Slaveholders could threaten enslaved women who were rebellious with the sale of their children to make them more compliant. This strategy is one of the reasons far fewer women than men fled from bondage. Most enslaved women were unwilling to abandon their children in order to increase their chances of escape; most fugitive women took their children with them. In 1786, the *Georgia Gazette* reported that only one female runaway, a mother named Hannah, had left a child behind. Although Hannah had taken her five-year-old daughter, Lydia, "she had 'inhumanely' left 'a child at her breast,'" the story quoted Hannah's enslaver as saying, castigating Hannah for shirking her maternal duty despite holding her baby in captivity.[10]

Born as an enslaved girl in 1813 North Carolina, Harriet Jacobs endured the relentless sexual abuse of her enslaver, Dr. James Norcom, for years. In her autobiography, *Incidents in the Life of a Slave Girl*, first published in 1861, Jacobs tells how Norcom deliberately used her children as pawns, thinking their presence on the plantation "would fetter me to the spot." Norcom's strategy worked for a time: "I could have made my escape alone; but it was more for my helpless children than for myself that I longed for freedom. Though the boon would have been precious to me, above all price, I would not have taken it at the expense of leaving them in slavery. Every trial I endured, every sacrifice I made for their sakes, drew them closer to my heart, and gave me fresh courage." Jacobs's children both bound her to slavery and gave her the courage to resist it. Jacobs eventually did flee without her children, spending seven years hiding in a crawl space in her grandmother's house before making the journey to Philadelphia. Years later, she bought her children's freedom.[11]

Harriet Jacobs's story tells not only of slavery's assault on Black families, but also of enslaved people's enduring love for their kin in the face of slavery's brutality. In *Help Me to Find My People: The African American Search for Family Lost in Slavery*, Heather Williams refers to the myriad slave narratives, letters, petitions, and newspaper advertisements that bonded and freed individuals wrote in desperate attempts to reunite with family members stolen by enslavers. Countering the lie that slavery diminished the significance of family to Black people, Williams observes that "despite painful losses during slavery, large numbers of African Americans continued to invest emotional capital in creating new families as well as finding those whom they had lost." Slaveholders were aware of the pain they were inflicting on Black mothers and children when they tore them apart, though they exploited it; that is why they could use the threat of forced separation as a means of preventing escape or rebellion. This remains a chief modus operandi of family policing today: child welfare agencies aim to keep Black mothers submissive by weaponizing their children, while denying the existence of loving ties between them.[12]

Even when enslaved families remained physically intact, Black parents were denied authority over their children. Slavery law installed the white patriarch as the head of an extended plantation family that included the Black people he enslaved. White people considered the plantation family, ruled by white men, to be the best institution to teach moral values to Africans, whom they deemed to be uncivilized. "Abrogation of the parental bond was a hallmark of the civil death that United States slavery imposed," writes law professor Peggy Cooper Davis in *Neglected Stories: The Constitution and Family Values*. Slaveholders proclaimed their moral authority by reinforcing the message of parental helplessness, frequently whipping enslaved parents in front of their children. "These messages of parental vulnerability and subordination were repeatedly burned into the consciousness of slave parents and children," Davis explains, "undermining their sense of worth, diminishing the sense of family security and authority, eroding the parents' function as a model of adult agency and independence, and, most importantly for our purposes, kindling a determination that freedom would entail parental prerogatives."[13]

The first act of many newly freed Black people was to search for their family members. During the chaotic period between the start of the Civil War in 1861 and its end in 1865, thousands of enslaved people abandoned farms and fled to Union army camps in search of freedom and their lost relatives. These congregations of Black refugees, considered to be contrabands, were often the site of glorious family reunions. As escaped Black people filed into Union-occupied Camp Hamilton in Virginia, missionary Charles Day reported, "Mothers are having restored to them their children whom they never expected to see again this side of eternity. Wives are brought upon their knees in praise to God at the appearance of husbands long ago torn from them and sold to the dreaded South and the meeting between these husbands and wives, parents and children no pen can describe."[14]

With the Thirteenth Amendment's passage, four million formerly enslaved people grabbed the opportunity afforded them by emancipation to create their own economic, social, and political lives independent of white domination. Establishing a family free from the sovereignty of white people formed the heart of Black liberation from captivity. Emancipated parents, determined to recover their children, "shared a passionate commitment to the stability of family life as a badge of freedom," writes historian Eric Foner. Over the course of her research, Heather Williams found more than a thousand "Information Wanted" or "Lost Friends" advertisements placed by Black people in search of their relatives. Six months after the Civil War ended, for example, Thornton Copeland placed an advertisement in the *Colored Tennessean* in Nashville: "INFORMATION is wanted of my mother, whom I left in Fauquier county, Va., in 1844, and I was sold in Richmond, Va., to Saml. Copeland. I formerly belonged to Robert Rogers. I am very anxious to hear from my mother, and any information in relation to her whereabouts will be very thankfully received. My mother's name was Betty, and was sold by Col. Briggs to James French."[15]

Black parents frequently located children who were still held by former enslavers and negotiated for their return. "If anyone has your children, go and get them," General John M. Palmer advised Black soldiers fighting in Kentucky in 1865. "If they will not give them to you, steal them out at night. I do not think that you will be committing any crime nor do I believe the almighty ruler of the universe will think you have committed any." Yet Black mothers and fathers encountered brutal repercussions from white men reluctant to give up the children they still viewed as their human chattel. Countless Black mothers endured vicious beatings when they demanded the return of their children. In a letter to his wife in 1864, a Union officer wrote that every day he was "visited by some poor woman who has walked perhaps 10 or 20 miles to try to secure the release of her children taken forcibly away from her and held to all intents and purposes in slavery." For these mothers, having custody of their children was essential to their freedom.

The rights of family had been central to the antislavery movement. In petitions to the government, enslaved people often based their claims for freedom on the natural right to family integrity. Abolitionists also focused their condemnation of slavery on its immoral destruction of families—"the greatest perceived sin of American slavery." Images of crying mothers and children clinging to each other as merciless slave traders wrenched them apart were widely circulated in antislavery pamphlets, slave narratives, and newspapers. In her celebrated abolitionist novel, *Uncle Tom's Cabin*, Harriet Beecher Stowe included such a drawing, captioned, "The Separation of the Mother and Child." Some scholars believe that the scene depicts the actual splintering of Josiah Henson's family as recounted in his autobiography, for which Stowe wrote the preface. "The worst abuse of the system of slavery is its outrage upon the family," Stowe wrote in her 1853 defense of the novel's realism. "It is one which is more notorious and undeniable than any other."[16]

Slavery's deprivation of family rights was a burning issue for the Reconstruction Congress as it drafted the Thirteenth Amendment prohibiting slavery and involuntary servitude and the Fourteenth Amendment protecting liberty and citizenship. Formerly enslaved people testified before Congress about their painful experiences of family disruption. Republican senator James Harlan of Iowa advocated for the Thirteenth Amendment by accusing slavery of causing "the abolition practically of the parental relationship, robbing the offspring of the care and attention of his parents, severing a relation which is universally cited as the emblem of the relation sustained by the Creator to the human family." The destruction of Black family ties meant slavery had to be abolished, for "according to the matured judgement of these slave States, this guardianship of the parent over his own children must be abrogated to secure the perpetuity of slavery," Senator Harlan argued. His colleague Senator Henry Wilson of Massachusetts promised accordingly, "When this amendment to the Constitution shall be consummated . . . the sharp cry of the agonizing hearts of severed families will cease to vex the weary ear of the nation." The legislators were moved both by the heart-wrenching accounts of family separation and by the argument that the right to family integrity is inalienable. Just as the child welfare system can trace its disruption of Black families to slavery, contemporary notions of family liberty can trace their roots to Black people's resistance against this form of state violence.[17]

FORCED APPRENTICESHIP OF BLACK CHILDREN

No sooner had Congress abolished slavery and its legalized control of Black families than a campaign of white supremacist terror, laws, and policies effectively nullified the Reconstruction Amendments and replaced Reconstruction with a Jim Crow regime. "How many black men and women were beaten, flogged, mutilated, and murdered in the first years of emancipation will never be known," writes historian Leon Litwack in *Been in the Storm So Long: The Aftermath of Slavery*. After Lincoln was assassinated, his successor, President Andrew Johnson, a white supremacist and former enslaver, quickly began pardoning ex-Confederates and returning confiscated and abandoned land to white planters. Instead of getting title to the property they had labored on and occupied, freed Black people were forced into wage servitude for the white landowners.[18]

Whereas the forced supervision and dissolution of Black families at the hands of white people is rooted in slavery, the systematic court-ordered displacement of free Black children to strangers' homes finds its origins in apprenticeship. Apprenticeship is the historical bridge that connects state disruption of Black families under the antebellum slavery system with state disruption of Black families under the twentieth-century foster care system.

A critical part of the white supremacist agenda was to restore Black children to white domination. After Emancipation, white planters exploited the apprenticeship laws already in place to wrest custody of Black children from their parents as a source of forced labor. Southern states also included provisions for compelled apprenticeship of Black children in the Black Codes, passed in 1865 and 1866 to control Black labor by prohibiting freedom of movement, contract, and family life. The Black Code passed by the North Carolina legislature in 1866 to return "lately slaves" to their prior status both restricted the working rights of Black adults and allowed Black children to be "bound out" to work for white planters without their parents' approval. These laws gave judges unfettered discretion to place Black children in the care and service of white people if they found the parents to be unfit, unmarried, or unemployed and if they deemed the displacement "better for the habits and comfort of the child."[19]

Of ninety thousand emancipated Black people in Maryland, some ten thousand were reenslaved under apprenticeship laws, typically to their former enslavers. A witness testified in 1867 that in some parts of the state, "the whites, the ex-masters of the slaves, had the children probably of about two-thirds of the families of the freedmen." Even the Freedmen's Bureau, an agency of the War Department established by Congress in March 1865 to provide relief to newly freed Black Americans and white refugees, sometimes chose apprenticeship over reuniting Black families. When it determined Black children to be abandoned or orphans, the bureau indentured them to white households instead of locating their free kin so they could remain with their families.[20]

Black parents resisted the legalized capture of their daughters and sons. Three hundred Black citizens sent a petition to President Andrew Johnson protesting their children's apprenticeship to former slaveholders. They charged that "our homes are invaded and our little ones seized at the family fireside, and forcibly bound to masters who are by law expressly released from any obligation to educate them in secular or religious knowledge." Masters were required by law to provide education to their white, but not their Black, apprentices. "God help us, our condition is better but little; free ourselves, but deprived of our children, almost the only thing that would make us free and happy," Lucy Lee wrote in a petition to regain her daughter. "It was on their account we desired to be free." A Black mother named Louisa complained to the Freedman's Bureau that "J.T. is whipping her children continually, and when she asked him not to do it, ordered her off his place and told her not to come back." The forced indentures to white planters also deprived Black families of the contributions their children could make to their own households as they transitioned from enslavement to economic survival. Freed parents sought not only affectionate and moral ties to their children but also "to wrest this important aspect of rural economic control from the hands of whites," notes historian Richard Paul Fuke.[21]

Black parents also fought the apprenticeship of their children in court. Prior to the Civil War, a laborer named Charles Snell petitioned for a writ of habeas corpus at the Circuit Court of Baltimore City to challenge the indenture of his seven-year-old daughter, Mary, to the mother of police officer James Maddox. Maryland's law, enacted in 1860, authorized courts to "summon before them the child of any free negro," and should it appear "better for the habits and comfort of said child," apprentice him or her to a white home "to learn to labor." According to census records, Mary eventually returned to her father's custody. Black parents continued to use habeas corpus to contest the indentures of their children after the Civil War. Some parents obtained relief from Radical Republican judges who took an abolitionist view of family rights.[22]

The most significant legal victory was decided in 1867 by Justice Salmon Portland Chase. Justice Chase was a leading antislavery lawyer and politician who served as Treasury Secretary during the Civil War and was appointed as Chief Justice of the United States Supreme Court by President Lincoln to succeed Roger Taney, the author of the white supremacist *Dred Scott* decision. While on federal circuit court duty in Baltimore, Chase agreed to hear a petition for habeas corpus brought on behalf of ten-year-old Elizabeth Turner, who was being held as an apprentice in Talbot County, Maryland, by a man named Philemon T. Hambleton. Hambleton had enslaved Elizabeth and her mother, Betsey Turner, until they were emancipated by Maryland's new constitution, which took effect on November 1, 1864. Two days later, Elizabeth was part of a group of Black children who were bound back to their former enslavers as apprentices. This was the fate of three thousand Black children across Maryland who were stolen back by white planters within days of emancipation under the apprenticeship provisions of the state's unrepealed slave code.[23]

The petition alleged that Betsey Turner was "able, ready, and willing" to care for Elizabeth and had not been summoned to court on the day the apprenticeship was authorized. Under that indenture, Hambleton had no duty to give Elizabeth "any education, in reading, writing, and arithmetic," though required by Maryland law "in the case of the binding of white children." Instead, Hambleton's contract provided he teach Elizabeth "the art or calling of a house servant." There were additional differences between the terms of Elizabeth's indenture and those of white apprentices: Hambleton's authority was described as a "property and interest," which permitted him to transfer Elizabeth at will to any person in the county. Those racial distinctions, the petition argued, violated the Thirteenth Amendment of the United States Constitution, ratified on July 31, 1865.

Justice Chase agreed. Finding that the indentures for Black children did not "contain important provisions for the security and benefit of the apprentice which are required by the laws of Maryland in indenture of white apprentices," he held that the state's apprenticeship law violated the Civil Rights Act of 1866, which Congress had enacted to enforce the Thirteenth Amendment. "Colored persons equally with white persons are citizens of the United States," he declared for emphasis. Elizabeth Turner was discharged from the custody of Hambleton. It appears that the decision led to the release of most Black apprentices held by white planters in Maryland by the summer of 1868.[24]

But Justice Chase's abolitionist reasoning was an aberration. Powerful white landowners across the South were determined to maintain their control of Black labor, and apprenticeship, along with sharecropping and the convict-leasing system, was a valuable instrument for extracting work from newly freed Black citizens. Most white southerners, like Frederick Eustace, a Georgia plantation superintendent, argued that Black children needed to be supervised by white masters because the Black race "was not prepared for freedom yet." Because enslaved children had been subject to the white plantation patriarch's authority, these white supremacists contended, their parents were incapable of raising them properly after the family was emancipated. Apprenticeship afforded Black children needed guidance that incompetent Black parents could not provide, and was "prompted by feelings of humanity towards these unfortunate young ones," the *Kent News* explained in December 1864. Although some Black parents signed contracts to apprentice their children, they were compelled by white violence, court order, or economic dispossession. "They sent for me to come to the court house," Maria Nichols of Kent County recounted about her son's indenture, "and i refuse to go and they sent high sheriffs after me and taken [me] by force then after i got there they did not ask me anything but they taken him and bound him and they would not let me say a word." Apprenticed children who escaped from bondage were recaptured and whipped.[25]

The view that Black children needed white supervision was bolstered by a mythology that disparaged Black mothers in particular. During the slavery era, white writers fabricated the image of a Black woman ruled by her sexual proclivities, identified by historian Deborah Gray White as "Jezebel" after the biblical wife of King Ahab. As early as 1736, the *South-Carolina Gazette* described "African Ladies" as women "of 'strong robust constitution' who were 'not easily jaded out' but able to serve their lovers 'by Night as well as Day.'" The icon of the lascivious Black temptress made white men's sexual violence against Black women seem like no violence at all. By law, enslaved women had no right to bodily autonomy, no right to consent or not to consent; their sexual violation was not recognized as rape. If Black women were inherently promiscuous, the thinking went, they could not be raped. The moniker "Jezebel" defined Black women in opposition to the prevailing image of the True Woman, who was virtuous, pure, and white. In his 1835 pamphlet *The Morals of Slavery*, the prominent South Carolina intellectual William Gilmore Simms wrote that Black women lacked the "consciousness of degradation" possessed by even the most disgraceful white prostitutes in the North.[26]

After the Civil War, white scholars justified the continued domination of Black children by linking Black women's presumed sexual depravity to Black women's presumed maternal deficiency. In *The Plantation Negro as a Freeman*, published in 1889, renowned historian Philip A. Bruce argued that Black women raised their daughters to follow their own depraved lifestyle, failing to "teach them, systematically, those moral lessons that they peculiarly need as members of the female sex." At the same time, books, newspapers, and merchandise circulated the caricature of the happily subservient Mammy. Unlike the tempting Jezebel, Mammy's sexuality was erased. She was depicted as dark-skinned, rotund, and dressed in an apron and head rag to accentuate her domesticity and lack of sex appeal for white men. For white people, Mammy symbolized the ideal Black woman and justified their exploitation of her labor in their homes.[27]

Mammy was trusted to care for white children only on condition that she remained under the constant supervision of her morally superior white mistress and that her complete devotion to white children superseded care for her own children. Black mothers were denied authority over either the white children they raised or the Black children they bore. White people considered Black mothers, like their apprenticed children, in need of guidance and discipline. "The modern negro woman has no such object-lesson in morality or modesty, and she wants none," Eleanor Tayleur complained in her 1908 essay, "The Negro Woman—Social and Moral Decadence." Tayleur charged Black mothers with abusing their children because they lacked "the brooding mother-love and anxiety which the white woman sends after her children as long as they live." This disparaging mythology originating in slavery continues to reverberate in the devaluation of Black mothers' bonds with their children that we see in child welfare policy and practice today.[28]

The experiences of Black families both as enslaved and as free dramatically change the origin narrative of America's child welfare system. The legalized breakup of Black families during the slavery and Reconstruction eras is as deeply embedded in US child welfare policy as the autonomy and benevolence accorded to white families, as well as coercive forms of addressing white childhood poverty, such as consigning children to poorhouses, orphanages, and foster homes. The court-ordered theft of emancipated children as apprentices in white people's homes reinstated the domination and destruction of Black families during the slavery regime. Apprenticeship also constituted a link between state separation of Black children from their families under the slavery system and state separation from their families under the foster care system. We should retell the historical narrative to center the reenslavement of Black children through apprenticeship to white people as America's first "child welfare system" for Black families.

DECIMATING NATIVE NATIONS

Today's child welfare system is rooted in settler colonialism as well as slavery. Another essential part of the history of child welfare in the United States is the federal government's forcible removal of Native children from their tribes. At the time the Civil War ceased, the United States was still waging wars against Native nations. Buoyed by the notion of Manifest Destiny, US forces were determined to expand the nation's borders westward at the cost of decimating the Indigenous peoples who lived there first. The federal government combined its dispossession of Native tribes with a policy to forcibly "civilize" them by erasing their culture. Congress passed the Civilization Fund Act in 1819, which paid for running Christian schools in tribal territories, and established the Bureau of Indian Affairs five years later to implement its programs.[29]

An alliance of the Lakota Sioux, Northern Cheyenne, and Arapaho defeated the Seventh Cavalry of the US Army in 1876 at the Battle of Little Big Horn in ongoing warfare over the Black Hills as white settlers sought to encroach on tribal lands. Just after "Custer's Last Stand," as the battle came to be called, the federal government devised a new military strategy to destabilize its Native opponents. It began stealing Native children from tribal communities and placing them in white-controlled boarding schools, where they were violently stripped of their languages, clothing, and customs and compelled to work without compensation. The Indian Boarding School Policy lasted until the 1970s, forcibly relocating more than one hundred thousand Native children among 460 Bureau of Indian Affairs–operated schools.

In 1879, the Department of Interior and the Department of War commissioned Lieutenant Richard Henry Pratt to establish the first off-reservation Indian boarding school in an abandoned military barrack in Carlisle, Pennsylvania. Pratt modeled the Carlisle Industrial Indian School after a detention center at Fort Marion, Florida, where Native prisoners of the Southern Plains Indian Wars were held without trial, some of them tortured and murdered. Based on Pratt's notorious philosophy of "kill the Indian and save the man," the federal boarding schools forced Native children to speak English, practice Christianity, and adopt white American ways. Their long hair was cut and their buckskin garments and moccasins replaced with Western dresses, suits, and oxfords. Their protective medicine bags and other belongings were set on fire. "The boys, one by one, would break down and cry when they saw their braids thrown to the floor," recalled a man named Lone Wolf from the Blackfoot in Montana. The captive children were often loaned out to do manual labor for white families who lived in the vicinity. Children who failed to submit were subjected to beatings and military-style punishments. Concluding that the boarding schools "operated below any reasonable standard of health and decency," a 1928 investigation described Native children living in overcrowded and squalid conditions without adequate food, clothing, or education.[30]

Congress encouraged the spread of boarding schools in 1881 by making attendance compulsory and authorizing the Bureau of Indian Affairs to "withhold rations, clothing, and other articles from those parents who resisted to send their children to school." Native children were also grabbed by force. "The wild Navajos, far back in the mountains, hide their children at the sound of the truck," wrote a witness about the arrival of government agents on the Navajo (Diné) reservation in 1930. "So stockmen, Indian police, and other mounted men are sent ahead to round them up. The children are caught, often roped like cattle, and taken away from their parents, many times never to return."[31]

The US dispossession of Native children was enacted in conjunction with the dispossession of tribal lands. The Dawes Act of 1887 divided Indian reservations into individual plots that the federal government allotted in its discretion to individual tribal members. The balance of lands the government left unassigned were opened up for non-Indian settlement and extraction. Taking Native children from their communities was part of a coordinated military plan to end the Indian Wars by annihilating Native nations, preventing the transfer of customs to the next generation, and weakening tribal solidarity. The US military weaponized Native children in its colonial terror against Indigenous people by taking them from their families and holding them hostage.

US presidents have continued to deploy the "plenary power" that gave the executive branch constitutional authority to conduct the so-called Indian Wars, enter into treaties with Native tribes, and take their land and children. The Bush, Obama, and Trump administrations all drew on legal precedents created during wars with Native nations to wield expansive powers in the War on Terror without judicial or congressional review. In fact, as legal scholar Maggie Blackhawk pointed out in a 2019 *New York Times* op-ed, the detention camps that confined Central American children seeking asylum at the southern border were justified by the same legal rationale used to establish the military-run boarding schools for stolen Native children.[32]

In the second half of the twentieth century, adoption became a central part of the federal policy to uproot Native children from reservations and assimilate them into white US culture. The Bureau of Indian Affairs and the US Children's Bureau launched the Indian Adoption Project in 1958 to stimulate transfers of Native children to white families nationwide. With federal funding and the cooperation of adoption agencies, the Child Welfare League of America relocated nearly four hundred Native children from reservations to white adoptive homes across sixteen states. When the project formally ended in 1966, it was succeeded by the Adoption Resource Exchange, which continued the government's mission of giving Native children to white parents into the 1970s. "One can no longer say that the Indian child is the 'forgotten child,'" the project's director, Arnold Lyslo, proclaimed at the time. The mass child removal dealt a grave blow to the very survival of many tribes. In 1971, for example, nearly one in four Native infants under age one in Minnesota was placed for adoption. Between 1961 and 1976, an estimated 12,486 additional Native children were placed for adoption by agencies that operated beyond the scope of the federal projects. During this period, the federal government continued to take Native lands in breach of treaties, while some states denied public benefits to Native families. In states that provided assistance to needy families, Native women reported that welfare workers forced them to be sterilized as a condition of keeping their children—a violation inflicted on Black women throughout the South.[33]

The federal government explained its widescale displacement of Native children with a familiar child-saving rationale. Key to the Indian Adoption Project's defense was a longitudinal study of a quarter of the Native children placed in white homes conducted by prominent Columbia child welfare researcher David Fanshel. Beginning in 1960,

Fanshel's research team interviewed the white parents annually to assess how well the Native children they'd adopted were progressing. In his 1972 report, *Far from the Reservation*, Fanshel described the relocation program as a response to the "tragic plight" of Native people, marked by unsanitary housing, illiteracy, unemployment, and alcoholism. "The children placed through the Indian Adoption Project," Fanshel wrote, "were those who, from the perspective of the social workers who intimately knew their situations, were doomed to lives of stark deprivation."[34]

Native tribes defiantly resisted the incursion. Tribal councils brought lawsuits against welfare officials and issued resolutions attempting to prevent welfare workers from taking children from reservations. In 1968, the Association on American Indian Affairs, a nonprofit organization directed primarily by Native board members, held a press conference for international reporters. "The Devil's Lake Sioux people and American Indian tribes have been unjustly deprived of their lands and their livelihood, and now they are being dispossessed of their children," executive director William Byler stated. That same year, grassroots activists in Minneapolis, a site of intense child taking, founded the American Indian Movement (AIM) to end discrimination against tribal residents. As the organization joined with tribes across the country to engage in militant protests, it broadened its reach to advocate for full restoration of tribal sovereignty and treaty rights, becoming part of a Red Power movement. Native tribes had forged a collective struggle to resist modern colonial assaults on their land, culture, and families.

Native activism pressured Congress to conduct hearings in 1974, 1976, and 1977 to listen to testimony from Native people on the damage inflicted by its child-taking policies. In the hearings, Native parents and tribal representatives presented evidence that between one-quarter and one-third of all Native children had been separated from their families. The tribal chief of the Mississippi Band of Choctaw Indians testified, "Culturally, the chances of Indian survival are significantly reduced if our children, the only real means for the transmission of the tribal heritage, are to be raised in non-Indian homes and denied exposure to the ways of their people." He highlighted the political impact of child removal on tribal sovereignty. "These practices seriously undercut the tribe's ability to continue as self-governing communities. Probably in no area is it more important that tribal sovereignty be respected than in an area as socially and culturally determinative as family relationships."[35]

At the close of the hearings, Congress acknowledged that the United States had waged a deliberate campaign to wrongfully remove Native children from their parents to place them in white homes and institutions. The lawmakers adopted the Native nations' perspective, expressly finding that "there is no resource that is more vital to the continued existence and integrity of Indian tribes than their children." In 1978, Congress passed the Indian Child Welfare Act (ICWA), establishing essentially a separate child welfare system that was supposed to be run by sovereign Native tribes. ICWA gives tribes control over child welfare decisions involving tribal members. Tribal courts have exclusive jurisdiction over custody proceedings involving Native children who are domiciled on a tribe's reservation. In adoptions of Native children, preference is given to placement with a member of the child's extended family, other members of the child's tribe, or other Native families. ICWA also sets the bar higher for termination of a Native parents' rights—the court must find beyond a reasonable doubt that continued custody will cause the child serious emotional or physical harm. It took two more decades for the Child Welfare League to apologize for its role in the Indian Adoption Project.[36]

Despite ICWA's transfer of child welfare decision making back to Native tribes, Native children remain horribly overrepresented in the US foster care system. The problem stems largely from the refusal of many state judges to recognize Native sovereignty and the jurisdiction ICWA granted to tribal courts. To make matters worse, the US Supreme Court has chipped away at ICWA's force in recent decisions. In a 2013 case, *Adoptive Couple v. Baby Girl*, a majority of justices sided with a white couple, the Copabiancos, who wanted to adopt a Native girl named Veronica over the objections of the Cherokee Nation. The custody dispute arose when Veronica's mother put the baby up for adoption while the father, Dusten Brown, a registered tribal member, was serving in Iraq. Before he was deployed, Brown had signed papers relinquishing his paternal rights, but thought Veronica would be raised by her mother. When he was served with a notice of adoption proceedings, he intervened to get custody of his daughter. The South Carolina Supreme Court affirmed a lower court ruling awarding custody to Brown pursuant to ICWA.[37]

The US Supreme Court reversed the ruling in a five-four decision, holding that ICWA didn't apply at all. The majority reasoned that ICWA's heightened scrutiny for terminating a Native parent's rights wasn't relevant because Brown never had custody of Veronica. For the same reason, the justices ruled that Veronica's placement with the Copabiancos didn't represent the "breakup of the Indian family." Justice Samuel Alito's opinion for the court displayed far more interest in protecting white people's ability to adopt Native children than protecting tribal sovereignty and rights. The court worried that a Native father "could play his ICWA trump card at the eleventh hour" to halt adoption proceedings. "If this were possible, many prospective adoptive parents would surely pause before adopting any child who might possibly qualify as an Indian under the ICWA." In her dissent, Justice Sonia Sotomayor noted that the majority had distorted the statutory language "in order to reach a conclusion that is manifestly contrary to Congress' express purpose in enacting ICWA: preserving the familial bonds between Indian parents and their children and, more broadly, Indian tribes' relationships with the future citizens who are 'vital to [their] continued existence and integrity.'" As a result, three-year-old Veronica was ripped from her father, who had cared for her for eighteen months, to be adopted by the white couple.

SAVING WHITE CHILDREN

It is against this backdrop of child removal as a terroristic weapon against Black and Native communities that we can now consider the emergence of modern child welfare agencies for white children in the United States. On one hand, "the very existence of slavery meant that child welfare institutions could develop in this country without concern for the majority of Black children," note Andrew Billingsley and Jeanne M. Giovannoni in *Children of the Storm*. "This factor alone ensured an inherently racist child welfare system." On the other hand, the brutal domination and destruction of enslaved families profoundly shaped the development of child welfare institutions.[38]

The colonial approach to child welfare for white families was imported from the Elizabethan Poor Laws of 1601, which provided for state-supported assistance to the needy outside the church. Public relief operated within a dual legal system based on wealth. Poor families were subject to government supervision for the public good; disputes in wealthier families over marriage, inheritance, or child rearing were treated as private matters. "For the poor, state intervention between parent and child was not only permitted but encouraged in order to effectuate a number of public policies, ranging from the provision of relief at minimum cost to the prevention of future crime," writes legal scholar Judith Areen. "For all others, the state would separate children from their parents only in the most extreme circumstances and then only when private parties initiated court action." America's earliest form of state aid derived from a class-based structure that permitted the government to intervene coercively in poor families in order to control them and exploit their labor.[39]

The English Poor Laws made three types of provisions for paupers: aid within their own homes; contractual arrangements with private individuals, such as indenture; and institutional congregate care in workhouses and almshouses. The American colonies adopted indenture and the poorhouse as the primary means of addressing family destitution, rejecting the option of offering direct relief to the poor. There were no separate services for impoverished children; children accompanied their parents to the deplorable institutions for the poor or were confined there by themselves.[40]

By the nineteenth century, poorhouses had been established across the nation to warehouse economically desperate families. "Despite optimistic predictions that poorhouses would furnish relief 'with economy and humanity,'" writes political scientist Virginia Eubanks, "the poor house was an institution that rightly inspired terror among poor and working-class people." Not only were poorhouses frigid and filthy, but they also kept mentally ill people confined to tiny cells for months at a time and sold the labor of those who were able-bodied.[41]

At the turn of the nineteenth century, wealthy reformers in northern cities began a charitable mission to rescue poor children from parental and institutional cruelty. The idea that childhood was its own stage of development that made (white) children innocent and in need of protection was taking hold. A wave of immigrants from Europe into urban centers hit by economic recession left thousands living in overcrowded slums without secure housing, jobs, or resources to care for their children. The new child welfare services concentrated on the effects of poverty on children, which they treated as symptoms of parental deficits—an offshoot of the general belief that poverty is the result of individual inadequacies. Between 1800 and 1850, at least sixty-two private charities were established to provide care for children deemed orphaned, abandoned, or neglected. The reformers were motivated by a child-saving philosophy that saw destitute children as the victims of neglect who could be properly trained by placement in arrangements more suitable than poorhouses and indenture. The emerging child welfare agencies also served to assimilate children of Irish, Italian, and Jewish immigrants living in urban slums to white US culture.[42]

Over the course of the 1800s, two institutions arose to deal with the care of poor children apart from almshouses and indentured servitude— the orphanage and the "free" foster home. The main child welfare reform of the early nineteenth century was the establishment of orphanages to salvage children from the "evil influences" of the poorhouse. Orphanages took in children whose parents were unable to care for them, as well as those whose parents had died. New York passed a law in 1875 that moved children from poorhouses to orphan asylums while providing for the involuntary commitment of children. As child protection societies began to appear throughout the East and Midwest, they persuaded states to pass laws that defined child maltreatment and to give them the authority to investigate poor parents and seek court orders removing children from their homes to be placed in orphan asylums.[43]

The second major innovation emerged when, in 1853, Reverend Charles Loring Brace, a twenty-seven-year-old missionary from New England's elite, founded the New York Children's Aid Society (CAS), the model for agencies that placed children in private foster homes. At the time, out of New York City's population of five hundred thousand, there were an estimated ten thousand to thirty thousand children from impoverished families consigned to overcrowded orphanages or surviving in the streets. Brace believed that these children were destined to become criminals unless they were transferred from the slums to more wholesome environments. CAS responded to "the deeply settled feeling of our citizens that something must be done to meet the increasing crime and poverty among the destitute children of New York," claimed its first circular.[44]

In his 1872 book, *The Dangerous Classes of New York and Twenty Years' Work Among Them*, Brace explained that "the cheapest and most efficacious way of dealing with the 'Dangerous Classes' of large cities, is not to punish them, but to prevent their growth; to throw the influences of education and discipline and religion about the abandoned and destitute youth of our large towns; to so change their material circumstances, and draw them under the influence of the moral and fortunate classes, that they shall grow up as useful producers and members of society, able and inclined to aid it in its progress." In a set of four drawings, Brace portrayed "the fortunes of the street waif," morphing over time from an unhoused child sleeping under a stairwell to a teenage thief, a drunkard at a saloon, and an incarcerated convict.

Although Brace designed the foster home as an alternative to indenturing children, it was actually a form of indenture without the contract. Impoverished children were expected to work for their foster families indefinitely in exchange for their keep. In 1874, news of Mary Ellen Wilson, a New York City child who was starved and beaten by the caretaker she called "Mamma," sparked the founding of the New York Society for the Prevention of Cruelty to Children. Although foster care advocates have traditionally used Mary Ellen's story as a justification for child removal, it turns out the case teaches the opposite lesson. Mary Ellen was taken from her impoverished mother and indentured to her abuser by the New York Board of Charities. Mary Ellen was not saved from abuse by foster care; she was abused while in foster care.[45]

Brace's program of modified indenture for children from poor immigrant families gave rise not only to "placing out" children across the Northeast, but also to shipping children to supply free labor in more distant locations. Determining that "the best of all asylums for the outcast child is the farmer's home," in 1854 Brace dispatched forty-seven children in CAS's care on a train from Grand Central Station bound for Michigan to be taken in by farm families. Brace's idea launched the so-called orphan train movement that transported children by the thousands from their impoverished families to provide free labor on farms in New York and in the Midwest, the South, and the West. CAS hoped to "be the means of draining the city of these children by communicating with farmers, manufacturers, or families in the country who may need such employment." With the help of charitable donations and reduced fares, the trains carried as many as three thousand children each year, mainly to states stretching across the Midwest, but also as far as Texas and Arizona. Between 1854 and 1929, the orphan trains relocated some two hundred thousand children to distant farms, where they were often overworked, underfed, and abused—and returned at will. Strong, able-bodied, and attractive children under the age of fourteen were preferred by the host families, as indicated by an 1893 newspaper ad announcing the arrival of an orphan train in Tecumseh, Nebraska: "All children received under the care of this Association are of SPECIAL PROMISE in intelligence and health, and are in age from one month to twelve years, and are sent FREE to those receiving them, on ninety days trial, UNLESS a special contract is otherwise made."[46]

The class divide between coercive public measures for poor families and private disputes for the wealthy families was mirrored by a racial divide between poor white families and poor Black families. Black families were largely excluded from openly segregated child welfare services until the end of World War II. Most of the orphanages and foster homes established to rescue destitute white children refused to accept Black children. The few "colored orphan asylums" were even worse than the ones for white children. By the time of the 1920 census, thirty-one northern states reported a total of 1,070 child-caring agencies. Of these agencies, 35 were for Black children only, 264 accepted children of all races, 60 took nonwhite children except Black children, and 711 were reserved for white children. The first orphanage for Black children in New York, the Association for the Benefit of Colored Orphans, was established in 1836. Its founders set eight years as the maximum age for admission, based both on the belief that older children would be impossible to rehabilitate and on the expectation that Black children would be indentured by age twelve. During a riot in 1863, a gang of white people broke into the New York colored asylum and set it on fire.[47]

Black children were more likely to be labeled delinquent than needy. The main child-caring institution for them was prison or the nascent reformatory for juvenile delinquents. Child-saving advocates established institutions for "dependent children" and "juvenile delinquents" simultaneously. Both were considered reforms that rescued indigent children from their inappropriate confinement with adults in almshouses and penitentiaries. At the same time that northern reformers were moving dependent children from almshouses to orphanages, the Society for the Prevention of Pauperism founded the New York House of Refuge in 1825 for juvenile offenders who had previously been incarcerated at Bellevue Prison. Black children not only were more likely than white children to be adjudicated delinquent, but they also were kept segregated and treated more harshly once confined to reformatories. A "Jim Crow juvenile justice system," as African American Studies professor Geoff K. Ward calls it, unjustly punished and exploited Black children for most of the twentieth century. Judges and administrators denied them the assumption of intrinsic innocence accorded to white children and instead believed that Black children were incapable of rehabilitation.[48]

As novelist Colson Whitehead made vivid in *The Nickel Boys*, Black boys found to be delinquent were subjected to unspeakable horrors in reform schools that were as brutal as prisons. Whitehead's protagonist, Elwood Curtis, is about to graduate from high school in 1960s Tallahassee when he is unjustly accused of stealing a car and sentenced to

Nickel Academy, where discipline is meted out with vicious whippings or worse. His lawyer tells him he got off lucky because "most of the kids had been sent here for much lesser—and nebulous and inexplicable—offenses. Some students were wards of the state, without family, and there was nowhere else to put them." Whitehead based his novel on a real-life reform school, Dozier School for Boys, that operated in Florida for 111 years, from 1900 to 2011. A secret graveyard in the back, bearing the bodies of at least eighty boys, and the testimonies of survivors have exposed the rape, torture, and murder that terrorized the children confined there. Black girls, too, were sent to reformatories at high rates, often as punishment for minor infractions. White administrators believed they possessed an innate sexual deviance that threatened to corrupt their white peers.[49]

But the state's main approach to Black children's needs in the first decades of the twentieth century was to ignore them. Black people relied primarily on extended family networks and community resources such as churches, women's clubs, and benevolent societies to take care of children whose parents were unable to. Booker T. Washington took Black communities' care for children as a point of pride, noting in 1909 that the "number of dependents among my own race in America is relatively small as compared with the number of dependents among the white population." While white-run child welfare systems either excluded Black children or forced them into the most inferior and violent institutions, "the negro, in some way, has inherited and has trained into him the idea that he must take care of his own dependents," Washington stated.[50]

SEGREGATED PUBLIC AID

During the Progressive Era (1890s–1920s), feminist activists successfully exploited the ideology of motherhood to win public relief for unmarried and widowed mothers living in poverty. They argued that husbandless mothers needed government aid so that they would not have to relinquish their maternal duties in the home to join the wage labor force. Supporting struggling mothers also avoided the need to place their children in orphanages and asylums. The nation's leading child welfare experts declared welfare's mission at the first White House Conference on Children, convened in 1909: "Children of reasonably efficient and deserving mothers who are without the support of the normal breadwinner should, as a rule, be kept with their parents, such aid being given as may be necessary to maintain suitable homes for the rearing of children." Mothers' pensions, initially provided through state and local programs, helped lay the groundwork for the modern federal welfare system.

The welfare programs were severely limited, however, by their patriarchal assumptions. The reformers adhered to the traditional notion that wives should rely on their husbands' wages to support the family and to a mission of controlling poor immigrant families. Aid generally was conditioned on compliance with "suitable-home" requirements and administered by juvenile courts that specialized in punitive and rehabilitative judgments.

The first maternalist welfare legislation was meant for white mothers only. Black single mothers were practically excluded from state aid for the first half of the twentieth century. Administrators either failed to establish programs in locations with large Black populations or distributed benefits according to standards, such as the suitable-home tests, that disqualified Black mothers. In 1931, the first national survey of mothers' pensions broken down by race found that only 3 percent of recipients were Black; 96 percent of welfare recipients were white. The majority of Black recipients resided in two states—California and Ohio—and there were only two Black mothers in all the South who received benefits. "The goal of withholding welfare from Black mothers was to keep them in the workforce rather than home caring for their own children," writes Laura Briggs. The New Deal solidified the racist exclusion of most Black mothers from its Aid to Dependent Children (ADC) program, which was based on discretionary eligibility standards. Those who qualified received stingier stipends, on the grounds that "blacks needed less to live on than whites."[51]

It took the midcentury Black freedom struggle to open the welfare system to Black people. But it was a Pyrrhic victory. As more and more

Black families began receiving benefits, the image of welfare recipients began to transmute from the worthy white widow to the immoral unwed Black mother. Southern states devised ways to throw Black mothers and children off the rolls in retaliation against civil rights gains. On the heels of the US Supreme Court's 1954 decision in *Brown v. Board of Education*, striking down state segregation of public schools as unconstitutional, southern states responded by slashing welfare. Within days of the *Brown* ruling, the Mississippi state legislature "attached a rider to an appropriations bill cutting children off welfare if their mothers failed to keep a suitable home," writes Briggs. A decade later, the city of Birmingham was the epicenter of civil rights conflict: in May 1963, the Children's Crusade, a series of demonstrations against racial segregation, was met with ferocious police violence ordered by Public Safety Commissioner Bull Connor; in September that year, the Klan bombed the 16th Street Baptist Church, killing four Black girls. In the decade between 1957 and 1967, the city decreased its total expenditures on welfare from $31,000 to $12,000. According to Briggs, these exclusionary welfare laws and budget cuts constituted a "campaign to punish the most impoverished Black households for the NAACP's desegregation work."[52]

The Mississippi rider also outlawed common law marriage as "an illicit relationship or promiscuity." As a result, between 1954 and 1960, 8,392 children, most of them Black, were dropped from the welfare rolls because they or a sibling were "illegitimate." Louisiana followed suit, enacting in 1960 a provision that denied benefits to children born out of wedlock. Again, upwards of 90 percent of the families affected were headed by Black women. Many states also implemented "man-in-the-house" rules to deny benefits to Black mothers suspected of living or having a sexual relationship with a man, who would be deemed a "substitute father" and expected to support the children financially. Social services workers routinely raided homes to try to catch a man on the premises or to look for evidence, such as male clothing. By providing an excuse to cut off state support for Black children, suitable-home and other eligibility laws, passed in states across the South, became an effective means for white lawmakers to economically assault Black communities in the battle over civil rights.[53]

Up to this point, state child welfare agencies had virtually ignored Black families and focused their attention on providing in-home services to white families receiving public assistance. Policies took a dramatic turn for the worst as southern states waged a backlash against the civil rights rebellion and Black mothers' claims to public aid. States began to punish poor mothers who failed to meet suitable-home standards by separating them from their children. In 1959 and 1960, respectively, the Tennessee and Florida legislatures enacted new suitable-home statutes that directed welfare workers to pressure mothers who were denied benefits to "voluntarily" relinquish custody of their children to relatives. Mothers who refused were charged with neglect and referred to juvenile court. A 1960 study of the Florida program revealed that "state welfare workers challenged the suitability of 13,000 families; of these, only 9 percent were white, even though white families made up 39 percent of the total caseload."[54]

During the 1960s, congressional debates over welfare policy prominently featured white people's interest in keeping poor Black mothers available for cheap domestic labor. Southern white politicians helped to defeat the Family Assistance Plan, which President Richard Nixon proposed in 1969 to provide a guaranteed minimum income for poor families, by arguing, "There's not going to be anybody left to roll these wheelbarrows and press these shirts." The federal government also cemented the policy of removing Black children from homes receiving welfare, paving the path to today's destructive foster care system. In 1961, Arthur Flemming, the head of the Department of Health, Education, and Welfare, directed states that they could not deny ADC based on suitable-home tests unless they took steps to rehabilitate the family. For families that could not be rehabilitated, Flemming allocated federal funds to put the children in foster care. Flemming reasoned that it was "completely inconsistent . . . to declare a home unsuitable for a child to receive assistance and at the same time permit him to remain in the same home, exposed to the same environment."[55]

Later that year, Congress amended Title IV of the Social Security Act to provide federal funding to maintain these children apart from their families. Now, with a federal mandate that homes must be suitable to receive ADC benefits and funding for foster care, local child welfare agencies had license to escalate the removal of Black children. State ADC eligibility workers began snatching Black children away from mothers deemed unsuitable instead of simply denying benefits. The foster care population mushroomed, with 150,000 children placed in out-of-home care in 1961 alone. The central mission of the child welfare system transformed from providing services to intact white families to taking Black children from theirs. The simultaneous shift in US child welfare policy from neglecting Black families to intervening in them marked another milestone in the history of Black family destruction that began with chattel slavery. Family separation served as a white supremacist strategy to quell Black rebellion during slavery, Reconstruction, and the civil rights movement.

As the Black freedom struggle gained momentum, southern states also debated legislation that would impose sterilization as the remedy for Black women's perceived reckless fertility and overreliance on public assistance. "The negro woman, because of child welfare assistance, [is] making . . . a business . . . of giving birth to illegitimate children," declared the sponsor of a 1958 sterilization bill in Mississippi. "The purpose of my bill was to try to stop, or slow down, such traffic at its source." Government officials achieved their goal by implementing federally funded family-planning programs that coerced Black women and girls into submitting to the operation.[56]

Fannie Lou Hamer, the celebrated leader of the Mississippi Freedom Democratic Party, told a Washington, DC, audience in 1965 that 60 percent of the Black women in Sunflower County, Mississippi, were subjected to postpartum sterilizations at Sunflower City Hospital without their consent. The practice of sterilizing southern Black women and girls through trickery or deceit was so common it became known as a "Mississippi appendectomy." Hamer had suffered this violation herself when she went to the hospital for the removal of a small uterine tumor in 1961 and later discovered that the doctor had performed a complete hysterectomy without even telling her. In a civil rights lawsuit challenging the sterilization abuse of people on Medicaid, federal district judge Gerhard Gesell noted in his 1973 ruling against this practice that "over the last few years, an estimated 100,000 to 150,000 low-income persons have been sterilized annually under federally funded programs." While most unmarried white women who became pregnant were pressured to put their babies up for adoption, Black women were subjected to state vilification, starvation, and sterilization.[57]

As with the white backlash against Reconstruction, government efforts to stamp out Black uprisings in the 1960s were reinforced with disparaging portrayals of Black mothers as dangerous reproducers. Despite the history of relentless state assaults on Black families, many white sociologists blamed unwed Black mothers for creating a dysfunctional family structure by displacing Black men as the heads of households. Daniel Patrick Moynihan's 1965 report, *The Negro Family: The Case for National Action*, promoted the theory that Black mothers were responsible for the disintegration of the Black family, the failure of Black people to succeed in US society, and rioting in urban centers. Moynihan, then assistant secretary of labor and director of the Office of Policy Planning and Research under President Lyndon Johnson, argued that reforming the Black family was vital to President Johnson's War on Poverty. "At the heart of the deterioration of the fabric of the Negro society is the deterioration of the Negro family," Moynihan wrote. "In essence, the Negro community has been forced into a matriarchal structure, which, because it is so out of line with the rest of the American society, seriously retards the progress of the group as a whole." By attributing urban crisis and Black militancy to Black family pathology, Moynihan's analysis furthered policies that tied poverty-relief programs to both harsh child welfare and crime control interventions in Black neighborhoods.[58]

TO FAMILY PRESERVATION AND BACK

In the 1970s, Congress began to examine the skyrocketing foster care population and the toll that foster care was taking on children and their families. Leading scholars criticized the child welfare system for unnecessarily removing children from their homes and leaving them to languish in foster care. Hearings on Capitol Hill revealed that federal policy created financial incentives for state child welfare authorities to prefer placing children in foster care over keeping families intact. The federal government reimbursed states for the cost of out-of-home placements but not for services provided to families within the home.

Congress took steps to ease the overemphasis on foster care by passing legislation that tied federal funding to reforms in states' approaches to child welfare. The Adoption Assistance and Child Welfare Act of 1980, signed by President Jimmy Carter, requires that state agencies make "reasonable efforts" to keep children safely at home, as well as to return children in foster care safely to their parents. In 1993, Congress enacted the Family Preservation and Family Support Program in response to concerns that child welfare agencies were not doing enough to keep families together, doubling federal funding for family preservation and support services intended to avoid taking children from their homes.

Although these efforts have been characterized as policy shifts toward family unity, they do not represent a radical change in the system's historic focus on policing and separating families. Child welfare scholars typically treat family preservation and child safety as two opposing ends of the spectrum of child welfare concerns. It is often said that American child welfare policy operates like a pendulum swinging from one objective to the other. The pendulum metaphor is mistaken. To begin with, it assumes a false opposition between keeping families together and keeping children safe. What's more, child welfare policy has never swung decisively toward preserving families. Even the most supportive federal legislation still centers on threatening parents with taking their children and devotes the bulk of funding to maintaining children away from home. For Black families, the pendulum of child welfare services has stayed firmly on the side of child removal and foster care.

The nod to preserving families was short lived, however. In the late 1990s, Congress passed back-to-back major legislation simultaneously stripping away support for struggling parents and speeding their children into adoptive homes. In 1996, Congress passed the Personal Responsibility and Work Opportunity Reconciliation Act, which ended the federal guarantee of cash assistance to families living in poverty and gave states wide latitude to decide how to spend federal funds and to implement extensive welfare reform policies. President Bill Clinton signed the law to great fanfare, pledging to "end welfare as we know it." The federal entitlement program Aid to Families with Dependent Children (AFDC) was replaced by Temporary Assistance to Needy Families (TANF), which provides reduced cash benefits for a limited time while recipients look for work. The myth of the Black welfare queen, constructed during the Reagan era as a Black woman who had babies just to get a government check, helped to fuel the bipartisan measures. Public aid is no longer supposed to support families but was transmuted instead into a behavior modification program designed to pressure impoverished mothers to meet their children's needs by getting married, having fewer babies, and finding low-wage jobs without adequate child care.

A year later, in 1997, President Clinton signed the Adoption and Safe Families Act (ASFA) after directing the federal government to take steps to double the number of foster children adopted annually by 2002. As First Lady, Hillary Clinton made adoption a centerpiece of her children's rights platform and was a vocal supporter of the federal adoption legislation. ASFA implemented the preference for getting foster children adopted over reunifying them with their parents through a set of mandates and incentives to state child welfare departments. Although the new law retained the requirement that agencies make reasonable efforts to preserve or reunify families, it drastically weakened the mandate, which already was not being enforced, by falsely equating child removal with child safety and permanency with termination of parental rights and adoption. The new law identified circumstances when the reasonable-efforts requirement can be waived altogether and established swifter timetables for terminating parents' rights to "free" children for adoption. These deadlines have little to do with child safety; they instead concern the length of time a child has spent out of the parents' custody, effectively shifting the presumption in favor of termination when children have spent more than fifteen of the previous twenty-two months in state custody.

ASFA also offers financial incentives to states to get more children adopted. The federal government pays states a bonus for every foster child adopted during the fiscal year that exceeds a baseline of prior average annual adoptions. Congress additionally funds technical assistance to states to boost their adoption numbers. By 2014, the federal government had handed states $424 million in adoption-incentive subsidies, exceeding the amount saved in foster care costs. To add insult to injury, Congress offset the difference by drawing from the TANF contingency fund, which is meant to supplement aid to impoverished families when states are undergoing budget crises. Congress appropriated diminishing funds for family preservation and reunification while spending increasing amounts on foster care and adoption assistance.[59]

Foster children's ties to their parents had become a nuisance. Under the new legislation, parents' rights were treated as the chief impediment to permanency (read as adoption) for children in foster care. Terminating parental rights was seen, in the words of Republican senator John Chafee, as "the critical first step in moving children into permanent placements." Chicago, where virtually all the children in foster care were Black, felt an immediate shock wave from the push to shatter family bonds. According to the *Chicago Reporter*, by 1999, just two short years after ASFA's enactment, "terminations grew from 958 to 3,743 in that period, meaning that three out of every five cases ended with parents losing custody." Some transracial adoption advocates cast terminations of Black mothers' rights in particular as a welcome means for facilitating adoptions of Black children by white middle-class couples. In January 2003, the National Association of Black Social Workers amended its policy statement "Preserving Families of African Ancestry," which was initially issued in 1972, to call for the repeal of ASFA.[60]

The coincidence of the welfare and adoption laws marked the first time in US history that the federal government mandated that states protect children from parental neglect but failed to guarantee a minimum economic safety net for impoverished families. The federal government's expenditures on foster care increased by 30 percent between

1996 and 2000, while spending on food stamps and welfare benefits fell by 33 percent and 19 percent, respectively. If we follow the money, we can see that federal child welfare policy shifted even further away from financially supporting poor and low-income families to relying more aggressively on child removal and adoption to deal with child poverty, especially in Black families.[61]

Added to these punitive, market-based responses to structural inequality was the controversial 1994 federal crime law, the Violent Crime Control and Law Enforcement Act, which was touted at the time as an aggressive response to rising crime rates. Its authorship by then Senator Joe Biden became a sore point during his 2020 presidential campaign, as he tried to distance himself from attempts that he and other Democrats had made in the 1990s to shake the impression they were soft on crime. The law imposed harsher prison sentences for federal offenses and showered states with funds to expand their police forces and build more prisons, while winning sympathy from more radical Democrats, like Senator Bernie Sanders, by including the Violence Against Women Act, which also relied on law enforcement to deal with domestic violence. Taken together, all three Clinton-era laws formed a trifecta of welfare contraction and carceral expansion. The family-policing system played an integral, though largely overlooked, role in the 1990s federal consolidation of capital accumulation, welfare retrenchment, and punitive containment.[62]

Since then, federal and state policies continued to shrink the financial safety net for poor and low-income families while responding to the resulting deprivation in Black communities by escalating police presence, incarceration, and child removal. Although the numbers of Black men, women, and children confined to jails, prisons, juvenile detention centers, and foster care have vacillated in recent years, the basic formula of addressing the suffering from state disinvestment with intensified state coercion has remained constant. In December 2018, Jazmine Headley, a twenty-three-year-old Black mother, found a space on the floor of the crowded New York City public benefits office where she could sit down with her one-year-old son. She was exhausted from waiting for hours to find out why her child care benefits had been stopped abruptly. A guard approached her and ordered her to move. When she stayed put, police were called to arrest her. A video shows two officers restraining Headley while two guards yanked the screaming toddler from her arms. One of them can be heard threatening to have CPS take her son. Headley was charged with resisting arrest and child endangerment and spent several days locked in a Rikers Island cell, for this and other unrelated charges, before attorneys were able to get the charges dropped. The public aid office has become a site for threatening Black mothers with arrest and child removal for the crime of seeking help to raise their children.[63]

Examining the roots of America's child welfare system, marked by tearing apart families to uphold white supremacist regimes, buttresses Malcolm X's words about the state's breakup of his own family: "nothing but legal modern slavery." Throughout its history, US family policing has revolved around the racist belief that Black parents are unfit to raise their children. Beginning with chattel slavery and continuing through the Jim Crow, civil rights, and neoliberal eras, the white power structure has wielded this lie as a rationale to control Black communities, exploit Black labor, and quell Black rebellion by assaulting Black families. Placing Black children in the state's custody implements the quintessential racist insult—that Black people are incapable of governing themselves and need white supervision.

Malcolm X also diagnosed the demise of his family as resulting from "a society's failure, hypocrisy, greed, and lack of mercy and compassion." These deeply rooted features of US society, ruled by a racial capitalist logic that values building the wealth of a white elite over meeting everyone else's basic needs, have turned the child welfare system into the destructive force it is today. To borrow Malcolm X's words, family policing sustains "a society that will crush people, and then penalize them for not being able to stand up under the weight."[64]

FIVE

STRONG-ARMED

PRESIGNED ORDERS

The Home of the Innocents on Market Street in Louisville, Kentucky, was opened in 1880 to rescue children from parents who were unable to care for them. The home, which still exists, includes "a safe haven for at-risk children" and provides care for "children who are victims of abuse, abandonment, and neglect," its website soothingly boasts. "This can mean a couple of days, or in some cases, several years." Its emergency shelter is available around the clock for children taken from their homes by CPS workers employed by the state's Cabinet for Health and Family Services.[1]

For years, the home kept stacks of blank forms with judges' signatures copied at the bottom to be used by CPS staff. The forms were emergency custody orders, required to be signed by a judge before caseworkers could separate children from their parents without a hearing. During regular business hours, a caseworker who decided a child should be removed filled out a form and ran it over to the courthouse for a judge to approve. After reading a written affidavit spelling out the reasons for removal, the judge had to find that the child was in serious risk of death or imminent physical injury before signing the order.

If the order was granted, CPS took the child from their home, and a custody hearing was scheduled for three days later. At that hearing, the parents had their first opportunity to challenge the emergency placement of their child in state custody and to plead with the judge for their child's return.

The pile of blank forms with judges' signatures were for after-hours removals. After the court closed at 4:30 p.m., or on weekends, caseworkers phoned an on-call judge to get verbal approval to remove children. The caseworkers filled out one of the blank forms that had been presigned by a judge and used it, along with the on-call judge's verbal okay, as authorization to snatch children from their beds in the middle of the night. But the after-hours judges never saw the completed forms, so they couldn't evaluate the allegations or evidence in writing beforehand. It was as if police officers began inscribing their own search warrants without judges reading them. A judge saw the order for the first time at the custody hearing three days after the child was taken to the home's emergency shelter.

A 2019 investigative report by the Louisville TV station WDRB found that this phony approval process had operated for at least three years. In one case, a CPS worker took three children from their parents after mentioning the need to remove only one child to the judge on the phone. The caseworker simply filled out three presigned forms, one for each child taken. "Our concern, which we have reason to believe has occurred, is that workers can take the blank signed orders and just fill it out to say whatever they want," explained Sarah Clay, a Louisville attorney appointed by the court to represent parents. "The current system that's in place allows a worker for the cabinet to essentially create their own court order without a judge ever seeing it."[2]

The local district court judges defended the practice on grounds that the law allowed for verbal approval of emergency removals. "It just means they have to have some form of an order," Jefferson District Court chief judge Anne Haynie noted. "That's all verbal means. That does not mean in person." Judge Haynie seemed to have misinterpreted the relevant Kentucky statute, which states, "In no event shall a child be removed pursuant to KRS 620.060 only on a verbal order."

Surely verbal approval of a written removal order is meaningless if the judge has no idea what the order says. The nonchalance displayed by the home, the CPS workers, and the district court judges resembled approving a lunch order, not the seizure of children from their parents. Only after WDRB's exposé went public did the district court begin to require caseworkers to email the completed forms to the judges so they could read them before signing them electronically. Louisville is not alone: in 2012, WXYZ Action News in Detroit revealed that probation officers in juvenile court were literally rubber-stamping a judge's name onto orders permitting CPS to take children from their homes without the judge ever having read the order.[3]

Although the practice in Louisville was abandoned, it gives an accurate indication of how poorly judicial proceedings protect families from government abuses of power. Even after the judges in Jefferson District Court began to actually read and sign the child removal orders they issued, they continued to grant emergency requests to the CPS workers who had previously engaged in the ruse. Judges routinely grant ex parte orders to remove children and place them in foster care, relying solely on the word of a CPS investigator, without first giving the parents a chance to defend themselves in court.

A powerful branch of the family-policing machinery consists of family court professionals who converge in hearings to determine the fate of families—including judges, lawyers representing CPS, court-appointed special advocates, experts who provide testimony on behalf of CPS, and court officers who stand guard. Judges decide whether to permit allegedly maltreated children to remain at home while the parents are monitored or to put the children in foster care. Often, caseworkers or police officers immediately remove children without a court hearing on grounds they are at risk of imminent harm. That means these children are already in foster care when the judge first reviews the case and must decide whether to reunite them with their parents. Judges also review agencies' recommendations for children's placements, how long to keep them there, when to move them to new placements, and when to return them, if ever, to their homes. Judges usually approve the requirements CPS imposes on parents, and if parents fail to comply, they may permanently terminate parents' legal rights to a relationship with their children. The child welfare system has a legal design that gives CPS workers enormous power to control families and parents little protection against them. Parents are strongarmed into following their dictates by the very credible threat of losing their children.

"Over nearly two decades of representing children in the foster care system, I can only recount a handful of times—maybe five or fewer—in which my clients had not already been removed prior to the first court hearing," writes Vivek Sankaran, the clinical professor at University of Michigan Law School. In one of his cases, CPS had been working with a family for many months when it became dissatisfied with the family's engagement in the mandated services. A caseworker made a middle-of-the-night call to a judge, who signed an emergency removal order. The next day, without any warning to her parents, CPS workers seized Sankaran's client—a nine-year-old girl—while she was eating lunch at school, despite lacking any evidence the child was in imminent danger. "Parents are considered guilty until proven innocent," Kimesha McDonald, a social worker at the Bronx Defenders, told me, referring to New York City's Administration for Children's Services (ACS). "ACS removes the child, then does the investigation afterward to see if you're a fit parent."[4]

Emergency removals not only deny parents the right to be heard before their children are taken; they also put parents at an unfair disadvantage once they appear in court. For now they must persuade a judge to rescind the existing order they never had a chance to contest. This biases the judge's consideration of the pros and cons: Wasn't there a good reason to urgently put the child in foster care in the first place? Suppose I return the child home, and the parents harm the child? Isn't it much safer to maintain the status quo while CPS has a chance to investigate? The rushed decision to place children in foster care makes it much easier to keep them there and then schedule a hearing to reconsider the placement at a future date.

This tendency toward emergency removal followed by judicial stagnation is exacerbated by fear on the part of caseworkers and judges of being spotlighted in the media as the person responsible for the death of a child "known to the system." Such stories always get newspaper headlines and wide circulation on the internet. Caseworkers may err on the side of taking children from their homes so a judge has to decide whether or not to return them to their parents. For their part, judges may be inclined to keep children in foster care, at least for a while, to mitigate accusations of doing nothing to prevent a tragedy. Joyce McMillan, a parent activist in New York City, calls the practice "*New York Post* law," indicating the desire to avoid appearing on the front page of the *New York Post*.[5]

Family court judges tend to rubber-stamp CPS determinations. "Most of the time judges deferred to ACS in terms of assessing risk and authorized their proposed solution with very little, if any, questioning or scrutiny," writes anthropologist Tina Lee about her observation of numerous initial hearings involving New York City's child welfare agency, ACS. A ruling in favor of foster care was so taken for granted that even lawyers assigned to represent parents rarely challenged the placement with any seriousness. Attorneys from the Bronx Defenders' family defense unit, dedicated to "really litigate these cases," told Lee that, when they insisted on questioning ACS's position, "they were heckled by fellow attorneys." Despite this bias in favor of approving emergency removals, many are reversed once the cases go to court. In testimony to the New York City Council, for example, ACS conceded that around 20 to 25 percent of its ex parte removals in 2018 were reversed by a judge—"meaning that something like 400 children were subject to emergency removals who were not in imminent risk of serious harm," observes journalist Molly Schwartz. We would find the number of unnecessary removals to be far higher if all of them received robust scrutiny in court.[6]

The odds are stacked against parents in other ways, as well. Most start out from a disenfranchised status: Black, Native, or Latinx; female; poor or low income; unfamiliar with their legal rights. Typically, a lone, frightened mother sits next to her public defender or court-appointed attorney, whom she may be meeting for the first time. If assigned by a judge, the lawyer may not want to be there. In legal circles, a judicial

assignment to represent parents in family court is considered the bottom of the barrel. The mother is confronted by an opposing battalion
of state-paid lawyers, caseworkers, and expert witnesses, all trying to
prove that she is a bad parent. Lee found she could observe family
court freely when she sat by herself, but was questioned about her
presence and usually barred from entering when accompanied by a
parent. "I came to attribute this difference to officials being suspicious
of anyone who might be present as an outside advocate for a parent."[7]

Child welfare proceedings position parents as adversaries of their
children, while casting everyone else in the courtroom as there to protect children from their parents. Judges frame the legal issues as a contest between the child's safety and the parents' rights, giving a moral
advantage to CPS. The legal standard of proof is accordingly designed
to tip the scales in the state's favor. In criminal cases, the prosecution has the burden of proving beyond a reasonable doubt that the
defendant is guilty. In family court, CPS needs to meet a test known
as preponderance of the evidence, showing only that it is more likely
than not that the alleged maltreatment occurred. This standard is often
interpreted to accept the state's claim that the parents pose a risk to
their children and to shift the burden to the parents to prove that their
children are safe. What little legal protection the state's statutes afford
parents may be cast aside, considered an irrelevant obstacle to quickly
ruling on the children's status. One judge told a mother seeking more
time with her children, "I know there's a legal right to ask for more
visits. But if I gave it to you, then I'd have to give it to every parent."
In 2018, the Colorado Office of Respondent Parents' Counsel, a government agency that advocates for poor parents, persuaded appellate
courts to find procedural violations in nearly one-third of the state's
child welfare cases.[8]

Imani Worthy, the parent organizer at *Rise*, the magazine devoted to
system-impacted parents, recalled, "While in the courthouse I couldn't
help but notice a separation when you enter. Lawyers, judges, clerks,
ACS caseworkers and staff walk in on the left side. On this side, I notice a lot of Caucasian people entering. The right side is for the general
public. The general public had so many Black and Brown faces. . . .

Why did it feel like only a certain type of people were going in and out of the general public doors?" Worthy realizes that it was their subordinated race and class status that distinguished policed family members who were relegated to entering on the degraded side of the court.[9]

Everyone in the courtroom treats mothers as if they are children in need of supervision. Mothers are to be seen and not heard, silent and with head hung low while disciplined for their inadequacies. "They are spoken about but not called to speak," says Kathleen Creamer, managing attorney of the family advocacy unit at Community Legal Services in Philadelphia, describing how judges interact with her clients, mostly low-income Black mothers. "It's enraging to stand next to a parent who is a whole human being and spoken about in terms of her obedience," Creamer went on. "Or in terms of her failures as a mother."[10]

There is something particularly debasing about being infantilized as a mother, whose identity is partly defined by her competence to care for her children. Her helplessness before the court is also particularly terrifying, not only because the fate of her children lies in others' hands, but also because she sees through the system's benevolence to its terror. Black mothers have reason to doubt that the state will take good care of their children, given its history of hatred toward Black girls and boys. "One characteristic of racism is that children are treated like adults and adults are treated like children," Cathy Park Hong writes in *Minor Feelings: An Asian American Reckoning*. The ritual played out in family court humiliates Black mothers while tossing their supposedly rescued children into a system that treats Black children as potential criminals.[11]

The silence demanded of parents is violently enforced by armed officers in uniform who stand guard in the courtroom, a constant reminder that the parents are viewed as dangerous. Nila Natarajan, a supervising attorney in the family defense practice at Brooklyn Defender Services, told me she has witnessed court officers physically assault clients who show emotion during judicial proceedings. Any display of anger or grief is seen as evidence of parental pathology. When a distraught mother whose child was placed in foster care ran out of the courtroom, the judge reprimanded her by reducing the time she could spend in visits with her child. A teenager who responded emotionally to a judge's order was hauled off to jail.[12]

Natarajan says the worst violence occurs when, without warning, the judge orders CPS to seize children from their parents in the midst of a hearing, right there in the courtroom. A dozen armed officers surround the family. Other officers block the doors to prevent anyone from escaping. Guards once ripped a breastfeeding baby from one of Natarajan's clients. Judges always exit the courtroom before the capture begins, so as to avoid facing the harrowing aftermath of their decisions. Natarajan has tried to get the New York City family court administration to consider at least implementing a trauma-informed approach to proceedings that cause such distress. But no one in charge is interested in alleviating the pain inflicted by the forced family separations.

Most parents don't need armed guards to wrestle them into compliance. Parents know that if they don't cooperate, they risk losing custody of their children for good. "The consequences of refusing to comply are too great, and resisting child protection's conditions is at a parent's own peril," says Emma Ketteringham, managing director of the Family Defense Practice at the Bronx Defenders. "The difference between parents who successfully avoid losing their children and keep their families intact and those who fail is rarely the type or severity of neglect or abuse involved, but is the degree to which the parent is willing to surrender their humanity, individuality and pride to the system and the court." Parents are put in the excruciating bind of having to succumb to the dictates of state agents bent on destroying their families. Their children are weaponized against them.[13]

SHORT-STAYERS

The trauma inflicted on children by family separation increases with the length of time spent apart. But CPS workers also cause tremendous harm when they casually remove children from their homes on flimsy grounds even for a matter of days. Taking children away from their parents for any amount of time is a violent exercise of state power. Yet research shows that caseworkers and police officers routinely take children from their parents for short placements in foster care. Each year CPS agencies remove about twenty-five thousand children from their homes who spend less than thirty days in foster care, with seventeen thousand returning home within ten days. Most of these "short-stayers" are placed in an unfamiliar environment—a nonrelative foster home or a congregate facility—and spend less than two weeks there. Ashley Keiler-Green, a doctor who regularly opened her home in Albuquerque, New Mexico, to foster children, compared the constant turnover to working in the emergency room. Of the fifty children who were placed with her and her husband from 2017 to 2019, more than three-quarters left within days.[14]

Furthermore, after being briefly consigned to foster care, the vast majority of the children were returned to the very homes from which they were taken. The remaining children were typically released to the custody of relatives. "What imminent risk of harm was mitigated during their brief stay in foster care that could not have been mitigated absent their removal?" two experts ask. Most likely, there was no such risk. The quick turnaround suggests there was no need to remove the children in the first place; they and their parents endured the terrifying seizure for no reason at all, except for the biased and callous snap judgments of CPS workers and police officers.[15]

New Mexico stands out for quickly returning 40 percent of its foster children—more than four times as many short-stayers as the national rate. In most states, CPS must get a court order allowing it to take protective custody of a child, or a law enforcement officer may remove a child without a warrant when the officer reasonably believes the child is injured or in imminent danger. When the removal hasn't been authorized by a judge, the state must simultaneously seek a prompt hearing to justify continued custody of the child. But New Mexico's law contains a loophole: it provides a forty-eight-hour window in which police may take children from their homes and place them in foster care before the Child, Youth and Families Department (CYFD) decides whether or not to file a removal petition in court.[16]

At least in part, the discretionary forty-eight-hour remove-then-reunify formula is driving New Mexico's enormous short-stayer population. Police officers responding to a domestic call can apprehend the children based on their unqualified sense that the home isn't safe. Or their reasons may be less benign—to threaten the parents or retaliate against them. The officers can hold the children in custody for two whole days, then return them to their parents if CYFD finds no reason to keep them, without ever having to justify the seizure in court. Essentially, New Mexico law enforcement can abduct children for two days without any authorization or review by CYFD or a judge. It "felt like being kidnapped, even though it was just for a few days," one child told the Marshall Project. "I didn't know how long it would last." Even children who have unstable home lives felt like casualties of a haphazard process, that of being shuffled into and out of foster care, like "being luggage, kind of—just tossing me around," a fifteen-year-old girl said.[17]

MORE POWER THAN THE PRESIDENT

My mother used to quote the English politician Lord Acton: "Power tends to corrupt, and absolute power corrupts absolutely." The authority to seize children can be wielded as a crushing threat in the hands of state agents who have virtually limitless leeway to maneuver without meaningful oversight. "I have more power than the president of the United States. I can come to your house and take your children away," a Black father declared, repeating what a caseworker told him in order to force his compliance with CPS commands. I heard the father testify at a hearing in Seattle that the Braam Oversight Panel held as we began reviewing problems with Washington's foster care system. Unfortunately, our efforts did nothing to diminish the child protection department's dictatorial power.

When CPS receives allegations of child maltreatment, caseworkers often coerce the parents to accept restrictive conditions on their family life by threatening to place their children in foster care. Imagine this typical scenario. A caseworker arrives at the home of a mother and her children, accompanied by an armed police officer. The caseworker informs the mother that an unnamed person accused her of child neglect, providing a sketchy description of the allegation. With the police officer standing watch, the caseworker proceeds to inspect the home and interrogate the mother and the children. For whatever reason, the caseworker decides the mother should be supervised or separated from the children and gives the mother a terrible choice: agree to CPS arrangements for your family or CPS will file a petition in court to put your children in foster care. The mother knows that many families in her neighborhood have been torn apart by judicial order. She knows the police officer could summarily take her children or arrest her for not being cooperative enough. She is terrified. Even in the absence of any evidence to support the accusations, the threat of foster care usually works.[18]

The agency, parents, and other relevant relatives then agree to a "safety plan"—a custody arrangement designed to keep the children safe while CPS investigates the allegations. Some safety plans allow children to remain at home but place constraints on other family members. Safety plans have required one of the parents to keep out of the house, both parents to participate in therapy, a mother to stand guard over her sleeping teenage son all night, and siblings not to interact with each other while living in the same home. Others require parents to relinquish physical custody of their children and allow them to move in with other family members, godparents, or family friends. Some states issue forms with blank spaces for CPS to spell out the safety plan requirements over the parents' signature. Often CPS simply gives parents verbal directives. The specific terms of safety plans, including their end dates, are left to the discretion of the CPS worker and supervisor—without any judicial review. The plans are "just a big old sign that says 'CPS is involved in my life,'" said San Antonio court administrator Barbara Schaefer. "It's not a legal binding document, it's not filed into court. CPS uses it as leverage to say, 'If you violate it, we'll remove the kids.'"[19]

Safety plans are considered to be voluntary because the parents ostensibly agree to them by signing a form or giving verbal consent. But they are coerced by an agency ultimatum: agree to let us transfer your children to Grandma or we'll immediately file a petition in court to transfer them to foster care. The form for safety plans used in South

Carolina states bluntly, "If the parent(s) refuse to sign a valid safety plan, an out of home placement must be sought by Law Enforcement or Ex parte Order to keep the child safe, pending the completion of the investigation." Parents typically lack a lawyer to advise them on the validity of the agency's threats or to negotiate the safety plan terms. Afraid of the potential consequences of a formal judicial proceeding—their children sent to live with strangers or, worse still, permanently estranged from their family—most parents give in. "Once the government gets involved, relatives and parents don't always have real choices," one caseworker acknowledged. "Sometimes it's auntie or else."[20]

In 2000, Diane Redleaf, a pioneering family defense lawyer, filed a class action lawsuit, *Dupuy v. Samuels*, challenging the constitutionality of Illinois safety plans. She argued that the plans interfered with the fundamental rights of parents and children to live together and therefore required due process review. It was estimated that as many as ten thousand families per year were being separated under safety plans in the state. During a twenty-two-day trial in Chicago federal court, Redleaf put on the stand parent after parent who recounted heartbreaking stories of how their families were wrecked by safety plans CPS forced them to sign. The state's sole defense was that safety plans were voluntary waivers of parents' rights to due process protections.[21]

In March 2005, Judge Rebecca Pallmeyer, a liberal nominated to the bench by President Bill Clinton in 1997, issued a lengthy decision that rejected CPS's position, finding that safety plans were plainly coerced and violated parents' constitutional rights. But her remedy was disappointing: she permitted safety plans to be based on mere suspicion, to remain in place for fourteen days, and to be reviewed by an administrator rather than a judge. Redleaf and her legal team appealed the decision, hoping the Seventh Circuit would issue stronger due process protections for parents.

In hindsight, Redleaf concedes that the appeal was a mistake. The Seventh Circuit reversed Judge Pallmeyer's decision, not by requiring greater protections for families, but by finding no constitutional violation in the first place. The opinion, written by Judge Richard Posner, a former University of Chicago law professor who helped found the conservative law and economics field, "made mincemeat of the fundamental rights of families," Redleaf writes. Judge Posner reasoned in abstract economics terms that the safety plans were voluntary because they constituted an offer CPS provided to parents as an alternative to opening a case in family court, which parents were free to accept or reject. "We can't see how parents are made worse off by being given the option of accepting the offer of a safety plan," Posner wrote. "It is rare to be disadvantaged by having more rather than fewer options." Judge Posner belittled the decision about child custody in a mystifying analogy: "If you tell a guest that you will mix him either a Martini or a Manhattan, how is he worse off than if you tell him you'll mix him a Martini?"[22]

That an appellate judge could find any resemblance between picking a cocktail at a dinner party and deciding the future existence of a family reveals a baffling failure to appreciate the weight of both state power and family integrity. Even if some parents decide they are better off with the less intrusive alternative, why should caseworkers be able unilaterally to intrude on their families at all? How many parents are bullied into signing safety plans when there was insufficient evidence to involve CPS in the first place? CPS isn't doing families a favor; it is imposing its unbridled and unjustified authority on them. A guest at a dinner party not liking Martinis or Manhattans could simply decline to have cocktails that evening. Parents told to choose between a safety plan and foster care don't have the option of telling CPS to leave their family alone. In June 2008, eight years after the *Dupuy* lawsuit was filed, the US Supreme Court turned down Redleaf's petition to review the Seventh Circuit's decision. The family police could continue the farce that parents agreed to safety plans voluntarily despite being threatened with foster care.

THE SHADOW SYSTEM

The clandestine nature of safety plans means that the reach of family policing is far greater than official statistics suggest. Safety plans allow CPS to change the physical custody of children outside of judicial or federal oversight. State agencies transfer custody of children from parents to family members or friends without any court proceeding, without placing the children in state custody, and without reporting the changes in custody to the federal government.[23]

At first blush, these informal transfers of physical custody from parents to relatives may seem less intrusive than the state taking legal custody of children and putting them in foster care. But this practice has created a shadow system of family policing that is hidden from scrutiny by courts, policy makers, and the general public. Agencies file no petitions alleging abuse or neglect, so there is no judicial review of their actions, no legal protection of parents' rights, and no federal tracking of these arrangements. Agencies evade federal requirements to make reasonable efforts to reunify the children with their parents, as well as to pay stipends to the relatives coerced to care for the children, leaving the families without the financial support foster kinship caregivers receive. The pretense that parents have voluntarily agreed to government management exempts agencies from these legal requirements.

University of South Carolina law professor Josh Gupta-Kagan calls this shadow practice "America's hidden foster care system." We can't know precisely how large the hidden foster care system is; states don't track the number of children it transplants off the record, nor are they required to by federal funding statutes. However, using a variety of empirical studies and state-specific documentation, Gupta-Kagan calculates that agencies surreptitiously separate 250,000 or more children from their parents annually, often for long periods of time and sometimes permanently. In other words, the secret foster care system affects roughly the same number of children as the formal one and has a similar impact on families—with the important distinction that it avoids judicial oversight and federal data tracking.[24]

"The state thus effectuates the children's loss of their parents' care and the parents' loss of physical custody of their children without any other branch of government checking or balancing the agency's actions and without anyone getting a lawyer," Gupta-Kagan writes. "It is as if a police department investigated a crime, concluded an individual was guilty, did not file charges or provide him with an attorney, and told him he had to agree to go to jail for several weeks or months, or else it would bring him to court and things could get worse."[25]

Child welfare agencies are able to force parents into these hidden arrangements because they can deploy benevolent terror. Caseworkers can credibly threaten parents with losing their children forever while we entrust them with the power to do so. Why? Because they are supposedly wielding this weapon to protect children—other people's children. Constitutional norms constrain the power of police and prosecutors with legal conventions like Miranda warnings, grand juries, and trials that require unanimous findings of guilt beyond a reasonable doubt. Of course, these legal constraints don't work well to protect the accused in real life. Police officers routinely stop, harass, arrest, and brutalize residents of Black neighborhoods based on race rather than culpability. People charged with crimes languish in jail without being convicted because they can't afford bail. Prosecutors overcharge defendants to compel them to plead guilty regardless of the evidence against them. But the public recognizes that limits on state power should exist when it comes to criminal punishment. There is a movement protesting these violations of constitutional norms and a robust public debate about how to ensure justice for people accused of committing crimes.

Child protection workers similarly infringe constitutional norms of family integrity and due process yet draw little public scrutiny or outrage. They coercively rearrange custody of children without a thought of protecting parents' rights through a lawyer or a court hearing. They have complete discretion to decide which families to offer informal arrangements to and which to break up through formal judicial proceedings. The fact that this secret system exists because CPS has the power to tear families apart calls into question the very legitimacy of a family-policing system.

SIX

THE FOSTER-INDUSTRIAL COMPLEX

SWOLLEN FUNDING STREAMS

Tens of billions of dollars flow each year from federal, state, and local government budgets to the coffers of child welfare agencies. Those agencies, in turn, employ cadres of staff, make payments to foster and adoptive parents, and enter into contracts with private businesses, programs, and professionals. On top of the monies disbursed by local CPS offices are piled those paid to the bureaucrats in government departments tasked with managing the assortment of child welfare activities. All the money coming in and flowing out from CPS operations nationwide shapes child welfare priorities and gives everyone cashing in a financial stake in keeping the machine well oiled.

Authorized by Congress, the US Department of Health and Human Services (HHS) directs child welfare policy by conditioning billions of dollars distributed to the states on compliance with federal guidelines. There are many possible ways the government could support the welfare of children. The most successful approach would be to invest in the things that have been proven to promote children's well-being: a living wage and income supports for parents; high-quality housing, nutrition, education, child care, and health care; freedom from state and private violence; and a clean environment. The United States doesn't focus on providing these things to families. In fact, it ranks the worst among industrialized nations for guaranteeing the resources children need to be healthy and happy. Instead, US child welfare policy centers on protecting children from alleged parental maltreatment by investing primarily in tearing families apart.

The Children's Bureau, established by President William Taft in 1912 as the first federal agency charged with investigating and reporting "upon all matters pertaining to the welfare of children and child life," still operates today, now within the HHS Administration for Children and Families. Since its inauguration, the bureau's focus has narrowed from a broad concern with children's welfare to child abuse prevention, foster care, and adoption. Its annual budget of almost $10 billion goes mostly to supporting and monitoring local child protection agencies that respond to reports of child abuse and neglect. Child protection agencies are also financed by state and local funding streams, and their budgets vary widely from one location to another. According to Child Trends, a leading child welfare research organization, the collective federal, state, and local investment in child protection activities across the nation totaled $29.9 billion in 2016.[1]

The child welfare service our nation spends the most money on is separating children from their parents. In 2019, the federal government alone devoted $8.6 billion to maintaining children in foster care and providing adoption subsidies—more than ten times the amount allocated to services aimed at keeping families together, either by preventing foster care placement or returning foster children to their parents. The lopsided expenditure on foster care reflects the government's reliance on child removal as its central child protection approach. A 2015 analysis by the Children's Research Center at the National Council on Crime and Delinquency calculated total national expenditures allocated to foster care in particular. Multiplying four hundred thousand children in foster care by an average annual cost of approximately $57,000 per child, it estimated the grand total at $22.8 billion.[2]

Whether spent on putting children in foster care, keeping them out, or returning them home, all the money and effort of America's family-policing system revolve around taking children from their families. This is not to say the child welfare system involves child removal alone. But its agents get their power to regulate and terrorize parents and children from the constant and realizable threat of taking children away and making them wards of the state. "Prevention" services aren't resources state agencies freely provide to families who request them; they are forced on parents whose children have been identified as candidates for foster care, as a condition of forestalling or shortening family separation. Under the current approach to child welfare, all this CPS funding is spent on policing families—keeping an intrusive watch on parents accused of child maltreatment and requiring them to engage in services on pain of losing custody of their children.

A complex web of congressional funding streams, dispersed through multiple programs administered by various federal agencies, is organized to feed the foster care apparatus. The convoluted child welfare financing structure rests on two main federal statutes: Title IV-B and IV-E of the Social Security Act. Title IV-B, making up only 4 percent of child welfare spending, provides grants to states for family preservation and reunification services. The bulk of child welfare spending—about half—comes from Title IV-E, which funds five federal programs supporting foster care, guardianship, and adoption.[3]

The largest by far is the Federal Foster Care Program, an open entitlement grant that reimburses states and local governments for the administrative and maintenance costs for every eligible child placed in foster care. Eligibility for Title IV-E reimbursement is determined by whether the child's parents meet the 1996 standards for Aid to Families with Dependent Children (AFDC)—the federal welfare program that was abolished when Congress passed the 1997 welfare-restructuring law. In other words, the federal government reimburses the foster care costs for those children whose parents are poor enough to have qualified for welfare benefits in 1996. More than half of children in foster care are that poor. Linking federal foster care reimbursement to family poverty is another sign that family policing is designed to regulate poor people.[4]

Title IV-E offers enormous federal backing for the philosophy of addressing the needs of impoverished families by destroying them. Not only do the Title IV-E funds for foster care far outstrip those for family preservation, but they are also open-ended entitlements, whereas Title IV-B funds are capped at paltry amounts that depend on annual congressional appropriations. When Congress enacted across-the-board spending cuts to take effect in 2013, known as sequestration, Title IV-B took a severe hit, contributing, along with other changes in appropriations, to a 29 percent decrease in Title IV-B spending by child welfare agencies between 2006 and 2016. Title IV-E funds, by contrast, kept flowing to reimburse states and localities for foster care costs. The Adoption and Safe Families Act gives states extra incentives to move children quickly from foster care to adoption and pays relatively generous subsidies, amounting to $2.6 billion annually, to the adoptive homes.[5]

Bottom line: most federal funding for child welfare services becomes available to families only after their children have been placed in state custody, and the money is spent primarily on the costs of family separation. The benevolent terror machine is strategically and amply fueled.

Responding to criticism of this skewed financing scheme, Congress passed the 2018 Family First Prevention Services Act, giving states more flexibility to use some Title IV-E money ordinarily restricted to foster care for alternative services for children "at imminent risk of entering foster care." But the act hews to the overall child removal mantra: it severely restricts states' ability to repurpose the funds by narrowly specifying which prevention services qualify for them and setting time limits on the "demonstration projects" that receive funding. Congress passed the Family First Act without repealing ASFA, with its speedier timelines for termination of parental rights and bonuses for adoption. While appearing to diversify its investments in child welfare services, Congress barely scratched its principal financial stake in family disruption. As with Title IV-B, moreover, the paltry prevention services permitted by the Family First Act, forced on parents with the ever-present threat of taking their children, are still designed to police families. The act achieves its aim of preventing foster care placements by providing CPS-involved families with "mental health and substance abuse prevention and treatment services, in-home parent skill-based programs, and kinship navigator services," all of which subject families to state monitoring and fail to meet their material needs.[6]

You might say these figures aren't that impressive. After all, $10 billion is a drop in the bucket of the multitrillion-dollar federal budget. What matters, though, is where these billions of dollars are directed— mainly, at breaking up families. The Title IV-E reimbursement structure creates an incentive for child welfare agencies to prefer services that split families apart over ones that keep them together, especially in the case of very poor parents who meet the AFDC eligibility standard. The remaining, diminutive portion of federal funds is still spent on family regulation. In cases that don't qualify for federal reimbursement, CPS agencies may have a financial incentive to pressure families into the hidden foster care system, by agreeing to informal safety plans, to avoid paying subsidies and providing services.[7]

In any case, the billions of dollars invested in the child welfare system prop up an overall paradigm that relies on destroying families rather than supporting them. The problem isn't only the size of federal, state, and local budgets allocated to child welfare services—whether too large or too small—but that the funds are spent unjustly. Our nation should devote even more billions to creating the societal institutions and structures that promote children's well-being. Instead, it powers a policing engine designed to buttress its stingy and brutal approach to meeting families' needs.

The inverse relationship between the federal funding for aid to families, on the one hand, and for foster care, on the other, became painfully clear under the Trump administration. As right-wing members of Congress pursued their agenda to slash public assistance programs, such as Medicaid, food stamps, and Temporary Assistance to Needy Families (TANF), the federal family aid program, the numbers of children entering foster care grew. By February 2018, the number of children in foster care exceeded the number of children being cared for at home with the support of TANF benefits in at least seven states, reported Shawn Fremstad, a senior fellow at the Center for Economic and Policy Research. In twenty-one states, for every two children receiving TANF while living with their families, one or more were living in foster care. A 2017 University of Kansas study found that when states imposed more restrictive policies for receiving TANF benefits, foster care placements increased. Moreover, states can and do use federal TANF funds to pay for CPS activities, including foster care costs and adoption payments. These recent developments reflect a basic principle of family policing: as social problems worsen as a result of policies that intensify income and racial inequality while shrinking the welfare safety net, government expands its policing of families that suffer the most.[8]

FEEDING THE LION

I once met with a city's top child welfare administrator who agreed with my criticisms of his department's devastation of families. But he told me candidly that there was nothing he could do to fundamentally change its practices. "Do you know how many people make money from this system?" he asked me. "There's no way they will let me destroy their income and profits." In addition to weaponizing children by threatening to take them away, the family-policing system monetizes children once it casts them into foster care.

The monies federal, state, and local governments collectively budget for child welfare services not only skew public policies toward breaking up families; they also facilitate a cabal of private and public enterprises that profit off child removal. A conglomerate of CPS agencies, government bureaucracies, hired professionals, and business contractors sustains itself financially by regulating families, taking children from their homes, and maintaining them in foster care. "Similar to how the coal mining industry mines rock for coal ore that can be converted into profit, the poverty industry mines children and the poor for aid funds and resources that are converted into private profits and government revenue," wrote law professor Daniel L. Hatcher in a meticulous 2016 exposé of poverty-program exploitation. Foster care is a key mechanism for siphoning money from poor families to state bureaucracies and their corporate partners.[9]

State Senator Nancy Schaefer launched a crusade against the Georgia Department of Children and Families after receiving a call from a woman whose granddaughters were taken when CPS pressured her daughter, a resident of the senator's district, to sign an agreement to place them in foster care. A staunch Christian evangelical who served for eight years as a trustee of the Southern Baptist Convention's religious liberty commission, Schaefer advocated for displaying the Ten Commandments in the Georgia senate building. The resistance even she, a "rock star of the Christian right," encountered when she took aim at the child welfare department's financing demonstrates how lucrative family policing is. When Senator Schaefer drafted a law, Senate Bill 415, to place a number of restraints on the state's power to take children from their parents, she was immediately confronted by fierce opposition. "If I help that family or if I help you, I'll lose my job," she was told by legislators whose endorsement she sought. At the last minute, the chair of the Georgia Senate's judicial committee presented her with a substitute bill deleting all the strong provisions from the original. Schaefer refused to accept the watered-down replacement.[10]

After her bill was torpedoed in the judicial committee, Schaefer penned a scathing report, *The Corrupt Business of Child Protective Services*, issued in November 2007 under official letterhead from her legislative desk, listing multiple ways state agencies and private businesses profit off family separation. She pointed to all the costly services parents are required to engage in—"parenting classes, anger management classes, counseling referrals, therapy classes and on and on." "The 'snatching of children' is growing as a business," she wrote, not only because "local governments have grown accustomed to having these taxpayer dollars to balance their ever-expanding budgets," but also because a large assortment of people received income from their involvement. "There are state employees, lawyers, court investigators, guardians ad litem, court personnel, and judges," the report stated. "There are psychologists, and psychiatrists, counselors, caseworkers, therapists, foster parents, adoptive parents, and on and on. All are looking to the children in state custody to provide job security."

Schaefer blamed animosity over her exposé of CPS corruption for her defeat by Jim Butterworth in the 2008 Republican primary. "The report cost me my senate seat," Schaefer would later say. But she continued her crusade to topple CPS's financial scaffolding, even traveling to Amsterdam in August 2009 to testify before the World Congress of Families. "These are crimes against humanity for financial gain," Shaefer told the international audience in a bone-chilling speech. "How do you tame a lion who has been well-fed?" she asked in a methodical tone, quoting Charles Spurgeon, the fiery nineteenth-century English preacher. "First, he must be brought down."

Whether social justice activists on the left or Republican legislators on the right, opponents of family policing must confront a well-fed, profitable, and entrenched foster care industry that has every incentive to stand its ground.

PREYING ON FAMILIES

If the family-policing system is a well-fed lion, vulnerable parents and children are its prey. Child welfare agencies and the private companies they collude with make up what has been referred to as the foster-industrial complex: they profit off families not only by receiving government funds for taking children, but also by extracting payments and property from the very families they break up.

In her pathbreaking book *Are Prisons Obsolete?*, published in 2003, renowned scholar and activist Angela Y. Davis defined the prison-industrial complex as "an array of relationships linking corporations, government, correctional communities, and the media." Although Davis is often credited with coining the term in 1998, she attributed its introduction to social historian Mike Davis, who first used it in a 1995 article in *The Nation*, "Hell Factories in the Field: A Prison-Industrial Complex," in reference to the expansion of California's penal system as an economic and political powerhouse. Pointing to the prison-industrial complex contested the belief that the prisons grew in response to rising crime rates. Instead, Angela Y. Davis argued, "prison construction and the attendant drive to fill these new structures with human bodies have been driven by ideologies of racism and the pursuit of profit." Corporations profited not only by running privatized prisons, but also by exploiting imprisoned labor and selling products to correctional facilities.[11]

The term originated from an unlikely source: President Dwight D. Eisenhower's farewell address on January 17, 1961. After noting that the century had already experienced four major wars involving multiple nations, Eisenhower, the only military general to be elected president in the twentieth century, alerted Americans to a looming "military-industrial complex" created by the compromising entanglements between the military and defense contractors. Eisenhower warned that "this conjunction of an immense military establishment and a large arms industry" wielded "influence—economic, political, even spiritual—[that] is felt in every city, every statehouse, every office of the Federal government." According to Eisenhower, the power that corporate money had to sway government policy threatened US liberties and democratic processes. Although entailing less money than the $700 billion defense budget or $80 billion prison system, the profitable business of family separation that merges government and corporate interests is aptly labeled the foster-industrial complex.[12]

One of the most insidious aspects of the foster-industrial complex is its theft of belongings from the children it claims to care for. A Nebraska statute, for example, provides that the "Department of Health and Human Services shall take custody of and exercise general control over assets owned by children under the charge of the department." The regulations implementing the law include a laundry list of children's property that the state can seize, from cash on hand or in bank accounts to insurance policies, household goods, and even burial plots. Some state and local governments require parents to pay for the services CPS forces on them. It is as if a kidnapper justified demanding a ransom as reimbursement for the kidnapped victim's living expenses.[13]

Danny Keffeler had already been placed in foster care by the Washington State Department of Social and Health Services (DSHS) when his mother died in 1990. Danny's grandmother, Wanda Pierce, was appointed as a fiduciary—called a representative payee—to manage Danny's Social Security Insurance (SSI) survivor benefits in a way that best met Danny's needs and furthered his well-being. Federal regulations require that a representative payee must either spend the funds on the beneficiary's current living expenses, such as food, shelter, clothing, and medical care, or conserve them in savings or investment accounts in the beneficiary's name. That is exactly what Ms. Pierce did for Danny, devoting some of the money he received to items he was missing in foster care and saving a portion for his future enrollment in college. Then DSHS applied to replace Ms. Pierce as Danny's representative payee so it could divert the SSI payments to reimburse itself for the costs of keeping Danny in foster care. When an administrative law judge sided with Danny's grandmother, DSHS filed an appeal with the Social Security Administration. Ms. Pierce fought Washington State over rights to manage her grandson's survivor benefits all the way to the United States Supreme Court—a case that would help to determine control over more than $100 million in SSI benefits that states were confiscating from foster children.[14]

On February 25, 2003, the Supreme Court handed down its decision in *Washington State Department of Social and Health Services v. Guardianship Estate of Danny Keffeler*. The US Solicitor General and thirty-nine states had joined an amicus brief supporting the DSHS position. Writing for a unanimous court, Justice David Souter framed the legal question as if Washington were simply recouping payment from a customer for services rendered. "At its own expense, the State of Washington provides foster care to certain children removed from their parents' custody, and it also receives and manages Social Security benefits for many of the children involved," the court's opinion began. "The question here is whether the State's use of Social Security benefits to reimburse itself for some of its initial expenditures violates a provision of the Social Security Act protecting benefits from 'execution, levy, attachment, garnishment, or other legal process.'" Given that setup, the blunt answer seemed perfectly reasonable: "We hold that it does not."[15]

Justice Souter rehearsed the SSI regulations that require that representative payees who receive benefits on behalf of beneficiaries spend them "only for the use and benefit of the beneficiary" and in the beneficiary's "best interests," and prohibit their attachment by creditors. Focusing on the term "other legal process," the court reasoned that Washington's reimbursement policy didn't violate the federal protections because the state wasn't acting as a creditor using a judicial proceeding to claim someone else's property. Paradoxically, because Washington State was obligated to provide foster care without charge and foster children therefore didn't owe it a debt, the state couldn't be considered a creditor. Instead, as the court saw it, the state was merely acting on behalf of foster children to use their benefits to recoup their maintenance costs. Somehow the court failed to see the reimbursement scheme as forcing foster children to cover the outlays the state was already obligated to make. Didn't taking their payments, then, aid Washington State alone and provide no extra benefit whatsoever to the children?

The court's parsing of the statutory terminology prevailed over the argument that the best interests of foster children meant maximizing the resources they had available for their well-being. As if to accentuate the stingiest possible interpretation of the law, Justice Souter pointed out that, according to federal regulations, the Social Security Act provided only a "minimum level of income" to children who otherwise would fail to "maintain a standard of living at the established Federal minimum income level." Heaven forbid that children in the state's care have more than the bare minimum needed to subsist! "A representative payee serves the beneficiary's interest by seeing that basic needs are met," the court concluded, "not by maximizing a trust fund attributable to fortuitously overlapping state and federal grants." The court's description conjured up a spoiled child of wealthy parents selfishly grasping an unearned and overflowing trust fund, not a ward of the state who likely needed every available resource to make ends meet.

The court ignored that the State of Washington confiscated what for many foster children is the only source of savings to prepare for their futures. Youth who might have aged out of foster care with their accumulated SSI benefits in hand are abandoned by agencies with no savings to cushion the fall. "It's really messed up to steal money from kids who grow up in foster care," Tristen Hunter, twenty-one, told the Marshall Project and NPR. When he aged out of foster care in Alaska, Tristen found out that the Office of Children's Services had pocketed nearly $700 a month in his federal survivor benefits, starting when he was twelve. "We get out and we don't have anybody or anything," he said. "This is exactly what survivor benefits are for." Malerie Shockley was pregnant at eighteen years old and living in a tent in the woods in Anchorage after running from her foster home when she learned that the agency had been confiscating her disability checks. Fortunately for Danny, his grandmother had saved his benefits for his college education before the state could expropriate them, and he graduated from Central Washington University in June 2002. The court didn't address, however, the constitutional objections raised by seizing foster children's benefits, such as whether the practice violates children's due process and equal protection rights or constitutes an unconstitutional taking. These questions remain ripe for future court challenges on behalf of children in foster care.[16]

Danny Keffeler's case is far from unique. With the help of corporate consultants, government authorities regularly divert federal benefits to which foster children are entitled to augment state coffers without benefiting the children or letting them know about it, turning foster children themselves into a source of revenue. A 2021 investigation by the Marshall Project and NPR found that in at least thirty-six states and Washington, DC, state child welfare agencies "comb through their case files to find kids entitled to these benefits," apply to Social Security to become each child's representative payee, and, once approved, take the payments. Daniel Hatcher calculates the value of assets state agencies take from foster children each year at more than $250 million. This public-private partnership has become such a regular feature of CPS and other government poverty programs that it has generated a cottage industry of "revenue maximization" companies. The Marshall Project and NPR report that child welfare departments in at least ten states hire for-profit companies to acquire benefits owed to children in foster care.[17]

Child welfare departments routinely enter into contracts with private corporations that specialize in using funding for poverty programs, such as Medicaid and Title IV-E, to expand government revenues. Some revenue-maximization schemes target the Title IV-E Foster Care Program in particular. Government agencies pay the private consultants to develop "penetration rate" strategies to extract the most federal funding possible from children in foster care—including diverting benefits that belong to the children. Revenue maximizers devise ways to increase the percentage of foster children from families poor enough to qualify for Title IV-E reimbursement. Another tactic is to multiply the number of children in foster care who are designated as disabled so states can grab their SSI disability payments. Children, like Danny Keffeler, whose parents have died are viewed as profitable, as well, because agencies can filch their SSI survivor benefits or Veteran's Assistance benefits if the parents died serving in the military. Medicaid funds and child support payments are also fair game. Decisions to separate children from their parents that may seem to be based on individualized risk assessments are actually determined by the potential revenue streams that are activated when children are placed in foster care.[18]

Daniel Hatcher's first job after graduating from law school was as a Legal Aid attorney representing children in the Baltimore foster care system. Most of the foster children in Baltimore come from the city's segregated Black neighborhoods. One of his clients was a young man Hatcher calls Alex, who had entered foster care at age twelve when his mother died and spent the next six years shuffling at least twenty times between short-term placements and group homes. It was only after he aged out of foster care, penniless, that Alex discovered he had been eligible to receive SSI survivor benefits ever since his father had died during Alex's time in state care. No one had told him that Maryland became his representative payee and confiscated every single payment he'd received. As a law professor, Hatcher would later conduct a painstaking investigation of the "poverty industry," the vast public-private partnership that extracts revenues by "strip-mining billions in federal aid and other funds," as Hatcher puts it, from vulnerable people like Alex. Among the alarming revelations Hatcher uncovered, the machinations of one thriving revenue maximizer, Maximus, Inc., stands out.[19]

With corporate headquarters in Virginia, Maximus is a global leader in private contracting for government services, including public aid programs. Established in 1975, the company enters into agreements with governments worldwide, including the United States, United Kingdom, Canada, Australia, Singapore, and Saudi Arabia, to tweak the efficiency of their public health and human services operations or to operate the programs outright. For example, Maximus has run the Georgia Families program for the Georgia Department of Community Health since 2005, facilitating enrollment in Medicaid and in Peach-Care for Kids, the state's Children's Health Insurance Program, commonly known as CHIP. An upbeat website advertises the company's services with the trademarked tagline "Helping Government Serve the People." Maximus runs a division euphemistically called "Benefits & Eligibility Advocacy Services," which is dedicated to advising governments on wringing their eligible residents for the last drop in federal funds.[20]

In 2012, the Maryland Department of Human Services contracted with Maximus to figure out ways to capitalize on foster children's SSI disability and survivor benefits. According to the agreement, the company's target was to achieve "maximum revenue impact" by increasing the percentage of Maryland's foster care population designated as disabled from 2 percent to 20 percent so the state could acquire up to $6 million of their disability benefits per year. "We will be looking for children with identifiable physical or mental disabilities," a Maximus executive explained to a Maryland official in a January 2013 email. "Generally, we encourage caseworkers to refer any child suspected from suffering from any illness—from a quadriplegic to ADHA [sic]—to be referred to us for evaluation." Maximus made clear its aim to financially exploit foster children with disabilities in its February 2013 report to the Maryland department, where it blatantly referred to them as a "revenue generating mechanism." In a similar deal that produced approximately $16.2 million for the state of Iowa over four years, Maximus proposed a pricing structure that treated foster children as monetary "units."[21]

In its June 2012 proposal to Maryland's DHS, Maximus described its overall strategy as "identifying the greatest stream in each case." This meant pinpointing children with disabilities who were *not* already eligible for Title IV-E reimbursement. In order to deliver "the greatest positive financial impact from the SSI advocacy operations," the proposal detailed, the team ranked children "in order of receiving the least Title IV-E revenue to the greatest." That way the state could collect the maximum allowable amounts of both Title IV-E payments for poor children and SSI payments for disabled children. Foster children poor enough to be eligible for Title IV-E funding didn't escape the Maximus gaze either. Under a different contract, Maximus operated the Baltimore City Office of Child Support Enforcement. In that capacity, Maximus pursued the parents of Title IV-E foster children for child support payments.[22]

Federal law requires that state child welfare agencies refer cases of children eligible for Title IV-E to child support enforcement. The enforcement systems then sue the primary caregivers, usually mothers, or go after absent fathers, sometimes tracking them down and establishing their paternity. Charging parents for child support is seen as fair reimbursement of the federal funds spent on maintaining their children in substitute care. But this recovery mechanism robs struggling parents of income they desperately need not only for their own survival but also to recover their children. A 2017 University of Wisconsin study found convincing empirical evidence of this destructive impact on families. The research team sought to determine whether "reducing resources by ordering child support payments may increase barriers to reunification and permanency." For example, charging a single mother for child support or diverting child support she's owed might make it harder for her to find secure housing, or it might compound the stress she's experiencing from an unstable economic situation. Pursuing the father for child support owed to the government, and not going to the mother, might drive him away from the family and deprive them of what support he would otherwise contribute.[23]

Merging administrative data from several state CPS and child support programs, the researchers found that cases in which child support is ordered or redirected were more likely to entail longer stays in foster care, "with a $100 increase in child support orders leading to a 6.6 month delay in reunification." The collateral damage inflicted on families kept apart longer lays bare the state's priorities: extracting more money from foster children rather than ensuring their well-being and return to their families.

When Maryland contracted with Maximus, the corporation had already built up a questionable track record. The District of Columbia hired Maximus as a revenue-maximization consultant to increase claims for foster children's federal Medicaid funds. In 2007, the corporation agreed to pay $30 million to settle an investigation by the US Department of Justice (DOJ) into alleged violations of the False Claims Act in connection with the DC contract. As part of the deferred prosecution agreement, Maximus admitted its involvement in making knowingly incorrect Medicaid claims. Fending off prosecution for Medicaid fraud only generated more government contracts between Maximus and a baffling array of state entities and services. "From the time of the settlement in 2007 through the end of 2008, Maximus entered into or extended contracts related to Medicaid or Medicare worth well over $200 million," Daniel Hatcher estimated. Like giving a foiled bank robber the combination to the vault, the District of Columbia extended the same Medicaid revenue-maximization contract with Maximus that produced the DOJ fraud charges. In addition, Hatcher tracked down Maximus contracts with New York State "to help prevent Medicaid fraud"; with the Centers for Medicare and Medicaid Services, "the federal agency to whom the allegedly fraudulent claims had been submitted"; and within the DOJ itself to provide investigative and analytical support in criminal cases.[24]

Maximus did so well that year that it distributed increased cash dividends to its shareholders as the national financial crisis sent stocks of most other corporations spiraling downward. Companies like Maximus that profit from poverty programs make a fortune off the misfortune of others. During hard times, as more and more parents become unemployed, rely on public assistance programs, and lose their children to foster care, the private sector that profits off aid programs cashes in. As Hatcher sees it, the intersecting ties between child welfare departments, corporate consultants, and state legislators form a self-serving "iron triangle" steered by profit. Poverty-industry contractors maintain their lucrative relationships with government agencies by engaging in "pay-to-play" tactics—making large campaign contributions to influential politicians and deploying lobbyists with insider connections—and by hiring or giving board positions to former government officials. The Maximus board of directors has included the former deputy associate commissioner for the Massachusetts Department of Public Welfare, the former mayor of Denver, Colorado, and the former governor of Illinois.[25]

To be clear, the federal funds extracted from foster children in revenue-maximization schemes don't even benefit the children by way of enhanced agency services. Instead, they often get diverted to general state and local treasuries and to the pockets of corporate contractors that are in on the deal. When Arizona hired Public Consulting Group (PCG) to increase claims for federal foster care funds, the state paid PCG's contingency fee first, then routed the remainder of the monies to offset "continuing budget shortfalls." A 2004 state report described how the "federal revenue maximization initiative," aimed at increasing both the number of foster children receiving Title IV-E assistance and the amount reimbursed by Title IV-E for administrative costs, was timed to cover the state legislature's prior budget reductions of $1.4 million. In other words, Arizona engaged in a three-card monte involving CPS, PCG, and legislators—the iron triangle—to boost federal foster care reimbursements that could plug the hole in the state budget that had been made in anticipation of the increased revenue.[26]

In her 2019 book, *Race for Profit: How Banks and the Real Estate Industry Undermined Black Homeownership*, Keeanga-Yamahtta Taylor, a professor of African American studies, introduced the concept of "predatory inclusion" to describe the way governments collude with banks and real estate agencies to draw low-income Black people into exploitative mortgage arrangements. Political scientist Joe Soss similarly describes the criminal punishment system's shift from prison labor extraction to financial extraction as corporations and local governments wrest fees and fines from Black residents unjustly arrested and jailed. In his project Preying on the Poor: Criminal Justice as Revenue Racket, Soss identifies a "predatory public-private partnership" that feeds revenues into city budgets and corporate pockets at the expense of criminalized Black populations. Like these facets of twenty-first-century racialized capital accumulation, the foster-industrial complex employs predatory practices in cahoots with big business to squeeze money from the very poor Black communities most oppressed by state policing and punishment.[27]

In 2018, after a hard-fought legislative battle against corporate lobbyists and Republican governor Larry Hogan, Maryland became the first state to enact legislation that gives some shield for foster children's benefits. With enough votes to override the governor's veto, the Maryland General Assembly passed a law named Protecting Resources of Children in State Custody, which requires foster care agencies acting as representative payees for children's SSI benefits to conserve specified amounts for the children. Instead of confiscating all the benefits for itself, the state now must save "at least 40% of the funds for the child starting at age fourteen, at least 80% of the funds starting at age sixteen, and 100% of the funds starting at age eighteen." At least now, children in Maryland's care who receive federal benefits will have a little money in the bank when the state abandons them upon their aging out of foster care.[28]

"I couldn't understand why my son was in the foster care system," says Angeline Montauban, the domestic violence survivor who spent five years retrieving her son from New York's ACS. "The executive of the foster care agency was making $600,000 a year, but the only type of housing they were offering families was a homeless shelter." Imagine if, instead of taking their children, states sent families an annual check for $50,000 for each child now kept in foster care and didn't strip them of federal SSI benefits, child support payments, and other resources. The legislators would have to rely on other revenue streams to make up for budget shortfalls and replenish agency coffers; the foster care caseworkers, agency heads, and bureaucrats would have to find new jobs; and the revenue-maximizing consultants would have to amend their corporate plans. But I have no doubt whatsoever that the children in these families would be far better off. If we cared about the welfare of children, we would dismantle the foster-industrial complex and send all the cash it sucks up directly to the family members who care for them.[29]

PART III
THE CARCERAL WEB

SEVEN

FAMILY SURVEILLANCE

BEYOND FOSTER CARE

Most people think of the child welfare system and the criminal punishment system as distinct parts of government. Child welfare is supposed to be based on civil law and therefore not entail the surveillance, punishment, and condemnation that characterize criminal justice. Whereas police investigate crimes to arrest lawbreakers, CPS workers investigate allegations of maltreatment to keep children safe. Whereas accused defendants stand trial to determine criminal culpability, family courts determine what's in the best interests of the child. Whereas people convicted of crimes are punished by imprisonment, parents found to have maltreated their children are served by social workers. Whereas children who commit offenses are delinquent and need to be rehabilitated, children who have been victimized by their parents are dependent and need to be rescued. Or so the official story goes.

In reality, the child welfare system operates surprisingly like its criminal counterpart. Everything about family policing I've described so far—the origins of child welfare institutions in slavery, settler colonialism, and hatred for the poor; the targeting of CPS interventions on Black people and other marginalized groups; and the terror the system inflicts on children, families, and communities—suggests that the claimed separation between criminal law enforcement and civil child protection is a sham. Recall the story of Vanessa Peoples that began the Introduction to this book. It is difficult to disentangle the threads of her encounter with the child welfare system that had to do with CPS from those that involved the Aurora police department. Being swept into one system puts parents and children at risk of being swept into the other. The child welfare system not only resembles the criminal punishment system; it also operates in tight conjunction with police and prisons. The more you consider all the ways the child welfare system parallels and intersects with the criminal punishment system, the more it looks like one integrated state apparatus for controlling Black communities—a giant carceral web.

One of the child welfare system's chief functions is to keep an eye on families in Black communities. CPS agencies investigate the families of 3.5 million children every year, with one in three children nationwide and the majority of Black children being subject to investigation at some point while growing up. Family surveillance extends far beyond the numbers of children placed in foster care, the measure most commonly noted to gauge the system's scope and impact. At the end of the 1990s, child welfare departments faced criticism for the outrageous volume of children they were taking from their parents and farming to foster care. As states around the country began to reduce their foster care populations, they simultaneously expanded their invasion into the private lives of families by investigating them and overseeing them with coercive services.[1]

Take New York City, for example. The Administration for Children's Services boasts that the number of children placed in foster care has dropped dramatically from a high of fifty thousand in the early 1990s—when the city responded to the crack cocaine "epidemic" by taking Black children from their families in droves—to seventeen thousand by 2007 and nine thousand a decade later. Yet the numbers of families under ACS surveillance mushroomed over that time. More than 20 percent of New York City's children interacted with ACS between 2015 and 2020, whether being checked for maltreatment, monitored by caseworkers, or put in foster care. In 2019 alone, ACS investigated more than eighty-four thousand children. It is estimated that one in three Black children has had some contact with ACS in the last several years.[2]

Identifying children as at risk for abuse or neglect gives caseworkers the authority to probe into and regulate every aspect of their family's life. "They retained all the money they were formerly using for the foster system and instead used that to build a very extensive apparatus for family surveillance and control," Lisa Sangoi, cofounder of the Movement for Family Power, explains. This shift toward monitoring families has not diminished the state's power to tear families apart. Family regulation still relies on the ever-present threat to take away children, and child welfare authorities still make good on that threat far too often. But it is equally important to take note of the child welfare system's sprawling reach beyond its placement of children in foster care.[3]

STOP AND FRISK

Comparing the powers of child welfare workers and police officers reveals a disturbing paradox. Child welfare authorities can wield greater control over families than cops while providing fewer legal protections to parents and children. Child welfare investigations are the stop and frisk of family surveillance without the safeguards of law and public scrutiny that are present in the criminal context. Indeed, some critical theorists have long argued that social welfare programs, including child protection, serve the purpose of allowing the state to manage members of oppressed communities without having to convict them of crimes. The rhetoric of saving children is merely a guise to justify expanding the government's power to investigate and regulate these communities beyond what would be permitted by criminal justice. "Child Protection has come to embody the legally sanctioned abuse of power," writes Lynne Wrennall, a child welfare researcher in Liverpool, UK.[4]

All it takes is a phone call from an anonymous tipster to a hotline operator about a vague suspicion to launch a life-altering government investigation. A child might seem unkempt or unattended. A parent might be observed smoking marijuana. A house might appear dirty.

Most of the people investigated by CPS are unaware of their rights or the name of a lawyer to call when a caseworker rings the doorbell without warning. But even legal advice about parents' rights is complicated in the case of child welfare investigations. "If it were law enforcement at the door, I could tell my client that they would be within their rights to refuse entry, to insist on a warrant, to decline to answer questions without an attorney, and, ultimately, to refuse a search of their home," New York City attorney and law professor Tarek Ismail writes.[5] The scope of parents' rights is less clear.

Because child welfare is classified as part of the civil legal system, CPS workers are not considered to be law enforcement officers. Moreover, although the Fourth Amendment applies to government maltreatment investigations, agencies and courts in effect have created a child welfare exception to the constitutional provisions that pertain to police searches. They treat protecting the privacy of family members as a risk to children and therefore an excuse to waive constitutional restraints. The United States Supreme Court has yet to decide whether the Fourth Amendment's requirements of a particularized warrant and probable cause apply to child welfare investigations.[6]

Even more significant, however, is the caseworker's threat to take children from the home, an action that could subject the family to years of separation, intense regulation, and, ultimately, permanent dissolution. Despite the fact that most child maltreatment accusations made to CPS are frivolous, investigations proceed from the assumption that parents are guilty of the reported suspicions. Any resistance on the part of parents to giving CPS full access to inspect their homes, children, and intimate lives is considered evidence of guilt. Caseworkers put notes about noncompliance in the case files to be deployed against the parents during a later proceeding. "Respondent mother was uncooperative." "Respondent mother had a negative attitude." "Respondent mother refused to allow a full search of the home." These are typical entries meant to indicate that the mother was either hiding past maltreatment or prone to committing it in the future. Parents are put in an impossible bind: in order to keep CPS from taking their children they must participate in an investigation that risks that very outcome.[7]

Given this sure-fire weapon, caseworkers regularly enter the homes of parents who have merely been accused of child maltreatment, without a warrant or a Miranda warning. CPS agents also show up at schools or day care centers to pull children aside and question them without parental permission. Whereas police officers arrest people suspected of criminal activity and interrogate them about their alleged wrongdoing, caseworkers delve deeply into everything about accused parents and initiate indefinite supervision of their lives. This power takes Big Brother's watchful eye from public spaces into intimate ones. Government surveillance "is typically envisioned as the state monitoring public activity, as in pedestrian police stops and closed-circuit cameras," notes sociologist Kelley Fong. But child protection investigations give government the opportunity to collect "substantial information about domestic life . . . ordinarily beyond the gaze of the state." The child welfare system's domestic surveillance augments law enforcement's growing practice of spying on and raiding residences in Black neighborhoods in addition to patrolling public streets.[8]

Compared with police stops and arrests, child protection investigations dig far deeper into the private lives of suspects. Caseworkers can make multiple unannounced home visits at any time of day or night, interrogate all household members, force children to disrobe, do criminal background checks, and request personal information from teachers, hospitals, therapists, and other service providers. In some cities, caseworkers force parents to sign blank releases to obtain their and their children's confidential records. As with other repressive aspects of the child welfare system, the public accepts this extraordinary state infringement of citizens' privacy and freedoms because it masquerades as benevolence.

DEPUTIZED AGENTS

Most agents who monitor families for the state don't wear uniforms and badges. Child welfare agencies enlist a vast cadre of ordinary civilians in their surveillance of families. By federal edict, every state must identify people who work in professions that put them in contact with children—such as teachers, health care providers, social services staff, and day care workers—and require them by law to report suspected child abuse and neglect to government authorities. These deputized agents are known as mandated reporters. States began enacting reporting laws in the 1960s, in response to the "discovery" of child abuse in 1962 when pediatrician Henry Kempe and his colleagues published a paper coining the term "battered child syndrome." In 1963, the federal Children's Bureau issued model statutes for states to adopt in their efforts to require reporting of child maltreatment. Almost every state had passed mandatory reporting provisions by 1967. As the meaning of what constitutes child abuse broadened and mandated reporting expanded, the number of maltreatment reports skyrocketed—from ten thousand in 1967 to more than two million annually two decades later.[9]

Eighteen states have gone even further, passing "universal" reporting legislation that requires all residents, with few exceptions, to convey their suspicions to CPS or police. All states have also established child abuse hotlines that anyone can call to report their suspicions—so everyone can patrol families. Still, professional reporters make the majority of calls. In 2019, over two-thirds of all reports of alleged maltreatment came from professionals. The most common mandated reporters were school personnel, followed by law enforcement, health care workers, social services staff, and mental health professionals. The remaining reports were made by nonprofessionals, such as friends, neighbors, or relatives, or by anonymous and unknown reporters.[10]

The tentacles of CPS surveillance spread throughout US society, far beyond the walls of child welfare agencies. Family policing relies on an expansive network of information sharing that spans the school, health care, public assistance, and law enforcement systems. This confluence of social services and child protective services directs state surveillance against poor and low-income families, especially Black families, who are more likely to rely on public service providers. Using social services, receiving welfare benefits, and living in public housing subject families to an extra layer of contact with mandated reporters. Public professionals are far more likely to report maltreatment than are private professionals who serve a more affluent, paying clientele.

At first blush, the government's encouragement of child abuse reporting may seem to be beneficial, if not imperative. Shouldn't the government ensure that someone is assigned to notice when children are at risk of harm? Isn't it our civic duty to help protect children by telling the government when they might be in danger? Even if we were not required to report maltreatment, we might want a way to seek help for a family in trouble. Although some people call the child abuse hotline as a form of retaliation, many professionals, relatives, and neighbors turn to CPS as a way to address the hardships they see families facing but not equipped to handle themselves. It may be the only avenue they know for getting help to children in need.[11]

Despite these benign intentions, reporting concerns about children's welfare to child protection authorities does not result in a beneficial response. Instead, CPS treats these calls as accusations to be investigated, not requests for support. Most reports are unsubstantiated by CPS caseworkers, so the families receive no response at all, other than being needlessly traumatized by an investigation. In fact, reports of suspected child maltreatment from teachers—the professionals most likely to call CPS—are the least likely to be substantiated. "In investigations, 50 percent of cases go right into the garbage," one caseworker observed. Substantiated reports launch even more intrusive oversight that does nothing to meet families' enduring material needs like secure housing, a reliable income, and decent health care.[12]

A therapist explained to sociologist Kelley Fong that she called CPS to get help for her fifteen-year-old client, Livia, and her mother, Gaby, who were having trouble dealing with Livia's mental health challenges. "There's not a lot of programs that we have available as clinicians here [and] we think CPS has all these resources at hand and they may not have these resources at hand," the therapist said. "That's the way we look at CPS, as like, oh, CPS has the resource for parenting, CPS has this, that, and the other thing." After the call triggered an unannounced visit from a caseworker who probed Gaby's personal life for an hour, Gaby felt the therapist had betrayed her. "She is not being helpful, she is just making my life more complicated," Gaby complained about the therapist. "I needed help from her and she did the opposite. . . . Instead of bringing peace, she messed everything up for us. . . . The confidence we have placed in her by telling her our life, making her part of our life, we lost that confidence in her." The therapist had intended to get additional parenting support for Gaby. Instead, she undermined what support her therapy offered the struggling mother and daughter. The caseworker interrogated Gaby two more times, then closed the case after the forty-five-day investigation period ended, leaving Livia with nothing but a strained relationship with her therapist.[13]

Fong found that "reporting professionals" like Livia's therapist typically contacted CPS not because they believed children were in imminent danger but because they "envisioned CPS as a sort of all-purpose agency, compensating for what they could not provide." Yet CPS routinely failed to meet their expectations. Professionals tend to overestimate how well CPS will address children's needs. This unwarranted faith in child welfare agencies encourages professionals to make calls based on sheer suspicion or concerns that don't amount to maltreatment. This helps to explain why teachers make so many unsubstantiated allegations: their daily interactions with their students reveal a myriad of needs schools haven't been equipped to handle. Instead of generously funding educational programs in Black communities, governments have intensified the police presence in schools, subjecting Black children to high rates of harassment, suspension, expulsion, and arrest. Many teachers may mistakenly see child welfare agencies as a lesser evil.[14]

These false expectations lead to especially damaging outcomes when medical professionals report their suspicions. Doctors' overestimation of how helpful CPS will be is matched by child welfare authorities' overinterpretation of doctors' reports as conclusive evidence of child abuse. While doctors assume CPS will respond to their concerns appropriately, caseworkers and judges assume doctors have accurately evaluated the risks to children. This mutually misguided deference leads many doctors to be shocked that their gut feelings caused the state to traumatize the very children they worried about. These faulty judgments are made most frequently about Black mothers, who experience the double whammy of fewer resources for caregiving as well as stereotypes about their caregiving deficits. What's more, social service workers, who may have low-wage jobs that are not unionized, feel pressure to report their suspicions for fear of getting fired if a child in their program is harmed at home. Although they will suffer no consequences from making an unwarranted call about Black parents, even if it traumatizes the family, they risk severe repercussions in the far, far less likely case that they fail to alert CPS to a child in serious danger.[15]

Mandated reporting drives parents from the very service providers that are most likely to support them. Many parents are deterred from fully engaging with health care, educational, and social service systems for fear the professionals who work there might turn them over to CPS. Some mothers hold off taking their children to the doctor for accidental injuries to avoid being wrongfully reported for suspected child abuse. "Say you take one of your kids to the hospital, the first thing they'll want to do is call Children and Family Services," one Black mother in Chicago told me. "Even if they know it's not your fault or nothing that could be helped, they will still call. If a child falls and hurt themselves or someone comes in with a sick baby, they don't care what the circumstances was or anything. That's the first thing that comes out of their mouth—'Call Children and Family Services.' That's why you find a lot of times people don't take their kids to the hospital." Because even baseless suspicions can lead to a terrifying encounter with CPS, parents trying their very best to care for their children are often reluctant to solicit aid from social service providers who might report them.

In her interviews with low-income mothers in Providence, Rhode Island, Fong found that their fear of CPS involvement didn't prompt the mothers to stay away from service providers altogether. Parents without an income or working for low-wage jobs have to rely on public services to meet their families' basic needs. They routinely encounter mandated reporters when going about their everyday lives. Missing school or medical checkups can trigger neglect allegations. Instead, the mothers strategically fashioned a "selective visibility" that allowed them to engage with doctors, teachers, and social services staff to a limited extent while shielding from view the aspects of their lives that made them most vulnerable to CPS involvement. They managed the information they disclosed to professionals, failing to confide any housing insecurity, drug use, or domestic violence, and preferred tapping services they could keep at a distance while eschewing intensive services like homeless shelters and home visiting programs that would give staff greater access to their intimate lives.[16]

When a Latina mother revealed to hospital staff that she was looking for housing for her newborn twins, the hospital notified CPS. "I was trying to be honest just so I can prepare myself . . . [but] that backfired on me," she told Fong. "After that moment I learned how to play the game." Like the mothers I interviewed in Chicago, the Providence mothers walked a fine line between needing to take advantage of available, though inadequate, resources the government offered while keeping at bay the unwanted intrusion that accompanied state support. Anthropologist Tina Lee found that the parents she interviewed in New York City were in the same boat. Many refrained from divulging their problems to service providers out of fear of "catching a case," as the mothers commonly called the arbitrary misfortune of being tagged for investigation—even if it meant sacrificing aid their families sorely needed.[17]

Enlisting service providers in CPS surveillance, then, weakens their capacity to improve children's welfare. Mandated reporting thwarts the potential for schools, health care clinics, and social programs to be caring hubs of community engagement that noncoercively help families meet their material needs. It also wastes millions and millions of dollars spent on investigating baseless allegations—money that could have provided concrete assistance to children and their family caregivers. These funds would bear far better fruit for children if given directly to their parents as cash allowances. Instead, professionals divert families to a system that has the potential to destroy them. "It's like Superman saving someone and throwing them in a lava pit," says Charity Toliver, founder of Black on Both Sides, a Chicago-based organization that amplifies the voices of Black foster youth. "Once a teacher called CPS about a student who was not dressed properly and received the reply that the child was already in foster care. That meant there was nothing else that could be done for him." Even if professionals bear no malice against the parents they report, it should be clear to them that their calls are causing more harm to families than good. Why continue to serve as deputized agents for a state surveillance system they can see is wrecking children's lives and pushing families away from what limited support public services offer?[18]

NEWBORN SCREENING

One of the most fraught arenas for mandated reporting is hospitals. Hospital staff routinely screen certain newborns for evidence of their mother's drug use during pregnancy and report positive results to child protection authorities. As we have seen, multiple studies show that doctors' screening and reporting of broken bones and skull fractures as suspected child abuse are biased against Black parents. The handling of prenatal drug use is no less discriminatory.

Over the last thirty years, states have increasingly included prenatal drug use in their definitions of child maltreatment. The jurisprudence crafted in the 1990s to criminalize pregnant Black women set the stage for a more widespread surge of fetal harm policies. The targets of prosecutions now extend from Black women accused of being pregnant and using crack cocaine to pregnant white women charged under laws intended to protect children from meth lab explosions. Between 1973—when *Roe v. Wade* was decided—and 2013, there were more than seven hundred documented cases in which women were arrested, detained, or subjected to forced medical interventions because of pregnancy-related accusations. Black women in particular were significantly more likely to be reported by hospital staff, arrested, and charged with crimes.[19]

As I argued in *Killing the Black Body*, these prosecutions followed a long history of devaluing Black women's childbearing and were efforts to control Black women, not to improve the health of their babies. The racist predictions by policy makers and the media that so-called crack babies were doomed to lives of welfare dependency and criminality have been soundly discredited. There is no reliable body of scientific evidence demonstrating that prenatal drug exposure necessarily causes long-term harms to children. As Movement for Family Power summarized in a 2020 report, "No literature to date has isolated any effects of prenatal drug exposure given the many confounding variables, such as poverty, other substance use, poor nutrition, etc." Moreover, studies have established that the best approach for infant health and development is keeping newborn babies with their mothers so they can bond and breastfeed.[20]

Despite the lack of scientific support, states began to define exposing a fetus to drugs as a form of child maltreatment or as evidence of unfitness as a parent. In 2003, Congress weighed in: it amended the Child Abuse Prevention and Treatment Act of 1974 (CAPTA) to require states to put in place policies and procedures "to address the needs of infants born with and identified as being affected by illegal substance abuse or withdrawal symptoms resulting from prenatal drug exposure." These measures must include a "requirement that health care providers involved in the delivery or care of such infants notify the child protective services system of the occurrence of such condition in such infants." Congress left it to the states to establish their own definitions of what constitutes child abuse and neglect. The number of states with prenatal drug use policies increased from one in 1974 to forty-two states and the District of Columbia in 2016. Whether considered a crime, infliction of civil child maltreatment, or reason to question the ability to parent in the future, using drugs during pregnancy is often seen as warranting a call to child protection authorities.[21]

The fact that doctors and nurses believe they are mandated by child protection laws to report prenatal drug use doesn't mean they implement this directive universally or uniformly. Instead, drug-screening and -reporting criteria are not standardized across hospitals in the United States. State laws defining child abuse and neglect and specifying when prenatal substance use must be reported vary drastically across the country. The American College of Obstetricians and Gynecologists found no consistency in health care providers' reporting obligations, noting, "South Carolina relies on a single positive drug test result, Florida mandates reporting newborns that are 'demonstrably adversely affected' by prenatal drug exposure, and in Texas, an infant must be 'addicted' to an illegal substance at birth."[22]

Another point of disagreement is when to test pregnant patients or newborns for evidence of drug use. Typically, it's a positive drug toxicology that triggers a report to CPS. Mothers and their babies who aren't screened are unlikely to be reported. Individual hospital protocols also vary drastically, even within states. In New York State, for example, although virtually all birthing hospitals screened some pregnant patients for drugs, only 15 percent screened all of them—meaning most hospitals used risk criteria to determine which patients to screen. The New York State Assembly has failed to pass a law requiring newborn screening or specifying when newborns should be screened, leaving each hospital to make up a procedure for itself. Only 60 percent of the hospitals put their policies for screening pregnant patients or newborns in writing.[23]

Like New York, most states don't have either universal drug testing or clear testing rules. Nor do they have any checks on when to report positive toxicologies to CPS. As a result, health care providers have wide latitude in determining which newborns exposed to drugs or alcohol get investigated. Their decisions whether or not to test and report rely on their subjective suspicions about the likelihood a mother used drugs—or, perhaps more telling, her fitness to care for her baby. This free-for-all invites rampant discrimination against Black mothers by hospital staff. Since the 1990s, numerous studies have shown that health care professionals report Black women who use drugs during pregnancy far more readily than they report their white patients. A widely cited study of pregnant patients in Pinellas County, Florida, published in 1990 in the prestigious *New England Journal of Medicine*, found that, although white women had a slightly higher rate of positive drug tests than Black women, Black women were *ten times* more likely to be reported to government authorities. Subsequent studies show a persistent willingness on the part of health care professionals to turn in Black women for using drugs while pregnant. In November 2020, New York City's Commission on Human Rights launched an investigation into whether or not three major private hospitals—Montefiore Medical

Center, Mount Sinai Health System, and New York-Presbyterian—were targeting Black and Latinx pregnant patients and newborns for drug testing in violation of the city's human rights laws. The City Health and Hospitals Corporation immediately announced that the city's public hospitals would end their practice of drug testing pregnant patients and newborns without consent.[24]

The prejudices of hospital staff are reinforced by racial inequities built into hospital-screening protocols. Hospitals serving white and affluent patients have more detailed screening criteria that may require a discussion with the mother or her consent prior to testing. By contrast, hospitals with a predominantly Black and lower-income patient population have less structured protocols that give staff more leeway to conduct newborn drug screenings. Moreover, the protocols themselves embed discrimination by including specific components that are more likely to pinpoint Black mothers. Identifying patients who had preterm births, limited prenatal care, or prior involvement with CPS all skew protocols toward testing babies born to Black women. Some hospitals use insurance status as a factor to determine which newborns to test, with reliance on Medicaid weighing in favor of testing. Adopting standardized protocols that rely on these discriminatory criteria will not stop the racial disparities in newborn testing and reporting.[25]

For example, a 2015 study of CPS reporting rates in California found that a hospital's adoption of a standardized protocol did nothing to reduce CPS reporting disparities. The hospital staff still reported almost five times more Black than white newborns based on the protocol's racially biased risk factors and staff discretion to report test results. Health care facilities structure their screening procedures to protect the privacy and integrity of the most privileged families and to invite intrusion into Black families.[26]

Instead of asking whether drug testing and reporting should be more standardized, we should be asking why hospitals are reporting newborns to CPS based on a single drug test in the first place. There is wide consensus among medical and child welfare experts that a positive toxicology simply captures any metabolites of certain substances that are circulating in the newborn's system at that moment. It can't predict health risks to the child, or the family's caregiving capacity. As an addiction medicine specialist told Movement for Family Power, "A drug test is not a test for addiction and certainly is not a parenting test."[27] A statement issued by the American College of Obstetricians and Gynecologists (ACOG) in 2020 acknowledged that "leading medical organizations agree that a positive drug test should not be construed as child abuse or neglect," noting that mandated drug testing "disrupts bodily autonomy of the pregnant person and their newborn and is inconsistent with treating substance use disorder as a health condition with social and behavioral dimensions." ACOG therefore recommended that health care providers rely on self-reporting instead. This is a hopeful sign that rampant surveillance of Black mothers and newborns by testing them for drugs and reporting the results to CPS may finally be on its way out.[28]

DIGITAL SURVEILLANCE

During the first months of the COVID-19 pandemic, Em Quiles found herself juggling full-time work with supervising her seven-year-old son's remote schooling at home. To keep her job, she put her teenage son in charge of keeping an eye on his younger brother's online class participation. One day in June 2020, Quiles was shocked to receive a call from the Massachusetts Department of Children and Families. The state's child welfare agency accused Quiles of neglect because her young son had missed virtual classes and homework assignments. During the 2020 school year, Massachusetts school officials in predominantly Black and Latinx districts reported dozens of parents to child protection authorities because their children failed to log in to classes. Quiles, who directs a Latinx advocacy organization in Worcester, was able to persuade a caseworker that the allegation was baseless. Still, Quiles's unexpected encounter with CPS reflects a new technology that child welfare agencies across the country have at their disposal to surveil families. Public education conducted via video cameras allows schools to monitor online truancy and to see inside a family's home during class. That information travels through the existing discriminatory pipeline between schools and CPS to accuse parents of child maltreatment.[29]

Child welfare agencies' extensive multisystem network of informants combined with their power to pry into a family's personal life and space give them access to massive amounts of information ordinarily beyond the government's reach. In recent years, agencies have begun adopting novel technological tools that are stretching the scope of family surveillance far beyond its current boundaries. The child welfare system has entered the digital age. Governments are increasingly employing big databases, computer programming, and artificial intelligence to monitor families and make automated decisions about intervening in them. Some of the nation's largest child welfare departments—in California, Florida, Illinois, Pennsylvania, and Texas—are using computerized risk assessment technologies to magnify family surveillance.

In another parallel between the child welfare system and the criminal punishment system, child protection agencies are following digital models already implemented by the police. Law enforcement agencies nationwide collect and store vast amounts of data about past crimes, analyze these data using mathematical algorithms to predict future criminal activity, and incorporate the forecasts into their strategies for policing individuals, groups, and neighborhoods. For example, the Los Angeles Police Department uses PredPol, the world's leading predictive-policing software, which analyzes ten years of crime data to produce boxes, each encompassing five hundred square feet, that overlay division maps, indicating where crimes are most likely to occur in the next twelve hours. LAPD officers receive printouts of the maps at the beginning of their shifts so they can concentrate their policing on the predictive boxes—a procedure known as "risk-based deployment." Similarly, the Memphis police department's Blue CRUSH program applies IBM predictive-analytics software to data on past crimes to identify "hot spots" where officers are directed to conduct sweeps and show a heightened police presence. A number of police departments have collected secret databases that list residents digitally predicted to be gang members.[30]

Government officials argue that computerized risk assessments can eliminate racial bias in policing decisions because they are more objective than police officers. Analyses of these predictive technologies, however, reveal that they disproportionately identify Black people as likely to commit crimes and Black neighborhoods as crime hot spots. When ProPublica studied a digital analytic tool used to predict recidivism, it found that Black people were almost twice as likely as white people to be identified as higher risk but not actually go on to commit other crimes. Although computer scientists create the predictive algorithms, they rely on crime databases created by the police, such as arrest records, that reflect prior racial profiling. When a predictive model identifies a trait or place based on structurally biased data or programming, the profiled trait or place garners heightened police attention. Risk assessment models that import data biased by racist policing practices become a "self-fulfilling feedback loop" where the prediction ensures future detection. This built-in discrimination subjects Black people to being further criminalized—not caught for committing crimes but predicted to commit crimes in the future.[31]

When employed by child welfare agencies, computerized risk assessment models operate the same way. Allegheny County, Pennsylvania, was one of the first places in the United States to pilot a predictive risk tool for child welfare decision making. In August 2016, the county adopted a model developed by researchers in New Zealand that scores families according to 132 variables, such as prior involvement in the child welfare or criminal punishment system, to predict future cases of child maltreatment. The county's software program, the Allegheny Family Screening Tool (AFST), aids staff in screening calls made to the child abuse hotline by displaying a risk assessment score of one to twenty for incoming referrals. Based on this information, the hotline staff and supervisors decide whether to screen out the referral or recommend an investigation.

In *Automating Inequality: How High-Tech Tools Profile, Police, and Punish the Poor*, political scientist Virginia Eubanks, who studied the Allegheny County system, argues that these technological innovations constitute a modern-day "digital poorhouse." The contemporary version is undergirded with the same ideologies that have long blamed poor people for their disadvantaged social position but has been upgraded with the digitized capacity to monitor and discipline them more efficiently. Like law enforcement predictive tools, inequality was coded into the child protection model's algorithms: AFST is structured to be biased against poor families.[32]

According to Eubanks, the dataset AFST uses to predict child maltreatment contains "only information about families who access public services." This not only discriminates against poor and low-income families on its face, but also builds in the bias inherent in mandated reporting by the staff of social service programs. Moreover, "one quarter of the predictive variables in the AFST are direct measures of poverty," Eubanks notes. Like predictive policing, Allegheny County's child maltreatment risk assessment creates a self-fulfilling feedback loop. Families scored as high risk by the AFST elicit extra scrutiny from child protection investigators, who know that screeners are using the algorithm, increasing the parents' odds of being found neglectful. If the investigation results in substantiating the allegation or removing a child from the home, county officials can claim an accurate prediction.[33]

The Allegheny predictive model omits data about middle-class and wealthy families. But the model's problem isn't just that the missing data make the predictions less accurate. The problem is that the model is structured to pull only poor and low-income families into the state's surveillance regime. The structure of algorithmic surveillance shows that its aim isn't to protect children; its aim is to regulate poor families. Maltreatment in wealthy families isn't missed; it's considered irrelevant.

The same social factors that skew risk assessments against poor families are even more likely to tag Black families. "We'd use all available data, including when dad was in jail three years before the call," boasted Erin Dalton, who served at the time as the deputy director of analytics, technology, and planning for the Allegheny County Department of Human Services and was named director in January 2021. Nevertheless, a 2019 study by two Stanford researchers found that AFST increased the rate of white children who were screened in, while slightly decreasing it for Black children. But they also noted that, before AFST was implemented, the county was experiencing a decline in the fraction of children who were screened in for investigation. The AFST halted that trend, especially for Black families. So it's possible that even fewer Black families would have been subjected to investigation had AFST not been in place.[34]

Predictive algorithms package the inequities embedded in the data into a score that necessarily reflects families' privileged or disadvantaged positions. Not only are structural inequities coded into the data and algorithms, but state agencies then use the results according to a predetermined philosophy to surveil instead of support Black communities. Of course, the impact of digital technologies would be very different if they were used to identify families that were struggling the most so the government could send them checks and supplies with no strings attached. But we don't need an algorithm to identify families who need more income. The government's failure to generously support families is not due to the lack of algorithms. The aphorism "garbage in, garbage out" captures an important aspect of data collection but doesn't capture the nature of built-in structural bias. "Inequality in, inequality out" is more apt.

As with their financial exploitation of families, public child welfare agencies engage the private sector to provide high-tech assistance with family surveillance. Child welfare departments are hiring global technology and consulting firms like IBM, SAS, Creative Information Technology (CITI), and Deloitte to develop and implement sophisticated risk assessment programs. Agencies no longer need to depend entirely on a multisystem network of mandated reporters to supply reconnaissance on families. They are contracting with fancy corporations to collect, store, and analyze previously unimaginable amounts of private information about children in targeted communities, their family members, and other individuals in their social networks. The size and breadth of these digital storehouses far surpass what we would expect democratic governments to hold on their citizens. The multimillion-dollar contracts with private enterprises to construct these expansive surveillance systems also eat up the budgets of child protection departments that refuse to provide the material resources that families need.

One of the chief players in child welfare analytics is SAS, the world's largest software company, founded in North Carolina in 1976. The SAS website describes how the firm is "combining its industry-leading data management and advanced analytics with proven models that can help save children's lives." Key to its predictive prowess is its ability to harvest enormous amounts of information about families from multiple sources. SAS professes the capacity to "access child-related data no matter where it is stored." The sources for such data include "social benefits, education, health care, law enforcement, criminal justice systems, etc." The company boasts of a "hybrid analytical approach" that applies "business rules, anomaly detection, predictive modeling, social network analysis, geospatial analysis, etc." to calculate "child safety risk scoring." Its surveillance tools dig deep into the lives of individuals associated with targeted children to "capture important data about them—criminal histories, behavioral health data, drug or alcohol treatment data, etc." Then all these data go into an automated monitoring system, where "risk scores are continuously recalculated based on the most up-to-date information, and an alert engine proactively notifies case workers when risk thresholds are exceeded." The SAS algorithm, like that used by most private tech companies, is a "black box": the mathematical formulas are proprietary trade secrets and safeguarded from disclosure by intellectual property law. So government agencies—and the public—have no idea how the risk scores are calculated.[35]

Los Angeles County's first experiment with child welfare analytics belies the claim that these technologies will improve outcomes for children. In 2014, the county's Department of Children and Family Services (DCFS), the largest child welfare department in the nation, hired SAS to develop Project AURA (Approach to Understanding Risk Assessment), a pilot that employed the company's predictive tools to assign risk scores for each child in contact with the department. Fortunately, the first phase was to test how well the model worked by applying it to DCFS referrals from 2013: could the risk scores identify which children were victims of maltreatment in the prior year? In a May 2017 memo to the LA County Board of Supervisors, Michael Nash, executive director at the county's Office of Child Protection, revealed, "While the tool correctly detected a high number of children (171 cases) at the highest risk for abuse, it also incorrectly identified an extremely high number (3,829 cases) of false positives (i.e., children who received high risk scores who were not at risk for a negative outcome)." Nash reported that DCFS "is no longer pursuing Project AURA." Instead, the county continued to rely on a different model. Structured Decision Making (SDM), a series of prompts caseworkers fill out to assess child safety and risk, is currently used by child welfare agencies in all California counties and in many other states. Like Allegheny County's AFST, its variables include family characteristics—such as criminal history and living in a home with broken windows and roaches—that skew the outputs toward tagging Black families. A study by the Washington State Institute for Public Policy found that, after Washington adopted the SDM risk assessment tool in 2007, Black children were more likely to have CPS referrals and to be removed from their homes than in earlier years.[36]

A different algorithmic model used by the Illinois Department of Children and Family Services, the Rapid Safety Feedback program, met a similar demise in December 2017 when it, too, was plagued by false positives. "More than 4,100 Illinois children were assigned a 90 percent or greater probability of death or injury," the *Chicago Tribune* reported from its review of internal DCFS records. "And 369 youngsters, all under age 9, got a 100 percent chance of death or serious injury in the next two years." False positives generated by predictive analytics are not just a matter of statistical imprecision or increased CPS workload. These algorithmic predictions initiate state investigations that terrorize the identified families and turn their lives upside down.[37]

The disastrous experiences with predictive analytics challenge the claim that machines are fairer than human decision makers because they are more objective. The opposite may be true: digitized systems are antidemocratic *because* they remove human discretion. Shifting control over decision making from caseworkers to corporate computer analysts doesn't eliminate bias; it embeds bias deeper into the system, making it less amenable to change. Parents snared by Allegheny County's digitized system told Virginia Eubanks "they'd rather have an imperfect person making decisions about their families than a flawless computer. 'You can teach people how you wanted to be treated.'" Human biases can be exposed, resisted, and potentially transformed, whereas computer algorithms cement biases into automated systems.[38]

This lack of government accountability is accentuated by placing the data extraction and risk assessments in the hands of seemingly objective private companies. "Administrative opacity is a deliberate strategy to manage regulatory environments," sociologist Tressie McMillan Cottom reminds us. "It shields organizations, both public and private, from democratic appeals for access and equity." By contracting with private firms like IBM, SAS, and CITI, whose algorithms are encased in proprietary black boxes, child welfare administrators can evade public scrutiny of high-tech family surveillance. As these firms make our private information increasingly accessible to public child welfare agencies, they simultaneously make the agencies' operations more private and less accessible to the public. Automating child welfare decision making concentrates control over surveillance technologies in an exclusive private-public alliance, squelching opportunities for appeals to justice, mass resistance, and social change.[39]

We need to evaluate the rise of computer analytics in child welfare by more than the claimed accuracy of its predictions. Modern law enforcement and child welfare systems are not identifying individuals who need to be watched based on their risky behavior. Rather, they use mathematical models to statistically identify targets of investigation within giant databases. Risk assessment has been detached from any regard for actual responsibility for causing harm. This promotes the state's carceral logic that aims to control populations rather than to adjudicate individual guilt or innocence, to manage social inequities rather than to aid those who are suffering from them. Algorithmic forecasts are based on data that were produced under the influence of existing racial discrimination in systems such as policing, housing, education, health care, and public assistance. A future predicted by today's algorithms, therefore, is predetermined to correspond to past racial inequality. In short, prediction becomes a way for the carceral state to foreclose visions of a more humane future.[40]

The pinnacle of this predictive approach is to identify subjects of government regulation from the moment of birth. Police gang databases have included toddlers. Riverside County in California instituted a probation program that monitors children identified to be "predelinquent." A 2011 paper concluded that "a prenatal maltreatment-predicting algorithm was theoretically possible: 'a risk assessment tool that could be used on the day of birth to identify those children at greatest risk of maltreatment holds great value.'"[41]

In August 2019, Allegheny County DHS director Mark Cherna announced precisely such a plan to proactively identify newborns predicted to be in danger of maltreatment. Dubbed Hello Baby, the pilot analyzes human services data using an algorithm that assesses children's future odds of being abused or neglected as soon as they are born. Hello Baby also gives information about resources to all families of newborns while they are still in the hospital. "Even if we make perfect hotline [screening] decisions, many . . . of those families will never come to our attention prior to the critical incident," DHS deputy director Erin Dalton told the *Pittsburgh Post-Gazette*. Dalton touted Hello Baby as a way to get support to needy families sooner. But, as with mandated reporting by social service providers, offering help within a coercive system is a Trojan horse: the gift of aid draws families into a snare that can lead to crushing state intrusion. Digitally expanding family surveillance even beyond the current network of reporting systems will only make child welfare agencies more efficient at destroying Black families, deterring the families from getting the resources they need, and perpetuating the myth that policing families is the solution to the structural inequities that plague them.[42]

FORCED TO BE SERVED

For families that are screened into the child welfare system, the next phase of surveillance entails forced compliance with services mandated by agencies and rubber-stamped by judges. It is Orwellian to call this process "serving" families when the vast majority of families are "served" against their will. The agency's "service plan" usually has nothing to do with providing the tangible things families need. Instead, it consists of a list of requirements parents must fulfill in order to keep their children at home or get them back from foster care. Rarely are parents asked what services they would find helpful. Parents are accused, investigated, and prosecuted just like defendants in criminal court. Service plans are akin to probation orders that list requirements and restrictions judges impose on people convicted of crimes. In the criminal context, violation of a single provision lands the offender in prison. In the child welfare system, parents who fail to comply risk having their rights terminated and never seeing their children again. Service plans are another sure indication that the system's aim is to police and punish families, not protect and care for children.

Service plans are typically cookie cutter. Many agencies use a form with a generic list of tasks that they may give to parents as is or with certain items highlighted. There is rarely any real attempt to tailor the services to the specific needs of individual families and children. A typical service plan includes the following requirements: attend parent training, anger management, and special needs classes; participate in a substance abuse treatment program; make random urine drops; participate in individual and family counseling; submit to unannounced visits and home inspections from CPS; make scheduled visitations with all children in foster care (who may be spread among multiple placements); maintain employment; find adequate housing; regularly contact the caseworker assigned to each child; complete psychological evaluations; participate in all family court conferences and hearings.

For the Black mothers I got to know, the prescribed solutions to their problems were a far cry from material things they said they needed, such as cash, affordable housing, furniture, food, clothing, education, and child care. Often, the requirements had nothing to do with their needs at all—like ordering them to attend anger management classes or treatment for drug addiction when they didn't have a problem with anger or drugs. The mothers regarded them more as assignments they had to complete to get their children back than as real assistance to their families. Angeline Montauban describes the meetings she had with her caseworker as a "compliance dog-and-pony show." In fact, the dizzying catalogue of burdensome and conflicting obligations made it harder for the mothers to take care of their children or prepare to reunite with them. "There's this judgment that these mothers don't have the ability to make decisions about their kids, and in that, society both infantilizes them and holds them to superhuman standards," Scott Hechinger, a lawyer at Brooklyn Defender Services, says. Sometimes permanency plans are so complicated or onerous that they seem designed to ensure failure. Nevertheless, mothers soon learn that expressing their families' true needs or complaining about the mandatory services will be interpreted as lack of cooperation, which will only extend the investigation or delay reunification with their children.[43]

The approach child welfare agencies take to addressing children's welfare is therapeutic. The services imposed on parents focus on fixing their perceived parenting deficits with skills classes and psychological counseling. Just as Black children's problems are deemed to stem from maltreatment by their parents, so the solutions to the problems are framed as rehabilitating parental pathologies. Compelling parents to undergo psychological evaluations is especially insidious: it provides a capacious avenue for agencies to find flaws in parents' behaviors or psyches that can justify perpetual family surveillance and separation. Psychological probing by a battery of state-hired therapists is bound to turn up some anxiety, hostility, depression, or improper attitude, especially when the client has gone through the traumatic experience of losing her children. This ploy allows agencies to avoid both admitting that the family was targeted because of its social adversities and doing anything to resolve them.

It is also highly unethical for agencies to force parents into therapy with counselors paid to collect private information to use against the parents. The contractual relationship between CPS and the therapists creates two egregious conflicts of interest. It violates the trust patients should be able to put in their therapists, and it biases the therapists' evaluations of the parents. This arrangement creates financial incentives for evaluators to write reports that confirm the caseworkers' view of the parents. And caseworkers are apt to hire evaluators who tend to agree with them, without regard for the quality of the mental health assessments they churn out. A 2017 investigation by ProPublica revealed that, for more than a decade, New York City family court judges had relied routinely on faulty mental health evaluations provided by Montego Medical Consulting, a for-profit company under contract with the city's child welfare department. The evaluators often based their reports on a brief session without observing any parent-child interaction. They failed to follow professional guidelines and employed questionable tools, such as Draw-a-Person where the evaluators made inferences about a subject's parenting ability based on a sketch. New York City's experience reflects a problem with state-hired psychologists that is endemic to family policing. As Georgia public defender Emma Brown-Bernstein decries, "I have seen the same evaluators marched into court over and over and over again to produce the same findings, give the same recommendations, and receive the same payment from the Department." It would be ludicrous to expect therapists and evaluators to provide any genuine help to parents under these treacherous conditions.[44]

The child welfare system generally treats having a mental or cognitive disability as evidence of parental unfitness and sometimes takes children from parents with mental health problems based on the false presumption they are incapable of caring for their children. According to ProPublica, about thirty states allow courts to terminate the rights of parents who have a mental illness that renders them incapable of safely raising their children. Judges often conclude that a mental illness diagnosis alone puts the child at risk without any evidence that the parents have caused harm. "Parents are often evaluated without a real analysis of their supports, of the life they actually live," psychiatry professor Joanne Nicholson told ProPublica. As a result, "the diagnosis starts to speak louder than real life." In addition, children with mental health issues are more vulnerable to being labeled maltreated. Poor and low-income parents often can't afford specialized care for their children, and CPS interprets their unmet needs as medical neglect. Agencies rarely provide the high-quality health care and services that would enable parents who are disabled or whose children are disabled to keep their families together.[45]

In November 2020, the Massachusetts Department of Children and Families settled a US Justice Department investigation into its practice of using these "unsupported stereotypes" to justify separating children from parents with disabilities. The civil rights probe was sparked in 2012 when the department took a newborn from a nineteen-year-old mother with a "mild intellectual disability," without evaluating her ability to care for the child. Under the settlement, "the child welfare agency must make a case-by-case assessment about whether the child faces imminent risk of abuse or neglect, and may not make that determination solely on a parent's disability, diagnosis, IQ or other 'intelligence measures.'" The settlement represents one positive step toward ending the discriminatory presumption that parents with disabilities pose a danger to their children.[46]

Like the rest of child welfare decision making, presumptions based on mental health assessments are biased against Black mothers, who are stereotyped as being intellectually impaired, irrational, and angry. Recall the story of Jornell from the Prologue. I was struck by how often references to her cognitive skills appeared in her mandated psychological evaluations, and how much they weighed against her being reunited with her son. When a therapist concluded "a diagnosis of bipolar disorder is not justified," the agency report stated that Jornell's problem instead was that she behaved like "an unsophisticated person from a cognitive point of view." A few months later, a new diagnosis appeared in Jornell's records. Now the evaluators worried about a "cognitive disorder" evidenced by Jornell's "disorganization in thinking," which allegedly put her at risk for "poor judgment." This was a further excuse to keep her son, David, in foster care so the agency could send Jornell for a new round of thorough evaluations. This time the purpose was to assess her "cognitive functioning" to determine whether her scattered thinking was caused by "borderline intellectual functioning," a "characterological defensive style," or a mental illness apparently undetected by the numerous psychiatric evaluations she had undergone for nearly three years. It seemed the child welfare department was conducting psychological surveillance of Jornell that would persist regardless of the diagnosis or assessment of risk to her son, as long as it could hire a therapist to question any aspect of her cognitive abilities.

Michelle Burrell, a New York City Legal Services attorney, asks pointedly, "How come a white mother in Fort Greene, Brooklyn, can struggle with depression and anxiety, dabble in therapy and medication inconsistently, refuse treatment altogether, and remain unbothered by child welfare officials, while her Black counterpart in Brownsville, Brooklyn, dealing with mild symptoms of depression, is required by the Court to participate in therapy until a social worker, most likely a young white intern who is providing her therapy at a public hospital, determines that she can stop?" The double standard puts in stark relief an ugly truth about family surveillance: child welfare investigations assemble a giant cadre of mostly white professionals to oversee the parenting of Black mothers.[47]

THE PRICE OF NONCOMPLIANCE

Families captured by the surveillance grid pay a heavy price if they fail to obey its arbitrary commands. Their fate becomes focused on a list of tasks a caseworker has copied or scribbled on a generic form. Compliance overshadows the child's needs or parent's caregiving or even the truth of the original allegations of maltreatment. The issue is no longer whether the child will be safe at home, but whether the mother has attended every parenting class, made every urine drop, participated in every therapy session, shown up for every scheduled visit, arrived at every appointment on time, and always maintained a contrite and cooperative disposition. Judges have dinged parents for missing a service assignment even when it conflicts with another one in the plan or even when the service is unavailable.

Many courts apply a rule that failure to complete the permanency plan is prima facie evidence that children should not be returned home. This heartless edict is reinforced by the Adoption and Safe Families Act's imposition of a fifteen-month time frame for agencies to file petitions to terminate parents' rights. The main reason families are permanently torn apart is that parents took too long to jump through the hoops. Keith Baumann, a supervising attorney at the Bronx Defenders, hears family court judges essentially saying, "You have failed to navigate the labyrinth we set up for you, so we will terminate your rights." As incredible as it sounds, parents' ties to their children are routinely severed for good because the parent failed to fulfill some provision on the caseworker's list. In other words, parents' rights are usually terminated for noncompliance, not harm to children. The parents are made legal strangers to their children; their children can be adopted by others; they may lose touch with their children forever.[48]

PERPETUAL SUSPECTS

Even when parents fully comply with the service plan or resolve the allegations quickly, they remain entangled in the surveillance grid. Parents indicated for child maltreatment are entered in a statewide registry, regardless of the circumstance of their case. Being a registered child maltreater seriously hobbles a parent's ability to find a job, secure housing, and serve as a caregiver for other children—even children in their own extended family. An indicated case disqualifies parents from many of the jobs most accessible to them, such as bus driver, teacher's or nurse's aide, and day care worker, and functions to blacklist them whenever a potential employer checks the registry.

Landing on the registry also bans people from being licensed as a foster caretaker. Agencies typically look for any CPS involvement of family members who are considered for child placements. In some states, appearing on a registry automatically disqualifies someone from becoming a kin caregiver, posing a significant impediment to families staying together. Until very recently, an entry in New York's Statewide Central Register of Child Abuse and Maltreatment stuck until the parent's youngest child turned twenty-eight, short of a hearing to have the report amended and sealed. In 2021, after a three-year campaign by parent activists and family defense attorneys, the New York legislature enacted a measure lowering the time a parent's name can remain on the registry to eight years in neglect cases.[49]

Once caught in the family surveillance machine, parents find it hard to emerge in one piece. Children, parents, and other family caregivers, including information about their intimate lives, not only are noted in registries; those details are perpetually stored in a vast, multisystem network facilitated by digital data gathering and predictive analytics in the hands of unaccountable corporate partners. Precisely because it seems to operate outside criminal law enforcement, the child welfare system has become an extremely useful arm of the carceral state, for it has the power to intensively monitor entire communities—all the while escaping public scrutiny and bypassing legal protections by claiming to protect the children of those communities.

EIGHT

CARCERAL ENTANGLEMENTS

PARTNERS WITH GUNS

Aurora, Colorado, police officers played multiple roles in the events that led to the arrest of Vanessa Peoples. The young mother's entanglement with the child welfare system began when an officer cited her for child endangerment at the park after her toddler son, Malik, strayed away. As a consequence of that criminal ticket, two CPS workers arrived at her house the next day. Then three police officers pulled up when one of the caseworkers summoned them to assist her in a routine investigation of Vanessa's home. The officers went room by room, inspecting every corner of the house. They stood guard to intimidate Vanessa and her mother and children as she negotiated with the caseworkers. In the end, a total of seven police officers got involved, ultimately hog-tying and arresting Vanessa for protesting their intrusion in her family's life.

CPS staff not only act like police officers; they also work hand-in-hand with police officers. Local child welfare and law enforcement authorities increasingly enter into contracts to create various types of collaborations—from sharing information to engaging in common trainings, cooperating in investigations, and jointly responding to reports. Police officers accompany caseworkers in investigations of maltreatment reports. They stand by while caseworkers conduct home visits to check up on families involved in child welfare proceedings. They help caseworkers forcibly tear children from the arms of their parents. Being able to enlist armed officers for backup adds extra credibility and terror to caseworkers' threats to remove children. Officers sometimes take the initiative. In some jurisdictions, police themselves conduct investigations of noncriminal maltreatment cases and may even seize children without a court order, with CPS workers following up afterward. Many police departments have installed special units devoted to detecting child abuse and neglect that may, in turn, have CPS workers on board to orchestrate a joint response.[1]

The mutual reinforcement that CPS and the police lend each other magnifies the capacity of each to terrorize families. On one hand, CPS can take advantage of its veneer of benevolence to escape public criticism for its brutality and bypass the constitutional provisions that place restraints on police officers' actions. On the other hand, police officers gain license to enter homes, restrain parents, and remove and detain children because they are acting in the name of child protection. When caseworkers are accompanied by cops on a visit, they carry both the moral imprimatur of child saving and the brute force of the officers' guns. Family defenders in New York like to quote C. S. Lewis: "Of all tyrannies, a tyranny sincerely exercised for the good of its victims may be the most oppressive. . . . Those who torment us for our own good will torment us without end for they do so with the approval of their own conscience." Caseworkers' power to torment families with a clear conscience is extended by and to the police officers who accompany them on their destructive missions.[2]

Police and CPS also serve as pipelines that drive parents from capture by the child welfare system to capture by the criminal punishment system. While each system targets Black mothers independently, each also draws Black mothers into the other's net. Police are mandated reporters of child abuse and neglect in every state. Law enforcement personnel place a close second only to teachers in the number of maltreatment allegations they convey to child protection authorities. In 2019, police made nearly one-fifth of 4.4 million total referrals received nationally by child welfare agencies. Police departments and child welfare offices also share allegations against parents. Most states have statutory procedures for child protection and law enforcement agencies to exchange information about suspected abuse and neglect. In nine states and the District of Columbia, all reports of child maltreatment made initially to CPS or to law enforcement must be cross-reported to the other agency.[3]

One of the reasons Black families are reported and investigated at such high rates is because racist policing practices put them in frequent contact with police officers. Policing is most aggressive precisely in the same segregated Black neighborhoods where child welfare agency surveillance is concentrated. Police are routinely deployed to patrol the streets of Black neighborhoods, which are increasingly identified by predictive technologies as criminal "hot spots" based on prior racial profiling. Police are installed at housing projects and keep their residents under constant surveillance. Police conduct surprise raids of homes—like the one that killed Breonna Taylor in March 2020 as she slept in her Louisville, Kentucky, apartment. These practices not only put police in constant contact with Black residents, but also place police and residents in an adversarial stance, increasing officers' inclination to suspect and report child maltreatment. Intensive policing in Black neighborhoods, in turn, stigmatizes the residents as dangerous, influencing CPS caseworkers' determinations about the risks the homes pose to children.[4]

At the same time, whenever caseworkers investigate a home for child maltreatment, it creates the possibility that they will find evidence of a crime. As they conduct their thorough inspection of every room in the dwelling, they may discover illegal drugs and make a report to 911. If the caseworker is accompanied by police officers, the officers may notice a reason to arrest someone in the family. In states where the cross-reporting is automatic, maltreatment allegations phoned in to the hotline are conveyed to prosecutors and police, even though the call may turn out to be baseless.[5]

A police department in Keizer, Oregon, launched a pilot project to partner more closely with child protective services. "The project places two CPS case managers at the police station, and when a call comes in about alleged abuse or neglect, the CPS case manager and a police officer make the visit together to interview the parents," explains a Casey Family Foundation report on child welfare and police collaborations. The project's asserted aim is to soften the police department's "culture of engaging families." But joining police and caseworkers together doesn't make police more like social workers; it makes social workers more like cops.[6]

Frank Edwards, a professor of criminal justice, dug into the federal data system that tracks all investigated reports of child maltreatment to determine whether the rate of contact between police and neighborhood residents is systematically related to the rate at which police report suspected child abuse and neglect. As a preliminary matter, Edwards found that police reporting follows a similar pattern as reporting by other professionals: most police-filed reports are for suspected child neglect, not physical abuse. Edwards also discovered that reporting by police influences child welfare decision making: the accusations made by police are considered more credible. "Children are far more likely to be classified as victims of child abuse and neglect following a child welfare agency assessment when they are reported by police than when reports originated from another source," Edwards observed.[7]

Edwards's analysis also confirmed that average levels of arrests were closely tied to the rates at which police report child maltreatment across counties. Although further research is needed to determine the reasons behind the link between arrests and CPS reports, the study found that contact with police often leads to a child welfare investigation. "These results suggest that involvement with the child welfare system is a spillover consequence of arrest," Edwards concluded. This pathway between arrests and CPS entanglement was especially striking for Native children, but also contributed to CPS cases in Black communities.[8]

Policing by law enforcement officers and by child welfare workers converges in Black neighborhoods to subject families to intense state surveillance and disruption. Because police deliberately patrol Black neighborhoods more aggressively, the association between exposure to police and child maltreatment reports generates a great deal of "spill-over" ensnaring of Black residents in child protective services. The racial geography of child welfare, with CPS cases concentrated in Black communities, results in part from the racist targeting of those communities by police. The symbiotic relationship between law enforcement and child welfare agencies systematically buttresses a police state in Black communities by triggering investigations into family life, reinforcing family surveillance with armed might, and threatening families with both prison and child removal.

Furthermore, engaging law enforcement in child welfare investigations increases the frequency of encounters between Black residents and police officers—encounters that carry a heightened risk of police violence. One of the reasons Black people experience such high rates of brutality at the hands of police is because they come in regular contact with police officers. Including a law enforcement presence in child welfare interactions with Black families adds a layer of potentially violent engagement. When the CPS worker in Aurora, Colorado, called for police assistance, Vanessa Peoples was viciously hog-tied and carried out of her home like an animal.

Taking police officers along on home visits can turn deadly. In 2017, the Baton Rouge, Louisiana, child protection department was investigating allegations of child abuse against a woman who took her toddler son to the hospital with burns. The caseworker assigned to question the woman's boyfriend, Calvin Toney, a twenty-four-year-old Black man, requested an escort from the Baton Rouge Police Department to his home. Toney had pled guilty to child abuse charges in 2014, but his family said he had turned his life around, obtaining a GED and a job working in construction machinery. Footage from the police officer's body camera reveals that the officer was standing off to the side as the caseworker, holding a clipboard, rang the doorbell and Toney let her in. Only then does the officer move forward to follow the caseworker into the apartment. Toney, looking surprised by the officer's sudden appearance, tries to leave. The officer tackles him to the ground in the hallway outside the door, shouting obscenity-laced commands. It is not entirely clear what happened during the struggle that ensued. What is clear is that it ended with the officer fatally shooting Toney. An investigation resulted in no charges being brought against the officer.[9]

Toney was not even a suspect in a criminal investigation, let alone charged with a crime. The officer had no warrant to enter Toney's apartment. There was no child in danger inside. He gained access only because Toney opened the door for the CPS caseworker. By hanging on the caseworker's coattails, the cop gained a reason to confront Toney and to sidestep his constitutional rights. Had the caseworker not rung Toney's doorbell, the young man probably would be alive today.

Protesters across the nation were still calling for justice in the killing of Alton Sterling, a Black man who was shot six times while on the ground by a Baton Rouge police officer less than a year earlier. For young Black men, the risk of being killed by police is shockingly high, and police use of force is among the leading causes of death. In recent years, we have witnessed police killings of unarmed Black men, women, and children when stopped for minor traffic violations, sleeping in their beds during a no-knock raid, being detained for petty offenses like passing a fake twenty-dollar bill, playing with a toy gun in the park, and walking in a suspicious manner. Being investigated by child welfare workers belongs on this list of circumstances that put Black people in danger of lethal encounters with the police.[10]

PUNISHING SURVIVORS

Another sphere where the entanglement of law enforcement and child welfare decreases safety for families is domestic violence. When mothers call the police to report being beaten by an intimate partner, the police often report the mothers to child protective services. Mothers may also be reported by social services agencies they turn to for protection. A plea for help may lead to losing your child to foster care, as Angeline Montauban learned after calling a New York City domestic violence agency while crouched in her bathroom. In some states, it is considered neglect to permit a child to witness violence inflicted on adults in the home or to reside in a home where violence occurs. When a mother calls 911 or a domestic violence hotline to confide that she is being abused, she may be confessing to child neglect.[11]

Across the nation, children are routinely taken from mothers experiencing domestic violence even if the children have not been physically harmed. Mothers are blamed for failing to protect their children even if they themselves are struggling to survive severe abuse in the home. According to a recent *USA Today* investigation, the Florida Department of Children and Families (DCF) "cited domestic violence as the reason it removed more than 3,500 children from biological parents in 2018, an increase of nearly 1,400 from 2013." Domestic violence was the primary reason for a quarter of removals in the state. "DCF considers exposing children to domestic violence as a form of child abuse and holds victims responsible when their kids witness it," the report stated, calling it "a system stacked against women who are abused." A recent comprehensive review of research similarly found that children are more likely to be placed in foster care if the allegations against their parent involved domestic violence compared to other reasons for investigation.[12]

Caseworkers find it easier to regulate the behavior of nonviolent mothers than to discipline their violent partners. The common CPS remedy for intimate partner violence is to coerce survivors to engage in therapeutic services aimed at rehabilitating them instead of taking steps to help the family end or avoid the assaults. The onus falls on the mother to protect herself and her children in the face of a doubly terrorizing situation: fear of the abuser compounded by fear CPS will take the children. Mothers must cease contact with violent partners and obtain orders of protection against them. In some cases, mothers are compelled to leave their homes and find shelter for themselves and their children. The ensuing requirements to attend multiple parent training classes, therapy appointments, and home visits make it all the harder for mothers to ensure their financial security by finding or keeping a job.

Maura Keating, director of litigation at the Center for Family Representation in New York City, calls it a "one-size-fits-all, bullying approach" that gives survivors no say in the plans that are supposed to protect their families. "So many of our clients have their housing by the skin of their teeth," Keating says. Forced to separate from a partner who paid the rent without material assistance from CPS means the family might be driven to homelessness. And recording their names in a child abuse registry may disqualify survivors from employment.[13]

Two decades ago, a landmark case in New York federal court seemed to signal change. In January 1999, Sharwline Nicholson, a thirty-two-year-old Black mother of two young children, waited at her Brooklyn apartment for Claude Barnett, the father of her three-year-old daughter, to arrive from South Carolina. Her daughter was asleep in a crib, and her eight-year-old son from a previous relationship was at school. Nicholson planned to tell Barnett she was breaking off their long-distance arrangement. When she delivered the news, Barnett erupted in rage and began to beat her, battering her face and fracturing her arm and ribs. Nicholson called 911 as soon as Barnett left and asked a neighbor who had babysat for her in the past to take care of her children while she was in the hospital. Three police officers came to her hospital room to inquire about the incident, and Nicholson arranged with them to take her children to stay with relatives while she recuperated. Instead, Nicholson learned the following day, while still hospitalized, that ACS had placed her children in foster care with strangers.

"When I called 911, I was bleeding so badly I knew I needed medical attention," Sharwline Nicholson would recall. "I didn't know I'd end up down that road, that calling for help would escalate and I'd end up losing my kids." ACS took her children despite the fact that they never saw Barnett assault their mother. Besides, Barnett didn't have keys to Nicholson's apartment and lived hundreds of miles away—the reason why a judge had previously denied Nicholson's application for an order of protection against him.[14]

In July 2001, federal judge Jack Weinstein heard testimony in a class action lawsuit brought by Nicholson and other survivors of domestic violence who alleged that New York City child welfare officials violated their constitutional rights by taking custody of their children. During the twenty-four-day trial, April Rodriguez told the judge that ACS had put her three children, ages seven, three, and one, in foster care when she called the police to report abuse by the father of two of the children. The agency refused to return them until Rodriguez moved into a shelter, forcing her to lose her job at a Manhattan video store. Although the children spent only a week in foster care, Rodriguez testified that "they weren't the same children" when they returned. "My baby's shirt was filthy and her diaper was disgusting," she said. "My son, his face was bruised and bloody, and he had pus coming from his lip."

But it was the testimony of Nicholson's caseworker that seemed to turn the case in favor of the survivors. He admitted that the city's policy had more to do with policing the mothers than protecting their children. He didn't consider Nicholson to be neglectful, nor did he bother to file a petition in family court until three business days after he placed her children in foster care. The purpose of taking the children, he conceded, was to coerce Nicholson into compliance. "After a few days of the children being in foster care," he explained, "the mother will usually agree to ACS's conditions for their return without the matter even going to court." It was plain for everyone to see that "ACS is just like the batterers," recalled the lead attorney for the plaintiffs, Carolyn Kubitschek. Once again, child welfare agents took children hostage to assert control over their mothers—at the expense of the family's safety.[15]

Judge Weinstein responded to the testimony in March 2002 by issuing a preliminary injunction in *Nicholson v. Williams*, ordering ACS to stop its practice of removing children solely because their mothers were victims of domestic violence. In a blistering opinion, the judge castigated ACS for blaming mothers who had done nothing wrong instead of providing the means to protect themselves and their children. "As a matter of policy and practice, ACS does not merely fail to advance the best interests of children by these unnecessary separations—they harm children," Judge Weinstein wrote. He concluded, "The removals of abused mothers' children, even when summarily approved by a court based on ACS representations, infringe on mothers' substantive due process rights." The city could no longer "penalize a mother, not otherwise unfit, who is battered by her partner, by separating her from her children," he ruled, "nor may children be separated from the mother, in effect visiting upon them the sins of their mother's batterer." Two years later, a unanimous New York Court of Appeals agreed, holding that parental failure to protect a child from witnessing abuse could not be equated automatically with neglect.[16]

The *Nicholson* case was supposed to radically change New York City's approach to domestic violence and serve as a model for other jurisdictions. But the experiences of Montauban and numerous other survivors tell a different story. In 2018, 25 percent of the fifty-six thousand investigations conducted by ACS were flagged as high priority for domestic violence in the family. Between 2016 and 2018, close to ten thousand children were placed under court-ordered ACS monitoring at least partially because of an allegation of domestic violence. Although child removals based strictly on exposure to domestic violence have decreased, ACS caseworkers have continued to find reasons to monitor survivors and take their children. Even if they don't remove children automatically from mothers who report intimate partner abuse, child protection workers can easily find a related pretext for intervention. Violent partners often control mothers in ways that sabotage the mother's caregiving. They may deny the mother access to needed assets, interfere with her employment, impair her physically, and cause her emotional distress. Any of these deficiencies can become grounds for CPS to charge a mother with vague allegations of neglect, endangerment, or inadequate guardianship. Caseworkers supervising survivors can evade the *Nicholson* ruling by accusing mothers of failing to comply with CPS mandates.[17]

It is no wonder that the child welfare system's punitive treatment of domestic violence survivors endangers them and their children. A 2020 study investigating the impact of laws that mandate reporting of domestic violence found alarming implications involving the child welfare system. The study analyzed a survey of more than two thousand survivors of intimate partner violence to explore how mandatory reporting laws affected their efforts to seek help. The researchers found that reporting requirements often deterred survivors from reaching out for support and reduced their ability to receive the support they sought. When triggered, domestic violence reports made the situation worse for most of the survivors. A third of the survivors surveyed said they did not ask at least one person for help because they were afraid information about the abuse would be reported to authorities.[18]

The survivors were mainly afraid of two types of state inference in their lives: by law enforcement and by CPS. The most common fear was involvement in the criminal punishment system. Many of the women surveyed expressed worry that their partners would be arrested or jailed. Incarcerating a partner could lead to dire consequences, from the abuser's deadly retaliation to losing a critical source of income and a valued relationship. The survivors wanted to end their partners' violence against them, not necessarily their connection to their partners. This finding helps to explain why a CPS requirement that mothers obtain orders of protection and cease all contact with an abusive partner can harm the family—especially when the mother's failure to comply leads to child removal, as happened to Angeline Montauban.[19]

The fear of police intervention also corresponds to Black feminists' opposition to relying on arrest, detention, and prosecution as solutions to interpersonal violence. Black women in the antiviolence movement have warned against participating in a regime that is eager to incarcerate large numbers of Black men but will not invest in resources like housing, education, and employment that would make Black women less vulnerable to violence. They point out that police officers often arrest, injure, and kill Black victims of domestic violence who call them for help. A study of mandatory arrest policies in New York City found that 27 percent of women who called a law enforcement hotline to report experiencing violence were arrested, even though 85 percent of them had been injured. Sixty-six percent of the women arrested were Black or Latina. A grassroots organization called Survived and Punished is devoted to freeing survivors who were imprisoned for defending themselves against a violent partner, like Marissa Alexander, a Black mother who was sentenced to twenty years in prison after she fired a warning shot at her husband who was threatening to kill her.[19]

Second only to fear of criminal legal involvement was fear of losing their children to foster care. "My children would be removed by CPS from my care," one woman stated as the reason she refrained from seeking help. Another feared "that my children would be removed and I would be blamed for everything, or called crazy." Other study participants explained that they dared not reach out for help because it might lead their abusers to follow through on threats to exploit CPS to punish them. Battered mothers in Florida whose children had been removed similarly told *USA Today* that they were afraid to ever call the police again. In one case, a mother lost custody of her children for failing to protect them from witnessing her husband's beatings, yet her husband was granted custody of their daughter. "The thing I regret most is that I ever called 911," said a mother whose children spent eight months in foster care after her boyfriend hit her and brandished a gun. "But I could also have been killed that night. Which one do you pick?" On the other side of the country, a Los Angeles mother whose three children were taken after she sought protection answered this way: "I called the police for help, but I should have just let my husband beat my ass."[20]

The CPS response to domestic violence, often triggered by a police report, makes mothers and their children less safe from the perpetrators of violence in their homes. The child welfare system blames and punishes battered mothers for exposing their children to violence, just as it blames and punishes mothers for other family problems caused by structural inequities beyond their control. A child welfare system that relies on forcing mothers into therapeutic remedies and taking their children isn't capable of providing safety for families. Instead, mothers are victimized twice—not only by their violent partners, but also by law enforcement and child welfare agencies that address domestic violence with a coordinated carceral approach.

"GROUND ZERO FOR THE WAR ON DRUGS"

As we saw with newborn screening, a single positive drug test can instigate CPS to take babies from their mothers and intrusively monitor their lives. Treating drug use by parents as child maltreatment and grounds for investigating families extends beyond the maternity ward. When children are placed in foster care, drugs are often claimed to be a factor. According to the National Center on Substance Abuse and Child Welfare, for 35 percent of all children in foster care nationally in 2016, parental drug or alcohol use was a contributing reason for their removal. A review of federal data from 2012 to 2017 found that 44.2 percent of entries of children under one year old into foster care involved their parents' alleged substance use. These statistics don't mean that in all these cases parents were so dependent on drugs that they were neglecting or harming their children. The children's problems may be unrelated to drug use in the home. Or drug use in the home may not cause any problems for the children. Drug use all by itself is commonly seen by CPS as evidence of bad parenting.[21]

The child welfare system's targeting of parental drug use has become an arm of the government's overall punitive assault on drug possession, especially in Black neighborhoods. In a major report on the topic, the New York City–based Movement for Family Power calls family policing "ground zero for the war on drugs." Even as some states are liberalizing their drug laws, including legalizing marijuana use and allowing its sale, child protection authorities continue to treat drugs as a reason to tear families apart.[22]

It is widely acknowledged today that the war on drugs has been a war on Black people, helping to drive the explosion of the prison population over the last forty years. The discriminatory impact of the child welfare system's drug policy is similar. Although drug use has become a ubiquitous excuse for investigating families, CPS directs its drug surveillance disproportionately at Black communities. "It's only specific people for whom using marijuana while also being a parent is deemed not appropriate," says Miriam Mack, an attorney with the Bronx Defenders. "And that is poor Black and Brown people." Most of us are well aware of wealthy white friends, neighbors, or celebrities who are parents yet make no attempt to hide their habit of smoking marijuana or consuming other mind-altering substances. They have no reason to fear a knock on their door by CPS caseworkers coming to investigate their homes.[23]

Child protection authorities assume that drug use by certain parents is harmful to children on its own. But that assumption is demonstrably false. To begin with, there is no evidence that drinking alcohol or using drugs by itself makes a parent dangerous or unfit. Much of what the public believes about the harms of drug use is based on flawed research or media hype. Psychologist Carl Hart, one of the world's leading experts on the behavioral and neuropharmacological effects of psychoactive drugs in humans, sparked controversy in 2021 when he published his book *Drug Use for Grown-Ups: Chasing Liberty in the Land of Fear*. Hart not only demonstrates empirically the folly of America's policies that vilify and criminalize drug users, but touts his own experiences injecting heroin recreationally to enhance his social and work life. The media, drug-abuse scientists, and government officials have promoted a fictitious view of drugs that exaggerates the minority of detrimental effects while ignoring the majority of benefits. "Over my more than twenty-five year career, I have discovered that most drug-use scenarios cause little or no harm and that some responsible drug-use scenarios are actually beneficial for human health and functioning," Hart concludes.[24]

Hart recognizes that some people who use drugs are addicts (or have a substance use disorder). According to the official psychiatric definition, their drug use must distress them and interfere with important life functions. Nevertheless, Hart argues, it is morally and scientifically wrong to equate any and all drug use with addiction, as if addiction were inevitable. Seventy percent of drug users don't meet the definition of addiction. It is also counterproductive to treat the health problem of addiction with cruel punishments that are ineffective and deter people from getting high-quality health care. Pointing the finger at drugs fails to address the underlying psychiatric and socioeconomic problems that can lead to addiction. It also papers over how the criminal drug laws have enabled federal and state governments to target Black communities for policing, arrest, and imprisonment. You don't have to agree with Hart's endorsement of recreational drug use by adults to accept his argument that not all drug use is harmful. His cogent analysis belies the child welfare system's approach to parents who use drugs as if they are categorically neglectful.

What's more, the equation of substance use with child maltreatment ignores the actual care parents are giving their children. "Often as public defenders in Bronx Family Court, we see family court petitions that only read, 'A parent uses xyz substance, a parent uses marijuana.' No connection whatsoever to the child," Bronx Defender Mack says. "Yet they're hauled into court and their life is regulated." Sometimes, caseworkers will tack on accusations of neglect based on evidence they gathered from inspecting the home and interrogating family members. But the alleged neglect is typically related to the family's lack of material resources—resources child welfare agencies rarely provide. Instead, the agencies typically require the parents to undergo intensive supervision related to their drug use, regardless of its relevance to the family's needs.[25]

As with drug arrests in Black neighborhoods, drug use has become a convenient pretext for branding Black parents as neglectful and trapping them in the carceral web.

WAR ON IMMIGRANT FAMILIES

During the Trump administration, the American public became painfully aware that the federal government was deploying child removal as a weapon to deter migration to the United States. Images of migrant children ripped from their parents and detained in crowded concentration camps flooded the media, evoking widespread condemnation of the inhumane family separation policy. The public is less aware that taking children as an anti-immigration measure extends beyond the southern border. US Immigration and Customs Enforcement (ICE) collaborates with local child welfare agencies throughout the United States, not only to police parents but also to deport them. The coordinated operation of ICE and CPS is yet another way the state tears apart Black and Brown families and sucks them into a carceral machine that encompasses detention centers, jails, and prisons.

Hailing from African and Caribbean nations, many undocumented families are part of Black communities and face discrimination based on their race and immigration status. Between 2012 and 2017, migrants from Haiti were the second most likely to be denied asylum, with odds close to those from Mexico. Jamaicans and Somalians also had high rates of asylum denial. Black immigrants are also the most likely to be targeted for deportation. According to the Black Alliance for Just Immigration, although only 7 percent of noncitizens in the United States are Black, they are 20 percent of those facing deportation based on criminal charges.[26]

Like the collaboration between the child welfare system and police, immigration and CPS officials share information to use against parents. Sometimes all three punitive systems—child protection, criminal, and immigration—conspire to tear families apart. Having an open CPS investigation can be a strike against parents in immigration proceedings. When an undocumented parent is picked up in a raid, the immigration judge may view any child maltreatment allegations CPS brings against the parent as grounds for deportation—even if the criminal case is dismissed. Roshell Amezcua, a family defense immigration attorney at the Bronx Defenders, has known ACS caseworkers to inform law enforcement when they discover that a parent they are investigating is undocumented.[27]

The immigration system also converges with the child welfare system when children who are separated from parents seeking asylum at the border are held in foster care while federal authorities determine the family's fate. The US held nearly seventy thousand migrant children in government custody in 2019. Children who don't have a relative in the United States who is willing to sponsor them—often out of fear of being deported—are typically relocated to federally licensed group homes and shelters. Some are placed with foster families through arrangements with child welfare agencies. Although federal officials promised that children would be held in government custody for only a week or two, migrant children have been held for months or even years.[28]

In 2018, during the Trump administration, the *Washington Post* reported that "new statistics show the government is placing a growing number in long-term foster care, sometimes hundreds of miles from their jailed parents." Some parents are deported without their children, and the long distances between those detained in the United States and the foster care facilities make it unlikely they can be reunited with their children. The children are left in limbo, lingering in foster care indefinitely. A class action lawsuit filed against the US government in 2019 by the families of migrant children seeks hundreds of millions of dollars for harms the children experienced in government custody, including sexual and physical abuse inflicted while they were in foster care.[29]

An Associated Press investigation uncovered cases of migrant parents fighting in state courts to keep their children from being adopted by US families who were supposed to be temporary caretakers. Due process rights protected by the US Constitution apply to all "persons" within the nation's borders, and immigration status alone should not be grounds to terminate the rights of parents who haven't been ruled unfit. Both the Obama and Trump administrations pledged to return children to their parents after splitting them apart at the border. But these safeguards may prove inadequate to ensure that migrant parents can withstand the devaluation of their bonds with their children by state child welfare agencies and judges.

In 2015, during the Obama administration, Araceli Ramos fled El Salvador with her two-year-old daughter, Alexa, to escape a violent partner. In one incident, the man kicked her so forcefully he left a permanent dent in the center of her forehead. At the end of their fifteen-hundred-mile journey, the mother and child crossed the Rio Grande into Texas, where they were arrested by US Customs and Border Protection. A border agent denied Ramos asylum, despite the evidence of domestic violence, when he detected criminal charges in her record from El Salvador, and snatched Alexa from her mother's arms. ICE held Ramos in a detention facility in rural Louisiana. Federal immigration authorities labeled Alexa an "unaccompanied minor"—as if she had crossed the border by herself—and placed her in the care of Bethany Christian Services, three thousand miles away from her mother. Since 2014, Bethany Christian Services, one of the nation's largest foster care and adoption agencies, has contracted with federal authorities to place children in shelters and homes in Maryland and Michigan. According to its website, the Michigan-based global nonprofit arranged for 266 foster families to provide care for 667 unaccompanied children in 2019. Bethany moved Alexa in with a local white family who had joined Bethany's evangelical crusade to address the "global refugee crisis" by fostering children.[30]

In 2016, a federal immigration judge ordered Ramos to be deported; Alexa was to be returned to her mother. But the Michigan couple refused to release the girl. Instead, they filed a petition in state court alleging that Alexa's life would be threatened if she went back to El Salvador with her mother, persuading a judge to grant them continued custody pending a full guardianship hearing. Eventually, after Ramos circulated her story on Facebook and the US Justice Department intervened on her behalf, she was reunited with Alexa in El Salvador. "If they give our children up for adoption without our permission, that isn't justice," Ramos told AP reporters. "They are our children, not theirs."[31]

CAGING BLACK MOTHERS

Black mothers are at the center of another crossroad in the carceral web. The child welfare and prison systems intertwine when parents are incarcerated, and Black mothers suffer the brunt of this collision. Black mothers make up a disproportionate share of women in prison, as well as of parents with children in foster care. As a result of the political choice to fund punitive instead of supportive policies, criminal punishment and child welfare regulation of mothers is pervasive in poor Black communities. Prisons and CPS function together to discipline and control poor and low-income Black mothers by keeping them under intense state supervision and punishing them for the hardships their families face as a result of structural racism and other inequities.

The United States stands out from all other nations on Earth for its reliance on caging human beings. The number of incarcerated Americans increased by nearly 700 percent between 1972 and 2009. Today, two million prisoners are locked up in local jails or state or federal prisons. We have both the largest number of incarcerated individuals and highest rate of incarceration in the world. Like the child welfare system, the prison system is marked by glaring racial disparities. Most people sentenced to prison in the United States today are from politically marginalized groups—poor, Black, and Brown. Not only are Black people five times as likely to be imprisoned as white people, but also the lifetime probability of incarceration for Black boys born in 2001 is estimated to be 32 percent, compared to 6 percent for white boys.[32]

A compelling body of social science research demonstrates how the astronomical escalation of imprisonment inflicts devastating havoc on the neighborhoods where most incarcerated individuals come from and return to. Legal scholar Michelle Alexander demonstrated that mass incarceration functions like a modern-day Jim Crow caste system because it "permanently locks a huge percentage of the African American community out of the mainstream society and economy," replicating the subjugated status of Black people that prevailed before the civil rights era. We can trace today's prison-industrial complex back to the convict-lease system installed after the Civil War to reinstate the white power regime and exploit Black people's labor. Southern states targeted Black men, women, and children for imprisonment by passing laws known as Black Codes, which criminalized their everyday lives, including appearing in public without adequate reason. Police picked up Black men and women on trumped-up charges and consigned them to toil on chain gangs or leased them to coal mines, railroads, and plantations until they met an early and miserable death. A similar white backlash against the civil rights movement launched the war on drugs and extreme sentencing policies that incarcerated large segments of Black communities. Mass imprisonment of Black people is a way for the state to exert direct control over poorly educated, unskilled, and jobless people who have no place in the market economy because of racism and capitalism, while preserving a racial caste system that was supposed to be abolished by civil rights reforms.[33]

One of the most powerful ways prison exerts this oppressive function is through its devastating impact on families. Locking up Black mothers and fathers transfers racial disadvantage to their children. "The collateral effects of mass incarceration cut through the immediate family fabric first, then penetrate the entire extended family for generations," writes journalist Sylvia A. Harvey. More than half the people caged in the nation's prisons and jails are parents of minor children. By 2007, there were 1.7 million children in America with a parent in prison, more than 70 percent of whom were children of color—an 82 percent increase since 1991. The number of children with a mother in prison more than doubled during that period. A decade later, close to six million children in the United States had experienced having a parent behind bars. In 2018, one in ten Black children had a parent in prison, making them six times more likely to have an incarcerated parent than white children. By age fourteen, one in four Black children born in 1990 had a parent imprisoned, compared to one in twenty-five white children.[34]

Imprisoned parents can no longer take care of their children either physically or financially. Children are deprived of the emotional support and guidance parents provide. Incarceration deprives millions of children of important material and social support from their parents, placing extra economic and emotional burdens on remaining family members. A 2015 study revealed that children whose parents were incarcerated suffered a host of negative educational outcomes as well; after controlling for poverty and other social factors, the researcher found that children with parents in prison "were less happy in school settings than their counterparts, achieved lower grades in adolescence," and attained lower levels of education in adulthood. Separation from imprisoned parents also has serious psychological consequences for children, including depression, anxiety, feelings of rejection, shame, anger, and guilt. One study found that children of incarcerated mothers experienced a trauma from the separation so profound that they displayed symptoms of post-traumatic stress disorder (PTSD).[35]

Most incarcerated women are mothers. Although there are far fewer incarcerated women than men, women are the fastest-growing segment of the prison population—and Black women are the most overrepresented group behind bars. Black women's incarceration hike surpasses that of Black men; their incarceration rate is double that of white women. Between 1985 and 1991, there was an astounding 828 percent increase in the number of Black women behind bars for drug offenses. In California, with more people behind bars than any other state, Black women make up close to 30 percent of the female prison population but only about 6 percent of women in the state. For most of these women, prison constitutes a culminating victimization that results from multiple forms of vulnerability and violation, including domestic violence, sexual abuse, drug addiction and other health problems, and homelessness.[36]

Most incarcerated mothers were convicted of nonviolent drug-related offenses or property crimes. As a result of harsh sentencing laws, they receive long prison terms for these relatively minor offenses. Women who depend on public assistance to care for their children are increasingly treated as criminals. Accusations of welfare fraud are brought as felony charges and punished with prison terms, rather than as administrative violations garnering civil penalties. Tens of thousands of Black women in prison today need treatment for a substance abuse problem, support for their children, or safety from an abusive partner instead of being caged. Putting Black mothers behind bars also strains the extended networks of kin and friends that have traditionally sustained Black families in difficult times, weakening communities' ability to withstand economic and social hardships and opening them to greater child welfare surveillance.[37]

The same mythology about Black maternal depravity legitimizes the massive disruption that both prison and child welfare systems inflict on Black families and communities. The mythology is reinforced when these systems leave the impression that Black mothers are prone to commit crimes and neglect their children. As Angela Y. Davis observed, the prison-industrial complex "relies on racialized assumptions of criminality—such as *images of black welfare mothers reproducing criminal children*—and on racist practices in arrest, conviction, and sentencing patterns." Stereotypes of maternal irresponsibility re-created by the child welfare system's disproportionate supervision of Black children help to sustain mass incarceration, and stereotypes of Black female criminality help to sustain family policing.[38]

Incarcerating large numbers of Black mothers and fathers throws thousands of Black children into foster care. It is impossible to calculate based on current data-collection systems precisely how often parental imprisonment itself causes foster care placement. Some incarcerated parents had their children taken prior to entering prison. Recent research demonstrates, however, a significant link between locking up Black parents and sending their children to foster care. It is safe to estimate that, in the last decade, tens of thousands of children were placed in foster care solely because a parent was imprisoned. The escalation of imprisonment between 1985 and 2000 has been tied to the growth of the foster care population during that period. Today, children are taken from their families and placed in foster care most frequently in states with higher incarceration rates. A 2016 analysis of Wisconsin administrative data discovered that 28 percent of children involved in the Milwaukee child welfare system between 2004 and 2012 had a parent in jail or prison within a year of their contact with CPS.[39]

The astronomical rates at which Black men are imprisoned contribute to Black families' intense involvement in the child welfare system. Locking up fathers diminishes family economic stability, caregiving capacity, and emotional support, putting more strain on Black mothers as they care for their children under already daunting conditions. Although the relationship between CPS involvement and paternal incarceration in the United States is understudied, an analysis of Danish data suggested that putting fathers in prison doubled children's risk of foster care placement. But incarcerating mothers has a greater and more direct impact on custody of children. The 2016 analysis of Milwaukee data found that "female prisoners are substantially more likely to have a CPS-involved child following their incarceration and black prisoners are disproportionately likely to have CPS-involved children." Many of these children end up in foster care.[40]

Black children aren't being put in foster care because their mothers went to prison for abusing or neglecting them. Most child maltreatment allegations are based on neglect that isn't serious enough for a prison sentence; it is extremely rare for mothers to be incarcerated for child abuse or neglect. The crimes committed by most mothers in prison were not against their children. Putting mothers behind bars results in foster care placements because mothers are typically the primary—if not sole—caretakers of their children, and child welfare authorities treat their imprisonment as neglect. Child welfare and prison policies come together to make it extremely tough for incarcerated women to retain legal custody of their children.

Prisons degrade parenting by incarcerated women in multiple ways. Even while giving birth, mothers are commonly devalued by prison administrators who insist on shackling them during labor. In many states, when pregnant prisoners go into labor, they are routinely chained to a hospital bed, their legs, wrists, and abdomens shackled together throughout the entire delivery of their babies. Prisoners enduring labor under the watchful eye of a guard pose no threat of flight. Strapping them down only intensifies the labor pains and can cause serious physical injuries. The only reason for restraining birthing prisoners this way is to torture them. Immediately after delivery, their newborns are automatically taken from them in the vast majority of states.[41]

Incarcerated mothers are much more likely than incarcerated fathers to be living with their children when they are sent to prison, often providing their children's sole economic and emotional support. About one-third of incarcerated mothers were living alone with their children when they were arrested, compared to only 4 percent of incarcerated fathers. Therefore, when mothers go to prison, the father often is not readily available or offered assistance to care for the children, increasing the chances of foster care placement. Children of imprisoned mothers must usually leave home. Relative caregivers who fill in for incarcerated mothers receive little government support, and most can't meet the increased caregiving expenses, let alone the cost of keeping the children in touch with their mothers. Many families don't have the financial, social, and emotional wherewithal to raise children of incarcerated relatives, and the only option available is foster care. What's more, a felony conviction often disqualifies family members from becoming legal caregivers, making it more likely that the children will be placed in foster care with strangers.[42]

Losing a parent to prison or jail is traumatic for a child; having to endure it while in the custody of strangers can be devastating. A Black mother from a Northeastern city who spent six years in prison told researchers the toll her incarceration had on her children:

> Two of my children lived in foster care for four years of my incarceration, and they're very angry. I left when they were 13 and 11, and they're 16 and 18, and they're still very angry. My son, he was six, and he's 11 going on 12, and he cries, and he's frustrated, and he can't tell me why. They're angry. They're very hurt. They know that I was taken from them for no reason. . . . My 20-year-old, she's 26 now, she had to step up and be a mom, a parent to five other kids. My other daughter had a nervous breakdown, and the oldest one tried to commit suicide since I've been gone. And then, my 16-year-old, she just tried to commit suicide.[43]

It is extremely hard for incarcerated mothers to hold on to legal custody of their children who have been placed in foster care. As we have seen, child welfare authorities typically mandate that parents complete a "service plan" with onerous requirements that are unrelated to the family's needs. Incarcerated women are expected to meet conditions that are challenging even for people living in the community. They are supposed to participate in case planning and court hearings, stay involved in their children's lives, attend parenting classes and therapy sessions, and ensure that stable employment and housing will be available following reunification with their children. The conditions of incarceration coupled with the inhumane policies of the prison and child welfare systems make it practically impossible to meet these requirements from inside prison walls.[44]

Barriers to spending time with children while in prison are a chief threat to later reunification. Child welfare agencies usually construe a parent's failure to visit and communicate with children as abandonment. Despite—or because of—being the primary caretaker of their children before arrest, incarcerated mothers are less likely than fathers to have family visits. When fathers are imprisoned, the mother usually

continues as the child's primary caregiver. She may maintain a relationship with the father while he is in prison and help him keep in
touch with the children. Mothers who are locked up find themselves at
the mercy of the substitute caregivers—whether relatives, friends, foster caretakers, or CPS staff—to maintain contact with their children.[45]

Most prisons are located in remote areas far away from where imprisoned mothers used to live. The cost of traveling long distances, including bus fare or gas, hotel, and time away from work, usually thwarts
personal visits. Child welfare agencies don't provide the means to take
children in foster care to visit their mothers in prison. Even telephone
calls to prison, which are typically saddled with exorbitant fees and
charges, may be too expensive for regular communication. Kinship
caregivers may not be able to afford these costs, and non-kin foster
caretakers may be less willing to put in the extra effort and expense.
Relatives and foster parents are discouraged further from arranging
visitation by the complicated and time-consuming logistics prison authorities make them navigate. As a result of all these obstacles, most
mothers in prison receive no visits at all from their children.[46]

Mothers risk permanently losing custody of their children because
judges consider it in children's best interests not to wait for their mother's release to issue a permanent custody decision. James Dwyer, a law
professor and zealous opponent of efforts to keep struggling families
together, believes courts shouldn't "hold a child hostage" while parents
are in prison. He argues that children who are placed in foster care before they are two years old should be put up for adoption immediately.
Dwyer also advocates that cities should be "zoned" for child protection
so that some "horrible" neighborhoods are declared "unfit" for child
rearing because they have high rates of poverty, drug use, and crime.
Many lawmakers and judges agree that parents forfeit their relationship with their children when they are imprisoned. Some states relieve
child welfare agencies from the duty to provide reunification services
in the case of parents who are convicted of felonies. Incarceration itself constitutes statutory grounds for termination of parental rights in
some states. The risk of termination was increased by the 1997 Adoption and Safe Families Act (ASFA), which places foster children on a

"fast track" to adoption. Child welfare authorities often point to the law's swift timetable for termination proceedings as grounds for severing incarcerated mothers' ties to their children. A 2003 study discovered that the number of cases terminating incarcerated parents' rights more than doubled in a few years after ASFA was enacted.[47]

Prison officials have no obligation to transport parents to family court hearings. Imprisoned parents may learn after the fact that a judge terminated their rights without a chance to defend themselves in person or say goodbye to their children. Judges often permanently fracture families without ever meeting the parents in court. A review of all San Francisco child welfare adoption files from the years 1997 and 2007 highlighted how frequently courts terminate the parental rights of incarcerated Black mothers and put their children up for adoption. Mothers were the primary caretakers of the children in all the adoption cases, and Black mothers were disproportionately represented. Only 2 percent of the mothers with a history of incarceration attended the court hearings in which their children were taken, reunification requirements were imposed, or their parental rights were terminated. Most of the parents were not represented by a lawyer. The findings paint a portrait of absolute disregard for the family ties of imprisoned mothers.[48]

According to a Marshall Project analysis of about three million child welfare cases between 2006 and 2016, at least thirty-two thousand parents were stripped of their rights while in prison without being accused of physical or sexual abuse, though neglect related to their poverty may have been involved. Of those, nearly five thousand appear to have lost their children permanently on account of their imprisonment alone. "Mothers and fathers who have a child placed in foster care because they are incarcerated—but who have not been accused of child abuse, neglect, endangerment, or even drug or alcohol use—are more likely to have their parental rights terminated than those who physically or sexually assault their kids," the Marshall Project's Eli Hager and Anna Flagg concluded. Given the exceptionally high percentage of Black children who have a parent behind bars, this annihilation has a severe impact on Black families in particular.[49]

The assault on their families continues even when imprisoned mothers are able to keep legal custody of their children. The penalties inflicted on formerly incarcerated people pose another set of impediments to these mothers maintaining a relationship with their children once they are released from prison. A host of state and federal laws places draconian obstacles in the path of even petty drug offenders by denying them federally funded benefits, public housing, education assistance, and job opportunities. Federal law imposes a lifetime ban on cash aid and food stamps to applicants with a felony drug conviction. Although individual states can opt out of this prohibition, most fully or partially enforce it. Housing insecurity is one of the chief reasons CPS takes children from their parents. The Anti-Drug Abuse Act of 1988 and the Quality Housing and Work Responsibility Act of 1998 make it even harder for mothers convicted of drug offenses to find a place to live. Under these laws, public housing authorities and landlords accepting Section 8 subsidies can deny leases to people tagged by criminal background checks. Mothers who can't afford rent or are excluded from housing assistance after they exit prison often end up living in homeless shelters.[50]

Another hurdle Black mothers must overcome is finding a job. Employers in most states can reject applicants who were convicted of a crime. Nearly every application for a job, regardless of the skills required, asks people with criminal records to "check the box." In a stunning 2003 study, sociologist Devah Pager set out to determine the consequences of incarceration for the employment prospects of Black and white job seekers—what she labeled "the mark of a criminal record." She conducted an audit experiment in which matched pairs of four male testers, two Black and two white, applied for entry-level jobs. Pager randomly assigned and rotated one of the Black testers and one of the white testers to have a criminal record and had them pursue a variety of actual job openings in Milwaukee. Pager discovered that a criminal record had a large and significant impact: even for white testers, a criminal record reduced the likelihood of a callback by 50 percent.[51]

But Pager's most striking finding was that white testers *with* criminal records were treated more favorably by employers than Black testers *without* criminal records. "Race continues to play a dominant role in shaping employment opportunities, equal to or greater than the impact of a criminal record," Pager concluded. Added to this racial discrimination, the effect of a criminal record was 40 percent larger for the Black testers than their white counterparts. Formerly incarcerated Black mothers searching for a job encounter triple discrimination on account of their race, gender, and criminal convictions. To make matters worse, they are disqualified from licenses for many occupations held predominantly by women, such as child care workers, certified nurse's aides, and beauticians. With no job, public assistance, or stable housing, many mothers released from prison find it impossible to meet agency demands for reuniting with their children.

Sociologist Susila Gurusami spent eighteen months in the early 2010s getting to know formerly incarcerated Black mothers who participated in a women's reentry program in Los Angeles. She witnessed how the mothers had to contend with a myriad of obstacles after leaving prison that complicated reuniting with their children. Even after serving their prison terms, the mothers were at the mercy of CPS caseworkers and parole or probation officers who "had the power to effectively interrupt their roles as mothers" by taking their children away or sending them back to prison or jail. "Fear of the foster care system structured parenting for all the mothers I spoke with," Gurusami observes.

Tragically, the work it took for mothers to comply with time-consuming state requirements often interfered with the work required to care for their children. Not able to afford childcare, mothers had to scramble to find someone to watch their children while they attended numerous mandatory appointments. They refrained from getting help for mental health and substance use problems for fear of seeming unfit to child welfare authorities. Their valiant efforts to keep their children safe from police violence, neighborhood predators, and other dangerous living conditions—what Gurusami terms "decarceral mother-work"—often undermined their ability to meet agency demands. CPS frequently interpreted their strategies for safeguarding their children as noncompliance and potential grounds for taking their children away from them. An especially pathological aspect of family policing is the way it punishes Black mothers for their fierce protection of their children.[52]

The convergence of prison and foster care in many Black women's lives means losing custody of their children permanently—for many mothers, the ultimate punishment the state can inflict. We must include state severing of family ties as a major penalty imposed by incarceration. It is one of the most brutal ways the carceral and child welfare systems unite to persecute Black communities.

———

IN AUGUST 2021, TYRON DENEER, A BLACK MAN WITH A BEARD and dreadlocks, broadcast an Instagram Live video showing armed deputies from the Manatee County Sheriff's Office detaining him, his partner Syesha Mercado (a former *American Idol* finalist), and their ten-day-old baby. The deputies had pulled the family's car over to the side of a highway to execute a family court judge's order to seize the couple's newborn daughter. The family's nightmare began in February of that year, when Mercado and Deneer took their thirteen-month-old son to a hospital in St. Petersburg, Florida, to seek medical care. Pregnant at the time, Mercado was having trouble transitioning the toddler from breastfeeding to eating solid foods and was concerned that he was dehydrated. Hospital staff called the child maltreatment hotline to report that the toddler was malnourished and failing to thrive, and the Department of Children and Families (DCF) took him from his parents.[53]

Because Mercado and Deneer were under CPS supervision when their daughter was born six months later, DCF considered the newborn to be at risk. The couple had hired an attorney to advocate for the return of their son and was embroiled in court proceedings, which led to the judge's "pick up" order to the sheriff's office. The video Deneer posted shows Mercado holding the infant wrapped in a pink blanket as she walks slowly from her car toward three white women who appear to be CPS staff, as if she were a condemned convict walking to the gallows. Mercado pauses in front of the workers.

"Do you not feel anything?" she asks the women desperately. "You guys, I'm human. This is my baby. My baby is days old and you're taking my baby away from me. You're taking my baby away from me. You have no heart."

As Mercado hands over her daughter, she pleads with the women once more: "My baby is healthy and happy. My baby is breastfeeding from me. What are you going to give my baby?" When the child began to cry, Mercado grows more distraught. "You're traumatizing my baby. . . . You have created so much trauma. . . . I'm not a danger to my baby. It's so wrong. It's so wrong." Then she collapses into Deneer's chest, weeping inconsolably.

With the help of the viral video, a team of lawyers, and media attention, Mercado and Deneer were reunited with their daughter nine days later while they continued to fight to recover their son. The terror inflicted by the armed officers who surrounded the peaceful family and the cruelty displayed by the CPS workers who tore the infant from her loving mother leave no doubt that the joint incursion was aimed at criminalizing the parents, not protecting their child.

NINE

STRUCTURED TO HARM

A TOXIC INTERVENTION

During lunchtime on April 29, 2020, a sixteen-year-old Black boy named Cornelius Frederick threw a slice of bread in the cafeteria at Lakeside Academy, the residential facility in Kalamazoo, Michigan, where the state child welfare department had placed him after his mother died and his father was unable to care for him. Lakeside boarded about 125 state wards who were considered to have behavior problems. Its management and staff were supplied by a for-profit corporation called Sequel Youth and Family Services, one of many private enterprises hired by child welfare agencies across the nation to operate their foster care programs. Workers watching the children quickly responded to the infraction by forcing Cornelius to the floor and holding him down, pressing their weight into his chest, abdomen, and legs for nearly ten minutes as the boy lost consciousness. Children who witnessed the incident said that as the men restrained Cornelius, he cried repeatedly, "I can't breathe, I can't breathe." A nurse on staff stood by the unresponsive teen, failing to offer him CPR or any other aid. Then she waited twelve minutes before calling 911 for medical assistance.[1]

Cornelius suffered cardiac arrest and was put on life support at the hospital, where he also tested positive for the COVID virus. He died on May 1. The local medical examiner ruled his death a homicide caused by "restraint asphyxia." That same month, on May 25, Minneapolis police officer Derek Chauvin murdered George Floyd by pressing his knee into Floyd's neck as the dying man uttered the same words Cornelius had: "I can't breathe." In June, the Michigan Department of Health and Human Services issued a blistering sixty-three-page report on its licensing investigation of Lakeside Academy, which cited numerous violations committed by the facility's employees. In words that depict a torture scene, the report disclosed that staff had put Cornelius in a similar restraint the previous January: "The resident was observed to stop moving or struggling within approximately 4 minutes of the restraint, however the restraint continued with unsafe positioning, in excess of 30 minutes, with up to 7 staff holding the resident." The state terminated its contract with Sequel Youth and Family Services and shut down Lakeside Academy. Only a year before, the corporation had closed two of its facilities in Utah as officials there investigated allegations of sexual abuse and violence inflicted on children they housed.[2]

We have seen how child welfare agencies collaborate with police departments, immigration authorities, and prison administrators to expand carceral control of Black communities. Although these alliances operate in the name of protecting Black children, they actually pull Black children into the state's punitive machinery. The trauma that children experience from being torn from their parents, siblings, and friends is compounded by conditions in foster care that continue to disrupt every aspect of their lives. Foster care is a toxic state intervention that inflicts immediate and long-lasting damage on children, producing adverse outcomes for their health, education, income, housing, and relationships. Black children trapped in foster care are also more vulnerable to arrest, detention, and incarceration—and early death.

It is hard to defend the US criminal punishment system when it locks up Black children in juvenile detention facilities and in adult prisons at rates every other nation would find unfathomable. Although the number of children confined by the juvenile justice system today is half its 2007 peak, more than forty-eight thousand children were locked in residential facilities on any given night in 2019. Black children were detained at nearly five times the rate of white children. Every year, seventy-six thousand children are prosecuted, sentenced, and imprisoned as adults. Although Black children comprised less than 15 percent of the child population in 2018, 52 percent of those prosecuted as adults were Black. The odds of a Black child receiving an adult prison sentence are nine times greater than for a white child.[3]

In the 2021 US Supreme Court decision *Jones v. Mississippi*, the conservative majority ruled, six to three, that judges may sentence children to life imprisonment without the possibility of parole. That means children as young as thirteen can be condemned to die in prison. Once again, this aspect of America's cruelty to juvenile offenders is marked by racism: 62 percent of children serving life without parole are Black. The public accepts this travesty because it fits the American affinity for caging people as punishment for crimes and the view of Black children as undeserving of compassion.[4]

The asserted rationale for tearing large numbers of Black children from their parents and relegating them to foster care is quite different, however. Black children are placed in foster care not to punish them for crimes they committed but purportedly to rescue them from maltreatment their parents are inflicting on them. For this logic to stand, state custody must make Black children better off than if they had been left with their parents. The government should be able to show that foster care puts Black children on a different trajectory, away from poverty, homelessness, juvenile detention, and prison and toward a brighter future. In this chapter, I demonstrate that the child welfare system does precisely the opposite. Foster care operates to contain Black children who are seized from their homes in conditions that crush their spirits and wreck their well-being. In the next chapter, I focus specifically on how foster care is structured to treat Black children as juvenile delinquents and to drive them into a prison-industrial complex designed to foreclose their chances for the future. Foster care criminalizes Black children.

DISPOSABLE CHILDREN

On March 26, 2018, Jennifer and Sarah Hart packed their six adopted children into the family's gold GMC Yukon SUV for a drive along the Pacific Coast Highway, with Jen at the wheel. The white married couple had adopted the two sets of Black siblings after CPS took the children from their homes and placed them in foster care. Jen stopped at a gravel pullout, then accelerated toward a cliff, deliberately plunging the car onto the rocks a hundred feet below. The two women and all six children—Markis, nineteen, Hannah, sixteen, Devonte, fifteen, Abigail, fourteen, Jeremiah, fourteen, and Sierra, twelve—perished.

Investigators trying to make sense of the mass murder-suicide discovered it was the culmination of prolonged child abuse in the Harts' home. The couple had bamboozled friends, neighbors, and child welfare authorities in three states for a decade. The women crafted a fake diorama of domestic bliss using the Black children as captive performers and casting themselves as their white redeemers. Jen meticulously curated a Facebook feed with photos of the children as they posed in endearing scenes in order to draw a social media following. Meanwhile, the couple subjected the children to routine and sadistic torment, isolating them from real contact with the outside world, starving them, and beating them with belts and their fists.[5]

In their comments, the Harts' devoted Facebook followers constantly refer to the women and their adopted children as "the perfect family." The couple convinced everyone that they had rescued the children by milking the twin tropes of virtuous white saviors and depraved Black mothers. Jen claimed that Devonte was born with "drugs pumping through his tiny body," and, by four years old, had "handled guns, been shot at, and suffered severe abuse and neglect." Yet there were numerous signs that the children were being victimized by their adoptive mothers. In September 2008, two years after she was adopted, Hannah, six, told a teacher that the bruises on her arm were from being whipped with a belt. After police investigated, the couple took Hannah and her two siblings out of school. Two years later, when Abigail was six years old, she told her teacher that Jen held her head under cold water and hit her after accusing her of stealing a penny. It was Sarah who pleaded guilty to misdemeanor domestic assault, and the couple pulled all the children out of school for good. CPS continued to receive calls reporting that the children were being denied food and subjected to cruel punishments. One night, Hannah showed up at the house next door to the Harts after escaping out a second-floor window, pleading to her neighbors, "Don't make me go back! They're racists, and they abuse us!"[6]

A photo Jen posted on Facebook shows three of the children dressed only in underpants sitting on a wood floor spread with newspapers. Each child is splattering colors on a sheet of paper from sticks dipped in open paint cans resting beside them. "Sometimes it feels good to crank up the tunes, shed your apparel, and throw your emotions onto canvas. Mini Jackson Pollocks going to town," Jen wrote. The cheery message stands in jarring contrast to the emaciated children in the picture, their ribs poking out and their arms and legs resembling toothpicks. When I saw the photo in a magazine article, my mind immediately went to the television commercials seeking donations for relief agencies that show images of starving African children. I wondered if the white Facebook followers were so accustomed to those images that the painting scene reinforced their view of the Harts as progressive saviors instead of raising concern about the children's well-being.[7]

Another photograph Jen posted went viral. Circulating on social media and television was a picture taken at a 2014 Black Lives Matter protest in Portland, Oregon, of a Black boy wearing a rust-colored leather jacket and sky-blue fedora hugging a white police officer as tears streamed down the boy's face. The boy was Devonte Hart. Isabel Wilkerson writes in *Caste: The Origins of Our Discontents* that when she saw the photo she detected something "deeply unsettling" about his face, which looked "contorted in anguish." "He did not have the carefree look of a child, nor the affectionate cheer of someone offering hugs to strangers," she recalls. While many people, like Wilkerson, were troubled by the sight of a distraught Black boy clutching a white cop, many others were comforted by its message of racial reconciliation. "People saw what they wanted to see and not the agony in the face of a

12-year-old boy who had the body of an 8-year-old due to starvation," writes Wilkerson. "People saw a picture of Black grace when what the world was actually looking at was an abused hostage."[8]

Devonte's death is made all the more tragic by the fact that his aunt, Priscilla Celestine, fought for more than two years to adopt him and his brother and sister, before a Texas judge handed the children to the Harts instead. Their mother, Sherry Davis, had lost custody of the children because of her drug addiction, and she and Clarence Celestine, father of two of the children, relinquished their parental rights in 2006, expecting Clarence's sister Priscilla to adopt the children. Priscilla, who had been caring for the children, had a clean record, a steady job as a receptionist at a hospital, and a five-bedroom apartment, but she ran afoul of child welfare authorities when a caseworker discovered Sherry watching her children while the aunt was at work. Arriving unannounced, the caseworker grabbed the children on the spot, telling them to kiss their mother goodbye. It was the last time Sherry saw them.[9]

Despite multiple investigations into evidence of maltreatment, the Harts were never separated from their adopted children. They repeatedly explained away their abuse by attributing the family's problems to defects the children had inherited from their mothers. The tragic ending resulted from "the latitude granted these white saviors to abuse children seen as throwaways," Wilkerson concludes. The deaths of the six Black children, though seemingly extreme, reflect a fundamental problem with the way the state treats Black children after taking them from their homes. Foster care compounds the lie that Black parents are incapable of caring for their children with the belief that Black children are damaged and disposable.

I am sure there are many people who become foster parents to provide a caring home for children until they can be reunited with their parents. In Black communities, grandmothers and aunties, like Priscilla Celestine, do their best to tend lovingly to children whose parents are unable to, typically without adequate support from the child welfare department. But these kindhearted foster parents exist in a system that operates based on perverse financial incentives, secrecy, and disruption. The foundational conditions of foster care are a formula for traumatizing children. The state forces children suffering from painful separations from their families into the hands of substitute caretakers—usually complete strangers—who often have unstable connections, lack oversight, and may be motivated strictly by the monetary rewards reaped from the arrangement.

ON THE MOVE

Foster caretakers typically don't develop strong bonds with the children they are paid to watch. One of the most egregious yet common ordeals imposed on foster children is moving them to multiple placements while in the state's care. Sociologist Nicole Rousseau describes the instability in foster homes she witnessed as a social worker. "I cannot count the number of times I rushed to work because the office secretary had called and told me a foster parent had dumped a child off at the front door of the agency when the doors opened," Rousseau recalls. "When I'd arrive, the child would always be sitting, all of his or her worldly belongings next to them in a trash bag, just waiting. Waiting for someone to take them to wherever they would sleep that night."[10]

Sometimes children spend only a few months, or even a few days, in a home or facility before being uprooted and transferred to another unfamiliar setting. The US Department of Health and Human Services sets the national standard at no more than four placements per one thousand days in foster care. Moving a child to a new home or facility more than once a year seems excessive enough, but states frequently fail to meet this goal. In 2019, 60 percent of children stayed in foster care for longer than twelve months, with the odds of moving increasing with time. In California, 44 percent of children who are in foster care for twenty-four months or longer experience three or more placements. The *Tampa Bay Times* reported that a child in Hillsborough County, Florida, moved more than fifty times in 2016, tossed between foster families, group homes, and the Salvation Army. That year, another Hillsborough child stayed in over forty-three different locations, with more than half lasting only two days or less. A lawsuit filed in 2019 by three organizations—National Center for Youth Law, Children's Rights, and Kansas

Appleseed—against the Kansas Department for Children and Families for violating the rights of foster children cited the case of a child who was relocated to 130 different placements.[11]

Athena Garcia-Gunn entered foster care as a teenager to escape the dangerous chaos that overtook her family when her mother died and her father turned to drugs to treat his depression. She discovered, however, that foster care imposed its own insecurity, shuffling her to eight different foster homes over the course of six years. "I was accustomed to instability, but no one really tells you about the mental abuse that the foster care system will put you through," Athena explained in a moving TEDx talk in 2017. "How you become more unstable than you probably were before. How you become a liability and you're bound by all these regulations for your 'well-being' and your 'safety.' How you really are treated like you're disposable: you really are given a trash bag—that's not just a story they tell. You are made to feel like you are temporary, and to not get too comfortable because you're not family."[12]

Children in foster care are more likely than average to enter the system with chronic health problems, stemming from the conditions of poverty and barriers to high-quality health care. Black children start out in poorer health than white children. The disruptions caused by foster care only make health issues worse and more difficult to treat. In addition to causing extreme psychological stress, moving children among multiple placements interrupts their medical appointments, the transfer of their medical records, and their relationships with health care providers. Doctors, foster caretakers, and caseworkers may fail to coordinate; foster caretakers may lack training for meeting children's particular medical needs or may simply neglect them; children may encounter long wait times for services; and state-run Medicaid programs may provide inadequate services or reimbursements.[13]

Serial displacement also impairs children's success in school. It is common for children to miss school days when they enter foster care because their enrollment is stymied by the need to transfer records. Children not only tend to switch schools when they are first placed in foster care, but also typically experience multiple school changes while in state custody. Each change may mean misplaced school records and adjusting to a new educational environment while also getting used to a new home. As a result, studies in cities nationwide have found that a third or more of foster youth report repeating a grade. For many, this educational instability means never completing high school.[14]

In Los Angeles County public schools, for example, Black children in foster care have the worst chronic absenteeism rate: they are twice as likely as the average Los Angeles County student to be chronically truant. They are also the most likely of all students to be placed in special-education classes and to be suspended, with one in six Black students in foster care experiencing suspension, compared to a 2 percent overall suspension rate. Only half of Black students in the LA foster care system graduated on time during the 2018–2019 school year. These dismal findings, reported by the UCLA Black Male Institute in October 2020, show that Black children in foster care "are being disenfranchised at almost every turn of their educational experiences," note Brianna Harvey and Kenyon Lee Whitman, two of the UCLA researchers.[15]

MASS CHILD ABUSE

Child protection workers often pull children from loving parents for being exposed to marijuana, living in insecure housing, or missing school, only to confine them to foster homes and facilities where they are physically and sexually abused. Whereas caseworkers monitor parents with voracious intensity, they devote far less oversight to the foster settings where they relegate the children. They are quick to remove children from their homes for minor parental mistakes yet slow to intervene when they learn that children are being harmed by the people hired to care for them.

The very same conditions that caseworkers deem too risky for children when present in their own homes are often overlooked when they exist in foster placements. In 2012, a ten-year-old girl with autism drowned in an open pond behind a Florida foster home, where a private agency had placed her despite noting the safety hazard. Another ten-year-old girl in Minnesota was sexually abused by her foster mother's adult son, who had moved back into the home and whose criminal record, according to state regulations, should have disqualified the placement. A two-year-old girl died from heat stroke in Massachusetts in 2015 while in the care of a woman who had four foster children, in addition to two of her own, although the home was licensed to foster only three, a physician had expressed concerns that she was overwhelmed by her children alone, and she had been reported twice for child maltreatment. An eleven-month-old infant died in 2017 while sleeping overnight in a car seat in a New Mexico foster home that was in disrepair, reeked of a foul odor, and lacked adequate bedding. In that instance, a caseworker had left the child and her two siblings there temporarily after taking them from their parents because the family was homeless.[16]

Many studies conducted since the 1980s have shown that children are much more likely to be maltreated in foster care than in their homes. To take one example, an analysis of Baltimore CPS records for the years 1984 to 1988 conducted by researchers at Johns Hopkins University and University of Maryland found that foster families had seven times the frequency of physical abuse reports compared to non-foster families. Moreover, foster homes had double the likelihood that a physical abuse report would be substantiated. At the time, 80 percent of the children in Baltimore's foster care system were Black.[17]

Physical and sexual abuse occur in all types of placements, whether private homes, group homes, or residential treatment facilities. Children who are moved to multiple placements may be assaulted by different adults or other foster children in each new setting. A study of young adults who had spent time in foster care in Washington State and Oregon found evidence in the case files that one in three had been abused by an adult in the foster home. Because this figure didn't account for abuse that was never officially reported or that was committed by other foster children, it is no doubt an undercount of the violence the children actually endured. In a follow-up study in Michigan, 29.2 percent of the adults formerly in foster care reported being neglected while in foster care, 21.5 percent reported experiencing physical abuse, and 12.3 percent reported experiencing sexual abuse. The researchers noted that these figures, too, likely reflected a reluctance of the participants to divulge the full extent of maltreatment they suffered. A 2020 *USA Today* investigation into Florida's child welfare system found rising numbers of allegations of abuse, neglect, and abandonment of children in foster care since 2015, as "caseworkers placed kids in dangerously overcrowded homes with foster parents who later faced civil or criminal charges of sexual assault and torture." In a 2021 follow-up investigation, the journalists discovered that abuse of foster children was more widespread than previously reported because the Florida child welfare department failed to count many incidents in its public figures—often renewing the licenses of abusive foster caretakers despite documented harm to children.[18]

TORMENTING LGBTQ CHILDREN

Foster care for gay and transgender children is almost uniformly nightmarish. LGBTQ children are more likely to be housed in congregate settings than their non-LGBTQ peers because child welfare agencies find it harder to locate foster homes for them. "I had to be placed in a residential facility under emergency shelter because there weren't any affirming placements available that would want to take a gay Black teenager," recalled twenty-two-year-old Weston Charles-Gallo, testifying before the US House Ways and Means Committee in 2021. These youth commonly report horrendous accounts of daily harassment and violence by bullies—abuse that is ignored or encouraged by agency staff or inflicted by staff members themselves.[19]

"I had at least two fights a day. The boys used to do stupid things because I was gay, like throw rocks at me or put bleach in my food," recounts Mariah Lopez, a transgender woman who lived in multiple group homes beginning at age eight. She continues:

> Once I was thrown down a flight of stairs and I've had my nose broken twice. They even ripped up the only picture of my mother that I had.
>
> Often the staff were bad, too. If I had had a fight with one of the staff earlier in the day, they would start conversations with the

other boys in the group home about the argument just to get them riled up, and then the boys would come up to me, challenging me and calling me names like f-ggot. Sometimes the staff would stand there while the kids jumped me. One time a staff member jumped me with the kids.[20]

"I would always have a butcher knife inside under my pillow because I didn't trust people," recalls a gay Black teen about his time in a group home. "I always felt that someone was going to try to attack me, so the only way I felt safe was with weapons."[21]

Foster caretakers frequently subject LGBTQ youth to inhumane isolation, discipline, or rejection for behavior they perceive as offensive, including attempts to "cure" their sexual or gender identity. State-accredited foster caretakers in a focus group described bisexual foster youth as "confused" because of assumed sexual abuse, and gay youth as sinful and dangerous because they were believed to be prone to committing sexual abuse. "I believe in all children deserving a home but you cannot watch them every second," one foster caretaker stated. "Being gay, you have less opportunities for sex and you might take it out on my own child." One foster caretaker explained why he called the social worker to remove a gay foster child from the home: "He never did anything to my grandbabies but as soon as I heard him on the phone with his boyfriends, that was it. I knew right then that he had the potential to hurt them and he had to go."[22]

The law in some states segregates foster children by gender or requires that homes and facilities where foster children above a certain age are housed provide separate bedrooms and bathrooms for boys and girls. Transgender children are typically misgendered and placed according to their sex assigned at birth, not their gender identity, mismatching them with their placements. State child welfare agencies' attempts to protect cisgender girls in foster care from rape by separating them from men and boys can fail to protect transgender girls (who are grouped with boys and male staff) from violence. Group-home staff routinely force gender nonconforming children to dress and act in ways that don't match their identities and punish them when their behavior violates gender norms. "When I was in a group home, I lost points because I didn't have long hair or wear dresses," a former foster child named Captain reports. "Even my mannerisms got me into trouble. The staff would tell me I wasn't 'talking like a lady' or that I was being 'too gentlemanly' when I opened doors for girls. They wouldn't let me be me because to them, I was outside of the gender boundaries they were comfortable with."[23]

The routine violence and discrimination against LGBTQ children in foster care results in catastrophic harm. A 2015 study of foster care in Los Angeles County reported that LGBTQ youth "are less satisfied with their child welfare system experience, are more likely to experience homelessness, are moved around to more placements, and are experiencing higher levels of emotional distress compared to their non-LGBTQ counterparts." A subsequent analysis of a nationally representative sample of youth in foster care found that those who identified as lesbian, gay, or bisexual (LGB) had a substantially higher risk of mental health and substance abuse problems than non-LGB foster youth, and were more than three times more likely to have run away in the prior six months. Child welfare authorities largely stand indifferent to the dehumanizing practices that endanger LGBTQ children in their care and implement policies that foment them. In June 2021, in *Fulton v. City of Philadelphia*, the US Supreme Court ruled that requiring a Catholic social service agency to approve same-sex couples as foster caretakers violated the nonprofit's First Amendment rights. Nevertheless, new statistics showing that youth who identify as LGBTQ make up as much as one-third of the foster care population in some cities have generated increased attention to the cruelty many of these children suffer while in state custody.[24]

DEATH BY FOSTER CARE

Foster care's systematic harm to children results in their death at horrifying rates. A major study of mortality statistics between 2003 and 2016, published in the *Journal of the American Medical Association Pediatrics* in 2020, found that the rate of death was higher for children in foster care than children in the general population across every age category, except for children aged fifteen to eighteen. Overall, children in foster care are 42 percent more likely to die than children who aren't in foster care. During that study period, mortality rates for children generally declined each year, but mortality remained constant for children in foster care—meaning the gap in death rates was widening. Although the researchers were unable to determine whether or not the experience of foster care itself caused the excessive deaths, they noted that less than half of the deceased foster children had a prior medical condition. At a minimum, the prevalence of deaths in foster care reinforces the evidence that the state does a terrible job of protecting the health and safety of children it forces into its custody.[25]

On January 22, 2017, a fourteen-year-old Black girl named Naika Venant began broadcasting on Facebook Live from the bathroom of her foster home in Miami Gardens, Florida. For two hours, she narrated to her followers why she no longer wanted to live. Then she hanged herself with a scarf in the shower stall in front of the live camera.[26]

Naika was first placed in foster care at age six, after her mother hit her with a belt and CPS became concerned that the little girl displayed "inappropriate sexualized behavior." Florida authorities returned Naika to her mother the following year and reported that the child said she had been raped in the foster home. Naika, a pretty girl with long hair, had a troubled relationship with her mother, Gina Alexis, who gave birth to Naika in Haiti at age seventeen. Alexis twice relinquished Naika to child welfare services when she felt unable to handle her daughter's emotional problems. Naika traveled back and forth between her mother and foster homes until she was placed in foster care for good at age thirteen. At the time she took her life, Naika had been shuttled between foster homes, group homes, and shelters fourteen times in the prior nine months. She attempted to run away and asked one of her foster caretakers to kill her because she didn't want to be in foster care. She had a pending criminal case arising from her recent arrest at her foster home. She told a caseworker she was "acting up" so she would be sent back to her mother. Four months before she took her life, Naika texted her mother, pleading to be reunited: "I wanna make this work betwn us," she wrote. "Tell me what I gotta Do & iLL Do iT Im Tired Of Us Fighting We Needa Make This Work Im Ready for Us to be a Team AGAIN."[27]

Suicide is perhaps the most heartbreaking sign of suffering foster care inflicts on children. Children in foster care are four times more likely to try to kill themselves than children in the general population. In a study of more than seven hundred children in California's foster care system, 41 percent reported they had thought about suicide, and nearly one in four had attempted it. Psychologist Lily Brown, director of the Center for the Study and Treatment of Anxiety, at University of Pennsylvania, recommends universal suicide screening of children in foster care.[28]

Suicide is extremely rare among preadolescent children, yet shockingly common among those in foster care. Over a quarter of foster children aged only nine to eleven in a Denver-area study exhibited suicidal thoughts and behaviors. In 2018, Hennepin County, Minnesota, paid $1.5 million to the grandmother of Kendrea Johnson, a six-year-old Black girl who hung herself with a jump rope from her bunk bed after being taken from her mother and placed in a foster home. Her grandmother alleged in a federal civil rights lawsuit that she had "lovingly and competently" cared for Kendrea in the past and had tried to gain custody of her, "but was informed by Hennepin County that her home was too small." Instead, Kendrea was put in a foster home where the caretaker's response to the girl's severe depression and repeated suicidal thoughts was to lock her in her room. Although Kendrea was eventually diagnosed with PTSD and referred to therapy at a "day treatment program," she remained in the same foster home and never got the kind of psychiatric care she needed.[29]

The child welfare system is clearly failing to heal whatever traumas children have when it places them in foster care. Like Naika, they may enter foster care because of their mental health challenges, which child welfare authorities promise—but fail—to treat. In fact, the high rates of suicidal thoughts among foster children suggest that being in foster care creates extreme mental distress that exacerbates many children's existing mental disorders and creates severe problems for others. Some children find foster care so unbearable they take their own lives. A 2020 review of the research on foster children's mental health concluded that "as many as half of children in foster care have clinically significant mental health difficulties while in care," with foster children being three to four times more likely to be diagnosed with a mental health disorder than children not in foster care from similar socioeconomic backgrounds. Another recent study based on caregiver reports found that children in foster care fared worse on every mental health outcome examined, including ADHD, depression, anxiety, and behavioral problems, than children in the general population. Because these results held true after controlling for child and household characteristics, they indicate that foster care itself has a detrimental impact on mental health.[30]

Instead of meeting children's psychological needs, agencies often cycle them through multiple foster homes or therapeutic facilities when their crises persist, only aggravating the problem. Children with clinically significant trauma symptoms are more likely to have unstable placements than others in foster care, especially if they are Black, older, male, or have any type of disability. And a 2020 study found that the likelihood of suicidal ideation—thinking about committing suicide—increased by 68 percent each time children experienced a foster placement. A 2017 US Senate investigation discovered that Illinois foster children in a private company's care waited an average of 122 days before receiving any contact with a therapist. In Florida, children were moved to new placements without ever having received court-ordered services. "Mental health was never really addressed. It was this vague, loose conversation to mark off on a box," explains Athena Garcia-Gunn in her TEDx talk. "This lack of regard for your mental, core emotional well-being is what I think makes or breaks a lot of foster youth, because foster care is so unstable, and foster care really does perpetuate all of the traumas you came in with and then gives you more while you're in it."[31]

The child welfare system also deals with the traumas it inflicts on children by drugging them. Foster children are given mind-altering medications ten times as frequently as low-income children living with their families. When Gabriel Myers hanged himself at age seven in a Florida foster home in 2009, it was revealed that among the psychotropic drugs prescribed for him was the antipsychotic Symbyax. Symbyax is not approved for children younger than ten, and one of its side effects is suicidal thoughts. In *Silent Cells: The Secret Drugging of Captive America*, sociologist Anthony Hatch ties together the forced administration of psychotropic drugs to Black adults in prison and to Black children in foster care, arguing that psychotropics have become central to various forms of "mass captivity within the U.S. carceral state." In prisons, psychotropic drugs are the most common type of mental health treatment, as well as a routine way to maintain order. In foster care, they are similarly used as "chemical straitjackets" to restrain children, in place of high-quality mental health care. "What if the new plan for governing and controlling the millions of people forced to live in captive America is to move them from their institutional cells to new locations *inside their own brain cells*?" Hatch asks provocatively. Tranquilizing children to mask the trauma inflicted by foster care and to pacify the rebellion it kindles is another carceral weapon the family-policing system wields against Black communities.[32]

HURT THAT LASTS A LIFETIME

In addition to its immediate toll, foster care has long-term consequences that gravely handicap children for the rest of their lives. Young adults who experienced foster care fare poorly on every measure of well-being, from health to education, employment, housing, and incarceration. A 2014 nationwide study found that former foster youth had a significantly higher risk of poor health outcomes, such as ADHD, asthma, cardiovascular disease, and other chronic problems, compared to both economically secure and economically insecure adults in the general population. Members of the foster care group also were more likely to lack insurance or Medicaid compared to those of the economically insecure group. Adults who experienced foster care as children, the researchers summed up, "have a higher risk of multiple chronic health conditions, above and beyond that which is attributable to economic insecurity." A 2012 study of adults in California similarly discovered that, even after adjusting for socioeconomic variables, those who had been in foster care were three times more likely to receive Social Security Disability Insurance or to report missing work during the preceding year due to health problems, suggesting an association between adult health status and morbidity and "a very specific adverse childhood event: placement into foster care." People who spend time in foster care have PTSD at almost twice the rate of US war veterans.[33]

In 2005, Casey Family Programs, one of the leading organizations working to improve child welfare, issued a major report on outcomes for young adults who had experienced foster care in Oregon or Washington State. Noting that "relatively few studies have examined how youth formerly in care ('alumni') have fared as adults," researchers with the Northwest Foster Care Alumni Study (the "Northwest Study") reviewed records of 659 adults who had been in foster care between 1988 and 1998 and interviewed 479 of them. The findings were dire: the foster care alumni had dramatically worse mental health, education, and employment outcomes than their counterparts who were never in foster care. The alumni had double the rate of mental illness and PTSD, were three times more likely to be living in poverty, and were fifteen times less likely to have finished college. Only 20 percent of the adults who had spent time in foster care were "doing well." As Richard Wexler, executive director of the National Coalition for Child Protection Reform, puts it, foster care has an 80 percent failure rate. We would not stand for such abysmal results from a doctor we trusted to improve our health or a builder we hired to renovate our home.[34]

There is some conflicting evidence on how foster alumni view their time in the system. Two years after the Casey report, Chapin Hall, a leading child welfare research institute at the University of Chicago, released a study of 591 twenty-one-year-old former foster youth in Illinois, Iowa, and Wisconsin. The Midwest Evaluation of the Adult Functioning of Former Foster Youth (the "Midwest Study") found similarly disturbing evidence that the young adults were not "doing well." For example, half of them reported at least one indicator of economic hardship in the past year: not enough money to pay rent or a utility bill; gas or electricity shut off; phone service disconnected; evicted. Despite their difficulties, however, 62.2 percent of the participants felt "satisfied with their experience in foster care," while 29.8 percent of their peers disagreed or strongly disagreed with that characterization. Although the Midwest youth seemed to have had a better experience than the Northwest youth, the difference may lie in the question asked. It's possible to be satisfied with poor outcomes if one's expectations are low. "During youths' formative years, the system repeated to them that there was nowhere else for them to go," notes a 2021 report on interviews with foster youth who experienced congregate care. "This killed youths' imaginative capacity to envision what could lie beyond institutional placements." Besides, a nearly one-in-three dissatisfaction rate is still a failing score.[35]

Casey Family Programs followed the Northwest Study with a smaller investigation of foster care alumni in Michigan. This time the researchers interviewed sixty-five adults in their twenties who had spent at least one year in foster care. Its findings, released in 2012, painted an equally alarming portrait of life after foster care. The young adults had spent an average of five years in foster care, and half of them had been moved to eight or more placements. Nearly a third reported running away from their foster homes at least once, while one in ten ran away five or more times. Health problems were common. Half reported having at least one mental health problem in the prior year, and a quarter reported having a chronic mental or physical health condition that required regular medical care. Most of the alumni were also struggling financially. Only 26.2 percent were working more than thirty-five hours per week. Two-thirds were living below the poverty line, less than half had health insurance, and nearly half reported being homeless or "couch surfing" since leaving foster care. The Michigan foster care alumni, like their Northwest counterparts, were not "doing well."[36]

FOSTER CARE IS WORSE

Many Americans are aware of these dismal outcomes for children who spend time in foster care. But they shrug off this awful reality by thinking it's less worrisome than the reality foster children would face at home. Proponents of foster care attribute its failures to the maltreatment and social disadvantages these children experienced before entering foster care. "Foster care isn't perfect," many tell themselves. "But it's still better than the terrible circumstances the children were rescued from." This rationale for foster care is shored up by the assumption held by many white child-savers that Black parents are so dysfunctional that relocating their children must produce at least some marginal improvement.[37]

The claim that foster care improves Black children's welfare has been demolished by recent research. The evidence is clear that putting children in the foster care system is itself harmful. Foster care does not just fail to remedy Black children's predicament; it makes Black children's predicament worse. Although few studies examine whether foster care causes greater harm to Black children in particular, we know that Black children are more likely to be placed in a harmful foster care system and to receive inferior services while in state custody. Foster care magnifies the societal barriers and assaults that Black children already face because of other forms of structural racism.

A 2006 study by researchers at University of Minnesota sought to correct the limitations of prior research by determining if foster care had a direct impact on child development apart from any disadvantages children brought from their homes. The team compared the development of behavior problems over time in forty-six children who were placed in the foster care system and forty-six children who were identified as maltreated but remained with maltreating caregivers. Although the children in the foster care group were developmentally similar to those in the maltreated group before they were placed, they began to exhibit an increase in behavior problems immediately upon entering foster care, which persisted after they returned home. "The increase in problematic behavior following departure from foster care significantly exceeded change in behavior problems among those reared by maltreating parental figures," the researchers found, "suggesting an exacerbation of problem behavior in the context of out of home care." In short, children exited foster care with more developmental problems than they had when they entered—and worse problems than the children who were left at home.[38]

Subsequent studies reinforced the conclusion that placing children in foster care impairs their developmental health. A 2015 project performed a series of meta-analyses of eighty-one studies published over the preceding three decades to examine what their combined findings revealed about the developmental outcomes of children in foster care. The researchers were dismayed by the results. "Contrary to our expectations," they wrote, "we found that generally foster children did not improve their functioning during their stay in foster care." Indeed, studies with larger sample sizes and time spans longer than a year showed a negative impact on adaptive functioning, suggesting that "adaptive functioning of children may deteriorate during their stay in foster care." The researchers found it "worrisome" that their analyses exposed that "foster care is incapable of reducing these problems or of improving the development of foster children."[39]

Joseph Doyle, a leading expert on the economics of government policy, has accumulated some of the most compelling evidence that foster care itself makes children worse off. Amazingly, before Doyle began his research, little attention was paid to whether placing maltreated children in foster care was actually beneficial or harmful for their life outcomes. To find out, he analyzed large datasets to compare outcomes for children on the margin of being taken from their parents to see which children have better outcomes: those who remain at home or those who are put in foster care. Doyle published the results of his first landmark study into "whether abused children benefit from being removed from their families" in a 2007 issue of the *American Economic Review*. Using a dataset that links children in Illinois with a wide variety of government programs, he estimated the causal effects of foster care placement on longer-term outcomes, including juvenile delinquency, teen motherhood, and earnings, for fifteen thousand children in Chicago between ages five and fifteen who were investigated for maltreatment from 1990 to 2002. Reflecting racial disparities in Chicago's child welfare system, Black children made up 76 percent of the sample, although they were only 26 percent of school-age children in Cook County.[40]

Doyle found that the children placed in foster care fared worse than those who remained at home on every outcome. The foster children had three times the juvenile delinquency rate and twice the teen birth rate, as well as lower earnings. Doyle noted limitations of the study design: it dealt with children at the margin of foster care placement and didn't consider whether foster care helped or harmed children in more extreme cases. Nevertheless, the results "suggest that large gains from foster care placement are unlikely for this group of children at the margin of placement, at least for the outcomes studied here," Doyle concluded. Rather, he observed, these children "tend to have better outcomes when they remain at home." Moreover, because the children who were left at home likely received inadequate resources from child welfare agencies, his findings understate the positive effects that could be achieved for children if their families were generously supported. Later, using the same Illinois dataset, Doyle investigated whether foster care kept children physically safer in the short term than being left at home. He found that emergency health care episodes were three times as likely for the children living in foster care.[41]

Taken together, Doyle's research indicates that foster care not only sets children up for adverse life outcomes in the future, but also endangers children in the present. These findings that taking children from their parents makes many worse off than if they had remained at home adds to other compelling evidence that foster care is bad child welfare policy. "Black children could be described as involuntary subjects in a government experiment in child rearing with no evidence that they have received any benefit from it," I wrote in *Shattered Bonds*. Two decades later, we have the proof that foster care not only fails to benefit Black children but in fact directly harms them.[42]

PERVERSE INCENTIVES

The mothers I interviewed in Chicago's Woodlawn neighborhood blamed the financial motives of some foster caretakers and the failure of DCFS to keep an eye on them for the poor quality of care received by foster children in their neighborhood. A common criticism of foster care was that caretakers tended to be neglectful because they were in it "just for the money." "Foster people don't give a care about them kids. All they want is the money, you know," a forty-eight-year-old mother told me. "And then a lot of times you see foster kids with foster parents, and the kids look like some thrift store reject, you know. And you get money for these kids. Ain't no way they should look like they look." The government prefers to pay substitute caretakers over providing income and other material supports directly to mothers in impoverished Black neighborhoods. Although Congress restructured welfare in 1996 by ending the federal entitlement to public assistance for children, foster care remains a well-funded entitlement program. The stipends paid to foster caretakers far exceed welfare benefits, and the monthly foster care payment is multiplied by the number of children in the foster home care, instead of the marginal increase per child provided under Temporary Assistance to Needy Families (TANF). Some states deny any increase in TANF payments at all if the mother became pregnant while already on welfare.[43]

The pernicious financial incentives of individual foster caretakers pales in comparison to the huge amounts made by private entities that operate many foster care systems. Over the last several decades, state child welfare departments have increasingly outsourced foster care services to private, for-profit corporations and nonprofit organizations, like the one responsible for Cornelius Frederick's death at Lakeside Academy. Privatizing foster care was seen as a market-based solution to the flaws in state-run systems. Competitive bidding by private entities to win lucrative contracts with child welfare departments was supposed to reduce government spending, increase efficiency, and improve service quality. After removing children from their homes, the state pays the private companies a monthly fee for each child placed in a company-run foster home or residential facility. The companies, in turn, recruit, screen, train, and pay foster caretakers, assign children to foster placements, and monitor the children's well-being, then pocket the balance of the fees left over. Florida, Kansas, and Nebraska depend entirely on private agencies to run their foster care systems. Other states, like California, which paid about $400 million for private foster care services in 2013, entrust substantial numbers of children to private management.[44]

These financial arrangements with private entities "introduced a powerful incentive for some to spend as little as possible and pack homes with as many children as they could," reported the *Los Angeles Times* after investigating abuse of foster children in California's private foster system. When enterprises—for-profit and nonprofit alike—are in the business of placing foster children in homes or facilities where caring for them is the sole source of income and income is the sole motivation, children can easily become commodities exploited by all the parties for monetary gain.[45]

When BuzzFeed News and *Mother Jones* exposed the 2013 murder of a blonde toddler in Texas at the hands of her foster caretaker, the stories caught the attention of Congress. In April 2015, the Senate Finance Committee, chaired by Utah Republican senator Orrin Hatch, launched a two-year bipartisan investigation into the failure of private companies to protect the children in their care. Its six-hundred-page report, *An Examination of Foster Care in the United States and the Use of Privatization*, presents a chilling portrait of rampant cruelty inflicted on children the state had relegated to its greedy corporate partners. The committee found that, despite monitoring procedures state agencies claimed to have in place, "these policies are not always followed; exceptions are made, waivers are granted, profits are prioritized over children's well-being, and sometimes those charged with keeping children safe look the other way." Overloaded public agencies and private companies seeking to maximize revenue operate like mercenaries whose mission is to kidnap children, then wash their hands of the captives once they hand the children over to accomplices.[46]

The committee focused on National Mentor Holdings, the largest for-profit foster care company in the nation, as a case study. Founded in Boston in 1980, Mentor had grown large enough to manage foster homes for more than ten thousand children spread over eighteen states. In 2006, the politically connected hedge fund Vestar Capital Partners bought out Mentor and, in 2014, began trading it on the New York Stock Exchange under the name Civitas Solutions, Inc. That year, the company reported $1.2 billion in revenue. In states that ban for-profit companies from securing contracts for foster care services, Mentor arranged with its nonprofit sister organizations, Alliance Human Services and Alliance Children's Services, to hire it as a subcontractor to run the operations, including recruiting, training, and monitoring foster caretakers. Although Mentor boasts on its website to offer "an array of quality, community-based services," the Senate uncovered "a company that prioritizes profits over children's well-being; a company that skirted corners when screening foster parents, that increased social workers' caseloads, that hired unlicensed workers, and whose primary mission was to 'fill beds' in order to increase company profits."[47]

The tragedy that triggered the Senate investigation was the 2013 murder of two-year-old Alexandria Hill by Sherill Small, a foster caretaker hired by Mentor. Texas child welfare authorities had removed the child at age one from her parents because they smoked marijuana and had "limited parenting skills," and because the mother suffered from grand mal seizures. Within a year of separation from her parents, Alexandria had been moved from her first foster home, where she had been neglected, and was already showing signs of distress in her second placement, with Small. A Mentor caseworker noted that Alexandria was pulling out so much of her hair that she was going bald in spots. Small began taking in foster children in September 2012, after she lost her job as a school bus driver; by December, all five of the children in her care prior to Alexandria had been removed as "failed placements." Small reported to Mentor "feeling stressed out" by fostering children. On a hot day in July 2013, Small put Alexandria in a "time out," making her face a wall in a dark room in the garage that everyone called a man cave. Small was annoyed that Alexandria had awakened before her that morning and had taken food and water from the kitchen. Later that day, Small swung Alexandria so violently that her head crashed into the floor, crushing her skull. As Alexandria lay dying in the hospital, Texas officials returned custody to her distraught parents so they could make the decision to take their daughter off life support.[48]

The Senate investigation uncovered that Mentor's horrendous neglect of the children parceled out to foster homes spread far beyond the death of Alexandria Hill. In numerous cases, Mentor failed to take steps either to protect foster children from harm or to investigate tragedies that occurred under its watch. After Alexandria Hill's murder, Texas regulators charged Mentor with more than one hundred serious violations committed from 2013 to 2015, including children being beaten, restrained, and forced into "inappropriate" sexual contact by adults in foster homes. Mentor ran a foster care compound on Maryland's Eastern Shore called Last Chance Farm, where it paid four related couples to keep foster children in their homes. For years, Mentor ignored the children's stories of being subjected to sexual assaults at the farm, as well as a warning letter expressing "extreme concern" about one of the foster caretakers, Stephen Merritt, that was sent to Mentor in 2010 by a psychotherapist. Mentor disregarded the red flags and renewed Merritt's foster care license a month after receiving the psychotherapist's letter. Merritt later pleaded guilty to eight counts of sexual offenses against minors who were in his care.[49]

As with Alexandria Hill, Mentor's slipshod care of foster children sometimes turned deadly. Mentor submitted to the Senate Finance Committee ninety-eight "level 4" incident reports dating from 2005 to 2014, which recorded the most serious occurrences of injury, assault, and abuse. An astounding eighty-five involved the death of a child in Mentor's care. The Senate investigation found evidence that Mentor actively covered up the deaths of foster children so it could continue placing children in dangerous homes for profit. The company conducted internal investigations in only thirteen of the fatalities. Incident reports were plagued by missing, inconsistent, and inaccurate information. Mentor paid millions of dollars in legal settlements to dozens of families of child victims. Its devious attempts to evade accountability make one wonder how many other families lost children to deadly abuse in foster homes, let alone the numbers of foster children who survived, scarred for life by the pervasive violence.[50]

Caseworkers hired by Mentor explained that the company was so fixated on extracting profits from foster children that it lost sight of protecting them. "You feel the pressure. You have to make those targets," a former worker told BuzzFeed News. "I went there because I care about services for kids. I eventually became a machine that cared about profits. I didn't care about kids." Each foster placement represents increased revenue for companies like Mentor. On one hand, there is every incentive to recruit more foster caretakers in order to place more children and to retain the money-generating arrangements regardless of the consequences for children. On the other hand, there is little incentive "to seek out reasons to reject a family, to investigate problems after children are placed, or to do anything else that could result in a child leaving the agency's program," says Roland Zullo, an expert on foster care privatization. Foster homes and residential treatment beds become money-making inventory to be expanded at all costs—even the deaths of children.[51]

At the sentencing hearing for Stephen Merritt, his lawyer presented another damning perspective on Mentor's culpability. Even though Merritt committed the crimes out of low cognitive capacity, she argued, Mentor deliberately sought out Merritt and put children in his care: "Because nobody else wanted these children and the Merritt home was an easy scapegoat, they continued to place the children year after year after year, ignoring disclosures of the victims, ignoring all of the warning signs that were there."[52]

We should also ask: what is the culpability of state child welfare departments that are ripping children from their homes only to leave them in the care of private enterprises with track records of child abuse? The Senate investigation uncovered widespread indifference to the well-being of children, a stunning lack of oversight of private foster care providers, and a clear pattern of putting children at risk of severe—even lethal—harm. The government officials in charge of the system are ultimately responsible for the mass abuse of children in state custody. Yet, even after the Senate committee uncovered a pattern of violence perpetrated against foster children, it did no more than recommend greater federal and state oversight to address "these shortcomings"—leaving in place the system whose fundamental philosophy and structure invite exploitation of the children shoved into it.[53]

Whereas the Senate's investigation and the media surrounding it highlighted cases involving white children, we should remember that Black children are more likely to experience these horrors in foster care—not only because Black children are thrown in foster care at higher rates, but also because government officials have historically cared less about their well-being. Deaths of Black children neglected by private foster care agencies have also caught the media's attention. It was the murder of Viola Vanclief, a two-year-old Black girl who had been placed by the Los Angeles agency United Care in the home of Kiana Barker, that led to the *Los Angeles Times* investigation into California's private foster care system. According to the newspaper, Craig Woods, a former carpet and hair care products salesman, started United Care in 1989 to benefit from the spike in state demand for foster homes for Black children taken from their parents during the crack epidemic.[54]

In 2010, a heavily intoxicated Barker beat Viola to death. United Care had ignored numerous prerequisites intended to protect children from dangerous foster homes. Barker and her live-in boyfriend both had been convicted of felonies. There were six complaints to the child abuse hotline lodged against them, and one was substantiated by the county child welfare department. The caseworker assigned to monitor Viola's well-being was overseeing more cases than state regulations permitted as she juggled three jobs at different foster care agencies. The county, United Care, and Barker were collaborating to get Viola adopted by Barker—which would mean a windfall of $10,000 for United Care and increased monthly payments for Barker. After Viola was buried in an unmarked grave, Barker was convicted of second-degree murder and United Care paid a $150 fine, the maximum penalty allowable.[55]

The child welfare system's treatment of children in its custody is appalling yet should come as no surprise: it is the predictable consequence of a system aimed at oppressing Black communities, not protecting Black children. The problem is not just that agencies bypass the procedures that are supposed to keep foster children safe; the problem is that foster care is inherently unsafe for children.

TEN

CRIMINALIZING BLACK CHILDREN

THE THIN LINE

On April 20, 2021, thirteen-year-old Ja'Niah Bryant called 911 for help. She and her sixteen-year-old sister, Ma'Khia, were being threatened by two women who used to live at the foster home in Columbus, Ohio, where they had been placed. "We got Angie's grown girls trying to fight us, trying to stab us, trying to put her hands on our grandma. Get here now!" Ja'Niah pleaded. When officers arrived twelve minutes later, they encountered several people engaged in a chaotic melee in front of the house. One of the officers stepped out of his car, shouting, "Get down, get down." At that moment, Ma'Khia, rainbow crocs on her feet and a steak knife in her hand, ran in front of the officer as she chased a woman, backing her against a car in the driveway. The officer fired at Ma'Khia four times, and she collapsed to the ground. She died at the hospital later that day from gunshot wounds to her chest.[1]

To many people, the police body-camera footage, showing Ma'Khia charging at a woman with a steak knife, seemed to justify the shooting. It looked on the surface as if the officer had saved the woman's life by stopping a violent attacker. But how did a teenage girl end up in a situation where she felt so threatened that she wielded a knife to protect herself?

In 2018, a judge ruled that Ma'Khia and her three younger siblings were neglected by their mother, Paula Bryant, and the children went to live with their paternal grandmother, Jeanene Hammonds, in her two-bedroom apartment for a little over a year. When the landlord discovered that the children had moved in, however, the family was evicted. Rather than help find housing that could keep Hammonds and her grandchildren together, Franklin County Children's Services put the four children in foster care. In December 2019, Hammonds filed a petition to regain custody of her grandchildren but was denied when the agency claimed she "does not understand the children's special needs" and she failed to facilitate their counseling sessions. The department also rejected Bryant's efforts to recover her children on grounds that she, too, fell short of meeting its prerequisites. Most of the children in the county's foster care system were identified as African American, like the Bryant siblings, or "multiracial."[2]

Ma'Khia and Ja'Niah were bounced between six different foster and group homes in two years, at first split apart, but later reunited at the foster home of Angela Moore on Valentine's Day, two months before Ma'Khia was killed there. Things were tense between Moore and the children she cared for. Three weeks before Ma'Khia's death, a girl called 911 from the house to complain about fighting there. "I want to leave this foster home!" she shouted to the dispatcher in desperation. Moore called police at least seven times between July 2018 and April 2021 to report foster children who had gone missing from her home.[3]

On the day of the shooting, Ma'Khia and Ja'Niah got into an altercation with two women, ages twenty and twenty-two, who had previously lived at the house and had come over while Moore was at work. The women berated the teenagers for not cleaning the house and, according to Ja'Niah, threatened to beat them. Hammonds raced to the house when Ja'Niah called her for backup. Hammonds says Ma'Khia grabbed the steak knife after one of the women brandished a knife first.

To her friends and classmates, Ma'Khia was a quiet and caring girl. To her teachers, she was a hardworking honor roll student. She had a penchant for inventively styling her curly hair, which she displayed in tutorial videos posted on TikTok. "She taught us how to love ourselves," one friend said. No one recognized the girl they saw on the body-cam footage waving a knife. Ja'Niah recalled how much Ma'Khia hated foster care and longed to return home. "We can go to Mommy or Grandma, it doesn't matter, as long as we can get off the system," Ma'Khia told her younger siblings. She had hoped for the family to be reunited before she "aged out" of the system—when the child welfare department would abandon custody of her because she turned eighteen. Instead, her exit from foster care was the result of a police officer's bullet.[4]

Just as the child welfare system entangles Black parents in a carceral web, so it throws many Black children into encounters with police officers and on a path to arrest, detention, and imprisonment. For Ma'Khia Bryant, foster care put her in a volatile situation that led to her death at the hands of police. There is a thin line between treating Black children as innocent victims in need of protection and treating them as delinquents in need of discipline. In some cities, the juvenile courthouse is divided into two sections. On one side, judges decide dependency cases involving children whose parents are charged with abusing or neglecting them. On the other, judges decide juvenile delinquency cases involving children charged with breaking the law. The Black adolescents and teenagers who were placed in foster care by judges on one side of the courthouse are often the same ones who are consigned to juvenile detention by judges across the hall.

When the juvenile court was first established, at the turn of the twentieth century, the line between dependency and delinquency was completely blurred for Black children. Excluded from white child welfare agencies, Black children whose families could not support them were labeled as delinquent. An eleven-year-old Black girl named Mary Tripplet was ruled to be a delinquent by Chicago's juvenile court in 1899 solely because she was an orphan. She was ordered to be admitted to the Illinois Industrial School for Girls at Geneva, where Black girls lived in segregated quarters and were treated with extra cruelty. Judges and guards denied them the assumptions of femininity and innocence accorded their white female counterparts. Today, although the state officially adjudicates Black children who are maltreated or delinquent through separate systems, their statuses can easily switch. This is not to say that Black children placed in foster care deserve to be treated well and those charged with offenses deserve to be treated poorly. Rather, the thin line between them shows that both systems are similarly structured to punish Black children, not to protect them. This chapter shows how the thin line between dependency and delinquency criminalizes Black children: foster care both treats Black children as if they were criminal offenders and pushes them into the criminal punishment system.[5]

TREATED LIKE DELINQUENTS

One way that the child welfare system criminalizes Black children is to compel those in foster care to live in violent and prison-like settings. Despite the popular image of rescued children living peacefully in private homes with caring foster "parents," the conditions of foster care are often quite the opposite. Large numbers of children are placed in some form of congregate care, whether group homes with a handful of children, dormitory-style facilities with dozens of residents, large "residential treatment centers," which may house more than a hundred adolescents and teens, or psychiatric hospitals. About fifty-five thousand foster children, mostly teenagers, are placed in group settings each year, and about one in five children will live in one at some point while in substitute care. In 2017, a third of teenagers in foster care were in a congregate placement. Black teens are much more likely than white teens to be placed in these environments that bear little resemblance to families.[6]

Group homes foment violence by cramming traumatized teens and staff—all strangers to each other—into one space while the teens are struggling to cope with extremely stressful life circumstances. Children interviewed for a 2011 study reported that some of the teens in their group homes used drugs, got in fights, and stole other residents' property. "I felt like I couldn't take it no more," a seventeen-year-old female resident said. "There was too many women and it was like 18 of us and it was like too much drama and I just felt like I didn't want to be a part of it. Some girls was like psychotic and they just put anybody in our group home cause it was a behavioral group home." Despite the chaos, the teens also complained about the excessive rules and restrictions the staff imposed on them. They expressed feeling "cooped up" with no productive or enjoyable activities to keep them occupied. Similarly, a teen in a 2021 study reported that for two years while living in congregate care, "I nearly had to physically fight every day. . . . It was like 'Fight Club.'"[7]

Black journalist and child advocate Stacey Patton spent most of her childhood in New Jersey's foster care system until she aged out in the late 1990s. Because she experienced "living in survival mode all the time," she understood why Ma'Khia Bryant picked up a knife to protect herself. Patton recalls resorting to violence at age fourteen, when an older girl in the group home who had been bullying her barged into her room to start a fight. Patton reacted by beating the girl with a spiked track shoe. "At that time, I didn't give one thought to the fact that I could have seriously injured or killed one of those kids, who had their own pent-up traumas, grief, losses, and anger," Patton writes. "My body and brain didn't work that way. Nobody was teaching us how to heal, how to manage our bodies and emotions."[8]

Patton describes how foster care felt like prison to her. "In some of my placements things were locked up—the refrigerator, food pantry and windows, and bedroom doors had alarms on them," she writes. "There were all these rules about how kids and staff were not allowed to hug or touch us. All the shrinks we were forced to see were white and had a hard time connecting with us and felt they didn't understand us. The staff were always walking around with logbooks and clipboards jotting down observation notes about us." Her experience in foster care straddled the thin line: "It was often hard to distinguish whether we were victims in protective care or if we were juveniles being treated like delinquents in some of these settings."[9]

The thin line between dependency and delinquency also marks the placement of foster children in so-called residential treatment centers that are supposed to provide specialized services to children with mental health or behavior problems. In many of these facilities, the conditions of confinement are exactly the same as in juvenile detention centers—or worse. Indeed, children in the foster care system and children in the juvenile justice system are often placed together. The residents are completely sequestered in secure facilities without any contact with the outside world, save possible visits from family members. Once locked in, children must attend "on-grounds" schools that are located at or near the institution, depriving them not only of interaction with nonresidential classmates but also of a meaningful education. Child welfare authorities treat foster children consigned to residential treatment centers in the same punitive manner that the juvenile justice system treats delinquents.[10]

In 2021, Think of Us, a research lab founded and directed by former foster youth, issued a scathing report, *Away from Home*, based on interviews with seventy-eight young people who had recently lived in institutional foster care placements. Among the study's numerous findings of dehumanizing conditions is the observation that youth "frequently compared institutional placements to prison, as institutional placements have many functions of a carceral environment: confined, surveilling, punitory, restrictive, and degrading." Youths recalled being "locked away" and treated like "a hostage," "a criminal," and "a dog in a cage." One teen described their room in painfully bleak terms: "Four plastic paneled white walls, small space. Bed is anchored to the floor. Bulletproof window that doesn't open. A little window in your door so the staff can view whatever you're doing whenever they want."[11]

Often, foster children with mental health or behavior problems are placed in out-of-state institutions far away from their homes, making family visits, as well as oversight by the state agencies responsible for their well-being, virtually impossible. A girl from Chicago with bipolar disorder was taken from her mother at age eleven and cycled through facilities in Arkansas, Illinois, Michigan, Ohio, and Tennessee. While at the Capstone Academy in Detroit, whose license was on provisional status, she "was sedated, subjected to bruising restraints and sexually assaulted by a facility employee," according to a 2020 investigation by

ProPublica and the *Chicago Tribune*. One-third of the children confined to Lakeside Academy in Kalamazoo, Michigan, where Cornelius Frederick was killed, were sent there by California's child welfare department. In the prior six years, California's Department of Social Services paid the for-profit Sequel Youth and Family Services $85 million to house children in eight residential treatment facilities spread across five states, skirting the state's ban on using for-profit services and ignoring reports of violent abuse by facility employees.[12]

Children may be confined to these prison-like facilities because they have mental disorders their families aren't able to handle without state assistance. Many parents have no choice but to let their children with mental health needs become state wards so the children can receive specialized services the family can't afford. Rather than providing mental health care directly to families, child welfare authorities require families to relinquish custody of children so they can be locked in residential treatment centers run by state and business partnerships.

Other foster children are confined to residential treatment centers simply because there is nowhere else available. Child welfare authorities sometimes consider these settings a last resort for difficult-to-place teens, many of whom end up in one after being shuttled among foster and group homes numerous times. A 2015 federal report found that over 40 percent of children placed in institutions had no clinical reason for such a restrictive setting, a finding confirmed by the 2021 Think of Us study, which also reported that institutions were the first placement for many of the youth interviewed. A federal lawsuit filed in 2018 by Children's Rights against the Florida Department of Children and Families (DCF) alleged that "children who have no clinical need are kept for months locked in psychiatric facilities solely because DCF has no other place to house them." At the same time, the complaint stated, DCF failed to provide therapeutic support to foster children who did have specialized mental health care needs—needs exacerbated by DCF's own disruption of their lives. Lawsuits making similar claims about the wrongful detention of foster children in therapeutic facilities have been filed recently in Alaska, the District of Columbia, Indiana, and West Virginia.[13]

In the last decade, an avalanche of scandals has rocked residential treatment facilities that detain foster children, exposing rampant verbal, physical, and sexual violence by staff, who act more like prison guards than substitute caregivers. Excessive restraints, like the one that killed Cornelius Frederick, are a routine form of discipline. In 2014, the *Miami New Times* reported on the brutality children experienced at the Center for Adolescent Treatment Services (CATS) in Pembroke Pines, Florida, run by the nonprofit Citrus Health Network. According to journalist Kyle Swensen, former residents describe the facility "as a gulag-like holding pen for damaged, low-income kids. Inside, children compete to earn 'points' while supervised by a low-educated and reportedly abusive staff—think *One Flew over the Cuckoo's Nest* meets *The Hunger Games*. Worse, residents claim they were regularly tied facedown to beds with four-point restraints and shot up with a mysterious chemical sedative they took to calling 'booty juice.'"[14]

Investigations into Pennsylvania's child welfare institutions were sparked by the 2016 killing of David Hess, a seventeen-year-old Black boy held at Wordsworth Academy in Philadelphia, a dilapidated residential treatment facility for youth with mental illness or behavior problems in both the foster care and juvenile justice systems. In 2017, more than thirty-seven hundred children in Pennsylvania were living in 541 state institutions, with nearly half of all foster children placed in one of them. Although only 49 percent of Philadelphia's population under age eighteen is Black, Black children make up 74 percent of those confined to residential treatment facilities. David died when three workers, who had entered his room in search of a stolen iPod, restrained him by punching him repeatedly in the ribs and pinning him to the ground in a headlock, suffocating him. The *Philadelphia Inquirer* and the *Philadelphia Daily News* discovered that Hess's killing was the culmination of massive child abuse at Wordsworth, which should have caught the attention of state authorities long before. Police had been summoned to the institution more than eight hundred times in the prior decade for incidents that included forty-nine sex crimes, broken bones, and other forms of child endangerment. The state closed Wordsworth as "an immediate and serious danger" to its residents, but no one was held accountable for killing Hess, though his death was ruled a homicide.[15]

In November 2020, the *San Francisco Chronicle* and *The Imprint* alerted California child welfare officials to their investigation into rampant physical and sexual violence perpetrated against foster children sent to residential treatment centers in far-flung states, half of which were run by Sequel Youth and Family Services. Its wrongdoing exposed, the state's Department of Social Services ended its use of all twelve out-of-state programs, based on numerous licensing violations, and brought back the 116 children trapped in them. In July 2021, California enacted a law prohibiting the future placement of foster children in out-of-state facilities. In all these cases, it has taken the murder of a child or a media exposé for child welfare authorities to terminate their contracts with euphemistically named residential treatment facilities that they know are torturing children in foster care.[16]

In its report *The State of America's Children 2021*, the Children's Defense Fund issued hopeful news. Between 2008 and 2018, twenty-six states and the District of Columbia decreased their use of congregate settings for children in foster care by at least 33.3 percent. The decline was 50 percent in fourteen states. With passage of the Family First Prevention Services Act of 2018 (Family First Act), Congress took steps to mitigate even more the harms inflicted on children placed in such institutions. Starting in 2019, the federal government will only reimburse states for two weeks of a child's stay in a congregate setting, with the exception of certain residential treatment programs. The law also limits the number of children allowed in a child care institution to twenty-five. But two weeks is still enough time to feel like a jail sentence for children placed in group facilities with as many as twenty-five residents. Moreover, the law contains loopholes that make it easy for an institution to evade the two-week limit. And the exception for residential treatment programs allows children to be confined in the most prison-like conditions. As of this writing, we know nothing about compliance with the group home restrictions or their impact on children's well-being because most states were granted a two-year delay to implement them.[17]

In October 2019, the Illinois Department of Children and Family Services transferred two teenagers from a shelter in Chicago to a new placement thirty miles away. The private contractor hired to transport the boys handcuffed their wrists and shackled their ankles for the entire journey. Although Illinois law prohibits minors from being "subjected to mechanical restraints in any facility licensed by DCFS," the contract with the transportation company provided for "secure transportation for DCFS Youth in Care" when regular transport was clinically determined to be unsafe. DCFS had approved secure transport more than one hundred times in the prior two years. "The foster care system is different from a penal system," an outraged Cook County Public Guardian Charles Golbert said. "It's not intended to punish children. Handcuffs and shackles are for adult criminals from whom the public needs to be protected." But, as we have seen, child welfare agencies routinely treat children in their custody as if they were criminals, deserving of punishment rather than protection.[18]

PATHWAY TO PRISON

"We Are Sending More Foster Kids to Prison than College." That is the headline of an investigative report on the pathway from foster care to prison published by the *Kansas City Star* in December 2019. The *Star* surveyed nearly six thousand people imprisoned in twelve states to examine the connection between foster care and incarceration. One in four of the prisoners had spent time in foster care. The state of Kansas arranged for all eight of its prisons to participate in the survey. Of the 1,200 incarcerated people who responded, 382—one-third—had been in foster care.[19]

The *Star*'s findings in Kansas are replicated in states across the nation. A recent review of the research concluded, "Studies that follow foster youth over time find that they are more likely to experience incarceration and that incarcerated adults are disproportionately likely to have been in foster care, suggesting a foster care-to-prison pipeline." The Midwest Study found that over half the children in its sample had been arrested, had been convicted of a crime, or had stayed overnight at a correctional facility. Analyzing Illinois records, economist Joseph Doyle found that foster care had a similarly detrimental effect: "The results suggest that among children on the margin of placement, children placed in foster care have arrest, conviction, and imprisonment rates as adults that are three times higher than those of children who remain at home." Doyle concluded it is unlikely that foster care is effective at preventing children from becoming involved in the criminal punishment system. To the contrary, foster care is a gateway to prison. Children who are wards of the state become involved in the criminal punishment system because of foster care, not in spite of it.[20]

Foster care often funnels children into the juvenile justice system even before they become adults. This path is so well worn that there are labels for children who are caught in both systems: crossover, dual system, dual status, and dually involved. "Crossover" refers to youth with current or past involvement in both systems at some point in their childhoods. The various "dual" terms apply more specifically to children who are adjudicated juvenile offenders while they are wards of the state. Typically, children cross into the juvenile justice system from foster care and not the other way around. According to the National Center for Juvenile Justice, there are no national statistics collected on the numbers of children who are in both systems. As of 2016, only six states published prevalence data on dual-status youth. An analysis of data from Chicago, Cleveland, and New York City found that between 7 percent and 24 percent of children in foster care went on to become involved in the juvenile justice system, with Black youth, youth who enter foster care as adolescents, and youth placed in congregate settings at the most risk. In Massachusetts, 40 percent of children held in juvenile detention in 2015 had open child protection cases. A recent Los Angeles case study found that "African American youth in Los Angeles County are disproportionately dually involved at a rate almost 6 times their general population numbers (7.4% vs. 43%)."[21]

The odds are stacked against foster children who are adjudicated as delinquent. Dual-system youth spend longer in the juvenile justice system and are more likely to be ensnared in the criminal punishment system as adults. They are detained for less serious offenses than their nondependent counterparts, receive harsher sanctions and fewer probation sentences and court dismissals, and are more likely to be placed on probation in a congregate setting rather than a home. In addition, the recidivism rate is higher for foster children than their delinquent peers who never experienced foster care. A study that checked on youth two years after they were released from juvenile justice found that 70 percent of those who were involved in the child welfare system had returned to the juvenile system, compared to 34 percent of those who had no contact with child welfare. Foster care makes it harder for children entangled in the juvenile justice system to escape it.[22]

ARRESTED IN FOSTER CARE

One way that foster care puts children at risk of juvenile detention is by traumatizing them. "Everyday occurrences in foster care, such as multiple placement moves and placement in congregate settings, often lead dependent youth to engage in externalizing, aggressive behaviors, landing them in the juvenile justice system," notes Sherri Y. Simmons-Horton, a social work professor who studies Black children caught in both systems. The dual-status youth she interviewed in Houston, Texas, felt that the circumstances that led to their arrest would not have occurred had they not been in foster care. Equally significant is that foster care is *structured* to make children vulnerable to arrest, prosecution, and detention. In other words, foster children are adjudicated delinquent not only because of their behavior but also because foster care systematically channels them to juvenile court.[23]

I first understood that foster care was a direct pathway to delinquency when I read a 2001 investigation by the Vera Institute of Justice into why so many teenagers in New York City were entering the child welfare system through juvenile justice. The Vera Institute estimated that more than one thousand teenagers were involved with both the Administration of Children's Services (ACS) and the juvenile justice system in 1997. Its analysis revealed that the teens were not entering foster care because they were delinquent, as ACS suspected. Rather, most of the adolescents ACS received from the juvenile justice system had actually been in the agency's care at the time of their arrest and were being returned to ACS.[24]

The researchers found that foster children were frequently detained because the child welfare system abandoned them when they got in trouble. When teenagers are picked up by the police, it is critical that their parents or another caregiver advocate on their behalf and offer to serve as an alternative to detention in a state facility. Black teens are already at a disadvantage because police, probation officers, prosecutors, and judges often view Black mothers as incapable of providing adequate discipline in the home. But Black teens in the foster care system don't even have their mothers to fight for them in police precincts and courts. Foster caretakers rarely advocate on behalf of an arrested child, deferring to unreachable caseworkers to intervene. Group homes typically discharge teens who are arrested instead of sending someone to take responsibility for them.

Even worse, foster caretakers not only desert children who are arrested; they are frequently responsible for getting children arrested. The Vera Institute found that teenagers in ACS custody were much more likely to be arrested at home than other teenagers in juvenile detention. Whereas only 4 percent of the non-ACS teens surveyed were arrested at home, 36 percent of the teens in foster homes and 55 percent of the teens in congregate care were arrested where they lived. In other words, the teens in the foster care system were being arrested for incidents related to their placements. One facility mentioned in the Vera Institute report called the police almost forty times over an eleven-month period.

More recent studies confirm that at least one-third of arrests of crossover youth are tied to their placements, usually the result of an incident that occurred in their group home. Randy was placed in foster care when he was ten and transferred to thirteen placements in three New York City boroughs while in ACS care. When he tussled with another boy in his foster home at age fourteen, "the foster parent was quick to call 911 instead of mediating and resolving the issue," Randy, now twenty-two, recently told *Teen Vogue*. Although it was his first arrest and no one was seriously injured, Randy was confined to juvenile detention for fourteen months. Then, when he was seventeen, a second altercation led to his prosecution as an adult and an eight-month incarceration on Rikers Island. Parents are extremely unlikely to call the police when sibling rivalry breaks loose at home. Foster caretakers frequently deal with teenagers who break the house rules, get into fights, or rebel against their placements by treating them as juvenile delinquents.[25]

RUNAWAYS

Foster care also pushes children into juvenile detention and jail by causing them to flee. Children living on their own not only may engage in delinquent conduct in order to survive, but also may be arrested simply because they fled. Once foster children run from their placements, they cross the thin line into delinquency. They are criminalized for trying to escape the prison-like conditions of foster care.

On any given day, thousands of children are missing from foster care because they absconded from state custody. Fleeing foster care is so common that these children have an official label: runaways. Studies of child welfare systems across the country estimate that anywhere from one-third to one-half of foster children have run away at least once while in care, and many have fled multiple times. The Midwest Study, for example, found that 46 percent of the youth surveyed had run away at some point, and nearly two-thirds of the runaways had escaped on numerous occasions. Children are more likely to run away if they are teens, Black, female, or LGBTQ, or if their parents' rights have been terminated. The type of placement also makes a difference. Children are more likely to run away from group homes, unstable placements, and residences where they are living with strangers and apart from their siblings. Being allowed to stay with family dramatically decreases the odds of fleeing.[26]

Unlike most children who run away *from* home, children in foster care are often running *to* home. Researchers who interviewed fifty young people who fled from foster care in Chicago and Los Angeles discovered that a key reason they ran was to be with family. About one-third spent their first night on the run at a relative's home. The youth explained that they missed their family and friends, who cared for them more than foster caretakers. "I ran away because I've been away from my family for a long time and I asked my caseworker could I go on the visits and see my mom for her birthday and he said no," a seventeen-year-old girl said. A sixteen-year-old girl attributed her decision to the group home staff: "Like literally, they didn't care about me, like they forgot about me. And I was like, hello, I'm kind of like going through a cycle right here where I'm becoming very depressed because the people, the environment, it's not getting anywhere," she explained.[27]

Most runaways return voluntarily to foster care after a week or two. But many others refuse to go back. Child welfare departments across the country can't account for hundreds of children in their custody. The crisis of missing foster children made national headlines in 2002 when a four-year-old Black girl named Rilya Wilson disappeared for fifteen months before Florida child welfare authorities even noticed. Other jurisdictions began to disclose the numbers of foster youth they lost track of each year: "Los Angeles County, 488; Oklahoma, 103; Tennessee, 496; and Massachusetts, 400," reported *Youth Today*. Most missing foster children are on the run. What happens to teens who run from foster care and don't want to go back? Some live under the radar with relatives or friends. A large number are left homeless. A recent survey of 693 homeless youth between ages fourteen and twenty-five living in Atlanta discovered that 43 percent of them had spent time in foster care. About one in ten of the former foster youth had not reached age twenty-one. Although they were eligible to return to foster care, they preferred to stay on the streets. Close to a third of them identified as LGBQ and 9 percent as transgender. A majority had not graduated from high school.[28]

Disconnected from their families and without state support, many runaways sell sex in order to survive or are coerced into commercial sex by adults, putting them at increased risk of arrest. In July 2013, the FBI announced that a nationwide sex-trafficking sting had recovered one hundred sexually exploited teenagers, some as young as thirteen years old. Sixty of them were missing from foster care. The federal government defines "sex trafficking" as "the recruitment, harboring, transportation, provision, obtaining, patronizing, or soliciting of a person for the purpose of a commercial sex act, in which the commercial sex act is induced by force, fraud, or coercion, or in which the person induced to perform such act has not attained 18 years of age." Law enforcement has used the term to vilify and control sex workers. Often the government's way of rescuing sex workers identified as trafficked is to arrest them and throw them in jail or force them into therapeutic programs. When runaway minors have sex with adults, either because they are physically threatened or because they need the money for food and shelter, they are being victimized. As we will see, state authorities typically criminalize them, much as they criminalize sex workers and adult survivors of sexual exploitation.[29]

Although most of the teenagers in the FBI sting were in the custody of child protection agencies, the officials in charge failed to hold the agencies responsible. "These kids are usually without an involved parent," said Staca Shehan, a director at the National Center for Missing and Exploited Children. "Pimps can come into their life and initially take on the role of protector." Somehow, Shehan forgot that the state had taken most of the children from their parents and was supposed to serve as their protector. Researchers who surveyed more than five hundred Black sex workers in Miami found that those who had been in foster care started sex work at a younger age and were also more likely to have been sexually abused as children—and for nearly half of them, the abuse began *after* they were placed in foster care.[30]

Foster care makes children vulnerable to sexual exploitation while they are in care as well as when they run away. Residential facilities can operate as recruitment stations for sexual exploitation of children. In December 2018, when federal prosecutors charged nineteen people in a sex-trafficking ring, they announced that fifteen of the exploited children were in the child welfare system. Nine of the girls were residents of Hawthorne Cedar Knolls, a residential treatment center in a small town in Westchester County, New York. The defendants lured the girls from the campus by pretending to have a romantic interest in them and offering them a place to stay, before coercing them into commercial sex. Hawthorne had gained a reputation for its high rate of runaways: 73 percent of its 188 residents were reported missing in a previous year. Yet New York continued to hold girls at the facility until the federal sting exposed the state's utter disregard for their safety.[31]

The Preventing Sex Trafficking and Strengthening Families Act, signed by President Barack Obama in 2014, addresses the trafficking of foster children. The law directs states to track victims of sex trafficking younger than age twenty-four under the national foster care–reporting system; to report children who are missing from foster care, within twenty-four hours, to law enforcement for entry into the National Center for Missing and Exploited Children database; and to put in place protocols to locate missing children, as well as screening to determine if they have been sex trafficked. But tracking missing foster children doesn't get to the bottom of why they ran away in the first place. Congress failed to acknowledge that foster care itself makes children vulnerable to sexual exploitation and, in many cases, actively facilitates it. Congress's wrongheaded approach to this problem is also reflected in the Family First Act's inadequate restrictions on congregate placements. Among the loopholes is a provision that allows continued federal funding for residential treatment centers that house "children and youth who have been found to be, or are at risk of becoming, sex trafficking victims." In other words, Congress addressed sex trafficking of foster children by supporting their confinement in institutions known to facilitate sex trafficking of foster children.[32]

To make matters worse, agencies revictimize sexually exploited foster youth by treating them as criminals. In many jurisdictions, these teens are arrested on prostitution charges even though they have been assaulted by adults and are too young to consent to sex. Not only does the foster care system drive children into the hands of traffickers, but it subsequently throws them into juvenile detention. In fact, because child welfare agencies are only interested in punishing parents, they may have no authority to protect the child victims in these cases of sexual abuse. "As a result, trafficked children, who are victims of statutory rape or child abuse, are sent into the juvenile justice system," notes a Georgetown

Law Center report, *The Sexual Abuse to Prison Pipeline*, "imprisoned as a direct consequence of their victimization." The child welfare system also treats sexually exploited children badly. Girls who are brought back into foster care after running away tend to be pathologized as having an "oppositional defiant disorder" and are subjected to draconian constraints on their activities and relationships, including their placement in restrictive and dangerous residential treatment facilities.[33]

In July 2021, I heard psychiatrist Dr. Bruce Perry, who coauthored the bestseller *What Happened to You* with Oprah Winfrey, describe his first experience with the foster care system as "really messed up." He had been asked to evaluate a girl in Chicago who kept running away from a foster home that was far away from her family. "They finally put her in a [psychiatric] hospital—because you have to be crazy to run away from a foster home, right?" he asked rhetorically. His critical question reminded me of Samuel Cartwright, an antebellum southern physician, who diagnosed enslaved people who ran away from plantations with a mental disorder he labeled "drapetomania," combining the Greek words for runaway and crazy.[34]

Foster care puts girls at especially higher risk of juvenile justice involvement. Although only one-fifth to one-quarter of the juvenile justice population is female, girls comprise one-third to one-half of dual-system youth. A Los Angeles survey of first-time offenders found that 37 percent of those who were also involved in the child welfare system were girls, whereas girls made up only 24 percent of those who were not involved in child protection. Another study discovered that 27 percent of Black girls in juvenile detention had an open child welfare case, compared to 13 percent of Black boys and only 7 percent of youth overall. This means that being in foster care increases the odds of juvenile justice involvement for girls even more than it does for boys. The Georgetown Law Center report suggests that "the reason for this increased risk of juvenile justice involvement for girls is unsafe living conditions in congregate care, including a higher risk of sexual abuse and physical abuse by staff and other youth." When girls develop "coping strategies" that break the rules, staff turn to law enforcement to control their behavior.[35]

Punishing children who have been sexually exploited follows the child welfare system's approach to runaways generally. In many jurisdictions, agencies' response to children who escape foster care is to call the police to have them arrested or to obtain civil arrest warrants so caseworkers can play the part of cops. Running away is one of the five most common juvenile-status offenses that can land a child in detention (the others are skipping school, drinking while underage, violating curfew, and "acting out"—also known as ungovernability, incorrigibility, or being beyond the control of one's parents). "I witnessed kids who ran away from their placement to go back home often get arrested and brutalized by cops when they were returned," Stacey Patton recalls from her time in New Jersey's foster care system. Until a New York State appellate court stopped the practice in 2019, New York City's ACS routinely applied for civil arrest warrants to detain foster children who ran away, 89 percent of whom were Black or Latinx in 2017. In Washington State, 123 foster children were jailed in juvenile detention facilities in 2017 for running away, with some confined multiple times.[36]

Criminalizing children who run away from the crushing conditions of foster care not only revictimizes them, but also deters them from seeking help for fear they will be thrown in jail. Despite all the hand-wringing about finding missing children, the child welfare system is driving children out in the street and across the thin line to delinquency, then putting up barriers to their safe return.

AGING OUT

Some children are never returned home from foster care. Like running away, there is a term to describe their exit from the system: they "age out." Also like running away, aging out of foster care channels many teens into prison. Children who aren't reunited with their families or adopted by new ones remain in state custody until they turn eighteen or, in some states, twenty-one. At that point, the state abruptly washes its hands of them. Because they are no longer state wards, they lose whatever services and supports they were receiving in foster care. Each year, more than twenty thousand youth age out of the system. After traumatizing them, disrupting their education, subjecting them to abuse and neglect, damaging their health, taking their benefits, and cutting them off from their families, child welfare authorities release them to manage on their own. Their parents' rights may have been terminated, making them "legal orphans." Caseworkers tell the teens to throw their belongings into a large black trash bag, then drop them off at a homeless shelter or give them bus fare, as if they had just been released from prison—often without a bank account, a high school diploma, or a job. As longtime family defense attorney Martin Guggenheim puts it, the system "spits out 20,000 children experiencing nothing but harm without any legal relationship to another human being."[37]

It is no wonder that young people who age out of foster care tend to have the most abysmal outcomes—putting them at risk of incarceration. All the long-term setbacks related to health, education, housing, income, and incarceration are made worse when teens transition to adulthood while in foster care and then are tossed aside, unprepared and unsupported. The 2016 National Youth in Transition Database, which tracks former foster youth at ages seventeen, nineteen, and twenty-one, discovered that 43 percent reported experiencing homelessness by age twenty-one. At age twenty-four, half will be unemployed. One in four will be incarcerated within two years of aging out. The prison system supplies Black children to the child welfare system when it incarcerates their parents. The child welfare system supplies young adults to the prison system when it abandons them.[38]

Federal, state, and local legislators have acknowledged the travesty of booting teens out of foster care to survive on their own, spurring many to pass measures to postpone or soften their landing. Under the federal foster care program, states are reimbursed for the cost of keeping youth in care until they reach age eighteen or, at the state's discretion, twenty-one. In 1999, Congress passed the John H. Chafee Foster Care Program for Successful Transition to Adulthood, which allocates Title IV-E funds to states for independent-living services for youth ages fourteen to twenty-one who are or were in foster care. Since 2018, states that extend foster care to age twenty-one can offer Chafee services up to age twenty-three. The Chafee program also authorizes vouchers worth $5,000 annually for eligible youth to attend college or postsecondary training. In addition, the Affordable Care Act makes aging-out youth eligible for Medicaid coverage until age twenty-six. Most states now offer foster youth some sort of extended support until they reach age twenty-one, with the help of matching federal funds.

Unfortunately, these belated efforts to mitigate foster care's damage have done little to spare young adults from life's harsh realities. The services offered by child welfare agencies to children when they age out of foster care are just as deficient as those they offer families when they put children in foster care. The Midwest Study, for example, found "sobering evidence" that child welfare agencies were not providing resources or skills needed for the transition to adulthood to many eligible youth through age twenty-one. At twenty-three years old, Joseph Jones was living in a transitional housing program for former foster youth in Oakland, California. He was moved to multiple foster placements, ending in residential facilities in distant states, until he turned twenty-one. A month before his birthday, the state cut off his housing and he shuttled from the streets to jail. "I feel like I started maturing about the age of 20," Jones told investigative journalists Karen de Sá and Sara Tiano. "And obviously at the age of 20, I only had one more year to really use services and the extended benefits."

Moreover, the extended foster care assistance comes with strings attached: unless they can demonstrate a disabling condition, youth must stay in school, keep a job, or be engaged in removing barriers to employment. These prerequisites are often piled on top of other obligations, such as participating in drug treatment, therapy sessions, or meetings with caseworkers. One slip-up can mean losing the safety net of housing and financial aid, and falling into life on the streets. In July 2021, California made a radical shift away from this precarious approach: the state legislature approved the first state-funded universal basic income plan for youth aging out of foster care, which will send them guaranteed and direct monthly payments of up to $1,000.[39]

California's plan to provide no-strings-attached payments to former foster youth is exceptional. I find it ironic that the chief reform of the aging-out policy has been to extend the deadline for foster care services. The solution to the damage inflicted by the system is to offer the injured more time in it. By the time the makeshift resources kick in, foster care has already set children back so far it is nearly impossible for them to catch up. The government gives teens a few more years of paltry services to recover from what might have been a childhood of traumatizing placements. "The precipice young people leaving foster care once faced at 18 has been shored up," de Sá and Tiano write. "But for far too many, it has simply been delayed three years into a lonely plunge at age 21." As with policing their parents, lawmakers refuse to give young adults what they need unless the recipients are tethered to programs that can regulate them.[40]

Of course, the provision of housing, education vouchers, and counseling is better than the prior practice of ruthless abandonment. A majority of youth who turn eighteen while in foster care opt for the extended programs. But the perversity of this stranglehold isn't lost on young people about to age out. "Walking into court for my very last time as a foster youth, I feel like I'm getting a divorce from a system that I've been in a relationship with almost my entire life," recounted Noel Anaya for NPR. "It's bittersweet because I'm losing guaranteed stipends for food and housing, as well as access to my social workers and my lawyer. But on the other hand, I'm relieved to finally get away from a system that ultimately failed me on its biggest promise. That one day it would find me a family who would love me."[41]

Rather than scraping together these inadequate fixes for children who age out of a system that failed them, why not keep them from entering the system in the first place?

This point is driven home by the numbers of teens who rekindle their relationships with their families once the state can no longer block their connection. Nearly all the former foster youth in the Midwest Study reported that they felt close to at least one family member, and more than three-quarters felt very close. Despite having been taken from their mothers, more than half the youth (55 percent) still felt somewhat or very close to them, with more than one in four living with a parent or other relative at age twenty-one. What's more, because many of the former foster youth relied on concrete assistance from their families, the renewed family bonds were critical to their success as they exited foster care. A more recent and larger study, based on a nationally representative sample of adolescents, found that foster children who reunified with their families had the lowest chance of becoming homeless, showing "the potential of families for promoting housing stability." Indeed, the researchers discovered that independent-living services and state policies that extend foster care failed to reduce the higher rate of homelessness among youth who aged out.[42]

Both studies emphasized the importance of families to the welfare of teens as they transition to adulthood, while putting in doubt the focus of child welfare reforms for preparing foster youth to try to make it on their own. "Our data highlight the need for child welfare practice and policy to pay closer attention to the family connections of foster youth," the Midwest researchers advised. These consistent findings beg the same question: why not strengthen valuable family relationships to begin with instead of trying to salvage them after children are harmed and abandoned by the foster care system?[43]

Black families often celebrate when their stolen children find their way back home, like hostages released from years-long captivity or prisoners who have served their time behind bars. It is a bittersweet scene—joyful because the family is reunited, yet tragic because tearing it apart was senseless.

CONFINING THE NEXT GENERATION

Babies born to Black mothers who are in foster care or have recently aged out are typically placed in state custody as newborns. The state consigns these teenagers to a *huis clos* situation where their forced involvement in the system is taken as evidence that their children need to be confined in it as well. The phenomenon of children who experience foster care having children who experience foster care is so common that it has spawned a focus of child welfare research. I was struck by the titles of recent studies on this topic: "Understanding the Intergenerational Cycle of Child Protective Service Involvement," "Intergenerational Pathways Leading to Foster Care Placement of Foster Care Alumni's Children," "Addressing Multi-Generational Dysfunction in Foster Care," "The Hidden Cost of Foster-Care: New Evidence of Inter-generational Transmission of Foster-Care Experiences."[44]

The very system that promises to break the cycle of family disadvantage by taking children from their homes creates its own cycle of intergenerational state entanglement. Agencies taking custody of babies born to children in their care is a signal of foster care's failure, a confession that foster care itself endangers children. Foster care is one of the chief ways the US state transfers the carceral containment of Black communities from one generation to the next.[45]

May 2021 marked the centennial of the Tulsa Race Massacre, when white mobs wiped out the thriving Black community of Greenwood, known as Black Wall Street, murdering hundreds of residents and destroying homes, businesses, and churches, leaving a generation's inheritance in ashes. In 2018, *New York Times* columnist Charles Blow interviewed one of the last known survivors, Olivia J. Hooker, at age 103, just two months before her death. She recalled hiding with her siblings beneath an oak dining table at six years of age as white men defiled their home. "They took a hatchet to my sisters' piano. They poured oil all over my grandmother's bed. They took all the silverware that Momma had just got for Christmas," she recounted. *"If anything looked precious, they took it."*[46]

The aim of white supremacy has long been to subjugate Black communities by taking what is most precious to them. As Blow observes, reflecting on Olivia Hooker's words, the Tulsa Massacre was "about the erasure of a Black excellence that by its very existence posed a fundamental threat to white supremacy. Black Wall Street represented Black prosperity even in an age of oppression, so white supremacy had to destroy it." Although foster care is often defended as the best we can do for damaged children, it actually is the worst we can do to precious children. The persistence of such a patently harmful system can't credibly be justified as protecting Black children. This government intervention does precisely the opposite: it drives Black children into a carceral web designed to contain Black communities and to maintain a punitive approach to meeting human needs, serving only a powerful elite. Truly valuing Black children would mean dismantling the destructive family-policing system and replacing it with a radically different way of caring for children, supporting families, and imagining safety.

PART IV
ABOLITION

CARE IN PLACE OF TERROR

THE NEW ABOLITIONISTS

On Martin Luther King Jr. Day in January 2021, about a hundred people dressed in winter jackets gathered on 125th Street in Harlem. The crowd stood on the sidewalk and sat in folding chairs beneath a newly installed billboard that proclaimed, "Some cops are called caseworkers. #AbolishNYCACS," referring to New York City's Administration for Children's Services. As Bob Marley's "Get Up, Stand Up" blasted from loudspeakers, a middle-aged Black woman sporting an afro and a black sweatshirt with "F##K ACS" displayed in white letters, took the microphone. The woman was Joyce McMillan, the activist who had planned the rally and whose organization, JMacForFamilies, had paid for the billboard. "The system is not designed to be of assistance. This system is designed to be harmful and to set people up for failure," she told the diverse gathering of parents, lawyers, and other supporters. "Everybody says I'm radical, but how much more radical can you be than snatching kids out of the home under the guise of protecting them and changing their rooms every three to four months?" Some of the protesters raised their fists in the air, while others clapped and cheered as McMillan spoke. A few of them carried signs with messages like "Abolish the Child Welfare Industrial Complex" and "Preventive Services Are Surveillance."[1]

McMillan is a veteran organizer of parents who have experienced ACS investigations. Over the last several years, she has led influential grassroots campaigns to dismantle New York's child welfare system, and the MLK Day protest was nothing new. In September 2019, she spoke alongside members of the city council's progressive caucus at a rally on the steps of city hall in Manhattan to support a legislative package that would impose greater oversight of ACS and give more rights to the parents it polices. A month before the MLK Day rally, McMillan coordinated a group of activists who spread across the city after dark to put up posters condemning the system's anti-Black racism. One was the sign at the entrance of the 125th Street subway station bearing the message "They separate children at the border of Harlem too." Another read, "From the plantation to the present, breaking up Black families has always meant profit."[2]

McMillan became a leader in an emerging movement to abolish the child welfare system after fighting to recover her own children from ACS. In 1999, when she gave birth to her second daughter, an anonymous caller to the hotline reported her for drug use, and ACS opened an investigation, directing McMillan to undergo a drug test. McMillan, who had no prior experience with child protective services, complied. "When they came into my life, I cooperated, not knowing who they were and what they did," McMillan told me. She assumed the caseworkers would close the investigation as soon as they saw that she only used drugs recreationally and her children were safe and well cared for. Instead, when the test results came back positive, "they immediately snatched the kids." McMillan's nine-year-old daughter went to live with the father. Her three-month-old baby was placed in a stranger's foster home.[3]

When ACS began its investigation, McMillan was enjoying a peaceful life with her newborn baby and older daughter, who was thriving in a private school. "I worked in the banking industry, and I had a place to live, a car, and a great credit score," she reminisced. "When they left me, I was addicted to drugs, I had no credit score, I lost my place to live, and ultimately was incarcerated. For an agency that calls itself a helping system, not only did they not help my children, they definitely tore me apart. They shredded me."

The tide turned when McMillan was able to get savvy and zealous representation from Lauren Shapiro, the managing director of the Family Defense Practice at Brooklyn Defender Services. Shapiro persuaded a judge to rule that McMillan could recover her children if she remained substance free for a year, dismissing ACS's insistence that completing a prescribed drug treatment program should be a prerequisite. McMillan, determined to be reunited with her children, met the challenge. She remembers crying "happy tears" on the day she was reunited with her younger daughter, who had turned two years old by then.

In 2013, McMillan decided to investigate the agency that was so intent on ruining her family. She vividly recalls coming across statistics on the race of the children ACS took from their homes, listed by borough and neighborhood. "I looked at Bed-Stuy"—one of Brooklyn's predominantly Black neighborhoods—"and there might have been twelve hundred removals," she said. Then she turned to the predominantly white neighborhoods. "I looked at Bensonhurst and there were two. My mind was blown." The stark racial disparities were replicated in each of the city's boroughs. "Everything I found indicated removals only involved Black and Brown people," she concluded. "In that moment, I knew it was no longer about me and my family; it was about the thousands of people represented in the numbers on that sheet who looked like me."

After volunteering and serving as program director at the nonprofit Child Welfare Organizing Project in Harlem, a pioneering organization founded in 1994 to advocate for parents in child welfare proceedings, McMillan founded JMacForFamilies in 2019. According to its mission statement, the organization "works to abolish the current punitive and harmful child welfare system, while creating a system that truly supports families and builds community." Awarded a visiting fellowship at the New School, which provides a stipend and an office, McMillan has been able to raise funds to support the campaign ideas percolating in her head. She created Parent Legislative Action Network (PLAN), a coalition of New York City's family defender services, professors from local law schools, and parent activists like Angeline Montauban to push for statutory changes that sustain family unity. PLAN's first victory was persuading the New York legislature to reduce the time someone's name potentially stays on the central registry from twenty-eight years to eight years.[4]

McMillan exemplifies a growing number of Black mothers across the nation who have felt the brunt of family policing and are fighting back. They have formed small, grassroots organizations that advocate for radical change in local child protection agencies and in our nation's approach to child welfare more broadly. They are spotlighting the racism in the child welfare system's design and practices, demanding that the system be dismantled, and working to replace it with concrete, community-based resources for children and their families.

For decades many Black mothers who've been caught in the child welfare system, like the ones I met in a Chicago church basement in 2000, have come together to give each other moral support and protest the removal of their children under daunting constraints. They have resisted a gargantuan system without funding or political support, while struggling to comply with the system's burdensome demands—a task made all the more difficult by the official view that their defiance constitutes evidence of parental unfitness. Today, Black mothers' calls for change are beginning to garner support from nonprofit foundations, policy centers, and activist organizations like Movement for Family Power, founded in New York City by two family defense attorneys, Erin Miles Cloud and Lisa Sangoi; California Families Rise, which evolved out of a Bay Area activist group called Parents Against CPS Corruption, founded by writer Michelle Chan; and the UpEND Movement, the brainchild of Alan Dettlaff, the dean of the University of Houston College of Social Work, and Kristen Weber, director of Equity, Inclusion, and Justice at the Center for the Study of Social Policy in Washington, DC.[5]

Rise Magazine, launched in New York City in 2005 to publish parents' stories, recently began developing a Parents' Platform that "crystallizes concrete steps toward child welfare abolition and centers the expertise of impacted parents and communities." In April 2021, *Rise*'s founder and longtime director, Nora McCarthy, a white woman, stepped down and handed the reins to former assistant directors Bianca Shaw, a Black mother, and Jeanette Vega, a Latinx mother. "Nothing about us, without us," says Halimah Washington, *Rise*'s community coordinator. "The people who are closest to the problems are the ones who are closest to the solutions but farthest from the resources. We already have the solutions." Black youth who are currently or were formerly in foster care, like Tymber Hudson, an outspoken advocate for LGBTQ foster youth, and the founders and directors of Think of Us, a research and development lab that centers the lived experiences of youth in foster care, are also increasingly calling for radical change.[6]

These activists, lawyers, and scholars are reaching a common conclusion: continuing to reform the child welfare system will never make it safe for children or supportive of families. The system and its foundational logic must be completely eradicated and replaced by a radically different approach to child safety and well-being.

YOU CAN'T FIX A SYSTEM THAT ISN'T BROKEN

A Litany of Reforms

We have tried ameliorating the devastation inflicted by family policing on children and their families. Over the last thirty years, child advocates have sued states across the nation for operating foster care systems that traumatize and endanger children. The child welfare departments in numerous states are currently governed by court-monitored settlement agreements that require them to make massive reforms. While some states have failed for decades to live up to old agreements, others have been taken to court recently for the same problems endemic to child removal. The Illinois Department of Children and Family Services is operating under more than ten consent decrees, one of which was filed in 1988. In 2020, nine years into federal litigation that had determined the Texas foster care system was violating children's constitutional rights, US District Judge Janis Jack held the state in contempt of court—for a second time—for its "stunning" failure to comply with court-ordered reforms. This track record of interminable court-supervised reform efforts forecasts little improvement in the treatment of children the state takes from their homes.[7]

Recently, more and more child welfare administrators and policy makers have conceded that the harm caused by family policing is excessive. The evidence of abysmal outcomes for system-impacted children is too voluminous and the financial cost of the government's failed investment in child protection too steep. Many acknowledge that families are being unnecessarily torn apart and that Black families are disproportionately affected. At the state and federal levels, legislators have implemented measures to reduce the foster care population and to increase services to families. Recall that Congress passed the Family First Prevention Services Act in 2018 to divert a small portion of Title IV-E funds from foster care to time-limited prevention services for children "who are candidates for foster care." Similarly, New York City drastically reduced the share of ACS-involved families whose children were placed in foster care while increasing the share of families involved in other mandated programs.

Yet these measures will likely prove as futile as class action lawsuits at ending the child welfare system's destructive policing of families. Indeed, such reforms have only increased the numbers of families regulated by child protection agencies and expanded state intrusion into Black communities through investigations, coercive service provision, and collaborations with police departments. The service providers are the very people hired by child welfare agencies to monitor families and report their failures to comply with agency dictates—infractions that can become the basis for severing family ties. Nor can the cruelty of family policing be mitigated by reforms focused on training caseworkers to be more caring when the system's very design is antithetical to care.

Designed to Destroy

The failure of child welfare reforms should not be surprising. We should expect it to be difficult to tweak a system so that it protects Black children when the system was established to oppress Black people. That conclusion would be obvious if the government hadn't run such an effective propaganda campaign, convincing most Americans that the trauma it inflicts on children is a form of child welfare, care, and protection. As demonstrated in Part II of this book, the roots of today's child welfare system lie in the forcible separation of enslaved families, the exploitation of Black children as apprentices to former white enslavers, and the exclusion of Black children from charitable aid. Throughout US history, the government has deployed child removal as a weapon to control Black people, as well as Indigenous, immigrant, and poor people, and to suppress their liberation struggles. Foster care was a reform that replaced orphanages and almshouses by putting impoverished children to work in local strangers' homes and dispatching them on orphan trains to distant farms without addressing their families' needs. Privatization was a reform to make foster care agencies run more efficiently while incentivizing even more abuse of children in state custody.

The litany of reforms has left undisturbed the false narrative undergirding the child welfare system: that children's hardships are caused by parental pathologies and child safety is achieved by policing families. Child protection still revolves around blaming parents for children's suffering that stems from an unequal society, and punishing them instead of making transformational social change. State authorities continue to target Black communities and to rely on the racist devaluation of Black families to legitimize the resulting devastation. Given the preservation of its foundational logic, the child welfare system has absorbed superficial measures to fix its defects and has persisted in its terror. The failures of foster care reform—the relentlessly abysmal outcomes, suicides, murders, trafficking, and detention of children—only lead to more reforms. Government authorities refuse to meet the needs of families with tangible resources, such as secure housing, food, and income, although they have the means to do so.

Why does the United States continue to invest billions of dollars in a broken system that fails so miserably at protecting children? Because the system is not broken. Those in power have no interest in fundamentally changing a system that is benefiting them financially and politically, one that continues to serve their interests in disempowering Black communities, reinforcing a white supremacist power structure, and stifling calls for radical social change. And they have persuaded most Americans to believe what policing abolitionist Geo Maher calls "the mirage of reform," which "tantalizes from a distance, promising relief that never arrives."[8]

Those who are committed to racial justice and ending the destruction of Black families must face the reality that the child welfare system can't be repaired. For decades, prison abolitionists have argued that incarceration's repressive outcomes for Black communities don't result from any system malfunction. To the contrary, the prison-industrial complex works so effectively to contain and control Black communities because that is precisely what it is designed to do. Prison abolitionists maintain, therefore, that reforms that correct what are perceived as aberrational flaws won't work to end racial injustice in the criminal punishment system. Reforms only help to legitimize and strengthen carceral institutions. Reforming prisons results in more prisons.[9]

The same is true for the child welfare system. Reforming family policing results in more family policing. We must abandon the fool's errand of tinkering with a system designed to tear families apart. Although it is important to expose the harms family policing inflicts, we must let go of the faith that awareness of the harms will stop them from occurring. Instead, we need to implement a paradigm shift in the state's relationship to families—a complete end to family policing by dismantling the current child welfare system and purging its punitive logic. At the same time, we need to build a safer society by reimagining the very meaning of child welfare and protection and by creating caring ways of supporting families and meeting children's needs. This is not just because reforms have failed to support families and keep children safe (which might appear to leave room for trying better reforms); it is because only by abolishing the child welfare system can we support families and keep children safe.

What About Abused Children?

Although the aim of abolition is to end the current system's harms to children and their families, many people fear that abandoning the system is dangerous. The most common objection I hear to abolishing the child welfare system is "How else will we protect children from severe abuse in their homes?" It is hard for many people to imagine any other way of protecting children than by taking them from their parents. Because the United States has relied on family policing as the main way it addresses the needs of Black children, it has guaranteed a sense that family policing is essential for their safety. By its very operation, family policing helps to manufacture the societal conditions that are the chief causes of harm to children—the same conditions that ostensibly justify the system's continued operation.

I know the headlines that are at the forefront of the minds of people who fear abolition:

> "Trial of 6-Year-Old's Killer Exposes Lapses in City's Child Welfare System" (*New York Times*, January 15, 2020)

> "A Dozen Calls to Child Abuse Hotline Did Not Save 8-Year-Old Boy" (*New York Times*, February 2, 2020)

> "A Young Father Was Investigated 4 Times. Then His Newborn Died" (*New York Times*, February 7, 2020)[10]

During my morning reading of the *New York Times* as I wrote this book, I started tearing out stories about children who had been killed by their parents. I carefully read the heartbreaking accounts of these children's deaths because I wanted to make sure I grappled with them in my commitment to abolish family policing. My aim is to work toward a society where children are no longer subjected *either* to the violence of family separation *or* to violence in their homes. One that hit me especially hard was the 2016 death of six-year-old Zymere Perkins. In January 2020, a jury found Rysheim Smith, a forty-five-year-old Black man, guilty of murdering Zymere, the son of his partner, Geraldine Perkins, in their Harlem apartment. At the trial, Perkins, who pleaded guilty to manslaughter and child endangerment, testified over five days about the starvation and beatings Zymere endured at the hands of Smith. Zymere's teachers had repeatedly reported bruises to New York's ACS. Although caseworkers investigated some of the calls, they never removed Zymere from his home. Perkins explained to the jury that she didn't intervene in the abuse because she was infatuated with Smith, a man twice her age, whom she called her "Prince Charming" for rescuing her and Zymere from a shelter for battered women in 2015.[11]

The most prominent news stories about the child welfare system report on child abuse scandals. These are cases where parents kill children "known to the system"—children who were allowed to remain at home after CPS conducted an investigation or were returned to their homes after a brief stay in foster care. These accounts of lethal abuse reverberate beyond the media to have a dramatic impact on public attitudes and child welfare policy making. Political scientist Juliet Gainsborough found that the occurrence of a child abuse scandal in a state was associated with a significant increase in the passage of child protection legislation, ranging from privatizing the system in Kansas to requiring FBI background checks for relative caregivers in Indiana. The most common response to child abuse scandals is to escalate taking children from their homes. Legislators and child welfare authorities are quick to react to a child's death by shoring up the very system that failed to protect the child in the first place. Richard Wexler, executive director of the National Coalition for Child Protection Reform, calls these government reactions "foster care panics." He has documented how child removals sharply increase after a high-profile tragedy but fail to prevent future deaths of children.[12]

ACS responded to Zymere Perkins's death with a foster care panic. According to the *New York Times*, "reports of children being abused or neglected in the city rose to nearly 69,000 in 2017 from about 65,000 in 2016." The Bronx saw a 40 percent increase in new cases between September 26, 2016, the day Zymere was killed, and December 21, 2016, compared to the same period in 2015. The flood of investigations may have contributed to ACS's failure to prevent Teshawn Watkins from smothering his six-week-old son, Kaseem, in their Bronx apartment in

2020. The twenty-seven-year-old Black man had been arrested twice for assaulting Kaseem's mother, Celicia Reyes, and ACS had investigated him four times over allegations that he abused their two older sons, ages three and four. The previous allegations had begun in 2016, during the period of escalating reports of child maltreatment to city authorities following Zymere's death. When Ms. Reyes's mother called 911 on December 28, 2016, out of concern for her grandsons' safety, "the police were already swamped."[13]

Overloading the system with children who could remain safely with their parents means that caseworkers have less time and money to find and follow the children who are in danger of severe abuse and neglect. The rising costs of foster care drain agencies of funds that could be used to support families, only worsening the conditions that can lead to serious maltreatment. Overzealous CPS authorities scare away families who might have sought help for domestic violence and other problems before they spiraled into deadly situations. This is why tragic cases of child abuse continue to appear even under the watch of the toughest child protection regimes. Children fall through the cracks not because child welfare agencies are devoting too many resources to family support. Children fall through the cracks because agencies are devoting too many resources to investigations and child removal.

The stories of children killed by their parents despite being "known to the system" may seem to send the message that more children could be saved if agencies worked harder at policing families. But ratcheting up investigations and removals has failed to reduce family violence. Texas CPS investigates a greater-than-average proportion of the referrals it receives, yet Texas has one of the highest child fatality rates in the nation. A study of child abuse deaths in the state concluded, "Surprisingly, the statistical analysis shows no relationship between a state's intervention with a family, as measured by its reporting rate, service rate, or removal rate, and its child abuse and neglect death rate." The report recommended reducing poverty and expanding access to proven violence-prevention programs as more effective at protecting children from lethal abuse than surveilling and separating families.[14]

Something is drastically wrong with a child protection approach that both breaks up families where children are safe and misses families where children are in grave danger. The problem isn't that there are too few people mandated to report their suspicions, too few caseworkers patrolling neighborhoods, or too few children taken from their homes. The problem is that a system based on surveillance and child-taking approaches child welfare in the wrong way. Intensifying surveillance and separation only intensifies their bad outcomes. The deaths of children known to the system don't prove that we need more family policing. They prove that family policing doesn't protect children. I am certain that the child welfare system causes unconscionable harm to children and their families. I am equally certain that it is incapable of protecting children from violence in their homes and that we can keep children safer without it.

Not Caring Enough

On top of the terror the family-policing system inflicts on investigated families, it also harms even more children who aren't forced into its clutches. The vast majority of US children who are denied adequate housing, nutrition, health care, and education by racial capitalist policies—by far, the greatest harms to children—are simply ignored by child welfare agencies. Among Western countries, the United States has the highest rate of childhood poverty, invests the least in supporting families, and spends the most on child removal and foster care. In 2019, more than ten million children—nearly one in seven of all the nation's children—were living below the federal poverty line, measured at $26,172 for a family of four. About 6 percent of children were living in "deep poverty," defined as having family resources less than one-half the poverty line. Child poverty rates for Black, Latinx, and Native children were more than double those of white children. More than half of all Black, Latinx, and Native children are poor or near poor.[15]

In 2015, Congress commissioned the National Academies of Sciences, Engineering, and Medicine to undertake a "nonpartisan, evidence-based report that would provide its assessment of the most

effective means for reducing child poverty by half in the next 10 years."
Aided by staff and funded by several foundations, a committee of leading social scientists engaged in research, commissioned papers, and so-
licited expert commentary to measure child poverty in the United States
and examine the most successful ways to shrink it. The resulting 2019
report recommended drastically expanding programs that give material supports to families, "either directly, by providing income transfers,
or indirectly, by providing food, housing, or medical care." A $3,000
per child per year child allowance would produce the largest poverty
reduction, but other policies, like raising the federal minimum wage,
providing paid family and medical leave, expanding the Earned Income
Tax Credit, and increasing child care, food, and housing subsidies are
also essential. None of the recommendations had anything to do with
increasing family surveillance and separation.[16]

The family-policing system embodies a cruel paradox. While it
brutally intrudes on too many families, failing to provide them true
safety or support, it also ignores the damaging impact of poverty,
racism, and patriarchal culture on even more children. Even worse,
the government's claim that CPS is protecting Black children serves
as a substitute for ending the racist social structures that endanger
them. The belief that Black children's problems are caused by their
families and the solution is to tear them apart secures policies that
criminalize Black children and their parents while impeding policies
that would help them thrive. By relying on policing families as the
way to protect children, the system blocks imagining a society that
is safer for children.

IMAGINING A SAFER WORLD

The only way to end the destruction caused by the child welfare system is to dismantle it while at the same time building a safer and more
caring society that has no need to tear families apart. If we reject the
carceral logic of policing families as the way to protect children, we can
reimagine what safety and well-being mean and work toward putting
that vision in place. The task for abolitionists "is not only, or not even

primarily, about abolition as a negative process of tearing down, but it is also about building up, about creating new institutions," explains renowned activist and scholar Angela Y. Davis, discussing W. E. B. Du Bois's concept of abolition democracy. "Du Bois pointed out that in order to fully abolish the oppressive conditions produced by slavery, new democratic institutions would have to be created."[17]

Liberation from enslavement was inseparable from creating a free society where slavery could not exist. Likewise, prisons will only cease to be built when social, economic, and political conditions eliminate the need for them. Abolitionists are working toward a society where prisons are inconceivable—a world where its inhabitants "would laugh off the outrageous idea of putting people into cages, thinking such actions as morally perverse and fatally counterproductive," writes Alexander Lee, founder of the Transgender, Gender Variant and Intersex Justice Project.[18]

Just imagine: a society where the needs of children and their families are generously met and where the idea of tearing children from their families as the way to care for them is laughable.

This vision of a safer society without family policing is not a pipe dream, an academic fantasy of pie in the sky, or a revolutionary utopia. We can imagine confidently a society that has no need for family policing because we are already creating it.

"An Unintended Abolition"

Anna Arons, an acting assistant law professor at New York University, stumbled across the unintended abolition of the child welfare system in New York City. It took place temporarily during the COVID-19 pandemic. When the city shut down in mid-March 2020, so did its family-policing apparatus. "This system shrunk in almost every conceivable way as mandated reporters retreated, caseworkers adopted less intrusive investigatory tactics, and family courts constrained their operations," notes Arons. "Reports fell, the number of cases filed in court fell, and the number of children separated from their parents fell." At the time, ACS authorities and the media speculated, with no evidence to back them up, that the pandemic put children at risk of abuse because they were "trapped" in their homes outside the watchful gaze of social workers, teachers, and other mandated reporters.[19]

But ACS data showed precisely the opposite. The forced experiment in abolition didn't endanger children; it arguably kept them safer. Reports of physical or sexual abuse in New York City decreased dramatically during the pandemic. ACS investigations related to child fatalities—which were required despite the lockdown—dropped by 25 percent between February 2019 and June 2019 and the same period in 2020. When the city bounced back in fall 2020, there was no deluge of child abuse cases that had gone unreported during the pandemic. ACS commissioner David Hansell told the city council that children remained equally safe in their homes during the shutdown as when family policing was in full effect. "ACS's data from the fall reveal that children stayed as safe with less surveillance, less government intrusion, and less family separation," Arons observes.[20]

New York City's children remained safe without ACS intervention because the pandemic generated more caring and effective ways to support families. Community-based groups sprang into action to provide tangible resources to residents who asked for assistance. By the end of July 2020, more than fifty mutual aid networks throughout the city were providing essential items like groceries and diapers and offering services like child care and mental health care. They deployed hundreds of thousands of dollars to meet people's needs through the work of thousands of volunteers. "The rapid expansion of mutual aid projects was breathtaking," writes Arons. Brooklyn-based Bed Stuy Strong built a network of twenty-seven hundred volunteers within a month, and Crown Heights Mutual Aid "made 1,300 grocery deliveries between mid-March and mid-May alone," Arons notes.[21]

The federal government also played a major role in keeping children safe during the pandemic. In April 2020, Congress rendered pathbreaking support to impoverished families by passing the CARES Act. As part of a stimulus package, the act provided a one-time payment of $1,200 for adults earning less than $75,000 a year, with an additional $500 payment for each child under the age of seventeen and $600 per week in extra unemployment benefits, through the end of July 2020. It was the largest distribution of direct aid to families in US history and larger than all other nonretirement programs combined. The checks went directly to parents without strings attached, forgoing the investigation, surveillance, and regulation entailed in child welfare programs.

"Though unintentional, this brief experiment shows that the typical outsized and reactionary family regulation system is not necessary to protect children," Arons concludes. "Abolition need not be a fantasy; New York City already made it, for a moment, a reality."[22]

CPS-Free Zones

New York City, like most places, had also engaged in another sort of experiment in abolition long before the pandemic. For decades, ACS has targeted almost exclusively Black and Latinx communities for intervention. Ninety percent of the families under investigation and children in foster care are from these communities. But there are other neighborhoods in New York City where CPS rarely, if ever, sets foot. Affluent white neighborhoods in US cities are CPS-free zones. This is not because the families who live there never experience problems or conflicts. It's because they have the privilege of addressing their problems and conflicts through private means and have no need to rely on a toxic child welfare system. Their needs for income, housing, and health care are all met, meaning they are able to avoid the types of problems families in poor Black neighborhoods must deal with on a daily basis.[23]

This nation has already created communities where the child welfare system has been abolished, but it has reserved them for elite white families. If America valued all children equally, it would ensure that the needs of all of them were met—and the child welfare system would cease to be necessary, like in those fancy neighborhoods.

History Lessons

The history of Black people building child-caring institutions within Black communities untethered to white-dominated ones also lends assurance that we can raise children safely without family policing. Excluded from nineteenth-century asylums and orphanages established by white charities, Black people relied primarily on extended family networks and community institutions to take care of children whose parents were unable to meet their needs. In the decades after Emancipation, Black women established hundreds of clubs and church groups dedicated to improving the status of Black families and providing services to Black mothers and children. Black club women emphasized social work that enhanced mothers' skills, families' material circumstances, and children's opportunities, an emphasis that stands in stark contrast to the child welfare system's reliance on punishing mothers and removing children from their homes.[24]

Black women's groups established schools and trained teachers, held mothers' meetings, ran day nurseries and kindergartens, and opened homes for working girls. They integrated child welfare work into an agenda that encompassed a broad range of antiracist activities, including agitation "against lynching, the convict lease system, the Jim Crow car laws, and all other barbarities and abuses which degrade and dishearten us," wrote Mary Church Terrell, first president of the National Association of Colored Women, in 1900. Ironically, because of white supremacist segregation, these women had the leeway to implement their vision within Black communities, perhaps with a freedom unparalleled in subsequent eras.[25]

A multitude of other Black community-based institutions have cared for Black children while resisting a racist child welfare system. When Black people in the South were shut out from hospitals that served white patients only, Black midwives routinely provided excellent labor and delivery care in their communities. In the 1970s, the Black Panther Party operated thirteen People's Free Medical Clinics, staffed by volunteer health care professionals, in urban neighborhoods across the country, which offered vaccinations and other basic services for children. With donations from local businesses, churches, and organizations, the party's Free Breakfast Program fed tens of thousands of children through its chapters in at least thirty-six cities.[26]

Kin Caregivers

The most ubiquitous form of help for struggling parents in Black communities is kinship care provided outside the foster care system. Black women share a rich tradition of women-centered, communal child care that draws on members of the extended family (grandmothers, sisters, aunts, and cousins), as well as close friends and neighbors. Their relationship with children ranges from daily assistance to long-term care, informal adoption, or taking turns assuming caregiving responsibilities for the child. Skyrocketing female incarceration rates, cutbacks in social services, the AIDS epidemic, and drug addiction led to a resurgence in caregiving by relatives, especially grandmothers, in the late 1980s. By 1994, nearly four million children lived in grandparent-headed households. More than one-third of these children lived in homes with no parent present. Almost half of the children being raised by grandparents were Black. Although state child welfare departments used to mistake shared caregiving among kin as child neglect, they increasingly rely on kin to care for a substantial segment of their foster care populations.[27]

Kinship foster care is better for children than foster care with strangers. Children are more likely to maintain contact with their parents, to stay with siblings, to avoid moving to multiple placements, and to receive loving attention. Kinship foster care also provides financial support for relative caregivers. But the price of foster care benefits is relinquishing custody of children to the state and submitting to supervision by the child welfare system. Families live under the perpetual threat that agencies will move the children to a stranger's foster home if relatives caring for them fail to comply with agency directives.[28]

At the Operation MOSES meeting I attended in Chicago in summer 2000, I met a woman named Devon whose nieces and nephews, whom she was raising as a licensed kinship caregiver, were seized from her and placed with a foster family in a distant suburb because her apartment was considered too small. Devon was allowed two supervised visits with the children in the first month after they were taken. Then the caseworker informed her that she couldn't see them again because they were being transitioned to adoption with the new foster caretaker. A year later, just as abruptly, Devon received a call from a DCFS caseworker informing her that the children would be returned to her. Unbeknownst to Devon, her children had been physically abused in the first foster home and were split up and placed in pairs with two different families. Apparently, Devon's relentless complaints to DCFS and to her state representative had triggered an internal investigation into the children's foster care placement.

"It's a happy time," Devon told me after the children's return. But she was grappling with the aftermath of the state's disruption of her family's life. While in foster care, the children had been given potent mood-altering drugs to make them more manageable, and Devon was working on weaning them from the medications. Because her foster care license had been revoked, DCFS drastically cut her monthly payment. Whereas some reformers have advocated reducing the abuses foster care inflicts on Black children by increasing foster kin placements, a better way to ensure their welfare would be to provide generous income and services directly to kin caregivers like Devon without requiring them to submit to family policing.[29]

BUILDING SAFER COMMUNITIES

There is a long way to go between our current destructive system, which upholds an unequal society, and an equal society that has no need for a destructive system. But this is a reason to start building safer communities now, not to lament the hopelessness of the task. The burgeoning abolitionist movement is working to strengthen and expand community-based efforts that already exist and to launch new initiatives that support families and care for children without relying on family policing. In this way, we can start dismantling the child welfare system while we create the conditions that make it obsolete.

Shrink the System Until It No Longer Exists

Two of the most helpful tools I learned from the prison abolitionists are the concepts of abolition as a horizon and engaging in "nonreformist reforms" that move us toward that vision. Prison abolition is a long-term project that requires strategically working toward the complete elimination of carceral punishment. No abolitionist expects all prison walls to come tumbling down at once. Yet abolitionist philosophy is defined in contradistinction to reform: reforming prisons is diametrically opposed to abolishing them. How can abolitionists take steps toward dismantling carceral institutions without falling into reformist traps? They have resolved this quandary with the concept of nonreformist reforms, which prominent abolitionist Ruth Wilson Gilmore defines in *Golden Gulag* as "changes that, at the end of the day, unravel rather than widen the net of social control through criminalization." To aid abolition, nonreformist reforms must shrink rather than strengthen "the state's capacity for violence" and facilitate the goal of building a society without prisons. By engaging in nonreformist reforms, in conjunction with other political strategies, abolitionists strive to make transformative changes in carceral systems with the objective of demolishing those systems rather than fixing them. For example, prison abolitionists have engaged in efforts to stop prison expansion by opposing prison construction or shutting down prisons that already exist; to defund police departments and end police stop-and-frisk practices; and to eliminate the requirement of money bail to release people charged with crimes.[30]

People working toward the horizon of demolishing the child welfare system are similarly fighting for nonreformist reforms that reduce the power of child welfare agencies to intervene in Black communities. The agenda of the Parent Legislative Action Network (PLAN), the initiative Joyce McMillan launched as part of JMacForFamilies, is a model of strategic strikes against the ability of ACS to regulate and destroy families. "Everything I think of now legislative-wise is how to shrink the system," McMillan told me. "When I think of divest and invest, I don't just think about money. Reduce, reduce, reduce until they're gone."

PLAN's collective of lawyers, law professors, and activists is pushing the New York State Legislature to enact three bills that would reduce the number of families investigated by ACS and empower parents and other family caregivers who become ensnared in child welfare proceedings. One proposed law requires CPS workers to give parents a Miranda notice, informing them of their right to refuse ACS entrance into their homes without legal representation. A second proposed law would change anonymous reporting to confidential reporting in hopes of deterring people from calling CPS to make baseless accusations. The third bill bans involuntary drug testing of pregnant patients and their newborns and reporting results to CPS. Another campaign launched by JMacForFamilies, Movement for Family Power, and other organizations is #RepealASFA, calling on Congress to rescind the 1997 Adoption and Safe Families Act, which accelerated the timeline for termination of parental rights.[31]

Family Defenders

One of the chief ways child welfare agencies exert power over parents is to steamroll over their legal rights. Most Black parents don't seek legal counsel before submitting to a CPS investigation, and they may meet with a lawyer for the first time after caseworkers have already taken their children. The rise of a cadre of attorneys known as family defenders, who provide legal services to CPS-impacted families, has improved children's chances of staying out of foster care or returning home swiftly. Vivek Sankaran, director of the Child Advocacy Law Clinic at University of Michigan Law School, reports that in a pilot program he ran in Detroit providing legal representation to parents, "not one of the children we worked with entered foster care. Lawyers can play a pivotal role in preventing government overreaching."[32]

Family defenders frame their representation of parents in child welfare proceedings as advocating for the entire family, contesting the view that parents are the adversaries of their children and recognizing that family unity is in children's best interests. Family defense has become increasingly effective as it broadens its services by including social workers and parent advocates in multidisciplinary teams that address their clients' social as well as legal needs. These teams keep families together by assisting them in obtaining secure housing, contesting evictions, accessing social services, and claiming benefits to help solve the problems that triggered the CPS investigation. "My lawyer's office is one of the only safe places where a mother can go to report that she's in crisis," says Kathleen Creamer, managing attorney of the Family Advocacy Unit at Community Legal Services in Philadelphia. "Pretty much anywhere else that she goes she's going to be surrounded by mandated reporters."[33]

Family defense services, like those at Community Legal Services, as well as Detroit Center for Family Advocacy, East Bay Family Defenders in California, and the New York–based Bronx Defenders, Brooklyn Defender Services, Center for Family Representation, and Neighborhood Defender Service of Harlem, provide critical advocacy against family policing inside and outside the courtroom, increasingly joining abolitionist campaigns. A key demand is legislation that guarantees parents high-quality, multidisciplinary legal defense at every stage of the CPS process, including at initial contact with caseworkers, before children are removed.

Fund Support, Not Terror

Another way for abolitionists to chip away at the child welfare system is to defund it. "While cutting police funding is not the same as abolishing the police," Geo Maher explains, "the hidden power of defunding as a strategy lies in how it can symbolically disrupt the world of police and provide a practical bridge toward a world with no police at all." Like defunding police, starting to divert the billions of dollars spent on investigating, regulating, and separating families to tangible resources provided directly to parents and other family caregivers, as well as to voluntary community-based supports for families, would be a tremendous step toward ending family policing altogether. The evidence is incontrovertible that wide-scale government policies that reduce childhood poverty by increasing family income and meeting families' material needs for housing, food, and health care would dramatically lessen the harms to children that child welfare agencies claim, but fail, to address. Government funds should also provide reparations to the children and families that child welfare agencies forcibly separated, to cover the costs of addressing the resulting physical, emotional, and economic injuries and to help separated family members reunite.[34]

Defunding CPS is a nonreformist reform only if it pulls money completely away from the family-policing apparatus. As I have noted, Congress and local governments have implemented measures, including the Family First Prevention Services Act, to shift some of the money child welfare departments spend away from maintaining children in foster care to providing services that prevent foster care placement. But as long as the funds remain in child welfare agency hands, the shift will expand, not shrink, the power these agencies have to police families. These programs continue to coerce parents to engage in therapeutic procedures—what legal services attorney Angela Burton and activist Angeline Montauban call "trauma pimping"—instead of giving them the material things their families need. The camouflage of offering help to parents on threat of losing their children to foster care legitimizes the assertion of control over more families.[35]

A far better policy is the part of President Joe Biden's pandemic stimulus, the American Rescue Plan, that provides for a one-year expansion of the child tax credit. Under the plan, the federal government sends monthly checks for up to $300 per child to poor and middle-income families to help them cover the costs of raising children. The guaranteed payments are projected to lift more than four million children out of poverty, cutting child poverty nearly in half. If Congress makes this regular infusion of income for families a permanent government program and revises its child-claiming rules to reach more children, it will keep children safer—what journalist Kendra Hurley calls "the most radical child protection plan this country has seen."[36]

Creating Our Own Way

As family-policing abolitionists push for nonreformist reforms that shrink the child welfare system, they are also growing community-based ways to provide support to families, known as mutual aid, that are completely disconnected from child welfare agencies. These networks, groups, and organizations are animated by an approach to child welfare that is diametrically opposed to family policing: they are caring instead of punitive, voluntary instead of coercive, generous instead of stingy. Mutual aid offers parents concrete goods and assistance to use however they determine will benefit their children, instead of mandating services based on parents' presumed pathologies. Activist and law professor Dean Spade aptly defines mutual aid as "collective coordination to meet each other's needs, usually from an awareness the systems we have in place are not going to meet them," and "in fact, have often created the crisis or are making things worse." Mutual aid projects work to meet survival needs alongside social movements to dismantle oppressive systems. Every social movement has been accompanied by mutual aid projects.[37]

As we saw in New York City during the pandemic lockdown, mutual aid groups can provide effective replacements for child welfare agencies, and many abolitionists are working collectively to put more in place. Joyce McMillan is teaming with another New York City abolitionist, Khadijah Abdurahman, to launch a project offering diapers to families for free. DHS Give Us Back Our Children, a self-help collective of mothers, other family caregivers, and their allies based in Los Angeles and Philadelphia, gives moral support and advice to families entangled in child welfare proceedings. The group has published guides—*How to Fight Your DHS Case* and *Know Your Rights: What to Do If Your Child Is Detained by the Los Angeles Department of Children & Family Services*—and gained permission to accompany mothers in dependency hearings to coach them in recovering custody of their children. Similarly, Milwaukee-based Welfare Warriors, which formed in 1986 as a small multiracial group of single mothers to start a newspaper, *Welfare Mothers Voice*, launched Mothers and Grandmothers of the Disappeared Children to aid family caregivers whose children have been removed from their homes.[38]

Rise Magazine recently issued a report, *Someone to Turn To*, written by a team of system-impacted mothers, that lays out a model for creating networks of parent peer supporters to lend caregiving assistance without involving child welfare agencies. *Rise* coexecutive directors Bianca Shaw and Jeanette Vega opposed New York City's plan to create "family enrichment centers" because the city-run centers were likely to become sites of family surveillance, recommending instead "peer support coordinated by trusted community organizations." Vega told journalist Kendra Hurley that she saw the potential for peer support during the COVID pandemic as residents of her Bronx neighborhood joined together, "taking turns with homeschooling, sharing washing machines, and, for material needs, turning to the local grassroots groups manned not by a government agency but by each other."[39]

For six months in 2020, a group of homeless mothers and children in Philadelphia took over fifteen vacant city-owned apartments and created two protest encampments to demand that city authorities provide housing for their families. In September 2020, the city of Philadelphia agreed to relinquish fifty vacant homes to a community land trust established by Philadelphia Housing Action, the coalition of housing activists that had organized the housing takeover.[40]

Black midwives and birthing doulas, like those affiliated with Ancient Song Doula Services in Bed-Stuy, Brooklyn, are reviving the tradition of delivering Black babies with a new political awareness. "You're not just a traditional doula," says Chanel Porchia-Albert, who founded Ancient Song in 2008 in her Brooklyn home. "You're understanding the intersections of care and of gender, sexuality and housing and all of these different things that show up for people when they're seeking out care, especially in Black, brown and Indigenous populations." The reproductive justice movement, launched by a group of Black feminist activists in 1994, has always advocated for the human right to raise children with dignity in safe, healthy, and supportive environments, along with the right to have or not have a child. Porchia-Albert considers her work at Ancient Song to be a form of mutual aid that advances reproductive justice. Black birth workers can help Black women have healthy pregnancies, give birth safely, and care for their babies instead of ripping babies from their mothers' arms.[41]

Family-policing abolitionists can also adopt transformative justice practices that prison abolitionists and anticarceral survivors of sexual violence are exploring apart from law enforcement. Transformative justice, Mariame Kaba explains, "is a community process developed by anti-violence activists of color, in particular, who wanted to create responses to violence that do what criminal punishment systems failed to do: build support and more safety for the person harmed, figure out how the broader context was set up for this harm to happen, and how that context can be changed so that this harm is less likely to happen again." Far from ignoring the harm caused by intimate violence, transformative justice holds individuals and institutions that caused the harm accountable and seeks to repair the harm done. Family, friends, and other community members (which may include those who experienced or committed the violence) come together to devise effective interventions in the sources of violence to prevent the violence from occurring in the future. This might entail creating more sustainable living conditions for families, providing high-quality mental health treatment for abusers, addressing the misogyny and other toxic gender norms that often underlie violence in the home, and working to end the systems and structures that foster domestic violence.[42]

Community-based support groups, mutual aid projects, and transformative justice processes allow for mass refusal to participate in family policing. They give struggling parents alternatives to relinquishing custody of their children to CPS as the price of support. They give relatives, neighbors, and mandated reporters ways to help families in need instead of calling the hotline. The graduate students at the Jane Addams College of Social Work at University of Illinois in Chicago published a resource list, "Alternatives to Calling DCFS," to guide well-intentioned people away from triggering a CPS investigation. As nonpunitive ways of caring for children flourish, the need for reporting suspected child maltreatment will diminish, garnering support for abolishing the practice altogether. More broadly, the growth of community spaces where children's needs are met will gradually shrivel those where family policing seems required. This is how we can work toward the horizon of a society that keeps children safe without tearing their families apart.[43]

———

In June 2020, about two hundred people marched from Brooklyn Family Court to Manhattan Family Court, chanting "ACS is the family police." When the protesters arrived at Foley Square, they encountered another, larger rally. The second group consisted of about a thousand Black Lives Matter marchers demanding an end to police violence against Black people. "We're supposed to feel safe with them," one of the protesters told the *New York Daily News*. "We're not supposed to be afraid of them." Those words might have referred to the reason either group was marching: to protest the city's child welfare agency or to protest the city's police department. The convergence of two marches symbolizes the deep connection between the new movement to end family policing and more seasoned movements to value Black lives and end the prison-industrial complex. There are promising signs that this connection is moving beyond symbolism and theory to collective action. In 2021, Black Lives Matter Los Angeles started a campaign called #ReimagineChildSafety to demand that the Los Angeles Board of Supervisors end the partnership between the city's child welfare department and the police.[44]

This book has demonstrated that the child welfare system's surveillance, control, and destruction of Black families is part of the same carceral regime as prisons and police. We should be on a common mission to bring down all the regime's damaging extensions and to create a common vision for meeting human needs, preventing violence, and caring for children, families, and communities. The unwillingness to confront the child welfare system's racist terror reminds me of a common scene in action/adventure movies. The hero, dangling from a cracking cliff, has to decide whether to let go and grab the hand of someone reaching down from a helicopter. Clinging to the crumbling rock means moving faster toward disaster. Only by releasing the grip on the cliff can the hero be brought to safety. We must stop clinging to a system that is propelling Black children to disaster out of fear of taking a fundamentally different path that would actually keep them safer. Instead, we can envision and build a world where tearing families apart to meet children's needs would be unimaginable.

Acknowledgments

*T*ORN *APART* IS THE CULMINATION OF 25 YEARS OF STUDYING and contesting racism in the child welfare system. During those years, I was blessed to collaborate with many individuals and organizations dedicated to resisting the system's destruction and to envisioning a better way to meet children's needs. They helped me to become a family-policing abolitionist. This book would not be possible without their support, insights, and inspiration. I would like to express my gratitude for some of them who made special contributions to this book project: Movement for Family Power and its directors, Erin Miles Cloud and Lisa Sangoi; National Coalition for Child Protection Reform and its executive director, Richard Wexler, president, Martin Guggenheim, and former board member Diane Redleaf; the UpEND Movement and its co-creators, Alan Dettlaff and Kristen Weber; and National Advocates for Pregnant Women and its founding executive director, Lynn M. Paltrow.

My greatest inspiration for this book comes from system-impacted mothers and their organizations—like Joyce McMillan, director of JMacForFamilies; Angeline Montauban and her reading group; the staff of *Rise Magazine*, including its founder, Nora McCarthy, co-executive directors, Bianca Shaw and Jeanette Vega, and Keyna Franklin, Imani

Worthy, and Halimah Washington; Philadelphia's DHS Give Us Back Our Children, especially Pat Albright, Carolyn Hill, and Phoebe Jones; and Elizabeth Brico. I owe them and other organizers dedicated to ending family policing my deepest gratitude, and my deepest hope for *Torn Apart* is that it advances their work for liberation.

Special thanks also to Nancy Polikoff and Jane Spinak, who encouraged me to mark the twentieth anniversary of *Shattered Bonds* with a new book and spearheaded the landmark symposium "Strengthened Bonds: Abolishing the Child Welfare System and Re-envisioning Child Well-Being," sponsored by the *Columbia Journal of Race and Law* and organized by its editors, Nicolás Quaid Galván, Jacob Elkin, and Vinay Patel. I greatly appreciate all the brilliant and dedicated activists, lawyers, and scholars who came together electronically over three glorious days in June 2021 to discuss why and how to abolish family policing.

The staff attorneys, social workers, and parent advocates at the family defense practices of the Bronx Defenders, Brooklyn Defense Services, Neighborhood Defender Service of Harlem, and Community Legal Services in Philadelphia, including managing attorneys Emma Ketteringham, Lauren Shapiro, Ryan Napoli, and Kathleen Creamer, graciously took time from their busy schedules to meet with me to discuss their exceptional advocacy for parents and their families. Their experiences benefited *Torn Apart* tremendously, and I am greatly inspired by their work. Sterling Johnson and Jennifer Bennetch of Philadelphia Housing Action also took time to speak with me about their remarkable direct action to demand homes for unhoused families in our city. As my argument in *Torn Apart* shows, I have also been profoundly influenced by prison abolitionists and especially appreciated engaging with Amna Akbar, Ruha Benjamin, Daniel Berger, Angela Y. Davis, Mariame Kaba, Robin D. G. Kelley, Victoria Law, Andrea Ritchie, Dylan Rodríguez, Angel Sanchez, Dean Spade, Maya Schenwar, and Keeanga-Yamahtta Taylor while writing this book.

I am indebted to Bernard Harcourt for inviting me to speak about family-policing abolition in his Abolition Democracy seminar at Columbia Law School, and to Tymber Hudson's dazzling contribution to the program. This book is also inspired by Tymber and other young

people who spent time in foster care and now advocate for its abolition. Other engagements that informed and inspired me while writing
this book include: a workshop on family-policing abolition at Penn
Law, organized by my student Lindsay Grier and sponsored by the Toll
Public Interest Center; a session on child welfare at the Eastern Sociological Association, organized by Kelley Fong; an UpFromTheCracks
podcast episode and other conversations with J. Khadijah Aburahman;
my podcast conversation with John Kelly of *The Imprint*, which published my article, "Abolishing Policing Also Means Abolishing Family Regulation"; and my plenary conversation with Kathleen Creamer
on "Demystifying Abolition," conducted at the American Bar Association's Center on Children and Law National Parent Representation
Conference.

My academic home at University of Pennsylvania, in the Department of Africana Studies, the Department of Sociology, and Penn Law,
has been an invaluable source of support. I am extremely grateful to
my Penn colleagues for their encouragement and to President Amy
Gutmann, Provost Wendell Pritchett, Dean Steven Fluharty, and Dean
Ted Ruger for generously providing financial and other resources to
facilitate my work.

I could not have written *Torn Apart* without the superb assistance
of a team of dedicated Penn Law students who conducted research and
met with me throughout summer 2020: Jacob Burnett, Vinita Davey,
Lauren Davis, Madison Gray, Lindsay Grier, Allison Kruk, Bridget Lavender, Michelle Mlacker, Claire Samuelson, Victoria Sanchez, and John
Santoro. Their voluminous files of sources and perceptive conversations about them provided up-to-date documentation for my ideas for
the book. Sociology PhD student Rebecca Schut, my teaching assistant for Race, Science, and Justice, and Dr. Ezelle Sanford, postdoctoral
fellow at my Program on Race, Science, and Society, went beyond the
call of duty and afforded me space to write during a busy spring 2021.
At the final stage of revisions, in summer 2021, Penn Law students
Nimo Ali and Nastia Gorodilova tirelessly and skillfully tracked down
needed information under a tight deadline. In addition, I had enlight-
ening conversations with my PhD students Victoria Copeland and

Brianna Harvey at UCLA and Isabella Restrepo at UC-Santa Barbara, who are all dedicated to a common mission. I am exceedingly grateful to these wonderful students for their commitment and camaraderie. Huge thanks also to Timothy Von Dulm and the entire Biddle Law Library research and scholarship staff for providing every source I ever requested with alacrity and expertise.

I am indebted to David Halpern of the Robbins Office for his steadfast support and sage advice at every phase of this book project. A long conversation with Brian Distelberg at Basic Books convinced me I needed to write this book, and his wise editorial guidance helped me get it in shape. I am thankful he believed in this project from the start. The manuscript benefited immensely from careful editing by Kyle Gipson at Basic Books. His astute queries and suggestions helped make my arguments sharper and stronger. Kelley Blewster's excellent copyediting improved the book's grammar and clarity. I thank everyone at Hachette Book Group, including Sharon Kunz and Melissa Veronesi, for their exceptional contributions to the publication of *Torn Apart*.

I am eternally grateful to my husband, sisters, and children for their love and devotion, which sustained me throughout this book project and all other aspects of my life. Thanks also to my African Episcopal Church of St. Thomas family, especially the Very Rev. Canon Martini Shaw, Barbara Savage, and Wendella Fox, for their prayers and support.

In February 2021, my daughter gave birth to my second granddaughter, Josephine. This book is dedicated to her and to my first granddaughter, Akari. May they grow up to see the abolitionist horizon become a reality and may they participate joyfully in its creation.

Notes

PROLOGUE

1. Dorothy Roberts, *Shattered Bonds: The Color of Child Welfare* (New York: Basic Civitas Books, 2001), 9.

2. Ira J. Chasnoff, Harvey J. Landress, and Mark E. Barrett, "The Prevalence of Illicit Drug or Alcohol Use During Pregnancy and Discrepancies in Mandatory Reporting in Pinellas County, Florida," *New England Journal of Medicine* 322 (1990): 1202–1206; Bryna Brennan, "'Boarder Babies': Abandoned by Addicted Mothers, and Still Unwanted," *Los Angeles Times*, July 30, 1989, www.latimes.com/archives/la-xpm-1989-07-30-mn-725-story.html; Ellen Hopkins, "Childhood's End: What Life Is Like for Crack Babies," *Rolling Stone*, October 18, 1990, www.rollingstone.com/culture/culture-news/childhoods-end-what-life-is-like-for-crack-babies-188557/; Peter Kerr, "Addiction's Hidden Toll: Poor Families in Turmoil," *New York Times*, June 23, 1988, https://timesmachine.nytimes.com/timesmachine/1988/06/23/044088.html?pageNumber=1.

3. Casey Quinlan, "New Data Shows the School-to-Prison Pipeline Starts as Early as Preschool," *Think Progress*, June 7, 2016, https://thinkprogress.org/new-data-shows-the-school-to-prison-pipeline-starts-as-early-as-preschool-80fc1c3e85be/. See also Monique W. Morris, *PushOut: The Criminalization of Black Girls in Schools* (New York: New Press, 2005); Carla Shedd, *Unequal City: Race, Schools, and Perceptions of Injustice* (New York: Russel Sage Foundation, 2015); Alexandros Orphanides, "The Dehumanization of Black Children: Tamir Rice, Kalief Browder and Dajerria Becton," *Huffington Post*, updated December 6, 2017, www.huffpost.com/entry/the-dehumanization-of-black-children_b_7581404; Johnny Diaz, "6-Year-Old Held in Facility for 2 Days Without Consent," *New York Times*, February 17, 2020, www.nytimes.com/2020/02/17/us/baker-act-love

-grove-elementary.html; Patrisse Cullors and Asha Bandele, *When They Call You a Terrorist: A Black Lives Matter Memoir* (New York: St. Martin's Press, 2018), 70.

4. Roberts, *Shattered Bonds*, 7.

5. Christopher A. Swann and Michelle Sheran Sylvester, "The Foster Care Crisis: What Caused Caseload to Grow?," *Demography* 43, no. 2 (May 2006): 309–333, Figure 1; Movement for Family Power, *"Whatever They Do, I'm Her Comfort, I'm Her Protector": How the Foster System Has Become Ground Zero for the U.S. Drug War* (New York: MFP, NYU Family Defense Clinic, Drug Policy Alliance, 2020), 18, www.movementforfamilypower.org/ground-zero.

6. Swann and Sylvester, "Foster Care Crisis," 310.

7. The story about Jornell is based on my interviews of her and my review of her court records in 2000 and borrowed from *Shattered Bonds: The Color of Child Welfare*. David is a pseudonym.

8. Washington State Department of Children, Youth and Families, "Braam Settlement Agreement," last updated 2017, www.dcyf.wa.gov/practice/practice-improvement/braam-settlement-agreement.

9. CR10 Publications Collective, *ABOLITION NOW! Ten Years of Strategy and Struggle Against the Prison Industrial Complex* (California: AK Press, 2008), xi; Rose Braz et al., "The History of Critical Resistance," *Social Justice* 27, no. 3 (Fall 2000): 6–10; Angela Y. Davis and Dylan Rodríguez, "The Challenge of Prison Abolition: A Conversation," *Social Justice* 27, no. 3 (Fall 2000): 212–218; Critical Resistance, *Critical Resistance: Beyond the Prison Industrial Complex* (Berkeley, CA: Critical Resistance Conference, September 25–27, 1998), http://criticalresistance.org/critical-resistance-beyond-the-prison-industrial-complex-1998-conference.

10. Dylan Rodríguez, "Abolition as Praxis of Human Being: A Foreword," in "Developments in the Law—Prison Abolition," *Harvard Law Review* 132 (2019): 1578.

11. In June 2021, the *Columbia Journal of Race and Law*, in collaboration with Columbia Law School, held a three-day symposium, Strengthened Bonds: Abolishing the Child Welfare System and Re-Envisioning Child Well-Being, marking the twentieth anniversary of *Shattered Bonds*. *Columbia Journal of Race and Law*, "The Columbia Journal of Race and Law Announces Its Volume 11 Symposium," February 4, 2021, https://journals.library.columbia.edu/index.php/cjrl/announcement/view/376.

INTRODUCTION: A BENEVOLENT TERROR

1. The boys' names are pseudonyms.

2. Author's interview of Vanessa Peoples, November 17, 2020; Aurora, Colorado, police officers' body camera footage and General Offense Reports from Vanessa Peoples's arrest on July 13, 2017; Diane L. Redleaf, "During a Routine Child Services Check, Cops Hog-Tied a Mom and Carried Her out 'Like a Pig Upside Down,'" *Reason*, September 24, 2020, https://reason.com/2020/09/24/aurora-police-hogtied-child-services-abuse/.

3. ACLU Colorado, "Interactive Map: Racialized Policing by the Aurora Police," 2021, https://aclu-co.org/interactive-map-racialized-policing-by-the

-aurora-police-department/; Michael Roberts, "Claim: At Least 13 People of Color Abused by Aurora Cops Since 2003," *Westword*, January 23, 2019, www .westword.com/news/claim-alberto-torres-one-of-at-least-13-people-of-color -abused-by-aurora-cops-since-2003-11026378.

4. Claire Lampen, "What We Know About the Killing of Elijah McClain," *The Cut*, updated August 11, 2020, www.thecut.com/2020/08/the-killing-of -elijah-mcclain-everything-we-know.html; Lucy Tompkins, "Here's What You Need to Know About Elijah McClain's Death," *New York Times*, updated February 23, 2021, www.nytimes.com/article/who-was-elijah-mcclain.html.

5. Gabriel L. Schwartz and Jaquelyn L. Jahn, "Mapping Fatal Police Violence Across U.S. Metropolitan Areas: Overall Rates and Racial/Ethnic Inequities, 2013–2017," *PLOS ONE*, June 24, 2020, https://journals.plos.org/plosone /article?id=10.1371/journal.pone.0229686; Frank Edwards, Michael H. Esposito, and Hedwig Lee, "Risk of Police-Involved Death by Race/Ethnicity and Place, United States, 2012–2018," *American Journal of Public Health* 108, no. 9 (September 2018): 1241–1248.

6. Chaz Puzzanchera and Moriah Taylor, "Disproportionality Rates for Children in Foster Care Dashboard," National Council of Juvenile and Family Court Judges, National Center for Juvenile Justice, 2021, http://ncjj.org/AFCARS /Disproportionality_Dashboard.aspx.

7. Casey Family Programs, "State-By-State Data," April 2021, www.casey.org /state-data/.

8. Hyunil Kim et al., "Lifetime Prevalence of Investigating Child Maltreatment Among US Children," *American Journal of Public Health* 107, no. 2, (February 2017): 278, www.ncbi.nlm.nih.gov/pmc/articles/PMC5227926/pdf/AJPH .2016.303545.pdf.

9. US Department of Health and Human Services, Children's Bureau, *The AFCARS Report: Preliminary FY 2019 Estimates as of June 23, 2020—No. 27* (Washington, DC: June 23, 2020), 1, www.acf.hhs.gov/sites/default/files/documents /cb/afcarsreport27.pdf; Josh Kagan-Gupta, "America's Hidden Foster Care System," *Stanford Law Review* 27 (August 2020): 852, https://ssrn.com/abstract =3437849; Christopher Wildeman and Natalia Emanuel, "Cumulative Risks of Foster Care Placement by Age 18 for U.S. Children, 2000–2011," *PLOS ONE* 9, no. 3 (March 2014): 5, https://doi.org/10.1371/journal.pone.0092785.

10. Chris Gottleib, "The Lessons of Mass Incarceration for Child Welfare," *Amsterdam News*, February 1, 2018, http://amsterdamnews.com/news/2018/feb/01 /lessons-mass-incarceration-child-welfare/?page=2; Christopher Wildeman, Frank R. Edwards, and Sara Wakefield, "The Cumulative Prevalence of Termination of Parental Rights for U.S. Children, 2000–2016," *Child Maltreatment* 25, no.1 (2019): 35, https://doi.org/10.1177/1077559519848499; Sylvia A. Harvey, "When the Clock Is Cruel: Parents Face Pandemic Hurdles as They Race to Keep Their Kids," *The Imprint*, May 2, 2021, https://imprintnews.org/child-welfare-2/parents -pandemic-hurdles-race-keep-kids/54024; The Imprint Staff Reports, "New Study Confirms High Percentage of Investigations, Loss of Parental Rights," *The Imprint*, April 22, 2021, https://imprintnews.org/youth-services-insider/study -high-prevalence-investigations-loss-parental-rights/53687.

11. Kelley Fong, "Concealment and Constraint: Child Protective Services Fears and Poor Mothers' Institutional Engagement," *Social Forces* 97, no. 4 (2019): 1785–1810.

12. Mariame Kaba, "Yes, We Mean Literally Abolish the Police," *New York Times*, June 12, 2020, www.nytimes.com/2020/06/12/opinion/sunday/floyd -abolish-defund-police.html.

13. Mariame Kaba and John Duda, "Towards the Horizon of Abolition: A Conversation with Mariame Kaba," Next System Project, November 9, 2017, https://thenextsystem.org/learn/stories/towards-horizon-abolition-conversation -mariame-kaba.

CHAPTER 1: DESTROYING BLACK FAMILIES

1. Molly Schwartz, "Do We Need to Abolish Child Protective Services?," *Mother Jones*, December 10, 2020, www.motherjones.com/politics/2020/12/do-we -need-to-abolish-child-protective-services/; Jaya Sundaresh, "New York Child Welfare Advocates Want Parents to Have Representation When Their Children Removed," *Youth Today*, June 5, 2019, https://youthtoday.org/2019/06/new-york-child -welfare-advocates-want-parents-to-have-representation-when-their-children -removed/; Angela Olivia Burton and Angeline Montauban, "Toward Community Control of Child Welfare Funding: Repeal the Child Abuse Prevention and Treatment Act and Delink Child Protection from Family Well-Being," *Columbia Journal of Race and Law* 11, no. 3: 639–680 (2021), https://doi.org/10.52214/cjrl.v11i3.8747; author's interview of Angeline Montauban, August 24, 2021.

2. Child Welfare Information Gateway, *Child Maltreatment 2019: Summary of Key Findings* (US Department of Health and Human Services, Administration for Children and Families, Children's Bureau, April 2021), ii, x, www.childwelfare .gov/pubPDFs/canstats.pdf.

3. Josh Kagan-Gupta, "America's Hidden Foster Care System," *Stanford Law Review* 27 (August 2020): 847, 857, https://ssrn.com/abstract=3437849.

4. US Department of Health and Human Services, Children's Bureau, *The AFCARS Report: Preliminary FY 2019 Estimates as of June 23, 2020—No. 27* (Washington, DC: June 23, 2020), 2, www.acf.hhs.gov/sites/default/files /documents/cb/afcarsreport27.pdf; Frank Edwards et al., "Contact with Child Protective Services Is Pervasive but Unequally Distributed by Race and Ethnicity in Large US Counties," *Proceedings of the National Academy of Sciences* 118, no. 30 (July 2021), www.pnas.org/content/118/30/e2106272118; Jerry Milner and David Kelly, "It's Time to Stop Confusing Poverty with Neglect," *The Imprint*, January 17, 2020, https://imprintnews.org/child-welfare-2/time-for-child -welfare-system-to-stop-confusing-poverty-with-neglect/40222.

5. Alicia Summers et al., *Disproportionality Rates for Children in Foster Care* (Reno, NV: National Council of Juvenile and Family Court Judges, May 2013), 66, www .ncjfcj.org/wp-content/uploads/2013/06/Disproportionality-Rates-for-Children -of-Color-in-Foster-Care-2013.pdf; Nicole Rousseau, *Black Woman's Burden* (New York: Palgrave Macmillan, 2013) 1, 149.

6. Hyunil Kim et al., "Lifetime Prevalence of Investigating Child Maltreatment Among US Children," *American Journal of Public Health* 107, no. 2 (February 2017): 278, www.ncbi.nlm.nih.gov/pmc/articles/PMC5227926/pdf/AJPH .2016.303545.pdf; Edwards et al., "Contact with Child Protective Services Is Pervasive but Unequally Distributed by Race and Ethnicity in Large US Counties." A study of vital and CPS records for California's 1999 birth cohort similarly found that "roughly 1 in 2 Black and Native American children were investigated during childhood." Emily Putnam-Hornstein et al., "Cumulative Rates of Child Protection Involvement and Terminations of Parental Rights in a California Birth Cohort, 1999–2017," *American Journal of Public Health*, May 5, 2021, https:// ajph.aphapublications.org/doi/10.2105/AJPH.2021.306214.

7. US Department of Health and Human Services, Children's Bureau, "CB Fact Sheet," June 29, 2021, www.acf.hhs.gov/cb/fact-sheet-cb.; US Department of Health and Human Services, Children's Bureau, *The AFCARS Report: Preliminary FY 2018 Estimates as of August 22, 2019—No. 26*, (Washington, DC: August 22, 2019), 2, www.acf.hhs.gov/sites/default/files/documents/cb/afcarsreport26 .pdf; US Department of Health and Human Services, Children's Bureau, *The AFCARS Report: Preliminary FY 2019 Estimates as of June 23, 2020—No. 27*, 2; Annie E. Casey Foundation, Kids Count Data Center, "Children in Foster Care by Race and Hispanic Origin in the United States," updated June 2021, https://datacenter .kidscount.org/data/tables/6246-children-in-foster-care-by-race-and-hispanic -origin?loc=1&loct=1#detailed/1/any/false/1729,37,867,38/2638,2601 ,2600,2598,2603,2597,2602,1353/12992,12993.

8. Christopher Wildeman and Natalia Emanuel, "Cumulative Risks of Foster Care Placement by Age 18 for U.S. Children, 2000–2011," *PLOS ONE* 9, no. 3 (March 2014): 5, https://doi.org/10.1371/journal.pone.0092785.

9. US Department of Health and Human Services, Children's Bureau, *The AFCARS Report: Preliminary FY 2019 Estimates as of June 23, 2020—No. 27*, 1; Shamini Ganasarajah et al., *Disproportionality Rates for Children of Color in Foster Care (Fiscal Year 2015)* (Reno, NV: National Council of Juvenile and Family Court Judges, September 2017), 5–6, www.ncjfcj.org/wp-content/uploads/2017/09 /NCJFCJ-Disproportionality-TAB-2015_0.pdf; Anita Ortiz Maddali, "The Immigrant 'Other': Racialized Identity and the Devaluation of Immigrant Family Relations," *Indian Law Journal* 89, (2014): 647, http://ilj.law.indiana.edu/articles/10 -Maddali.pdf.

10. Patrick McCarthy, "The Alliance for Racial Equity in Child Welfare— Yesterday, Today and Tomorrow," in *Disparities and Disproportionality in Child Welfare: Analysis of the Research* (Seattle, WA: Center for the Study of Social Policy, Annie E. Casey Foundation, December 2011), v, https://casala.org/wp-content /uploads/2015/12/Disparities-and-Disproportionality-in-Child-Welfare_An -Analysis-of-the-Research-December-2011-1.pdf; John Fluke et al., "Research Synthesis on Child Welfare Disproportionality and Disparities," in *Disparities and Disproportionality in Child Welfare*; Robert B. Hill, "Synthesis of Research on Disproportionality in Child Welfare: An Update," in *Disparities and Disproportionality in Child Welfare*.

11. Tanya A. Cooper, "Racial Bias in American Foster Care: The National Debate," *Marquette Law Review* 97, no. 2 (2013): 215. For example, Elizabeth Bartholet, *Nobody's Children: Abuse and Neglect, Foster Drift, and the Adoption Alternative* (Boston: Beacon Press, 1999); Elizabeth Bartholet, "The Racial Disproportionality Movement in Child Welfare: False Facts and Dangerous Directions," *Arizona Law Review* 51, no. 4 (2009): 871, http://nrs.harvard.edu/urn-3:HUL .InstRepos:2887034; Richard Barth, "Child Welfare and Race: Models of Disproportionality," in *Race Matters in Child Welfare: The Overrepresentation of African American Children in the System,* ed. D. M. Derezotes, J. Poertner, and M. F. Testa (Washington, DC: Child Welfare League of America, 2005), 25–46; Brett Drake, Sang Moon Lee, and Melissa Jonson-Reid, "Race and Child Maltreatment Reporting: Are Blacks Overrepresented?," *Children and Youth Services Review* 31, no. 3 (2009): 309–316; Sheila Ards and Adele Harrell, "Reporting of Child Maltreatment: A Secondary Analysis of the National Incidence Surveys," *Child Abuse and Neglect: The International Journal* 17, no. 3 (1993): 337–344; Sheila Ards, Chanjin Chung, and Samuel Myers, "Sample Selection Bias and Racial Difference in Child Abuse Reporting: Once Again," *Child Abuse and Neglect* 25, no. 1 (2001): 7–12.

12. Bartholet, *Nobody's Children,* 6; Elizabeth Bartholet, "Where Do Black Children Belong? The Politics of Race Matching in Adoption," *University of Pennsylvania Law Review* 139 (1991), 1222, https://scholarship.law.upenn.edu/penn _law_review/vol139/iss5/1/.

13. Bartholet, "The Racial Disproportionality Movement in Child Welfare," 871, 878.

14. Brett Drake, "Response to a Research Synthesis on Child Welfare Disproportionality and Disparities," in *Disparities and Disproportionality in Child Welfare,* 101.

15. Ben Baeder, "Studies: Disproportionate Number of Black Children End Up in L.A. Foster Care," *Whittier Daily News,* March 23, 2013, www.whittier dailynews.com/2013/03/23/studies-disproportionate-number-of-black-children -wind-up-in-la-foster-care/; National Coalition for Child Protection Reform, "Child Abuse Is Way Down (Don't Tell Anyone): An Analysis of NIS-4 from the National Coalition for Child Protection Reform," February 2, 2010, updated September 26, 2015, www.drive.google.com/file/d/0B291mw_hLAJsWEJfeWxBT2t XaUU/view?resourcekey=0-UpSY_riqtfirYghoxlcThg.

16. Child Advocacy Program, "Race and Child Welfare: Disproportionality, Disparity, Discrimination: Re-Assessing the Facts, Re-Thinking the Policy Options," Working Conference at Harvard Law School, Cambridge, MA, January 28–29, 2011, https://cap.law.harvard.edu/events-and-conferences/cap -conferences/race-and-child-welfare/; see also Race and Child Welfare: Archived Conference Videos, https://cap.law.harvard.edu/events-and-conferences /cap-conferences/race-and-child-welfare/conference-videos/.

17. Fluke et al., "Research Synthesis," 1, 23.

18. Don Lash, *"When the Welfare People Come": Race and Class in the US Child Protection System* (Chicago: Haymarket Books, 2017), 47; Fluke et al., "Research Synthesis," 25; Sandra T. Azar and Philip Atiba Goff, "Can Science Help Solomon? Child Maltreatment Cases and the Potential for Racial and Ethnic Bias in

Decision Making," *St. John's Law Review* 81, no. 3 (Summer 2007): 544, https://scholarship.law.stjohns.edu/lawreview/vol81/iss3/3/.

19. A. J. Sedlak et al., *Fourth National Incidence Study of Child Abuse and Neglect (NIS-4): Report to Congress* (Washington, DC: US Department of Health and Human Services, Administration for Children and Families, 2010), 2, www.acf.hhs.gov/sites/default/files/documents/opre/nis4_report_congress_full_pdf_jan2010.pdf; Andrea J. Sedlak et al., *Supplementary Analyses of Race Differences in Child Maltreatment Rates in the NIS-4* (Washington, DC: US Department of Health and Human Services, Administration for Children and Families, 2010), 1, www.acf.hhs.gov/sites/default/files/documents/opre/nis4_supp_analysis_race_diff_mar2010.pdf.

20. Sheila D. Ards et al., "Decomposing Black-White Differences in Child Maltreatment," *Child Maltreatment* 8, no. 2 (2003): 112–121, https://doi.org/10.1177/1077559502250817.

21. Andrew Billingsley and Jeanne M. Giovannoni, *Children of the Storm: Black Children and American Child Welfare* (New York: Harcourt Brace Jovanovich, 1972), vii.

22. Richard P. Barth et al., "Outcomes Following Child Welfare Services: What Are They and Do They Differ for Black Children?," *Journal of Public Child Welfare* 14, no. 5 (2020): 477–499, https://doi.org/10.1080/15548732.2020.1814541.

CHAPTER 2: "THEY SEPARATE CHILDREN AT THE HARLEM BORDER, TOO"

1. Colleen Kraft, "AAP Statement Opposing Separation of Children and Parents at the Border," American Academy of Pediatrics, press release, May 8, 2018, https://docs.house.gov/meetings/IF/IF14/20180627/108510/HMKP-115-IF14-20180627-SD011.pdf; Dana L. Sinopoli and Stephen Soldz, "Stop Border Separation of Children from Parents!," petition signed by 13,013 mental health professionals, June 2018, https://web.archive.org/web/20180710083801/https://childsworldamerica.org/stop-border-separation/organizations/.

2. William Wan, "What Separation from Parents Does to Children: 'The Effect Is Catastrophic,'" *Washington Post*, June 18, 2018, www.washingtonpost.com/national/health-science/what-separation-from-parents-does-to-children-the-effect-is-catastrophic/2018/06/18/c00c30ec-732c-11e8-805c-4b67019fcfe4_story.html. See also Allison Eck, "Psychological Damage Inflicted by Parent-Child Separation Is Deep, Long-Lasting," *NOVA Next*, June 20, 2018, www.pbs.org/wgbh/nova/article/psychological-damage-inflicted-by-parent-child-separation-is-deep-long-lasting/; Sara Goudarzi, "Separating Families May Cause Lifelong Health Damage," *Scientific American*, June 20, 2018, www.scientificamerican.com/article/separatingfamilies-may-cause-lifelong-health-damage/.

3. Shanta Trivedi, "The Harm of Child Removal," *New York University Review of Law and Social Change* 43 (2019): 530, https://scholarworks.law.ubalt.edu/all_fac/1085, citing Miriam Jordan, "A Migrant Boy Rejoins His Mother, but He's Not the Same," *New York Times*, July 31, 2018, www.nytimes.com/2018/07/31/us/migrant-children-separation-anxiety.html; American Immigration Council,

"Separated Family Members Seek Monetary Damages from United States: *C.M. v. United States*, Case 2:19-cv-05317-SRB (D. Ariz., filed Sept. 19, 2019)," http://americanimmigrationcouncil.org/litigation/separated-family-members-seek-monetary-damages-united-states; Brief of International Human Rights Organization and International Law Scholars as Amici Curiae in Support of Plaintiffs, D.J.C.V., Minor Child, and G.C., His Father v. United States of America (S.D.N.Y), filed December 22, 2020; Brief of Doctors Beth Van Schaack (J.D., Ph.D.), Daryn Reicherter (M.D.), and Ryan Matlow (Ph.D.) as Amici Curiae in Support of Plaintiffs' Opposition to Defendant's Motion to Dismiss the Complaint, D.J.C.V., Minor Child, and G.C., His Father v. United States of America.

4. Myah Ward, "At Least 3,900 Children Separated from Families Under Trump 'Zero Tolerance' Policy, Task Force Finds," *Politico*, June 6, 2021, www.politico.com/news/2021/06/08/trump-zero-tolerance-policy-child-separations-492099; Diane Redleaf, "When the Child Protective Services System Gets Child Removal Wrong," *Cato Unbound*, November 9, 2018, www.cato-unbound.org/2018/11/09/diane-redleaf/when-child-protective-services-system-gets-child-removal-wrong.

5. Monique B. Mitchell, *The Neglected Transition: Building a Relational Home for Children Entering Foster Care* (Oxford, UK: Oxford University Press, 2016), 12, 5.

6. Mitchell, *Neglected Transition*, 81; Trivedi, "The Harm of Child Removal," 533–534; Vivek Sankaran, Christopher Church, and Monique Mitchell, "A Cure Worse than the Disease?: The Impact of Removal on Children and Their Families," *Marquette Law Review* 102, no. 4 (2019): 1166–1167, https://repository.law.umich.edu/cgi/viewcontent.cgi?article=3055&context=articles; Kalina M. Brabeck, M. Brinton Lykes, and Cristina Hunter, "The Psychosocial Impact of Detention and Deportation on U.S. Migrant Children and Families," *American Journal of Orthopsychiatry* 84, no. 5 (September 2014): 500, citing Anna Freud and Dorothy T. Burlingham, *War and Children* (New York: Medical War Books, 1943).

7. Jason B. Whiting and Robert E. Lee III, "Voices from the System: A Qualitative Study of Foster Children's Stories," *Family Relations* 52, no. 3 (July 2003): 292, www.jstor.org/stable/3700280.

8. Kendra L. Nixon, H. L. Radtke, and Leslie M. Tutty, "'Every Day It Takes a Piece of You Away': Experiences of Grief and Loss Among Abused Mothers Involved with Child Protective Services," *Journal of Public Child Welfare* 7, no. 2 (May 2013): 182–183, 180, https://doi.org/10.1080/15548732.2012.715268. See also Elizabeth Wall-Wieler et al., "Maternal Health and Social Outcomes After Having a Child Taken into Care: Population-Based Longitudinal Cohort Study Using Linkable Administrative Data," *Journal of Epidemiology and Community Health* 71, no. 12 (December 2017), www.jstor.org/stable/10.2307/26896114.

9. National Advocates for Pregnant Women, Movement for Family Power, and nineteen other signatories, *Violence Against Women in the Medical Setting: An Examination of the U.S. Foster System*, joint submission to the United Nations Special Rapporteur on Violence Against Women, May 31, 2019, https://ccrjustice.org/sites/default/files/attach/2019/06/MFP_NAPW_UN_VAW_Submission-20190531-Final.pdf.

10. Sankaran, Church, and Mitchell, "A Cure Worse than the Disease?," 1171–1173; Trivedi, "The Harm of Child Removal," 560.

11. Donald Braman, *Doing Time on the Outside: Incarceration and Family Life in Urban America* (Ann Arbor: University of Michigan Press, 2007); Todd Clear, *Imprisoning Communities: How Mass Incarceration Makes Disadvantaged Neighborhoods Worse* (Oxford, UK: Oxford University Press, 2009); Jeffrey Fagan et al., "Reciprocal Effects of Crime and Incarceration in New York City Neighborhoods," *Fordham Urban Law Journal* 30, no. 5 (2003), https://ir.lawnet.fordham.edu/ulj/vol30/iss5/3; Dorothy E. Roberts, "The Social and Moral Cost of Mass Incarceration in African American Communities," *Stanford Law Review* 56 (2004): 1271.

12. Dorothy E. Roberts, "The Racial Geography of Child Welfare: Toward a New Research Paradigm," *Child Welfare* 87, no. 2 (2008):125–150, http://cap.law.harvard.edu/wp-content/uploads/2015/07/robertsrd.pdf.

13. Mark F. Testa and Frank F. Furstenberg, "The Social Ecology of Child Endangerment," in *A Century of Juvenile Justice*, ed. Margaret K. Rosenheim et al. (Chicago: University of Chicago Press, 2002), 237–263.

14. Kelley Fong, "Neighborhood Inequality in the Prevalence of Reported and Substantiated Child Maltreatment," *Child Abuse and Neglect* 90, no. 1 (2019):13–21; Molly Schwartz, "Do We Need to Abolish Child Protective Services?," *Mother Jones*, December 10, 2020, www.motherjones.com/politics/2020/12/do-we-need-to-abolish-child-protective-services/.

15. Isabel Wilkerson, *The Warmth of Other Suns: The Epic Story of America's Great Migration* (New York: Random House, 2010); Richard Rothstein, *The Color of Law: A Forgotten History of How Our Government Segregated America* (New York: Liveright, 2017); Keeanga-Yamahtta Taylor, *Race for Profit: How Banks and the Real Estate Industry Undermined Black Homeownership* (Chapel Hill: University of North Carolina Press, 2019).

16. Erin McElroy and Andrew Szeto, "The Racial Contours of YIMBY/NIMBY Bay Area Gentrification," *Berkeley Planning Journal* 29, no. 1 (2017): 13, https://escholarship.org/content/qt4sw2g485/qt4sw2g485_noSplash_a4a78f6499d4e010591b543fef163936.pdf.

17. All names used for respondents in this study have been changed to preserve their anonymity. Roberts, "Racial Geography," 131.

18. Roberts, "Racial Geography," 132.

CHAPTER 3: PROFESSIONAL KIDNAPPERS

1. Mary Jo Pitzl, "DCS Workers Apparently Fired over 'Professional Kidnapper' T-shirts," *Arizona Republic*, July 21, 2020, www.azcentral.com/story/news/local/arizona-child-welfare/2020/07/21/kidnapper-t-shirts-apparent-firings-arizona-department-child-safety/5448029002/; Mary Jo Pitzl, "'Professional Kidnapper' T-shirt Stunt Drains 22 Years of Experience from Prescott Child Welfare Office," *Arizona Republic*, August 8, 2020, www.azcentral.com/story/news/local/arizona-child-welfare/2020/08/08/eight-arizona-dcs-staffers-fired-professional-kidnapper-t-shirt-pic/3320014001/.

2. Chaz Puzzanchera and Moriah Taylor, "Disproportionality Rates for Children in Foster Care Dashboard," National Council of Juvenile and Family Court Judges, National Center for Juvenile Justice, 2021, http://ncjj.org/AFCARS /Disproportionality_Dashboard.aspx.

3. Kelley Fong, "'The Tool We Have': Why Child Protective Services Investigates So Many Families and How Even Good Intentions Backfire," briefing report for the Council on Contemporary Families, August 11, 2020, https:// contemporaryfamilies.org/cps-brief-report/.

4. Casey Family Programs, "State-By-State Data," April 2021, www.casey .org/state-data/; Duncan Lindsey, *The Welfare of Children* (New York: Oxford University Press, 1994), 155.

5. Diane L. Redleaf, "Where Is It Safe and Legal to Give Children Reasonable Independence?," American Bar Association, September 30, 2020, www .americanbar.org/groups/litigation/committees/childrens-rights/articles/2020 /where-is-it-safe-and-legal-to-give-children-reasonable-independence/.

6. Matthew Desmond, *Evicted: Poverty and Profit in the American City* (New York: Crown Publishers, 2016), 4; Emily Benfer et al., "The COVID-19 Eviction Crisis: An Estimated 30–40 Million People in America Are at Risk," Aspen Institute, August 7, 2020, www.aspeninstitute.org/blog-posts/the-covid-19-eviction -crisis-an-estimated-30-40-million-people-in-america-are-at-risk/; Bridget Lavender, "Coercion, Criminalization, and Child 'Protection': Homeless Individuals' Reproductive Lives," *University of Pennsylvania Law Review* 169 (2021), 1615–1686, 1659–1662.

7. Vivek Sankaran, "The Looming Housing Crisis and Child Protection Agencies," *The Imprint*, September 16, 2020, https://imprintnews.org/opinion /looming-housing-crisis-child-protection-agencies/47437; Kathryn Joyce, "The Crime of Parenting While Poor," *New Republic*, February 25, 2019, https://new republic.com/article/153062/crime-parenting-poor-new-york-city-child -welfare-agency-reform; National Coalition for Child Protection Reform, "Who Is in 'The System'—and Why," Issue Paper 5 (2015), https://drive.google.com/file /d/0B291mw_hLAJsT00wNkk5R1c1dWM/view?resourcekey=0-o3pjlZPJ5NCKS 3VNI88EmA.

8. National Coalition for Child Protection Reform, "Who Is in 'The System'—and Why"; Elizabeth Brico, "To 'Protect' My Kids, the State Made Me Homeless," Rewire News Group, July 31, 2020, https://rewirenewsgroup.com /article/2020/07/31/to-protect-my-kids-the-state-made-me-homeless/.

9. Stephanie Clifford and Jessica Silver-Greenberg, "Foster Care as Punishment: The New Reality of 'Jane Crow,'" *New York Times*, July, 21, 2017, www .nytimes.com/2017/07/21/nyregion/foster-care-nyc-jane-crow.html.

10. Clifford and Silver-Greenberg, "Foster Care as Punishment."

11. Lenore Skenazy, *Free-Range Kids: How to Raise Safe, Self-Reliant Children (Without Going Nuts with Worry)* (Hoboken, NJ: Jossey-Bass, 2009); Lenore Skenazy, "Why I Let My 9-Year-Old Ride the Subway Alone," *New York Sun*, April 1, 2008, www.nysun.com/opinion/why-i-let-my-9-year-old-ride-subway-alone /73976/.

12. Diane L. Redleaf, "Narrowing Neglect Laws Means Ending State-Mandated Helicopter Parenting," American Bar Association, September 11, 2020, www.americanbar.org/groups/litigation/committees/childrens-rights/articles /2020/fall2020-narrowing-neglect-laws-means-ending-state-mandated-helicopter -parenting/?.

13. Jessica Grose, "Mother's Little Helper Is Back, and Daddy's Partaking Too," *New York Times*, October 3, 2020, www.nytimes.com/2020/10/03/style/am-i -drinking-too-much.html.

14. Emma Ketteringham, "Families Torn Apart over Pot: As N.Y. Moves to Legalize Marijuana, It Must Fix Agonizing Disparities That Take Children Away from Black and Brown Mothers and Fathers," *New York Daily News*, May 8, 2019, www.nydailynews.com/opinion/ny-oped-families-ripped-apart-over-pot -20190508-qtrnmuyztzfr7let4vxjxga7zm-story.html.

15. Lacy Crawford, *Notes on a Silencing: A Memoir* (New York: Little, Brown and Company, 2020), 209.

16. Joanne N. Wood et al., "Disparities in the Evaluation and Diagnosis of Abuse Among Infants with Traumatic Brain Injury," *Pediatrics* 126, no. 3 (2010): 408, 413, https://doi.org/10.1542/peds.2010-0031, which notes that studies "suggest that the disparities are not limited to a few hospitals but exist across a wide network of pediatric hospitals"; Wendy G. Lane et al.,"Racial Differences in the Evaluation of Pediatric Fractures for Physical Abuse," *Journal of the American Medical Association* 288, no. 13 (2002): 1603–1609, https://jamanetwork .com/journals/jama/fullarticle/195342.

17. Jeff Guo, "Police Are Searching Black Drivers More Often, but Finding More Illegal Stuff with White Drivers," *Washington Post*, October 27, 2015, www.washingtonpost.com/news/wonk/wp/2015/10/27/police-are-searching -black-drivers-more-often-but-finding-more-illegal-stuff-with-white-drivers -2/; ACLU Illinois, "Racial Disparity in Consent Searches and Dog Sniff Searches," August 13, 2014, www.aclu-il.org/en/publications/racial-disparity -consent-searches-and-dog-sniff-searches; Emma Pierson et al., "A Large-Scale Analysis of Racial Disparities in Police Stops Across the United States," *Nature Human Behavior* 4 (July 2020): 739–740, https://doi.org/10.1038/s41562-020 -0858-1; Wood et al., "Disparities in the Evaluation," 408; Elizabeth Hlavinka, "Racial Disparity Seen in Child Abuse Reporting: Clinician Bias Suggested for Overdiagnosis in Certain Groups," *MedPage Today*, October 5, 2020, www .medpagetoday.com/meetingcoverage/aap/88958.

18. Heather T. Keenan et al., "Perceived Social Risk in Medical Decision Making for Physical Child Abuse: A Mixed Methods Study," *BMC Pediatrics* 17, no. 1 (2017): 2, https://bmcpediatr.biomedcentral.com/track/pdf/10.1186/s12887 -017-0969-7.pdf.

19. On physicians' misdiagnosis of accidental injuries as child abuse and the damaging consequences for families, see Stephanie Clifford, "When the Misdiagnosis Is Child Abuse," *The Atlantic*, August 20, 2020, www.theatlantic .com/family/archive/2020/08/when-misdiagnosis-child-abuse/615337/; Deborah Tuerkheimer, *Flawed Convictions: "Shaken Baby Syndrome" and the Inertia*

of Injustice (Oxford, UK: Oxford University Press, 2014); Kellie Lang et al., "Calling Out Implicit Racial Bias as a Harm in Pediatric Care," *Cambridge Quarterly of Healthcare Ethics* 25, no. 3 (2016): 540, https://doi.org/10.1017/S0963180116000190.

20. Imani Worthy, "Imani's Testimony to City Council," recorded on October 28, 2020, *Rise Magazine*, November 3, 2020, www.risemagazine.org/?s=testimony.

21. Ben Kesslen, "Actress Says She Accidentally Dropped Her Son on His Head, Sending Him to ICU," NBC News, April 19, 2019, www.nbcnews.com/news/us-news/actress-says-she-accidentally-dropped-her-son-his-head-sending-n996376; Jen Juneau, "Celebs Support Jenny Mollen After She Reveals She Dropped Son on His Head, Fracturing His Skull," *People*, April 18, 2019, https://people.com/parents/celebrities-support-jenny-mollen-after-son-skull-fracture-comments/; Paige Gawley, "Jenny Mollen's 5-Year-Old Son Fractures His Skull After She Accidentally Drops Him on His Head," *ET Online*, April 18, 2019, www.etonline.com/jenny-mollens-5-year-old-son-fractures-his-skull-after-she-accidentally-drops-him-on-his-head.

22. Sheila D. Ards et al., "Racialized Perceptions and Child Neglect," *Child and Youth Services Review* 34, no. 8 (2012): 1480; Christopher Magan, "Black Children Disproportionately Removed from Their Families; State Lawmakers Seek Fix," *Pioneer Press*, April 10, 2018, www.twincities.com/2018/04/10/black-children-are-disproportionately-removed-from-their-families-state-lawmakers-seek-legislative-fix/; Complaint, Mitchell v. Dakota County Social Services, No. 18-cv-01091-WMW-BRT (D. Minn. Apr. 24, 2018); Sylvia A. Harvey, "Minnesota Legislature Again Fails to Pass Bill Defending Black Families," *The Imprint*, August 23, 2021, https://imprintnews.org/child-welfare-2/minnesota-legislature-again-fails-to-pass-bill-defending-black-families/58034.

23. Ards et al., "Racialized Perceptions and Child Neglect"; Stephanie Rivaux et al., "The Intersection of Race, Poverty and Risk: Understanding the Decision to Provide Services to Clients and to Remove Children," *Child Welfare* 87, no. 2 (2008); Center for the Study of Social Policy, *Race Equity Review: Findings from a Qualitative Analysis of Racial Disproportionality and Disparity for African American Children in Michigan's Child Welfare System* (2009), https://ncwwi.org/files/race-equity-review-michigan.pdf. For additional studies demonstrating discrimination against Black parents in child welfare decision making, see Tricia Stephens, "Distinguishing Racism, Not Race, as a Risk Factor for Child Welfare Involvement: Reclaiming the Familial and Cultural Strengths in the Lived Experiences of Child Welfare–Affected Parents of Color," *Genealogy* 5, no.1 (2021): 11; Jude Mary Cénat et al., "Overrepresentation of Black Children in the Child Welfare System: A Systematic Review to Understand and Better Act," *Children and Youth Services Review* 120 (2021), https://doi.org/10.1016/j.childyouth.2020.105714; Vernon Brooks Carter and Miranda Myers, "Examination of Substantiated Lack of Supervision and Its Impact on Out-of-Home Placement: A National Sample," *Journal of Public Child Welfare* 2, no. 1 (2008): 51–70; Alan J. Detlaff and Reiko Boyd, "Racial Disproportionality and Disparities in the Child Welfare System: Why Do They Exist, and What Can Be Done

to Address Them?," *Annals of the American Academy of Political and Social Science* 692 (January 2021): 253–274.

24. Christopher Wildman et al., "The Prevalence of Confirmed Maltreatment Among US Children, 2004–2011," *JAMA Pediatrics* 168, no. 8 (2014): 706–713, https://jamanetwork.com/journals/jamapediatrics/fullarticle/1876686.

CHAPTER 4: ROTTEN AT THE ROOT

1. Malcolm X and Alex Haley, *The Autobiography of Malcolm X* (New York: Ballantine Books, 1965), 9–23; Les Payne and Tamara Payne, *The Dead Are Arising: The Life of Malcolm X* (New York: Liveright Publishing, 2020), 83–109.

2. Laura Briggs, *Taking Children: A History of American Terror* (Oakland: University of California Press, 2020), 8; Tierney Sheree Peprah, *Fostering False Identity: The Child Welfare System's Design of Social Control of the Black Family* (independently published, 2021).

3. Briggs, *Taking Children*, 3, quoting Hillary Clinton (@HillaryClinton), "There's nothing American about tearing families apart," Twitter, June 20, 2018, 9:34 a.m., https://twitter.com/hillaryclinton/status/1009434414986747906?lang=en.

4. Josiah Henson, *Truth Stranger than Fiction: Father Henson's Story of His Own Life* (Boston: John P. Jewett and Company, 1858), www.gutenberg.org/files/49129/49129-h/49129-h.htm.

5. Henson, *Truth Stranger than Fiction*. For more accounts of separation of enslaved children from their parents, see Heather Andrea Williams, *Help Me to Find My People: The African American Search for Family Lost in Slavery* (Chapel Hill: University of North Carolina Press, 2012), 21–45.

6. M'Vaughters v. Elder, 4 S.C.L. (2 Brev.) 307 (1809), https://cite.case.law/scl/4/307/; Angela Y. Davis, *Women, Race and Class* (New York: Vintage, 1983), 7; Williams, *Help Me to Find My People*, 25.

7. Toni Morrison, *Beloved* (New York: Vintage Books, 1987), 28.

8. Williams, *Help Me to Find My People*, 27–29.

9. Williams, *Help Me to Find My People*, 98.

10. Deborah Gray White, *Ar'n't I A Woman? Female Slaves in the Plantation South* (New York: W. W. Norton, 1999), 70–74; *Georgia Gazette*, April 20, 1786, quoted in Betty Wood, "Some Aspects of Female Resistance to Chattel Slavery in Low-Country Georgia, 1763 to 1815," *Historical Journal* 30, no. 3 (1987): 610, n. 24, www.jstor.org/stable/2639161.

11. Harriet Jacobs, *Incidents in the Life of a Slave Girl* (Boston: Thayer and Eldridge, 1861).

12. Williams, *Help Me to Find My People*, 11.

13. Peggy Cooper Davis, *Neglected Stories: The Constitution and Family Values* (New York: Hill and Wang, 1997), 98.

14. Williams, *Help Me to Find My People*, 141.

15. Eric Foner, *Reconstruction: America's Unfinished Revolution* (New York: Harper and Row, 1988), 88.

16. James M. McPherson, *Battle Cry of Freedom: The Civil War Era* (New York: Oxford University Press, 1988), 37; Harriet Beecher Stowe, *A Key to Uncle Tom's*

Cabin: Presenting the Original Facts and Documents upon Which the Story is Founded Together with Corroborative Statements Verifying the Truth of the Work (Boston: John P. Jewett and Co., 1853).

17. Briggs, *Taking Children*, 18, 27; Kurt Mundorff, "Children as Chattel: Invoking the Thirteenth Amendment to Reform Child Welfare," *Cardozo Public Law, Policy & Ethics* 1 (2003): 131.

18. Leon F. Litwack, *Been in the Storm So Long: The Aftermath of Slavery* (New York: Random House, 1979), 276–277.

19. Karen L. Zipf, *Labor of Innocents: Forced Apprenticeship in North Carolina, 1715–1919* (Baton Rouge: Louisiana State University Press, 2005); Richard Paul Fuke, "Planters, Apprenticeship, and Forced Labor: The Black Family Under Pressure in Post-Emancipation Maryland," *Agricultural History* 62, no. 4 (1988): 57–74, www.jstor.org/stable/3743375; David Zucchino, *Wilmington's Lie: The Murderous Coup of 1898 and the Rise of White Supremacy* (New York: Grove Atlantic, 2020), 35.

20. Fuke, "Planters, Apprenticeship, and Forced Labor," 63; Briggs, *Taking Children*, 28.

21. Fuke, "Planters, Apprenticeship, and Forced Labor," 57, 62; Zucchino, *Wilmington's Lie*, 8.

22. Martha S. Jones, *Birthright Citizens: A History of Race and Rights in Antebellum America* (New York: Cambridge University Press, 2018), 120–121.

23. In re Turner, 24 F. Cas. 337 (C.C.D. Md. 1867); Randy E. Barnett, "From Antislavery Lawyer to Chief Justice: The Remarkable but Forgotten Career of Salmon P. Chase," *Case Western Reserve Law Review* 63, no. 3 (2013): 677, https://scholarship.law.georgetown.edu/facpub/1027/; Fuke, "Planters, Apprenticeship, and Forced Labor," 58.

24. Fuke, "Planters, Apprenticeship, and Forced Labor," 73.

25. *Kent News*, December 7, 1864, quoted in Fuke, "Planters, Apprenticeship, and Forced Labor," 64; Maria Nichols to Oliver Otis Howard, October 11, 1866, Record Group 105, Maryland, Box Records, Letters Received, Assistant Commissioner (September 1865–October 27, 1866), quoted in Fuke, "Planters, Apprenticeship, and Forced Labor," 65.

26. Dorothy Roberts, "Race," in *The 1619 Project: A New Origin Story*, ed. Nikole Hannah-Jones and the editors of the *New York Times Magazine* (New York: One World, 2021); White, *Ar'n't I A Woman?*, 30; Estelle B. Freedman, *Redefining Rape: Sexual Violence in the Era of Suffrage and Segregation* (Cambridge, MA: Harvard University Press, 2013), 28.

27. Philip Alexander Bruce, *The Plantation Negro as a Freeman: Observations on His Character, Condition, and Prospects in Virginia* (New York: G. P. Putnam's Sons, 1889), 11; Patricia Hill Collins, *Black Feminist Thought: Knowledge Consciousness, and the Politics of Empowerment* (New York: Routledge, 1991).

28. Eleanor Tayleur, "'The Negro Woman—Social and Moral Decadence,' *Outlook* (1904)" in *The American New Woman Revisited: A Reader, 1894–1930*, ed. Martha H. Patterson (Ithaca, NY: Rutgers University Press, 2008), 71–77, https://doi.org/10.36019/9780813544946-014.

29. Maggie Blackhawk, "Federal Indian Law as Paradigm within Public Law," *Harvard Law Review* 132, no. 1787 (2019): 1831–1832; Briggs, *Taking Chil-*

dren, 46–75; Mary Annette Pember, "Death by Civilization," *The Atlantic*, March 8, 2019, www.theatlantic.com/education/archive/2019/03/traumatic-legacy-indian-boarding-schools/584293/; Harvard Law Review, "Recent Legislation: Truth and Healing Commission on Indian Boarding School Policy Act," *Harvard Law Review Blog*, November 21, 2020, https://blog.harvardlawreview.org/recent-legislation-truth-and-healing-commission-on-indian-boarding-school-policy-act/.

30. Peter Nabokov, *Native American Testimony: A Chronicle of Indian-White Relations from Prophecy to the Present, 1492–2000* (New York: Penguin Random House, 1999), 220.

31. Dane Coolidge, "'Kid Catching' on the Navajo Reservation: 1930," in *The Destruction of American Indian Families*, ed. Steven Unger (New York: American Indian Affairs, 1977), 21.

32. Maggie Blackhawk, "The Indian Law That Helps Build Walls," *New York Times*, May 26, 2019, www.nytimes.com/2019/05/26/opinion/american-indian-law-trump.html.

33. Ellen Herman, "Indian Adoption Project," Adoption History Project, Department of History, University of Oregon, 2012, https://pages.uoregon.edu/adoption/topics/IAP.html; Briggs, *Taking Children*, 64–65; Claire Palmiste, "From the Indian Adoption Project to the Indian Child Welfare Act: The Resistance of Native American Communities," *Indigenous Policy Journal* 22, no. 1 (Summer 2011), www.indigenouspolicy.org/index.php/ipj/article/view/4/3.

34. David Fanshel, *Far from the Reservation: The Transracial Adoption of American Indian Children* (Metuchen, NJ: Scarecrow Press, 1972).

35. Mississippi Band of Choctaw Indians v. Holyfield, 490 U.S. 30, 33 (1989).

36. Judith Graham, "Adoption Apology Too Late for Indians," *Chicago Tribune*, May 7, 2001, www.chicagotribune.com/news/ct-xpm-2001-05-07-01050 70184-story.html.

37. Adoptive Couple v. Baby Girl, 570 U.S. 637 (2013).

38. Andrew Billingsley and Jeanne M. Giovannoni, *Children of the Storm: Black Children and American Child Welfare* (New York: Harcourt, 1972), 24.

39. Judith Areen, "Intervention Between Parent and Child: A Reappraisal of the State's Role in Child Neglect and Abuse Cases," *Georgetown Law Journal* 63, no. 4 (March 1975): 887, 899; Walter I. Trattner, *From Poor Law to Welfare State: A History of Social Welfare in America* (New York: Free Press, 1989), 15–27.

40. Billingsley and Giovannoni, *Children of the Storm*.

41. Virginia Eubanks, *Automating Inequality: How High-Tech Tools Profile, Police, and Punish the Poor* (New York: St. Martin's Press, 2018), 15.

42. Trattner, *From Poor Law to Welfare State*, 108–115; Rebecca S. Trammel, "Orphan Train Myths and Legal Reality," *Modern American* 5, no. 2 (Spring 2009): 3–13.

43. Billingsley and Giovannoni, *Children of the Storm*, 26–27, 32; Trattner, *From Poor Law to Welfare State*; Catherine E. Rymph, *Raising Government Children: A History of Foster Care and the American Welfare State* (Chapel Hill: University of North Carolina Press, 2017); Tina Lee, *Catching a Case: Inequality and Fear in New York City's Child Welfare System* (New York: Rutgers University Press, 2016), 20–22.

44. Trattner, *From Poor Law to Welfare State*, 115–117.

45. Richard Wexler, "Real Origins of Child Welfare Points to Today's Foster Care Wrongheadedness," *Youth Today*, January 27, 2020, www.youthtoday.org/2020/01/real-origin-of-child-welfare-points-to-todays-foster-care-wrongheadedness/.

46. Linda Gordon, *The Great Arizona Orphan Abduction* (Cambridge, MA: Harvard University Press, 2001); Trattner, *From Poor Law to Welfare State*; Rymph, *Raising Government Children*; Andrea Warren, *Orphan Train Rider: One Boy's True Story* (Boston: Houghton Mifflin, 1996), 37; Andrea Warren, "The Orphan Train," *Washington Post*, 1998, www.washingtonpost.com/wp-srv/national/horizon/nov98/orphan.htm.

47. Billingsley and Giovannoni, *Children of the Storm*, 75–76, Table 4-1.

48. Tera Eva Agyepong, *The Criminalization of Black Children: Race, Gender, and Delinquency in Chicago's Juvenile Justice System, 1899–1945* (Chapel Hill: University of North Carolina Press, 2018); Geoff K. Ward, *The Black Child-Savers: Racial Democracy and Juvenile Justice* (Chicago: University of Chicago Press, 2012); David Rosner and Gerald Markowitz, "Race, Foster Care, and the Politics of Abandonment in New York City," *American Journal of Public Health* 87, no. 11 (November 1997): 1844–1849, https://doi.org/10.2105/ajph.87.11.1844.

49. Colson Whitehead, *The Nickel Boys: A Novel* (New York: Doubleday, 2019), 53.

50. Booker T. Washington, "Destitute Colored Children of the South," *Proceedings of the Conference on the Care of Dependent Children*, held on January 25–26, 1909 (Washington, DC: Government Printing Office, 1909), 113–117.

51. Linda Gordon, *Pitied but Not Entitled: Single Mothers and the History of Welfare 1890–1935* (New York: Free Press, 1994); Gwendolyn Mink, *The Wages of Motherhood: Inequality in the Welfare State, 1917–1942* (Ithaca, NY: Cornell University Press, 1995); Briggs, *Taking Children*, 31.

52. Briggs, *Taking Children*, 33–34; Kim Gilmore, "The Birmingham Children's Crusade of 1963," Biography, February 14, 2014, updated January 19, 2021, https://www.biography.com/news/black-history-birmingham-childrens-crusade-1963.

53. Rymph, *Raising Government Children*, 163; Peprah, *Fostering False Identity*, 168–173.

54. Briggs, *Taking Children*, 38.

55. Jill Quadagno, *The Color of Welfare: How Racism Undermined the War on Poverty* (New York: Oxford University Press, 1995); *Family Assistance Plan: Hearing Before the Subcommittee of Appropriations*, House of Representatives, 87th Cong. (1961) (statement of Arthur Flemming, Secretary of Health, Education, and Welfare).

56. Briggs, *Taking Children*, 36; Dorothy Roberts, *Killing the Black Body: Race, Reproduction, and the Meaning of Liberty* (New York: Pantheon, 1997).

57. Relf v. Weinberger, 372 F. Supp. 1196, 1199 (D.D.C. 1974), https://law.justia.com/cases/federal/district-courts/FSupp/372/1196/1421341/.

58. Elizabeth Hinton, *From the War on Poverty to the War on Crime: The Making of Mass Incarceration in America* (Cambridge, MA: Harvard University Press, 2016), 181.

59. Movement for Family Power, *"Whatever They Do, I'm Her Comfort, I'm Her Protector": How the Foster System Has Become Ground Zero for the U.S. Drug War* (New York: MFP, NYU Family Defense Clinic, Drug Policy Alliance, 2020), 48, www .movementforfamilypower.org/ground-zero.

60. Victoria Copeland, "Centering Unacknowledged Histories: Revisiting NABSW Demands to Repeal ASFA," *Journal of Public Child Welfare*, September 6, 2021, www.tandfonline.com/doi/full/10.1080/15548732.2021 .1976349; National Association of Black Social Workers, "Preserving Families of African Ancestry," January 10, 2003, www.nabsw.org/resource/resmgr /position_statements_papers/preserving_families_of_afric.pdf; Natalie Pardo, "Losing Their Children: As State Cracks Down on Parents, Black Families Splinter," *Chicago Reporter*, April 6, 2011, www.chicagoreporter.com/losing -their-children-state-cracks-down-parents-black-families-splinter/.

61. Christopher A. Swann and Michelle Sheran Sylvester, "The Foster Care Crisis: What Caused Caseload to Grow?," *Demography* 43, no. 2 (May 2006), 309.

62. German Lopez, "The Controversial 1994 Crime Law That Joe Biden Helped Write, Explained," *Vox*, September 29, 2020, www.vox.com/policy-and -politics/2019/6/20/18677998/joe-biden-1994-crime-bill-law-mass-incarceration.

63. Ashley Southall and Nikita Stewart, "They Grabbed Her Baby and Arrested Her. Now Jazmine Headley Is Speaking Out," *New York Times*, December 16, 2018, www.nytimes.com/2018/12/16/nyregion/jazmine-headley-arrest .html.

64. Malcolm X and Alex Haley, *The Autobiography of Malcolm X*, 22.

CHAPTER 5: STRONG-ARMED

1. Home of the Innocents, "About the Home," accessed July 2, 2021, www .homeoftheinnocents.org/the-home/; Norton Children's Medical Group, "Open Arms Children's Health to Become Part of Norton Children's Medical Group," news release, April 15, 2021, www.homeoftheinnocents.org/app/uploads/2021 /04/OACH.Norton-Press-Release_FINAL.pdf; "Overview" in "Residential Services," Home of the Innocents, accessed July 2, 2021, www.homeoftheinnocents .org/services/residential-treatment/.

2. Jason Riley, "Kentucky Workers Accused of Illegally Removing Children from Homes," WDRB, March 18, 2019, www.wdrb.com/in-depth/sunday-edition -kentucky-workers-accused-of-illegally-removing-children-from/article_5b42179c -474f-11e9-b44e-5b1688808fe4.html.

3. Heather Catallo, "Families Torn Apart Illegally? Heather Catallo Investigates," WXYZ-TV Detroit, May 9, 2012, video, www.youtube.com/watch?v =v6N19MSNDMQ.

4. Vivek Sankaran, "Is Every Foster Care Removal Really an Emergency?" *The Imprint*, July 6, 2020, https://imprintnews.org/opinion/is-every-foster-care -removal-really-an-emergency/44916; author's interview of the Bronx Defenders staff via Zoom, July 21, 2020.

5. Movement for Family Power, *"Whatever They Do, I'm Her Comfort, I'm Her Protector": How the Foster System Has Become Ground Zero for the U.S. Drug War* (New York: MFP, NYU Family Defense Clinic, Drug Policy Alliance, 2020), 57, www.movementforfamilypower.org/ground-zero.

6. Tina Lee, *Catching a Case: Inequality and Fear in New York City's Child Welfare System* (New York: Rutgers University Press, 2016), 61; Molly Schwartz, "Do We Need to Abolish Child Protective Services? Inside One Parent's Five-Year Battle with the 'Family Destruction System,'" *Mother Jones*, December 10, 2020, www.motherjones.com/politics/2020/12/do-we-need-to-abolish-child-protective-services/.

7. Lee, *Catching a Case,* 180–181.

8. Vivek Sankaran, "Child Welfare Is a System in Need of Umpires," *The Imprint*, August 12, 2019, https://imprintnews.org/child-welfare-2/the-child-welfare-system-needs-its-judges-to-be-umpires/36871; Colorado Office of Respondent Parents' Counsel, "Protecting the Fundamental Right to Parent," accessed June 26, 2021, https://coloradoorpc.org/.

9. Imani Worthy-Moore, "Imani's Testimony to City Council," *Rise Magazine*, November 4, 2020, www.risemagazine.org/?s=testimony.

10. Kathleen Creamer, remarks (Strategic Lawyering in the Public Interest Seminar, University of Pennsylvania Carey School of Law, October 27, 2020).

11. Cathy Park Hong, *Minor Feelings: An Asian American Reckoning* (New York: One World, 2020), 77.

12. Author's interview of the Brooklyn Defender Services staff via Zoom, July 22, 2020.

13. Emma Ketteringham, quoted in Movement for Family Power, *"Whatever They Do, I'm Her Comfort, I'm Her Protector,"* 30.

14. Vivek S. Sankaran and Christopher Church, "Easy Come, Easy Go: The Plight of Children Who Spend Less than Thirty Days in Foster Care," *University of Pennsylvania Journal of Law and Social Change* 19, no. 3 (2016): 209, https://scholarship.law.upenn.edu/jlasc/vol19/iss3/2/; Sankaran, "Is Every Foster Care Removal Really An Emergency?"; Eli Hager, "The Hidden Trauma of 'Short Stays' in Foster Care," Marshall Project, February 11, 2020, www.themarshallproject.org/2020/02/11/the-hidden-trauma-of-short-stays-in-foster-care.

15. Sankaran and Church, "Easy Come, Easy Go," 209.

16. Sankaran and Church, "Easy Come, Easy Go," 226; Hager, "The Hidden Trauma of 'Short Stays' in Foster Care."

17. Hager, "The Hidden Trauma of 'Short Stays' in Foster Care."

18. Diane L. Redleaf, *They Took the Kids Last Night: How the Child Protection System Puts Families at Risk* (Santa Barbara, CA: Praeger, 2018), 43–45; Josh Gupta-Kagan, "America's Hidden Foster Care System," *Stanford Law Review* 72, no. 4 (April 2020); Katherine C. Pearson, "Cooperate or We'll Take Your Child: The Parents' Fictional Voluntary Separation Decision and a Proposal for Change," *Tennessee Law Review* 65, no. 4 (Summer 1998): 835–874; Andrew Brown, "Shadow Removals: How Safety Plans Allow CPS to Avoid Judicial Oversight," *The Hill*, May 31, 2019, https://thehill.com/opinion/judiciary/446108-shadow-removals-how-safety-plans-allow-cps-to-avoid-judicial-oversight.

19. Roxanna Asgarian, "Hidden Foster Care: All of the Responsibility, None of the Resources," The Appeal, December 21, 2020, https://theappeal.org/hidden-foster-care/.

20. Annie E. Casey Foundation, *The Kinship Diversion Debate: Policy and Practice Implications for Children, Families and Child Welfare Agencies* (2013), 1, https://assets.aecf.org/m/resourcedoc/KinshipDiversionDebate.pdf, quoted in Gupta-Kagan, "America's Hidden Foster Care System," 850.

21. Dupuy v. Samuels, 465 F.3d 757 (7th Cir. 2006); Redleaf, *They Took the Kids Last Night*, 42–52.

22. Redleaf, *They Took the Kids Last Night*, 48; Dupuy v. Samuels. In 1997, the Third Circuit, in an opinion quite distinct from *Dupuy*, ruled in favor of a doctor who was ordered to leave the home when his little girl wandered to a neighbor's house, naked, and revealed she was "sleeping with mommy and daddy." "The threat that unless Dr. Croft left his home, the state would take his four-year-old daughter and place her in foster care was blatantly coercive," the Third Circuit held. Croft v. Westmoreland County Children and Youth Servs., 103 F.3d 1123 (3d Cir. 1997).

23. Gupta-Kagan, "America's Hidden Foster Care System," 848.

24. Gupta-Kagan, "America's Hidden Foster Care System," 844.

25. Gupta-Kagan, "America's Hidden Foster Care System," 843.

CHAPTER 6: THE FOSTER-INDUSTRIAL COMPLEX

1. Vivek Sankaran and Christopher Church, "Rethinking Foster Care: Why Our Current Approach to Child Welfare Has Failed," *SMU Law Review Forum* 73, no. 12 (April 2020): 124; Elizabeth Brico, "The Government Spends 10 Times More on Foster Care and Adoption Than Reuniting Families," *TalkPoverty*, August 23, 2019, www.talkpoverty.org/2019/08/23/government-more-foster-adoption-reuniting/; Children's Bureau, "CB Fact Sheet," accessed June 27, 2021, www.acf.hhs.gov/cb/fact-sheet-cb; Kristina Rosinsky and Sarah Catherine Williams, *Child Welfare Financing SFY 2016: A Survey of Federal, State, and Local Expenditures* (Child Trends, December 2018), 7, www.childtrends.org/wp-content/uploads/2018/12/CWFSReportSFY2016_ChildTrends_December2018.pdf.

2. Casey Family Programs, "State-by-State Data," May 13, 2019, https://perma.cc/PRG5-DGE5; Congressional Research Service, "Child Welfare: Purposes, Federal Programs, and Funding," updated June 30, 2021, https://fas.org/sgp/crs/misc/IF10590.pdf; Jesse Russell, "Child Welfare Finance and Foster Care Outcomes," *Journal of Public Child Welfare* 9, no. 2 (March 2015): 136, https://doi.org/10.1080/15548732.2015.1022277.

3. Rosinsky and Williams, *Child Welfare Financing SFY 2016*, 11.

4. The other Title IV-E programs are Adoption Assistance Program, Guardianship Assistance Program, Chafee Foster Care Program for Successful Transition to Adulthood/Education and Training Vouchers, and waiver demonstration projects. The rest of federal expenditures on child welfare services comes from Temporary Assistance for Needy Families, the Social Services Block Grant, and Medicaid.

5. Rosinsky and Williams, *Child Welfare Financing SFY 2016*, 25; Chris Gott-leib, "The Lessons of Mass Incarceration for Child Welfare," *Amsterdam News*, February 1, 2018, http://amsterdamnews.com/news/2018/feb/01/lessons-mass -incarceration-child-welfare/?page=2.

6. Miriam Mack, "The White Supremacy Hydra: How the Family First Pre-vention Services Act Reifies Pathology, Control, and Punishment in the Family Regulation System," *Columbia Journal of Race and Law* 11, no. 3: 767–810 (2021), https://doi.org/10.52214/cjrl.v11i3.8751.

7. Josh Gupta-Kagan, "America's Hidden Foster Care System," *Stanford Law Review* 72, no. 4 (April 2020), 883.

8. Shawn Fremstad, "Budget Cuts Are Putting More Kids in Foster Care," *TalkPoverty*, February 23, 2018, https://talkpoverty.org/2018/02/23/budget-cuts -putting-kids-foster-care/; Donna K. Ginther and Michelle Johnson-Motoyama, "Do State TANF Policies Affect Child Abuse and Neglect?" (presented at the APPAM Annual Research Conference, Chicago, October 27, 2017), www.econ .iastate.edu/files/events/files/gintherjohnsonmotoyama_appam.pdf; "Stateline Ex-poses Use of TANF as a Child Welfare Slush Fund," *NCCPR Child Welfare Blog*, July 28, 2020, www.nccprblog.org/2020/07/stateline-exposes-use-of-tanf-as-child.html.

9. Daniel L. Hatcher, *The Poverty Industry: The Exploitation of America's Most Vulnerable Citizens* (New York: New York University Press, 2016), 2.

10. Mark Davis, "What Really Took 2 Lives in Schaefer Case?," *Atlanta Journal-Constitution*, August 11, 2012, https://www.ajc.com/news/local/what -really-took-lives-schaefer-case/BF1mNNltQJBjJTv6xlfiPN/; Nancy Schaefer, Senator, 50th District of Georgia, *The Corrupt Business of Child Protective Services*, Georgia General Assembly, November 16, 2007, updated September 25, 2008, https://archive.org/details/pdfy-GPCopyJd2XQjvNIk.

11. Angela Y. Davis, *Are Prisons Obsolete?* (New York: Seven Stories Press, 2003), 84; Mike Davis, "Hell Factories in the Field: A Prison Industrial Com-plex," *The Nation*, February 1995.

12. President Dwight D. Eisenhower, "Farewell Address," transcript, January 17, 1961, www.ourdocuments.gov/doc.php?flash=false&doc=90&page=transcript.

13. Hatcher, *The Poverty Industry*, 76–77, 87.

14. Daniel L. Hatcher, "Foster Children Paying for Foster Care," *Cardozo Law Review* 27, no. 4 (February 2006): 1810–1813; Erik Eckholm, "Welfare Agencies Seek Foster Children's Assets," *New York Times*, February 17, 2006, www.nytimes .com/2006/02/17/us/welfare-agencies-seek-foster-childrens-assets.html.

15. Washington State Department of Social and Health Services v. Guard-ianship Estate of Danny Keffeler, 537 U.S. 371 (2003).

16. Katherine M. Krause, "Issues of State Use of Social Security Insurance Beneficiary Funds for Reimbursement of Foster-Care Costs," *Family Law Quar-terly* 41, no. 1 (Spring 2007), www.jstor.org/stable/25740601; Daniel L. Hatcher, "Stop Foster Care Agencies from Taking Children's Resources," *Florida Law Re-view Forum* 71, (2019): 109; Eli Hager with Joseph Shapiro, "Meet Malerie, Tris-ten, Katrina, Alex, Ethan, Mateo," Marshall Project in partnership with NPR, May 17, 2021, www.themarshallproject.org/2021/04/22/foster-care-agencies -take-thousands-of-dollars-owed-to-kids-most-children-have-no-idea; Joseph

Shapiro, "Consultants Help States Find and Keep Money That Should Go to Foster Kids," NPR, April 28, 2021, www.npr.org/2021/04/28/991503850/consultants-help-states-find-and-keep-money-that-should-go-to-foster-kids.

17. Hatcher, *The Poverty Industry*, 80; Eli Hager and Joseph Shapiro, "State Foster Care Agencies Take Millions of Dollars Owed to Children in Their Care," NPR, April 22, 2021, www.npr.org/2021/04/22/988806806/state-foster-care-agencies-take-millions-of-dollars-owed-to-children-in-their-ca.

18. Hatcher, *The Poverty Industry*, 46, 65–110.

19. Hatcher, *The Poverty Industry*, 1; Gillian B. White, "When Poverty Is Profitable," *The Atlantic*, June 22, 2016, www.theatlantic.com/business/archive/2016/06/poverty-industry/487958/.

20. Maximus, "Maximus Contact Centers in Georgia and New Jersey Awarded by Benchmark Portal," *PR Newswire*, April 18, 2018, www.prnewswire.com/news-releases/maximus-contact-centers-in-georgia-and-new-jersey-awarded-by-benchmarkportal-300631480.html.

21. Hatcher, *The Poverty Industry*, 2, 83, 89.

22. Hatcher, *The Poverty Industry*, 99, 145.

23. Eve A. Stotland, "Resolving the Tension Between Child Support Enforcement and Family Reunification," *Clearinghouse Review* 35 (September–October 2001); Daniel L. Hatcher, "Collateral Children: Consequence and Illegality at the Intersection of Foster Care and Child Support," *Brooklyn Law Review* 74, no. 4 (June 2009): 1334; Maria Cancian et al., "Making Parents Pay: The Unintended Consequences of Charging Parents for Foster Care," *Children and Youth Services Review* 72 (January 2017): 100–110, https://doi.org/10.1016/j.childyouth.2016.10.018.

24. Hatcher, *The Poverty Industry*, 30.

25. Hatcher, *The Poverty Industry*, 3, 37, 41.

26. Hatcher, *The Poverty Industry*, 30, 50.

27. Keeanga-Yamahtta Taylor, *Race for Profit: How Banks and the Real Estate Industry Undermined Black Home Ownership* (Chapel Hill: University of North Carolina Press, 2019); Rafael Khachaturian, "The Criminal Justice System as a Predatory Revenue Racket: Joe Soss," *Mitchell Center Podcast*, December 20, 2019, https://mitchellcenter.libsyn.com/episode-17-the-criminal-justice-system-as-a-predatory-revenue-racket-joe-soss.

28. Hatcher, "Stop Foster Care Agencies from Taking Children's Resources," 111.

29. Angeline Montauban, "Remarks, Panel 1: Legal Frameworks That Perpetuate Family Regulation" (presented at *Columbia Journal of Race and Law*, 11th Annual Symposium, Strengthened Bonds: Abolishing the Child Welfare System and Re-Envisioning Child Well-Being, Columbia Law School, June 17, 2021), https://virtual.eventmanagement.columbia.edu/strengthened_bonds.

CHAPTER 7: FAMILY SURVEILLANCE

1. Child Welfare Information Gateway, *Child Maltreatment 2019: Summary of Key Findings* (US Department of Health and Human Services, Administration for

Children and Families, Children's Bureau, April 2021), 3, www.childwelfare.gov /pubPDFs/canstats.pdf; Hyunil Kim et al., "Lifetime Prevalence of Investigating Child Maltreatment Among US Children," *American Journal of Public Health* 107, no. 2, (February 2017): 278, www.ncbi.nlm.nih.gov/pmc/articles/PMC5227926 /pdf/AJPH.2016.303545.pdf.

2. Movement for Family Power, *"Whatever They Do, I'm Her Comfort, I'm Her Protector": How the Foster System Has Become Ground Zero for the U.S. Drug War* (New York: MFP, NYU Family Defense Clinic, Drug Policy Alliance, 2020), 58–60, www.movementforfamilypower.org/ground-zero.

3. Molly Schwartz, "Do We Need to Abolish Child Protective Services? Inside One Parent's Five-Year Battle with the 'Family Destruction System,'" *Mother Jones*, December 10, 2020, www.motherjones.com/politics/2020/12/do-we-need -to-abolish-child-protective-services/; Miriam Mack, "The White Supremacy Hydra: How the Family First Prevention Services Act Reifies Pathology, Control, and Punishment in the Family Regulation System," *Columbia Journal of Race and Law* 11, no. 3: 767–810 (2021), https://doi.org/10.52214/cjrl.v11i3.8751; J. Khadijah Abdurahman, "Calculating the Souls of Black Folk: Predictive Analytics in the New York City Administration for Children's Services," *Columbia Journal of Race and Law* 11, no. 4: 75–110 (2021), https://doi.org/10.52214/cjrl.v11i4 .8741.

4. Michelle Burrell, "What Can the Child Welfare System Learn in the Wake of the Floyd Decision?: A Comparison of Stop-and-Frisk Policing and Child Welfare Investigations," *City University of New York Law Review* 22, no. 1 (Winter 2019), https://academicworks.cuny.edu/clr/vol22/iss1/14; Lynne Wrennall, "Surveillance and Child Protection: De-mystifying the Trojan Horse," *Surveillance and Society* 7, no. 3 (July 2010): 307, https://doi.org/10.24908/ss.v7i3/4.4158; Jacques Donzelot, *The Policing of Families* (New York: Pantheon, 1979); David Garland, "The Birth of the Welfare Sanction," *British Journal of Law and Society* 8, no. 1 (Summer 1981), https://doi.org/10.2307/1409833.

5. Tarek Z. Ismail, "The Consent of the Compelled: Child Protective Agents as Law Enforcement Officers," (unpublished manuscript, 2021).

6. Doriane Lambelet Coleman, "Storming the Castle to Save the Children: The Ironic Costs of a Child Welfare Exception to the Fourth Amendment," *William and Mary Law Review* 47 (2005), 413; in December 2021, the Pennsylvania Supreme Court held that Fourth Amendment protections extend to home inspections conducted by child welfare workers during civil investigations. Interest of Y.W.-B., 1 EAP 2021, _A.3d._, 2021 WL 6071747, (Pa. Dec. 23, 2021).

7. Ismail, "The Consent of the Compelled."

8. Kelley Fong, "Getting Eyes in the Home: Child Protective Services Investigations and State Surveillance of Family Life," *American Sociological Review* 84, no. 4 (August 2020): 610–611, 623; Susila Gurusami and Rahim Kurwa, "From Broken Windows to Broken Homes: Homebreaking as Racialized and Gendered Poverty Governance," *Feminist Formations* 33, no. 1 (Spring 2021): 1–32.

9. Mical Raz, *Abusive Policies: How the American Child Welfare System Lost Its Way* (Chapel Hill: University of North Carolina Press, 2020); Mical Raz, "Unintended Consequences of Expanded Mandated Reporting Laws," *American Acad-*

emy of Pediatrics 139, no. 4 (April 2017), https://doi.org/10.1542/peds.2016-3511; Jane Waldfogel, *The Future of Child Protection: How to Break the Cycle of Abuse and Neglect* (Cambridge, MA: Harvard University Press, 1998).

10. Child Welfare Information Gateway, *Child Maltreatment 2019: Summary of Key Findings*, 3.

11. Fong, "Getting Eyes in the Home," 611.

12. Brianna Harvey, Josh Gupta-Kagan, and Christopher E. Church, "Reimagining Schools' Role Outside the Family Regulation System," Columbia Journal of Race and Law 11, no. 3: 575–610 (2021); Fong, "Getting Eyes in the Home," 624.

13. Fong, "Getting Eyes in the Home," 619.

14. Fong, "Getting Eyes in the Home," 620.

15. Clara Presler, "The Dangerous Dynamic of Mutual Deference: A Case for Removing Doctors from Mandated Reporting," *Columbia Journal of Race and Law* 11, no. 3: 575–610 (2021), https://journals.library.columbia.edu/index.php /cjrl/article/view/8750; Charity Tolliver et al., "Policing by Another Name: Mandated Reporting as State Surveillance," webinar from Shriver Center on Poverty Law, November 14, 2020, www.povertylaw.org/article/webinar-policing-by -another-name-mandated-reporting-as-state-surveillance/; Burrell, "What Can the Child Welfare System Learn in the Wake of the Floyd Decision?," 136.

16. Kelley Fong, "Concealment and Constraint: Child Protective Services Fears and Poor Mothers' Institutional Engagement," *Social Forces* 97, no. 4 (June 2019), https://doi.org/10.1093/sf/soy093.

17. Fong, "Concealment and Constraint," 8; Tina Lee, *Catching a Case: Inequality and Fear in New York City's Child Welfare System* (New York: Rutgers University Press, 2016), 83–84.

18. Tolliver et al., "Policing by Another Name."

19. Lynn M. Paltrow and Jeanne Flavin, "Arrests of and Forced Interventions on Pregnant Women in the United States, 1973–2005: Implications for Women's Legal Status and Public Health," *Journal of Health Politics, Policy and Law* 38, no. 2 (2013), 299–343, https://doi.org/10.1215/03616878-1966324.

20. Movement for Family Power, *"Whatever They Do, I'm Her Comfort, I'm Her Protector,"* 20.

21. Sue Thomas et al., "Drug Use During Pregnancy Policies in the United States from 1970 to 2016," *Contemporary Drug Problems* 45, no. 4 (August 2018), https://doi.org/10.1177/0091450918790790; Children's Bureau, *Plans of Safe Care for Infants with Prenatal Substance Exposure and Their Families* (August 2019), www.childwelfare.gov/pubPDFs/safecare.pdf.

22. Committee on Health Care for Underserved Women, American College of Obstetricians and Gynecologists, *Substance Abuse Reporting and Pregnancy: The Role of the Obstetrician-Gynecologist*, Committee Opinion Number 473, January 2011, reaffirmed 2014, quoted in Khiara Bridges, "Race, Pregnancy, and the Opioid Epidemic: White Privilege and the Criminalization of Opioid Use During Pregnancy," *Harvard Law Review* 133, no. 3 (January 2020): 800.

23. Amanda Roy et al., "Toxicology Screening Practices for Perinatal Substance Use Among New York State Birthing Hospitals," New York State Perinatal Quality Collaborative, New York State Department of Health, SUNY Albany

School of Public Health, 2018, www.albany.edu/cphce/nyspqcpublic/Toxicology SurveyPosterAMCHP2018.pdf; Dorothy Roberts, *Killing the Black Body: Race, Reproduction, and the Meaning of Liberty* (New York: Pantheon, 1997).

24. Roberts, *Killing the Black Body*, 175–176; Ira J. Chasnoff, Harvey J. Landress, and Mark E. Barrett, "The Prevalence of Illicit-Drug or Alcohol Use During Pregnancy and Discrepancies in Mandatory Reporting in Pinellas County, Florida," *New England Journal of Medicine* 322, no. 17 (April 1990), https://doi.org/10.1056/NEJM199004263221706; D. R. Neuspiel et al., "Custody of Cocaine-Exposed Newborns: Determinants of Discharge Decisions," *American Journal of Public Health* 83, no. 12 (December 1993), https://doi.org/10.2105/ajph.83.12.1726; Sarah C. M. Roberts and Amani Nuru-Jeter, "Universal Screening for Alcohol and Drug Use and Racial Disparities in Child Protective Services Reporting," *Journal of Behavioral Health Service and Research* 39, no. 1 (June 2011), https://doi.org/10.1007/s11414-011-9247-x; Michael Fitzgerald, "New York City to Investigate Hospital Drug Tests of Black and Latino New Mothers, Which Can Prompt Foster Care Removals," *The Imprint*, November 16, 2020, https://imprintnews.org/child-welfare-2/new-york-hospital-drug-tests-mothers-foster 49384.

25. Sarah C. M. Roberts and Amani Nuru-Jeter, "Universal Alcohol/Drug Screening in Prenatal Care: A Strategy for Reducing Racial Disparities? Questioning the Assumptions," *Maternal and Child Health Journal* 15 (November 2010), https://doi.org/10.1007/s10995-010-0720-6.

26. S. C. M. Roberts et al., "Does Adopting a Prenatal Substance Use Protocol Reduce Racial Disparities in CPS Reporting Related to Maternal Drug Use?: A California Case Study," *Journal of Perinatology* 35, no. 2 (February 2015), https://doi.org/10.1038/jp.2014.168.

27. Movement for Family Power, *"Whatever They Do, I'm Her Comfort, I'm Her Protector,"* 31.

28. American College of Obstetricians and Gynecologists, "Opposition to Criminalization of Individuals During Pregnancy and the Postpartum Period: Statement of Policy," December 2020, www.acog.org/clinical-information/policy-and-position-statements/statements-of-policy/2020/opposition-criminalization-of-individuals-pregnancy-and-postpartum-period.

29. Bianca Vásquez Toness, "Your Child's a No-Show at Virtual School? You May Get a Call from the State's Foster Care Agency," *Boston Globe*, August 15, 2020, www.bostonglobe.com/2020/08/15/metro/your-childs-no-show-virtual-school-you-may-get-call-states-foster-care-agency/.

30. Sarah Brayne, *Predict and Surveil: Data, Discretion, and the Future of Policing* (New York: Oxford University Press, 2021), 70; Brian Jordan Jefferson, "Predictable Policing: Predictive Crime Mapping and Geographies of Policing and Race," *Annals of the American Association of Geographers* 108, no. 2 (May 2017), https://doi.org/10.1080/24694452.2017.1293500; Andrew Guthrie Ferguson, *The Rise of Big Data Policing: Surveillance, Race, and the Future of Law Enforcement* (New York: New York University Press, 2017); Kevin Miller, "Total Surveillance, Big Data, and Predictive Crime Technology: Privacy's Perfect Storm," *Journal of Technology Law and Policy* 19 (2014): 105–146.

31. Jeff Larson et al., "How We Analyzed the COMPAS Recidivism Algorithm," ProPublica, May 23, 2016, www.propublica.org/article/how-we-analyzed-the-compas-recidivism-algorithm.

32. Virginia Eubanks, *Automating Inequality: How High-Tech Tools Profile, Police, and Punish the Poor* (New York: St. Martin's Press, 2017), 183–184.

33. Eubanks, *Automating Inequality*, 156.

34. Daniel Heimpel, "Uncharted Waters: Data Analytics and Child Protection in Los Angeles," *The Imprint*, July 20, 2015, https://imprintnews.org/featured/uncharted-waters-data-analytics-and-child-protection-in-los-angeles/10867; Jeremy D. Goldhaber-Fiebert and Lea Prince, *Impact Evaluation of Predictive Risk Modeling Tool for Allegheny County's Child Welfare Office*, Allegheny County Analytics, March 2019, www.alleghenycountyanalytics.us/wp-content/uploads/2019/05/Impact-Evaluation-from-16-ACDHS-26_PredictiveRisk_Package_050119_FINAL-6.pdf; Kate Giammarise, "Can an Algorithm Help Keep Kids Safe? So Far, Allegheny County's Screening Tool Is Improving Accuracy," *Pittsburgh Post-Gazette*, May 6, 2019, www.post-gazette.com/news/social-services/2019/05/06/Allegheny-Family-Screening-Tool-County-DHS-children-child-welfare-safety/stories/201905020120.

35. CITI's 2019 announcement of its deal with Louisiana's Department of Children and Family Services to implement its comprehensive child welfare solution (CCWIS), called Unify, similarly boasts of providing a "360 degree view of the child and family." CITI, "Creative Information Technology Inc. Selected to Implement State of Louisiana CCWIS," September 23, 2019, https://citi-us.com/in-focus/latest-news/creative-information-technology-inc-selected-implement-state-louisiana-ccwis; SAS Institute Inc., "Analytics for Child Well-Being," accessed July 7, 2021, www.sas.com/en_us/software/analytics-for-child-well-being.html.

36. Michael Nash to Los Angeles County Board of Supervisors, "Memorandum: Examination of Using Structured Decision Making and Predictive Analytics in Assessing Safety and Risk in Child Welfare," County of Los Angeles Office of Child Protection, May 4, 2017, http://file.lacounty.gov/SDSInter/bos/bc/1023048_05.04.17OCPReportonRiskAssessmentTools_SDMandPredictiveAnalytics.pdf; Dina Gusovsky, "Can Life as a Data Point Save America's At-Risk Children?," CNBC, January 14, 2016, www.cnbc.com/2016/01/14/an-80-billion-annual-tax-bill-thats-failing-our-children.html; Richard Wexler, "Los Angeles County Quietly Drops Its First Child Welfare Predictive Analytics Experiment," *NCCPR Child Welfare Blog*, May 9, 2017, www.nccprblog.org/2017/05/; Stop LAPD Spying Coalition, *Abolishing the Surveillance of Families: A Report on Understanding Harm, Surveillance, and Information Sharing in the Department of Children and Family Services in Los Angeles County*, October 2020, https://stoplapdspying.org/wp-content/uploads/2020/10/LA-County-DCFS-Information-Sharing-Surveillance-Oct-2020.pdf; Washington State Institute for Public Policy, "Structured Decision Making Risk Assessment: Does It Reduce Racial Disproportionality in Washington's Child Welfare System?," May 2011, www.wsipp.wa.gov/ReportFile/1086.

37. David Jackson and Gary Marx, "Data Mining Program Designed to Predict Child Abuse Proves Unreliable, DCFS Says," *Chicago Tribune*, December 6,

2017, www.chicagotribune.com/investigations/ct-dcfs-eckerd-met-20171206 -story.html.

38. Eubanks, *Automating Inequality*, 166–167.

39. Tressie McMillan Cottom, "Where Platform Capitalism and Racial Capitalism Meet: The Sociology of Race and Racism in the Digital Society," *Sociology of Race and Ethnicity* 6, no. 4 (October 2020): 443, https://doi.org/10 .1177/2332649220949473.

40. Issa Kohler-Hausmann, *Misdemeanorland: Criminal Courts and Social Control in an Age of Broken Windows Policing* (Princeton, NJ: Princeton University Press, 2018); Dorothy E. Roberts, "Digitizing the Carceral State," *Harvard Law Review* 132, no. 6 (April 2019); Abdurahman, "Calculating the Souls of Black Folk: Predictive Analytics in the New York City Administration for Children's Services"; Simone Browne, *Dark Matters: On the Surveillance of Blackness* (Durham, NC: Duke University Press, 2015); Ruha Benjamin, *Race After Technology: Abolitionist Tools for the New Jim Code* (New York: Polity, 2019).

41. Eubanks, *Automating Inequality*, 137, quoting Emily Putnam-Hornstein and Barbara Needell, "Predictors of Child Protective Service Contact Between Birth and Age Five: An Examination of California's 2002 Birth Cohort," *Child and Youth Services Review* 33 (2011), 2400, 2406; Carimah Townes, "California County Law Enforcement Puts Kids on Probation for Bad Grades," The Appeal, July 10, 2018, www.theappeal.org/california-county-law -enforcement-puts-kids-on-probation-for-bad-grades/.

42. Kate Giammarise, "With 'Hello Baby' Officials Aim to Reach All Babies Born in Allegheny County—with An Algorithm Targeting Those Most at Risk," *Pittsburgh Post-Gazette*, August 5, 2019, www.post-gazette.com/news /social-services/2019/08/05/Hello-Baby-officials-aim-reach-all-babies -born-Allegheny-County-algorithm-targeting-most-at-risk/stories/2019 07240098.

43. Stephanie Clifford and Jessica Silver-Greenberg, "Foster Care as Punishment: The New Reality of 'Jane Crow,'" *New York Times*, July 21, 2017, www .nytimes.com/2017/07/21/nyregion/foster-care-nyc-jane-crow.html; Lee, *Catching a Case*, 140–181; Angela Olivia Burton and Angeline Montauban, "Toward Community Control of Child Welfare Funding: Repeal the Child Abuse Prevention and Treatment Act and Delink Child Protection from Family Well-Being," *Columbia Journal of Race and Law* 11, no. 3: 639–680 (2021), https://doi .org/10.52214/cjrl.v11i3.8747.

44. Joaquin Sapien, "Dysfunction Disorder," ProPublica, January 17, 2017, www.propublica.org/article/dysfunction-disorder-nyc-family-court-flawed -mental-health-reports; Emma Brown-Bernstein, "Evaluating Evaluations," *Rethinking Foster Care* (blog), August 23, 2021, https://rethinkingfostercare .blogspot.com/2021/08/evaluating-evaluations.html.

45. ProPublica, "Should a Mental Illness Mean You Lose Your Kid?," copublished with *The Daily Beast*, May 30, 2014, www.propublica.org/article/should -a-mental-illness-mean-you-lose-your-kid.

46. The Imprint Staff Reports, "U.S. Justice Department: Discrimination Settlement a 'Landmark' Moment for Disabled Parents," *The Imprint*, November

24, 2020, https://imprintnews.org/child-welfare-2/massachusetts-discrimination -settlement-a-landmark-for-disabled-parents/49686.

47. Burrell, "What Can the Child Welfare System Learn in the Wake of the Floyd Decision?," 126.

48. Author's interview of the Bronx Defenders staff via Zoom, July 21, 2020.

49. Emma Brown-Bernstein, "Child Welfare Must Face History to Get Past It," *The Imprint*, November 22, 2020, https://imprintnews.org/child-welfare -2/child-welfare-must-face-history-get-past/49352; Michael Fitzgerald, "New York Limits Access to Parents' Names in Child Abuse and Neglect Registry," *The Imprint*, April 3, 2020, https://imprintnews.org/news-2/new-york-access -names-neglect-registry/42044.

CHAPTER 8: CARCERAL ENTANGLEMENTS

1. Frank Edwards, "Family Surveillance: Police and the Reporting of Child Abuse and Neglect," *RSF: The Russell Sage Foundation Journal of the Social Sciences* 5, no. 1 (February 2019), 50–70, https://www.rsfjournal.org/content/5/1/50; Casey Family Programs, *Supportive Communities: Are There Good Examples of How Child Welfare Agencies Are Collaborating with Law Enforcement?*, January 2018, www.casey .org/media/SComm_Models_Law_Enforcement_fnl.pdf.

2. Tarek Ismail, "Family Separation in Our Backyard: The Cruelty of Prematurely Removing Children from Their Homes," *New York Daily News*, October 10, 2020, www.nydailynews.com/opinion/ny-oped-family-separation-in-our -backyard-20201010-igwsbzvkxrfvjfcaebbs5elgy4-story.html, quoting C. S. Lewis, *God on the Dock* (1948).

3. Child Welfare Information Gateway, *Child Maltreatment 2019: Summary of Key Findings* (US Department of Health and Human Services, Administration for Children and Families, Children's Bureau, April 2021), www.childwelfare.gov /pubPDFs/canstats.pdf; Children's Bureau, *Cross Reporting Among Responders to Child Abuse and Neglect* (Washington, DC: US Department of Health and Human Services, Child Information Gateway, 2016), www.childwelfare.gov/pubPDFs /xreporting.pdf.

4. Edwards, "Family Surveillance," 52.

5. Erica Meiners and Maya Schenwar, "'Stop-and-Frisk' for Caregivers: How Expanded Mandated Reporting Laws Hurt Families," *Truthout*, June 29, 2017, https://truthout.org/articles/stop-and-frisk-for-caregivers-how-expanded -mandated-reporting-laws-hurt-families/.

6. Casey Family Programs, *Supportive Communities*, 5.

7. Edwards, "Family Surveillance," 56.

8. Edwards, "Family Surveillance," 62–63.

9. Briana Augustus, "Raw Body Cam: Footage Released in 2017 Shooting of Calvin Toney," *brproud*, posted October 30, 2019, www.brproud.com/news /local-news/raw-body-cam-footage-released-in-2017-shooting-of-calvin -toney/; Emma Discher, Grace Toohey, and Lea Skene, "Child Abuse Case Central to Baton Rouge Fatal Police Shooting of Calvin Toney; Officer ID'd," *The

Advocate, November 14, 2017, www.theadvocate.com/baton_rouge/news/crime
_police/article_27d5c4ea-c973-11e7-890b-370fce65f7c1.html.

10. Frank Edwards, Hedwig Lee, and Michael Esposito, "Risk of Being Killed by Police Use of Force in the United States by Age, Race-Ethnicity, and Sex," *Proceedings of the National Academy of Science of the United States of America* 116, no. 34 (August 2019): 16, 793–794, https://doi.org/10.1073/pnas.1821204116.

11. Natalie Pattillo, "Victims of Spousal Abuse Are Losing Their Children to Social Services," *Pacific Standard*, March 5, 2018, https://psmag.com/social -justice/victims-spousal-abuse-children.

12. Suzanne Hirt, "Florida Blames Mothers When Men Batter Them—Then Takes Away Their Children," *USA Today*, December 16, 2020, www.usatoday.com /in-depth/story-series/2020/12/16/florida-blames-mothers-when-men-batter -them-then-takes-their-children/6507973002/; Ijeoma Nwabuzor Ogbonnaya and Cara Pohle, "Case Outcomes of Child Welfare–Involved Families Affected by Domestic Violence: A Review of the Literature," *Children and Youth Services Review* 35, no. 9 (September 2013), https://doi.org/10.1016/j.childyouth.2013.05.014.

13. Abigail Kramer, *Backfire: When Reporting Domestic Violence Means You Get Investigated for Child Abuse* (New York: Child Welfare Watch, New School Center for New York City Affairs, 2020), 3–4.

14. Somini Sengupta, "Tough Justice: Taking a Child When One Parent Is Battered," *New York Times*, July 8, 2000, www.nytimes.com/2000/07/08/nyregion /tough-justice-taking-a-child-when-one-parent-is-battered.html.

15. Kramer, *Backfire*, 3–4.

16. Nicholson v. Williams, 203 F. Supp.2d 153, 250-51 (E.D.N.Y. 2002); Nicholson v. Scoppetta, 820 N.E.2d 840 (N.Y. 2004).

17. Kramer, *Backfire*, 3–4; Lynn F. Beller, "When in Doubt, Take Them Out: Removal of Children from Victims of Domestic Violence Ten Years After Nicholson v. Williams," *Duke Journal of Gender Law and Policy* 22, no. 2 (Spring 2015): 205–239, https://scholarship.law.duke.edu/djglp/vol22/iss2/2/; Jaime Perrone, "Failing to Realize *Nicholson*'s Vision: How New York's Child Welfare System Continues to Punish Battered Mothers," *Journal of Law and Policy* 20, no. 2 (2012): 641–675, https://brooklynworks.brooklaw.edu/cgi/viewcontent.cgi?article=1083 &context=jlp; Tina Lee, "Child Welfare Practice in Domestic Violence Cases in New York City: Problems for Poor Women of Color," *Women, Gender, and Families of Color* 3, no. 1 (Spring 2015), https://doi.org/10.5406/womgenfamcol.3.1.0058.

18. Carrie Lippy et al., "The Impact of Mandatory Reporting Laws on Survivors of Intimate Partner Violence: Intersectionality, Help-Seeking and the Need for Change," *Journal of Family Violence* 35, no. 4 (April 2020), https://doi .org/10.1007/s10896-019-00103-w.

19. INCITE! Women of Color Against Violence, editors, *Color of Violence: The Incite! Anthology* (Cambridge, MA: Duke University Press, 2016); Beth E. Richie, "A Black Feminist Reflection on the Antiviolence Movement," *Signs: Journal of Women in Culture and Society* 25, no. 4 (2000): 1136, https://doi.org /10.1086/495533; Andrea J. Ritchie, *Invisible No More: Police Violence Against Black Women and Women of Color* (Boston: Beacon Press, 2017); Beth E. Richie, *Compelled to Crime: The Gendered Entrapment of Battered Black Women* (New York: Routledge,

1996); Survived and Punished, *Criminalizing Survival* Curricula, October 2018, https://survivedandpunished.org/criminalizing-survival-curricula; Victoria Frye et al., *The Family Protection and Domestic Violence Intervention Act of 1995: Examining the Effects of Mandatory Arrest in New York City* (New York: Family Violence Project, Urban Justice Center, 2001), https://doi.org/10.13140/RG.2.2.30058.31682.

20. Hirt, "Florida Blames Mothers When Men Batter Them—Then Takes Away Their Children"; Chris Martin, "Op Ed: She Reached Out for Help and Got Her Kids Taken Away," Witness LA, June 16, 2021, www.witnessla.com /op-ed-she-reached-out-for-help-and-got-her-kids-taken-away/.

21. National Center on Substance Abuse and Child Welfare, "Child Welfare and Alcohol and Drug Use Statistics," accessed July 9, 2021, https:// ncsacw.samhsa.gov/research/child-welfare-and-treatment-statistics.aspx; Tammy Richards et al., "Children Prenatally Exposed to Alcohol and Other Drugs: What the Literature Tells Us About Child Welfare Information Sources, Policies, and Practices to Identify and Care for Children," *Journal of Public Child Welfare*, published online October 23, 2020, https://doi.org/10.1080/15548732 .2020.1814478.

22. Movement for Family Power, *"Whatever They Do, I'm Her Comfort, I'm Her Protector": How the Foster System Has Become Ground Zero for the U.S. Drug War* (New York: MFP, NYU Family Defense Clinic, Drug Policy Alliance, 2020), www .movementforfamilypower.org/ground-zero.

23. "The New Jane Crow," #BHeard, Bric TV, February 13, 2020, video, www .youtube.com/watch?v=mGlM1EWzDy4.

24. Carl L. Hart, *Drug Use for Grown-Ups: Chasing Liberty in the Land of Fear* (New York: Penguin Press, 2021), 9.

25. "The New Jane Crow," Bric TV.

26. RAICES, "Black Immigrant Lives Are Under Attack," accessed July 9, 2021, www.raicestexas.org/2020/07/22/black-immigrant-lives-are-under-attack/; Jeremy Raff, "The 'Double Punishment' for Black Undocumented Immigrants," *The Atlantic*, December 30, 2017, www.theatlantic.com/politics/archive/2017/12 /the-double-punishment-for-black-immigrants/549425/; Black Alliance for Just Immigration webpage, accessed July 9, 2021, https://baji.org/.

27. Author's interview with the Bronx Defenders staff via Zoom, July 21, 2020.

28. Christopher Sherman, Martha Mendoza, and Garance Burke, "The US Held a Record Number of Migrant Children in Custody in 2019," *USA Today*, November 12, 2019, www.usatoday.com/story/news/nation/2019/11/12/border -crisis-us-government-held-70-000-migrant-children-2019/2572376001/.

29. Nick Miroff, "'Lost' Immigrant Children? Statistics Show the Government Is Keeping More of Them Far Longer," *Washington Post*, May 30, 2018, www.washingtonpost.com/world/national-security/theres-fury-over-lost -migrant-children-but-stats-show-trumps-government-is-holding-more-of -them-longer/2018/05/30/d179b334-6438-11e8-99d2-0d678ec08c2f_story .html; Emily Atkin, "The Uncertain Fate of Migrant Children Sent to Foster Care," *New Republic*, June 20, 2018, https://newrepublic.com/article/149161 /uncertain-fate-migrant-children-sent-foster-care; Associated Press, "The U.S.

Has Held a Record 69,550 Migrant Children in Government Custody in 2019,"
NBC News, November 12, 2019, www.nbcnews.com/news/latino/u-s-has
-held-record-69-550-migrant-children-government-n1080486; Associated Press,
"Migrant Kids Separated at Border Faced Abuse in Foster Homes," *Los Angeles Times*, August 15, 2019, www.latimes.com/world-nation/story/2019-08-16
/immigration-border-separations-foster-homes.

30. Bethany Christian Services, "About Us," accessed July 10, 2021, https://
bethany.org/about-us/impact.

31. Garance Burke and Martha Mendoza, "AP Investigation: Deported Parents May Lose Kids to Adoption," AP News, October 9, 2018, https://apnews
.com/article/97b06cede0c149c492bf25a48cb6c26f.

32. Thomas P. Bonczar, "Prevalence of Imprisonment in the U.S. Population, 1974–2001," Bureau of Justice Statistics, August 2003, https://bjs.ojp.gov
/content/pub/pdf/piusp01.pdf; Sentencing Project, "Criminal Justice Facts," accessed July 10, 2021, www.sentencingproject.org/criminal-justice-facts/.

33. Michelle Alexander, *The New Jim Crow: Mass Incarceration in the Age of
Colorblindness* (New York: New Press, 2010), 16; Douglas A. Blackmon, *Slavery
by Another Name: The Re-Enslavement of Black Americans from the Civil War to World
War II* (New York, Anchor Books, 2009), 99; Sarah Haley, *No Mercy Here: Gen-
der, Punishment, and the Making of Jim Crow Modernity* (Chapel Hill: University
of North Carolina Press, 2016); Ruth Wilson Gilmore, *Golden Gulag: Prisons,
Surplus, Crisis, and Opposition in Globalizing California* (Berkeley: University of
California Press, 2007); Angela Y. Davis, *Are Prisons Obsolete?* (New York: Seven
Stories Press, 2003).

34. Sylvia A. Harvey, *The Shadow System: Mass Incarceration and the American Family* (New York: Bold Type Books, 2020), 7; Lauren E. Glaze and Laura
M. Maruschak, "Parents in Prison and Their Minor Children," Bureau of Justice Statistics, August 2008, revised March 2010, 2, https://bjs.ojp.gov/content
/pub/pdf/pptmc.pdf; Annie E. Casey Foundation, "Nearly Six Million Kids
Are Impacted by Parental Incarceration," November 17, 2017, www.aecf.org
/blog/a-growing-number-of-kids-are-impacted-by-parental-incarceration/?gclid
=Cj0KCQjwppSEBhCGARIsANIs4p4X8ExXBSCm4AdPZ2SqKL-ZyoiDw_5ig
-jE7vbv7F0c_DaKkc4vZ5kaAtcoEALw_wcB; Eli Hager, "A Mass Incarceration
Mystery," Marshall Project, www.themarshallproject.org/2017/12/15/a-mass
-incarceration-mystery; Christopher Wildeman, "Parental Imprisonment, the
Prison Boom, and the Concentration of Childhood Disadvantage," *Demography*
46, no. 2 (May 2009): 270–271, https://doi.org/10.1353/dem.0.0052.

35. Sarah Wakefield and Christopher Wildeman, *Children of the Prison Boom:
Mass Incarceration and the Future of American Inequality* (New York: Oxford University Press, 2013); Christopher Wildeman, "Parental Incarceration, Child Homelessness, and the Invisible Consequences of Mass Imprisonment," *Annals of the
American Academy of Political and Social Science* 651, no. 1 (January 2014); Christopher Wildeman and Emily A. Wang, "Mass Incarceration, Public Health, and
Widening Inequality in the USA," *The Lancet* 389, no. 10077 (April 2017), https://
doi.org/10.1016/S0140-6736(17)30259-3; Holly Foster and John Hagan, "Punishment Regimes and the Multilevel Effects of Parental Incarceration: Intergen-

erational, Intersectional, and Interinstitutional Models of Social Inequality and Systemic Exclusion," *Annual Review of Sociology* 41 (August 2015), https://doi .org/10.1146/annurev-soc-073014-112437; Marcus Shaw, "The Racial Implications of the Effects of Parental Incarceration on Intergenerational Mobility," *Sociology Compass* 10, no. 12 (December 2016): 1105, https://doi.org/10.1111 /soc4.12440.

36. Susila Gurusami, "Motherwork Under the State: The Maternal Labor of Formerly Incarcerated Black Women," *Social Problems* 66, no. 1 (February 2019): 130, https://doi.org/10.1093/socpro/spx045; Jason M. Williams, Zoe Spencer, and Sean K. Wilson, "I Am Not *Your Felon*: Decoding the Trauma, Resilience, and Recovering Mothering of Formerly Incarcerated Black Women," *Crime and Delinquency* 67, no. 8 (November 2020), https://doi.org/10.1177/0011128720974316; Glaze and Maruschak, "Parents in Prison and Their Minor Children"; Beth E. Richie, *Compelled to Crime*.

37. Nekima Levy-Pounds, "Can These Bones Live? A Look at the Impacts of the War on Drugs on Poor African-American Children and Families," *Hastings Race and Poverty Law Journal* 7, no. 2 (Spring 2010): 353–380; Kaaryn S. Gustafson, *Cheating Welfare: Public Assistance and the Criminalization of Poverty* (New York: New York University Press, 2011); Holly Foster, "Strains of Maternal Imprisonment: Importation and Deprivation Stressors for Women and Children," *Journal of Criminal Justice* 40, no. 3 (June 2012): 221–229; Megan Comfort, *Doing Time Together: Love and Family in the Shadow of the Prison* (Chicago: University of Chicago Press, 2008); Sandra Braman, *Change of State: Information, Policy, and Power* (Cambridge, MA: MIT Press, 2007).

38. Angela Y. Davis, "Masked Racism: Reflections on the Prison Industrial Complex," *Colorlines*, September 10, 1998, www.colorlines.com/articles/masked -racism-reflections-prison-industrial-complex.

39. Youth.gov, "Child Welfare Services to Children and Families of Prisoners," accessed July 10, 2021, https://youth.gov/youth-topics/children-of -incarcerated-parents/child-welfare-services-children-and-families-prisoners #_ftn1; Christopher A. Swann and Michelle Sheran Sylvester, "The Foster Care Crisis: What Caused Caseloads to Grow?," *Demography* 43, no. 2 (May 2006): 309–335; Frank Edwards, "Saving Children, Controlling Families: Punishment, Redistribution, and Child Protection," *American Sociological Review* 81, no. 3 (April 2016), https://doi.org/10.1177/0003122416638652; Lawrence M. Berger et al., "Families at the Intersection of the Criminal Justice and Child Protective Services Systems," *Annals of the American Academy of Political and Social Science* 665, no. 1 (April 2016), https://doi.org/10.1177/0002716216633058.

40. Signe Hald Andersen and Christopher Wildeman, "The Effect of Paternal Incarceration on Children's Risk of Foster Care Placement," *Social Forces* 93, no. 1 (March 2014), https://doi.org/10.1093/sf/sou027; Berger et al., "Families at the Intersection of the Criminal Justice and Child Protective Services Systems."

41. Priscilla A. Ocen, "Punishing Pregnancy: Race, Incarceration, and the Shackling of Pregnant Prisoners," *California Law Review* 100, no. 5 (October 2012): 1239–1311; Amnesty International USA, *Abuse of Women in Custody: Sexual Misconduct and Shackling of Women* (New York: Amnesty International Publications, 2001).

42. Glaze and Maruschak, "Parents in Prison and Their Minor Children," 5; International Association of Chiefs of Police, "Safeguarding Children of Arrested Parents," August 2014, 5, https://bja.ojp.gov/sites/g/files/xyckuh186 /files/Publications/IACP-SafeguardingChildren.pdf.

43. Williams, Spencer, and Wilson, "I Am Not *Your Felon*," 21–22.

44. Eli Hager and Anna Flagg, "How Incarcerated Parents Are Losing Their Children Forever," Marshall Project, December 2, 2018, www.themarshall project.org/2018/12/03/how-incarcerated-parents-are-losing-their-children -forever; Ronnie Halperin and Jennifer L. Harris, "Parental Rights of Incarcerated Mothers with Children in Foster Care: A Policy Vacuum," *Feminist Studies* 30, no. 2 (Summer 2004): 340–341.

45. Sarah Schirmer, Ashley Nellis, and Marc Mauer, "Incarcerated Parents and Their Children: Trends 1991–2007," Sentencing Project, February 2009, 5, https://www.sentencingproject.org/wp-content/uploads/2016/01/Incarcerated -Parents-and-Their-Children-Trends-1991-2007.pdf.

46. National Resource Center on Children and Families of the Incarcerated, "Children and the Families of the Incarcerated Fact Sheet," Rutgers University, 2014, https://nrccfi.camden.rutgers.edu/files/nrccfi-fact-sheet-2014.pdf; Jill McCorkel, "Mothers in Prison Aren't Likely to See Their Families This Thanksgiving—or Any Other Day," The Conversation, November 22, 2019, theconversation.com/mothers-in-prison-arent-likely-to-see-their-families -this-thanksgiving-or-any-other-day-126134; Halperin and Harris, "Parental Rights of Incarcerated Mothers with Children in Foster Care," 342.

47. Hager and Flagg, "How Incarcerated Parents Are Losing Their Children Forever"; James G. Dwyer, "No Place for Children: Addressing Urban Blight and Its Impact on Children Through Child Protection Law, Domestic Relations Law, and 'Adult-Only' Residential Zoning," *Alabama Law Review* 62 (2011): 889–959; Deseriee A. Kennedy, "Children, Parents and the State: The Construction of a New Family Ideology," *Berkeley Journal of Gender, Law and Justice* 26 (November 2011): 78–138; Philip Genty, "Damage to Family Relationships as a Collateral Consequence of Parental Incarceration," *Fordham Urban Law Journal* 30 (2003): 1678.

48. Charlene Wear Simmons and Emily Danker-Feldman, "Parental Incarceration, Termination of Parental Rights and Adoption: A Case Study of the Intersection Between the Child Welfare and Criminal Justice Systems," *Justice Policy Journal* 7, no. 2 (Fall 2010), www.cjcj.org/uploads/cjcj/documents/Parental _Incarceration.pdf.

49. Hager and Flagg, "How Incarcerated Parents Are Losing Their Children Forever."

50. George Lipsitz, "'In an Avalanche Every Snowflake Pleads Not Guilty': The Collateral Consequences of Mass Incarceration and Impediments to Women's Fair Housing Rights," *UCLA Law Review* 59, no. 6 (2012): 1737–1809; Alexander, *The New Jim Crow*, 175–220; Rahim Kurwa, "The New *Man in the House* Rules: How the Regulation of Housing Vouchers Turns Personal Bonds into Eviction Liabilities," *Housing Policy Debate* 30, no. 6 (August 2020), https://doi .org/10.1080/10511482.2020.1778056.

51. Devah Pager, "The Mark of A Criminal Record," *American Journal of Sociology* 108, no. 5 (March 2003): 937–975.

52. Gurusami, "Motherwork Under the State," 134, 136.

53. *Black Enterprise* Editors, "The Power of Kim K: Syesha Mercado Got Her Baby Back After 'Medical Kidnapping,'" *Black Enterprise*, August 20, 2021, www.blackenterprise.com/the-power-of-kim-k-syesha-mercado-got-her-baby-back-after-medical-kidnapping/?test=prebid; Kiara Brantley-Jones and Sabina Ghebremedhin, "'American Idol' Finalist Syesha Mercado Fights to Regain Custody of Her Children," *GMA*, August 19, 2021, www.goodmorningamerica.com/family/story/american-idol-finalist-syesha-mercado-fights-regain-custody-79517748; Elizabeth Chuck, "Authorities Take 2nd Child from 'American Idol' Contestant, Prompting Outrage," NBC News, August 13, 2021, www.nbcnews.com/news/amp/ncna1276796. A month earlier, in July 2021, Los Angeles police officers drew guns on a Black couple and their newborn in their home after the USC Medical Center reported the couple for suspected medical neglect. Simone Stancil, "Los Angeles Couple Says LAPD Arrived at Home, Drew Guns After Giving Birth to Newborn Baby," Blavity, July 15, 2021, https://blavity.com/los-angeles-couple-says-lapd-arrived-at-home-drew-their-guns-after-giving-birth-to-newborn-baby?category1=news&category2=Social-Justice.

CHAPTER 9: STRUCTURED TO HARM

1. Lindsay Schnell, "Foster Care Teen's Death Draws Scrutiny to Group Home Outbreaks: Who Is Looking Out for These Children?," *USA Today*, May 15, 2020, www.usatoday.com/story/news/nation/2020/05/15/coronavirus-foster-care-death-draws-scrutiny-group-home-outbreaks/5196297002/; Christine Hauser and Michael Levenson, "Three Charged in Death of Michigan Teenager Restrained at Youth Academy," *New York Times*, June 24, 2020, www.nytimes.com/2020/06/24/us/cornelius-frederick-lawsuit-lakeside-academy.html; Vanessa Romo, "3 Children's Home Staffers Charged in Death of 16-Year-Old," NPR, June 25, 2020, www.npr.org/sections/live-updates-protests-for-racial-justice/2020/06/25/883189076/3-childrens-home-staffers-charged-in-death-of-16-year-old.

2. The Office of Governor Gretchen Whitmer, "Governor Whitmer Statement on Youth Death at Lakeside for Children in Kalamazoo," press release, June 20, 2020, www.michigan.gov/whitmer/0,9309,7-387-90499_90640-532682—,00.html; Associated Press, "Second Utah Facility for Troubled Teens Closes in a Month," *U.S. News*, July 16, 2019, www.usnews.com/news/best-states/utah/articles/2019-07-16/second-utah-facility-for-troubled-teens-closes-in-a-month; Michigan Department of Health and Human Service, Division of Child Welfare Licensing, *Special Investigation Report* (Lansing, MI: June 17, 2020), 10, www.michigan.gov/documents/mdhhs/CI390201235_SIR_2020C0207030_6_18_2020__Redacted_694555_7.pdf.

3. Wendy Sawyer, "Youth Confinement: The Whole Pie 2019," press release, Prison Policy Initiative, December 19, 2019, www.prisonpolicy.org/reports/youth2019.html; "United States of Disparities," A Data Project from the Burns

Institute, accessed August 26, 2021, https://usdata.burnsinstitute.org/#comparison
=2&placement=1&races=2,3,4,5,6&offenses=5,2,8,1,9,11,10&year=2017
&view=map; Children's Defense Fund, *The State of America's Children 2021* (Washington, DC: 2021), 30, www.childrensdefense.org/wp-content/uploads/2021/04
/The-State-of-Americas-Children-2021.pdf.

4. Children's Defense Fund, *The State of America's Children 2021*; Josh
Rovner, "Juvenile Life Without Parole: An Overview," Sentencing Project, May
24, 2021, https://www.sentencingproject.org/publications/juvenile-life-without
-parole/.

5. Lauren Smiley, "Two White Moms. Six Black Kids. One Unthinkable
Tragedy. A Look Inside the 'Perfect' Hart Family," *Glamour Magazine*, September 6, 2018, www.glamour.com/story/hart-family-tragedy-jen-and-sarah-hart
-case; Roxanna Asgarian, "Before Children's Grisly Deaths, a Family Fought
for Them and Lost," The Appeal, July 12, 2018, https://theappeal.org/before
-childrens-grisly-deaths-a-family-fought-for-them-and-lost/.

6. Asgarian, "Before Children's Grisly Deaths."

7. Smiley, "Two White Moms."

8. Isabel Wilkerson, *Caste: The Origins of Our Discontents* (New York: Random
House, 2020), 285–287.

9. Asgarian, "Before Children's Grisly Deaths."

10. Nicole Rousseau, *Black Women's Burden: Commodifying Black Reproduction*
(London, UK: Palgrave Macmillian, 2009), 148.

11. Christopher O'Donnell and Nathaniel Lash, "Nowhere to Call Home:
Thousands of Foster Children Move So Much They Risk Psychological Harm,"
Tampa Bay Times, December 27, 2018, www.tampabay.com/hillsborough/nowhere
-to-call-home-thousands-of-foster-children-move-so-much-they-risk
-psychological-harm-20181227/; Children's Law Center of California, "Foster Care Facts," accessed August 3, 2021, www.clccal.org/resources/foster-care
-facts/; US Department of Health and Human Services, Children's Bureau, *The
AFCARS Report: Preliminary FY 2019 Estimates as of June 23, 2020—No. 27* (Washington, DC: June 23, 2020), 5, www.acf.hhs.gov/sites/default/files/documents/cb
/afcarsreport27.pdf; Laura Bauer, "Settlement Could Take Kansas Foster Care
from 'Shockingly Broken' to Model for Nation," *Kansas City Star*, July 9, 2020,
www.kansascity.com/news/politics-government/article244104907.html.

12. Athena Garcia-Gunn, "A Former Foster Youth," TEDxMtSAC, August
3, 2017, video, www.youtube.com/watch?v=yy9iQ50N3Bo.

13. Yo Jackson and Lindsay Huffhines, "Physical Health and Foster Youth,"
in *Handbook of Foster Youth*, ed. Elizabeth Trejos-Castillo and Nancy Trevino
-Schafer (Abingdon, UK: Routledge, 2018).

14. Peter J. Pecora, "Maximizing Educational Achievement of Youth in Foster Care and Alumni: Factors Associated with Success," *Children and Youth Services
Review* 34, no. 6 (2012): 1121–1129, http://fostercarechildren.pbworks.com/w/file
/fetch/63728498/Maximizing%20Educational%20Achievement%20of%20Youth
%20in%20Foster%20Care%20and%20Alumni.pdf; April M. Moyer and Abbie
E. Goldberg, "Foster Youth's Educational Challenges and Supports: Perspectives of Teachers, Foster Parents, and Former Foster Youth," *Child and Adolescent*

Social Work Journal 32, no. 1 (2019): 2, https://wordpress.clarku.edu/agoldberg
/files/2020/04/Moyer_Goldberg-Foster-Youth-Educational-Challenges.pdf; Ely-
sia V. Clemens et al., "The Effects of Placement and School Stability on Academic Growth Trajectories of Students in Foster Care," *Children and Youth Services
Review* 87, no. 1 (2018), www.unco.edu/cebs/foster-care-research/pdf/Academic
-Growth-Trajectories.pdf.

15. Brianna M. Harvey et al., *The Disenfranchisement of Black Foster Youth:
An Analysis of Los Angeles County Public School Data* (Los Angeles: UCLA Black
Male Institute, 2020), https://blackmaleinstitute.org/wp-content/uploads/2020
/10/Final-Black-FY-Brief-2020.pdf; Kenyon Lee Whitman and Brianna Harvey,
"The Disenfranchisement of Black Foster Youth," *The Imprint*, December 2, 2020,
https://imprintnews.org/child-welfare-2/disenfranchisement-black-foster-youth
-students/49626.

16. Brian Joseph, "The Brief Life and Private Death of Alexandria Hill,"
Mother Jones, February 26, 2015, www.motherjones.com/politics/2015/02
/privatized-foster-care-mentor/; Abby Elizabeth Conway, "Report Finds Blatant Lack of Oversight by DCF in Licensing of Foster Home Where Toddler
Died," WBUR News, October 1, 2015, www.wbur.org/news/2015/10/01/auburn
-foster-child-death-investigation; Rick Nathanson, "CYFD and Foster Parent
Sued over Baby's Death" *Albuquerque Journal*, July 31, 2019, www.abqjournal
.com/1347737/cyfd-and-foster-parent-sued-over-babys-death-ex-respite-home
-didnt-have-adequate-bedding-11monthold-girl-died-while-strapped-in-car
-seat-for-the-night-lawsuit-says.html.

17. Mary Benedict et al., "Types and Frequency of Child Maltreatment by
Family Foster Care Providers in An Urban Setting," *Child Abuse and Neglect* 18,
no. 7 (1994): 577–585, https://doi.org/10.1016/0145-2134(94)90084-1. See also,
for example, J. William Spencer and Dean D. Knudsen, "Out-of-Home Maltreatment: An Analysis of Risk in Various Settings for Children," *Children and
Youth Services Review* 14, no. 6 (1992): 485–492; Brenda Morton, "Seeking Safety,
Finding Abuse: Stories from Foster Youth on Maltreatment and Its Impact on
Academic Achievement," *Child and Youth Services* 36, no. 3 (2015), https://doi.org
/10.1080/0145935X.2015.1037047.

18. Peter J. Pecora et al., *Improving Family Foster Care: Findings from the Northwest
Foster Care Alumni Study* (Seattle, WA: Casey Family Programs, 2005), www.casey
.org/northwest-alumni-study/; Catherine Roller White et al., *Michigan Foster Care
Alumni Study Technical Report: Outcomes at Age 23 and 24* (Seattle, WA: Casey Family Programs, 2012), www.casey.org/media/StateFosterCare_MI_fr.pdf; Suzanne
Hirt, Michael Braga, and Pat Beall, "Foster Kids Starved, Beaten and Molested.
Few Caregivers Are Punished," *USA Today*, March 18, 2021, updated March 21,
2021, www.usatoday.com/in-depth/news/investigations/2021/03/18/foster-care
-children-starved-beaten-molested-florida-reports-show/6782615002/.

19. Jeremy Loudenback, "LGBTQ Youth Make Up One Third of Foster
Care, but Are Often Poorly Served," *The Imprint*, July 6, 2021, https://imprintnews
.org/top-stories/lgbtq-youth-face-overrepresentation-challenges-in-foster
-care/56680; Michael Fitzgerald and Megan Conn, "LGBTQ Foster Youth in
New York City: Strong in Numbers, Struggling in Care," *The Imprint*, November

12, 2020, https://imprintnews.org/child-welfare-2/lgbtq-foster-youth-new-york
-numbers-survey/49316; Ariel Love, "A Room of One's Own: Safe Placement for Transgender Youth in Foster Care," *New York University Law Review*
89, no. 6 (2014): 2279, www.nyulawreview.org/wp-content/uploads/2018/08
/NYULawReview-89-6-2268-Love.pdf; Sarah Mountz et al., "'Because We're
Fighting to Be Ourselves': Voices from Former Foster Youth Who Are Transgender and Gender Expansive," *Child Welfare* 96, no. 1 (2018):103–125; Mad-
elyn Freundlich and Rosemary J. Avery, "Gay and Lesbian Youth in Foster Care:
Meeting Their Placement and Service Needs," *Journal of Gay and Lesbian Social
Services* 17, no. 4 (2004): 39–57, https://doi.org/10.1300/J041v17n04_03.

20. Mariah Lopez, "Trapped!," *Represent Magazine*, January 2, 2000, www
.representmag.org/issues/FCYU040/Trapped!.html?story_id=FCYU-2000
-01-02&printable=1.

21. Rosalynd Erney and Kristen Weber, "Not All Children Are Straight and
White: Strategies for Serving Youth of Color in Out-of-Home Care Who Identify as LGBTQ," *Child Welfare* 96, no. 2 (2018): 159.

22. Jennifer A. Clements and Mitchell Rosenwald, "Foster Parents' Perspectives on LGB Youth in the Child Welfare System," *Journal of Gay and Lesbian Social
Services* 19, no. 1 (2007): 57–69, https://doi.org/10.1300/J041v19n01_04.

23. Love, "A Room of One's Own," 2271; Jody Marksamer with Dean Spade
and Gabriel Arkles, *A Place of Respect: A Guide for Group Care Facilities Serving
Transgender and Gender Non-Conforming Youth* (New York: National Center for
Lesbian Rights, Silvia Rivera Law Project, Spring 2011), 6, www.nclrights.org/wp
-content/uploads/2013/07/A_Place_Of_Respect.pdf.

24. Bianca D. M. Wilson and Angeliki A. Kastanis, "Sexual and Gender Minority Disproportionality and Disparities in Child Welfare: A Population-Based
Study," *Children and Youth Services Review* 58, no. 11 (2015): 11, https://doi.org
/10.1016/j.childyouth.2015.08.016; Alan Dettlaff and Micki Washburn, *Out-
comes of Sexual Minority Youth in Child Welfare: Prevalence, Risk, and Outcomes: A
Guide for Child Welfare Professionals* (Houston: University of Houston, Graduate
School of Social Work, 2018), 12, https://cssp.org/wp-content/uploads/2018
/08/Sexual-Minority-Youth-in-Child-Welfare_providers_final.pdf; Loudenback,
"LGBTQ Youth Make Up One Third of Foster Care, but Are Often Poorly
Served"; Fitzgerald and Conn, "LGBTQ Foster Youth in New York City"; Fulton v.
City of Philadelphia, 593 US ___ (2021), www.supremecourt.gov/opinions/20pdf
/19-123_g3bi.pdf.

25. Barbara Chaiyachati et al., "All-Cause Mortality Among Children in the
US Foster Care System, 2003–2016," *JAMA Pediatrics* 174, no. 9 (2020): 896,
https://jamanetwork.com/journals/jamapediatrics/fullarticle/2764570.

26. Kristine Philips, "After a Lifetime of Foster Homes and Abuse, a 14-Year-
Old Broadcast Her Suicide on Facebook," *Washington Post*, March 16, 2017, www
.washingtonpost.com/news/post-nation/wp/2017/03/16/after-a-lifetime-of-foster
-homes-and-abuse-a-14-year-old-broadcast-her-suicide-on-facebook/.

27. Carol Marbin Miller and Audra D. S. Burch, "Before Suicide by Hanging,
Girl Pleaded in Vain for Mom's Acceptance," *Miami Herald*, updated March 19,
2017, www.macon.com/news/nation-world/national/article138831808.html.

28. Emily Gurnon, "Suicide Looms Large in Minds of Many Foster Youth," *The Imprint*, September 27, 2020, https://imprintnews.org/childrens-mental -health/suicide-looms-large-minds-many-foster-youth/47755; Lily A. Brown, "Suicide in Foster Care: A High-Priority Safety Concern," *Perspectives on Psychological Science* 15 (2020): 665–668, https://doi.org/10.1177/1745691619895076.

29. Rhiannon Evans et al., "Comparison of Suicidal Ideation, Suicide Attempt and Suicide in Children and Young People in Care and Non-care Populations: Systematic Review and Meta-analysis of Prevalence," *Children and Youth Services Review* 82, no. 1 (2017): 125, https://doi.org/10.1016/j.childyouth.2017.09.020; Gurnon, "Suicide Looms Large in Minds of Many Foster Youth"; Brown, "Suicide in Foster Care"; Samantha Schmidt, "Girl, 6, Died by Hanging in Foster Care. County Settles with Family for $1.5 Million," *Washington Post*, June 7, 2018, www.washingtonpost.com/news/morning-mix/wp/2018/06/07/girl-6-died -by-hanging-in-foster-care-county-settles-with-family-for-1-5-million/; Mary Broadus on behalf of KZJ and as trustee for the next of kin of KZJ vs. Hennepin County et al., CASE 0:16-cv-01211 (D. Minn., filed May 9, 2016), https://kstp .com/kstpImages/repository/cs/files/Broadus%20complaint(1).pdf.

30. Amy D. Engler et al., "A Systematic Review of Mental Health Disorders of Children in Foster Care," *Trauma, Violence, and Abuse* (2020): 1–10; Kristin Turney and Christopher Wildeman, "Mental and Physical Health of Children in Foster Care," *Pediatrics* 138, no. 5 (2016), https://pediatrics.aappublications.org /content/pediatrics/138/5/e20161118.full.pdf.

31. Shelby L. Clark et al., "Investigating the Relationship Between Trauma Symptoms and Placement Instability," *Child Abuse and Neglect* 108, no. 1 (2020): 8, https://doi.org/10.1016/j.chiabu.2020.104660; Engler et al., "A Systemic Review of Mental Health Disorders of Children in Foster Care," 6; US Congress, Senate, Committee on Finance, *An Examination of Foster Care in the United States and the Use of Privatization*, 115th Cong., 1st sess., S. Prt. 115-28 (Washington, DC: US Government Publishing Office, 2017),17, https://www.govinfo .gov/content/pkg/CPRT-115SPRT26354/pdf/CPRT-115SPRT26354.pdf; Phillips, "After a Lifetime of Foster Homes"; Garcia-Gunn, "A Former Foster Youth."

32. Deb Stone, "U.S. Foster Care: A Flawed Solution That Leads to Long-Term Problems?," *STIR*, May 12, 2014, www.stirjournal.com/2014/05/12/u-s -foster-care-a-flawed-solution-that-leads-to-more-long-term-problems/; Anthony Ryan Hatch, *Silent Cells: The Secret Drugging of Captive America* (Minneapolis: University of Minnesota Press, 2019), 9, 10, 13; Kathleen Noonan and Dorothy Miller, "Fostering Transparency: A Preliminary Review of 'Policy' Governing Psychotropic Medications in Foster Care," *Hasting Law Journal* 65, no. 6 (2014): 1526, https://hastingslawjournal.org/wp-content/uploads/Noonan-65.6.pdf.

33. Laura Gypen et al., "Outcomes of Children Who Grew Up in Foster Care: Systematic-Review," *Children and Youth Services Review* 76, no. 1 (2017): 80, https://doi.org/10.1016/j.childyouth.2017.02.035; Kym R. Ahrens et al., "Health Outcomes in Young Adults from Foster Care and Economically Diverse Backgrounds," *Pediatrics* 134, no. 6 (2014): 1073, https://pediatrics.aappublications.org /content/134/6/1067; Cheryl Zlotnick et al., "Life Course Outcomes on Mental and Physical Health: The Impact of Foster Care on Adulthood," *American*

Journal of Public Health 102, no. 3 (2012): 539, www.ncbi.nlm.nih.gov/pmc/articles/PMC3487656/pdf/AJPH.2011.300285.pdf; Candice N. Plotkin, "Study Finds Foster Kids Suffer PTSD," *Harvard Crimson*, April 11, 2005, www.thecrimson.com/article/2005/4/11/study-finds-foster-kids-suffer-ptsd/.

34. Pecora et al., *Improving Family Foster Care*, 9, 39; Richard Wexler, "80 Percent Failure: A Brief Analysis of the Casey Family Programs Northwest Foster Care Alumni Study," National Coalition for Child Protection Reform, updated March 2008, https://nccpr.org/80-percent-failure/.

35. Mark E. Courtney et al., *Midwest Evaluation of the Adult Functioning of Former Foster Youth: Outcomes at Age 21* (Chicago, IL: Chapin Hall Center for Children at the University of Chicago, 2007), 21, 73, www.chapinhall.org/wp-content/uploads/Midwest-Eval-Outcomes-at-Age-21.pdf; Sarah Fathallah and Sarah Sullivan, *Away from Home: Youth Experiences of Institutional Placements in Foster Care* (Think of Us, July 2021), 93, https://www.thinkof-us.org/awayfromhome.

36. White et al., *Michigan Foster Care Alumni Study Technical Report*, 11, 22–23.

37. Thomas P. McDonald et al., *Assessing the Long-Term Effects of Foster Care: A Research Synthesis* (Washington, DC: CWLA Press, 1996), https://irp.wisc.edu/publications/focus/pdfs/foc153j.pdf; June M. Clausen et al., "Mental Health Problems of Children in Foster Care," *Journal of Child and Family Studies* 7 (1988): 283–296, https://doi.org/10.1023/A:1022989411119; T. C. Hulsey and R. White, "Family Characteristics and Measures of Behavior in Foster and Non-foster Children," *American Journal of Orthopsychiatry* 59, no. 4 (1989): 502–509, https://doi.org/10.1111/j.1939-0025.1989.tb02739.x.

38. Catherine R. Lawrence, Elizabeth A. Carlson, and Byron Egeland, "The Impact of Foster Care on Development," *Development and Psychopathology* 18, no. 1 (2006): 71, https://cca-ct.org/Study%20Impact%20of%20Foster%20Care%20on%20Child%20Dev.pdf.

39. Anouk Goemans, Mitch van Geel, and Paul Vedder, "Over Three Decades of Longitudinal Research on the Development of Foster Children: A Meta-Analysis," *Child Abuse and Neglect* 42, no. 1 (2015): 130–131, https://doi.org/10.1016/j.chiabu.2015.02.003. See also Miriam J. Maclean et al., "Out-of-Home Care Versus In-Home Care for Children Who Have Been Maltreated: A Systematic Review of Health and Wellbeing Outcomes," *Child Abuse Review* 25, no. 4 (2016): 251–272, https://doi.org/10.1002/car.2437; Heidi Jacobsen et al., "Foster Children Are at Risk for Developing Problems in Social-Emotional Functioning: A Follow-Up Study at 8 Years of Age," *Children and Youth Services Review* 108 (2020): 1–10, https://doi.org/10.1016/j.childyouth.2019.104603.

40. Joseph J. Doyle Jr., "Child Protection and Child Outcomes: Measuring the Effects of Foster Care," *American Economic Review* 97, no. 5 (2007): 1584, 1591, https://www.jstor.org/stable/30034577.

41. Doyle, "Child Protection and Child Outcomes," 1607; Joseph J. Doyle, "Causal Effects of Foster Care: An Instrumental-Variables Approach," *Children and Youth Services Review* 35, no. 7 (2011): 23, http://hdl.handle.net/1721.1/120582.

42. Dorothy Roberts, *Shattered Bonds: The Color of Child Welfare* (New York: Basic Civitas Books, 2001), 20.

43. Dorothy E. Roberts, "The Racial Geography of Child Welfare: Toward a New Research Paradigm," *Child Welfare* 87, no. 2 (2008): 143–144, http://cap.law.harvard.edu/wp-content/uploads/2015/07/robertsrd.pdf.

44. Schnell, "Foster Care Teen's Death Draws Scrutiny"; Grace S. Hubel et al., "A Case Study of the Effects of Privatization of Child Welfare on Services for Children and Families: The Nebraska Experience," *Children and Youth Services Review* 35, no. 12 (2013): 2050, https://doi.org/10.1016/j.childyouth.2013.10.011; Garrett Therolf, "Private Foster Care System, Intended to Save Children, Endangers Some," *Los Angeles Times*, December 18, 2013, www.latimes.com/local/la-me-foster-care-dto-htmlstory.html.

45. Therolf, "Private Foster Care System."

46. US Congress, Senate, Committee on Finance, *An Examination of Foster Care in the United States and the Use of Privatization*, 115th Cong., 1st sess., S. Prt. 115-28 (Washington, DC: US Government Publishing Office, 2017), 5, 30, www.govinfo.gov/content/pkg/CPRT-115SPRT26354/pdf/CPRT-115SPRT26354.pdf.

47. Aram Roston, "Fostering Profits: Abuse and Neglect at America's Biggest For-Profit Foster Company," BuzzFeed News, February 20, 2015, www.buzzfeednews.com/article/aramroston/fostering-profits; Senate, *An Examination of Foster Care*, 5, 7, 11.

48. Roston, "Fostering Profits"; Joseph, "The Brief Life and Private Death of Alexandria Hill"; Ryan Grim and Aida Chavez, "Children Are Dying at Alarming Rates in Foster Care and Nobody Is Bothering to Investigate," *The Intercept*, October 18, 2017, https://theintercept.com/2017/10/18/foster-care-children-deaths-mentor-network/; Aram Roston, "In an Unmarked Grave, a Baby's Untold Story," BuzzFeed News, June 18, 2015, www.buzzfeednews.com/article/aramroston/in-an-unmarked-grave-a-baby-who-died-on-for-profit-foster-co.

49. DispatchAdmin, "Guilty Plea in Child Sex Abuse Case," *The Dispatch*, September 1, 2011, https://mdcoastdispatch.com/2011/09/01/guilty-plea-in-child-sex-abuse-case/; Roston, "Fostering Profits."

50. Senate, *An Examination of Foster Care*, 22–23.

51. Roston, "Fostering Profits"; Joseph, "The Brief Life and Private Death of Alexandria Hill."

52. Roston, "Fostering Profits."

53. Senate, *An Examination of Foster Care*, 2.

54. Therolf, "Private Foster Care System."

55. Therolf, "Private Foster Care System"; *Los Angeles Daily News*, "Agency: Half of Foster Parents Criminals," March 30, 2010, updated August 28, 2017, www.dailynews.com/2010/03/30/agency-half-of-foster-parents-criminals/.

CHAPTER 10: CRIMINALIZING BLACK CHILDREN

1. Nicholas Bogel-Burroughs, Ellen Barry, and Will Wright, "Ma'Khia Bryant's Journey Through Foster Care Ended with an Officer's Bullet," *New York Times*, May 8, 2021, www.nytimes.com/2021/05/08/us/columbus-makhia-bryant-foster-care.html; Nicquel Terry Ellis, "The Foster Care System Is Failing Black

Children and the Death of Ma'Khia Bryant Is One Example, Experts and Attorney Say," CNN, May 5, 2021, www.cnn.com/2021/05/06/us/makhia-bryant-foster -care/index.html; Megan Conn and Michael Fitzgerald, "Police Killing of Foster Child Ma'Khia Bryant in Ohio Wrenches Youth, Allies," *The Imprint*, April 22, 2021, https://imprintnews.org/child-welfare-2/police-killing-foster-makhia -bryant-ohio-biden/53696; Mark Ferenchik and Holly Zachariah, "Ma'Khia Bryant Was Helpful and Kind, Her Friends and Family Say," *Columbus Dispatch*, April 24, 2021, www.dispatch.com/story/news/2021/04/24/makhia-bryant-killed -police-shooting-described-helpful-kind/7341250002/; Kevin Williams, Jack Healy, and Will Wright, "'A Horrendous Tragedy': The Chaotic Moments Before a Police Shooting in Columbus," *New York Times*, April 21, 2021, www.nytimes.com /2021/04/21/us/columbus-police-shooting-bryant.html.

2. Bogel-Burroughs, Barry, and Wright, "Ma'Khia Bryant's Journey"; Ellis, "The Foster Care System Is Failing Black Children."

3. Bogel-Burroughs, Barry, and Wright, "Ma'Khia Bryant's Journey"; Ellis, "The Foster Care System Is Failing Black Children."

4. Bogel-Burroughs, Barry, and Wright, "Ma'Khia Bryant's Journey"; Ellis, "The Foster Care System Is Failing Black Children."

5. Tera Eva Agyepong, *The Criminalization of Black Children: Race, Gender, and Delinquency in Chicago's Juvenile Justice System, 1899–1945* (Durham: University of North Carolina Press, 2018).

6. Harmke Leloux-Opmeer et al., "Characteristics of Children in Foster Care, Family-Style Group Care, and Residential Care: A Scoping Review," *Journal of Child and Family Studies* 25 (2016): 2358, www.ncbi.nlm.nih.gov/pmc/articles /PMC4933723/pdf/10826_2016_Article_418.pdf; Amy J. L. Baker and Patricio Calderon, "The Role of Group Homes in the Child Welfare Continuum of Care," *Residential Treatment for Children and Youth* 21, no. 4 (2004): 39–58; Annie E. Casey Foundation and Kids Count, *Every Kid Needs a Family* (Baltimore, MD: 2015), www.aecf.org/resources/every-kid-needs-a-family; Annie E. Casey Foundation, *Keeping Kids in Families: Trends in U.S. Foster Care Placement* (Baltimore, MD: 2019), www.aecf.org/resources/keeping-kids-in-families; National Conference of State Legislatures, *Congregate Care, Residential Treatment and Group Home State Legislative Enactments 2014–2019* (Denver, CO: 2020), www.ncsl.org/research/human -services/congregate-care-and-group-home-state-legislative-enactments.aspx.

7. Michael R. Pergamit and Michelle Ernst, *Running Away from Foster Care: Youths' Knowledge and Access of Services* (National Runaway Switchboard, 2011), 26, https://monarchhousing.org/wp-content/uploads/2011/08/runawayyouth.pdf; Sarah Fathallah and Sarah Sullivan, *Away from Home: Youth Experiences of Institutional Placements in Foster Care* (Think of Us, July 2021), 36, www.thinkof-us.org /awayfromhome.

8. Stacey Patton, "The Foster Care System and Others Failed Ma'Khia Bryant—and Black Kids Like Her," *The Grio*, April 23, 2021, https://thegrio.com /2021/04/23/makhia-bryant-foster-system-black-children/.

9. Patton, "The Foster Care System."

10. David Jackson and Duaa Eldeib, "Thousands of Foster Children Were Sent Out of State to Mental Health Facilities Where Some Faced Abuse and

Neglect," ProPublica and *Chicago Tribune*, March 11, 2020, www.propublica.org /article/illinois-dcfs-children-out-of-state-placements; Wendy Sawyer, "Youth Confinement: The Whole Pie 2019," press release, Prison Policy Initiative, December 19, 2019, www.prisonpolicy.org/reports/youth2019.html; Emily Wax-Thibodeaux, "'We Are Just Destroying These Kids': The Foster Children Growing Up Inside Detention Centers," *Washington Post*, December 30, 2019, www.washingtonpost.com/national/we-are-just-destroying-these-kids-the -foster-children-growing-up-inside-detention-centers/2019/12/30/97f65f3a -eaa2-11e9-9c6d-436a0df4f31d_story.html; Elissa Glucksman et al., *Unsafe and Uneducated: Indifference to Dangers in Pennsylvania's Residential Child Welfare Facilities* (Philadelphia: Children's Rights, Education Law Center, 2018), www .childrensrights.org/press-release/unsafe-and-uneducated-new-report-reveals -dangers-for-youth-in-pennsylvania-foster-care/.

11. Fathallah and Sullivan, *Away from Home*, 68–69.

12. Joaquin Palomino, Sara Tiano, and Cynthia Dizikes, "Far from Home, Far from Safety," *The Imprint*, December 11, 2020, https://imprintnews.org/child -welfare-2/california-ends-out-of-state-placements/50095; Jackson and Eldeib, "Thousands of Foster Children."

13. Fathallah and Sullivan, *Away from Home*, 9, 26–28; Complaint, H. G. and M. G. v. Carroll, Case 4:18-cv-00100-WS-CAS (N.D. Fla., February 20, 2018), www.childrensrights.org/wp-content/uploads/2018/02/2018.021-Complaint .pdf; Jackson and Eldeib, "Thousands of Foster Children."

14. Kyle Swenson, "Teens Tied Down and Shot Up with Drugs at Pembroke Pines Facility," *Miami New Times*, February 20, 2014, www.miaminewtimes.com /news/teens-tied-down-and-shot-up-with-drugs-at-pembroke-pines-facility -6394901.

15. Glucksman et al., *Unsafe and Uneducated*, 5, 7; Nancy Phillips and Chris Palmer, "Death, Rapes, and Broken Bones at Philly's Only Residential Treatment Center for Troubled Youth," *Philadelphia Inquirer*, April 22, 2017, www.inquirer .com/philly/news/pennsylvania/philadelphia/Death-rape-Philadelphia-Wordsworth -residential-treatment-center-troubled-youth.html; Alicia Victoria Lozano, "New Probe Launched into David Hess' Asphyxiation Death at Philadelphia Wordsworth Academy," NBC Philadelphia, June 11, 2019, www.nbcphiladelphia .com/news/local/new-investigation-david-hess-death-at-philadelphia -wordsworth-academy/186049/; City of Philadelphia, Youth Residential Place- ment Task Force, *Report and Recommendations* (Philadelphia: 2019), www.jdapa .info/uploads/YOUTH%20Residential%20Placement%20Task%20Force %202019%20Report%20and%20Recommendations.pdf.

16. Joaquin Palomino, Sarah Tiano, and Cynthia Dizikes, "Confronted over Abuse, California Is Bringing 116 Kids Home from Far-Away Pro- grams. Counties Are Scrambling," *The Imprint*, December 18, 2020, https:// imprintnews.org/child-welfare-2/counties-scrambling-california-races-bring -kids-home/50410; Joaquin Palomino and Sara Tiano, "California Bans Out-of- State Treatment Programs After Reporters Investigate Abuse," *The Imprint*, July 19, 2021, https://imprintnews.org/child-welfare-2/california-bans-out-of-state -treatment-programs/56995.

17. Children's Defense Fund, *The State of America's Children 2021* (Washington, DC: 2021), 66, www.childrensdefense.org/wp-content/uploads/2021/04 /The-State-of-Americas-Children-2021.pdf; Teresa Wiltz, "This New Federal Law Will Change Foster Care as We Know It," PEW Trusts, May 2, 2018, www.pewtrusts.org/en/research-and-analysis/blogs/stateline/2018/05/02/this -new-federal-law-will-change-foster-care-as-we-know-it; Kalena Thomave, "Family First Act Brings Major Changes One Year After Passage," Spotlight on Poverty and Opportunity, February 27, 2019, https://spotlightonpoverty. org/spotlight-exclusives/family-first-act-brings-major-changes-one-year -after-passage/; National Conference of State Legislatures, *Congregate Care*; John Kelley, "Latest Family First Tally: 39 States Taking Delay for Up to Two Years," *The Imprint*, October, 21, 2019, https://imprintnews.org/child-welfare-2 /latest-family-first-tally-39-states-taking-delay-for-up-to-two-years/38513.

18. Elyssa Cherney, "2 Teens in DCFS Care Were Shackled and Handcuffed During Drive from a Youth Shelter: 'Totally Unacceptable,' Agency Says," *Chicago Tribune*, November 8, 2019, www.chicagotribune.com/news/ct-teens-shackled -illinois-dcfs-20191108-u2fdwp52kre77h2x4mudygyeji-story.html.

19. Judy L. Thomas and Laura Bauer, "Throwaway Kids: 'We Are Sending More Foster Kids to Prison than College,'" *Kansas City Star*, December 15, 2019, www.kansascity.com/article238206754.html; Judy L. Thomas and Laura Bauer, "'The State That Neglected Me as a Kid Is the Same State That Wants to Kill Me,'" *Kansas City Star*, December 15, 2019, www.kansascity.com/news /special-reports/article238280638.html.

20. Youngmin Yi and Christopher Wildeman, "Can Foster Care Interventions Diminish Justice System Inequality?," *Future of Children* 28, no. 1 (2018): 39, https://files.eric.ed.gov/fulltext/EJ1179175.pdf; Mark E. Courtney et al., *Midwest Evaluation of the Adult Functioning of Former Foster Youth: Outcomes at Age 21* (Chicago, IL: Chapin Hall Center for Children at the University of Chicago, 2007), 9, www.chapinhall.org/wp-content/uploads/Midwest-Eval-Outcomes-at-Age-21 .pdf; Joseph J. Doyle Jr., "Child Protection and Adult Crime: Using Investigator Assignment to Estimate Causal Effects of Foster Care," *Journal of Political Economy* 116, no. 4 (2008): 749, www.journals.uchicago.edu/doi/pdf/10.1086/590216.

21. Juvenile Justice Geography, Policy, Practice and Statistics (JJGPS), *Systems Integration* (Reno, NV: National Council of Juvenile and Family Court Judges, Center for Juvenile Justice, 2016), www.jjgps.org/systems-integration; J. J. Cutuli et al., "From Foster Care to Juvenile Justice: Exploring Characteristics of Youth in Three Cities," *Children and Youth Services Review* 67 (2016): 84, https://doi .org/10.1016/j.childyouth.2016.06.001. Denise C. Herz et al., "Challenges Facing Crossover Youth: An Examination of Juvenile Justice Decision-Making and Recidivism," *Family Court Review* 48, no. 2 (2010), estimated that between 9 and 29 percent of youth involved with child protective services also become involved with the juvenile justice system. See also Massachusetts Juvenile Detention Alternatives Initiative, "Massachusetts Juvenile Detention Alternatives Initiative Dashboard, Statewide Overview: July–September 2015 Update" (Boston: Department of Youth Services, 2015), www.mass.gov/doc/quarter-3-2015-data -dashboard/download; Carly B. Dierkhising et al., "System Backgrounds, Psy-

chosocial Characteristics, and Service Access Among Dually Involved Youth: A Los Angeles Case Study," *Youth Violence and Juvenile Justice* 17, no. 3 (2019), https://doi.org/10.1177/1541204018790647.

22. Sherri Y. Simmons-Horton, "A Bad Combination: Lived Experiences of Youth Involved in the Foster Care and Juvenile Justice Systems," *Child and Adolescent Social Work Journal* (2020): 2, https://doi.org/10.1007/s10560-020-00693-1; Sherry Lachman, "The Opioid Plague's Youngest Victims: Children in Foster Care," *New York Times*, December 28, 2017, www.nytimes.com/2017/12/28/opinion/opioid-crisis-children-foster-care.html; Sara Goodkind et al., "From Child Welfare to Jail: Mediating Effects of Juvenile Justice Placement and Other System Involvement," *Child Maltreatment* 25, no. 4 (2020): 410–442, https://doi.org/10.1177/1077559520904144; Michael T. Baglivio et al., "Maltreatment, Child Welfare, and Recidivism in a Sample of Deep-End Crossover Youth," *Journal of Youth and Adolescence* 45, no. 4 (2016): 625–654, https://doi.org/10.1007/s10964-015-0407-9.

23. Simmons-Horton, "A Bad Combination," 2. See also Jennifer Yang, Evan C. McCuish, and Raymond Corrado, "Foster Care Beyond Placement: Offending Outcomes in Emerging Adulthood," *Journal of Criminal Justice* 53, no. 3 (2017): 46–54, https://doi.org/10.1016/j.jcrimjus.2017.08.009.

24. Dylan Conger and Timothy Ross, *Reducing the Foster Care Bias in Juvenile Detention Decisions: The Impact of Project Reform* (New York: Vera Institute of Justice, June 2001), 18, www.vera.org/downloads/Publications/reducing-the-foster-care-bias-in-juvenile-detention-decisions-the-impact-of-project-confirm/legacy_downloads/Foster_care_bias.pdf.

25. Rachel Anspach, "The Foster Care to Prison Pipeline: What It Is and How It Works," *Teen Vogue*, May 25, 2018, www.teenvogue.com/story/the-foster-care-to-prison-pipeline-what-it-is-and-how-it-works.

26. Courtney et al., *Midwest Evaluation*, 18–19; Mark E. Courtney and Andrew Zinn, "Predictors of Running Away from Out-of-Home Care," *Children and Youth Services Review* 31, no. 12 (2009): 1298–1306, https://doi.org/10.1016/j.childyouth.2009.06.003; Pergamit and Ernst, *Running Away from Foster Care*; Amy Dworsky, Fred Wulczyn, and Lilian Huang, "Predictors of Running Away from Out-of-Home Care: Does County Context Matter?," *Homelessness* 20 (2018): 101–116, www.jstor.org/stable/26524874; Natasha E. Latzman et al., "Human Trafficking Victimization Among Youth Who Run Away from Foster Care," *Children and Youth Services Review* 98 (2019): 113–124, https://doi.org/10.1016/j.childyouth.2018.12.022.

27. Pergamit and Ernst, *Running Away from Foster Care*, 25.

28. *Youth Today*, "Foster Care Tragedies Send States Scrambling," February 1, 2003, https://youthtoday.org/2003/02/foster-care-tragedies-send-states-scrambling/; Nicholas Forge et al., "Out of the System and Onto the Streets: LGBTQ-Identified Youth Experiencing Homelessness and Past Child Welfare Involvement," *Child Welfare* 96, no. 2 (2018): 47.

29. Latzman et al., "Human Trafficking Victimization," 114; D. A. Gibbs et al., *Report to Congress: The Child Welfare System Response to Sex Trafficking of Children* (Washington, DC: US Department of Health and Human Services,

Administration for Children and Families, 2018), www.acf.hhs.gov/sites/default
/files/documents/cb/report_congress_child_trafficking.pdf; Malika Saada Saar,
"Stopping the Foster Care to Child Trafficking Pipeline," *Huffington Post*, October 29, 2013, updated January 23, 2014, www.huffpost.com/entry/stopping
-the-foster-care-_b_4170483; Malika Saada Saar interviewed by Michel Martin, "Finding and Stopping Child Sex Trafficking," *Tell Me More from NPR News*,
August 1, 2013, www.npr.org/templates/story/story.php?storyId=207901614;
Office on Trafficking in Persons, "Fact Sheet: Human Trafficking," Administration for Children and Families, 2017, www.acf.hhs.gov/otip/fact-sheet/resource
/fshumantrafficking; Molly Smith and Juno Mac, *Revolting Prostitutes: The Fight for
Sex Worker's Rights* (New York: Verso Books, 2020).

30. Alexei Koseff, "Sex Trafficking Sting Highlights Vulnerability of Foster Care Children," *Los Angeles Times*, July 29, 2013, www.latimes.com/nation
/la-xpm-2013-jul-29-la-na-child-sex-20130730-story.html; Hilary Surratt and
Steven P. Kurtz, "Foster Care History and HIV Infection Among Drug-Using
African American Sex Workers," *AIDS and Behavior* 16, no. 4 (2012): 982, 986,
www.ncbi.nlm.nih.gov/pmc/articles/PMC3234336/.

31. David Jackson and Duaa Eldeib, "Youths Drawn into Prostitution While
Living at Residential Facilities," *Chicago Tribune*, December 8, 2014, www.chicago
tribune.com/investigations/ct-youth-treatment-prostitution-met-20141203
-story.html; Dawn Post, "Why Human Traffickers Prey on Foster-Care Kids,"
City Limits, January 23, 2015, https://citylimits.org/2015/01/23/why-traffickers
-prey-on-foster-care-kids/; Nikita Steward and Benjamin Weiser, "Troubled
Girls Were Sent to This Town to Heal. Many Were Lured into the Sex Trade
Instead," *New York Times*, December 13, 2018, www.nytimes.com/2018/12/13
/nyregion/sex-trafficking-hawthorne-cedar-knolls.html.

32. Gibbs et al., *Report to Congress*, 1–6; National Coalition for Child Protection
Reform, "The *Philadelphia Inquirer* Exposes Devereaux—and Devereaux Exposes
the Entire Residential Treatment Industry," *NCCPR Child Welfare Blog*, August 14,
2020, www.nccprblog.org/2020/08/the-philadelphia-inquirer-exposes.html.

33. Malika Saada Saar et al., *The Sexual Abuse to Prison Pipeline: The Girls'
Story* (Washington, DC: Human Rights Project for Girls, Georgetown Law Center on Poverty and Inequality, and Ms. Foundation for Women, 2015), 19, www
.law.georgetown.edu/academics/centers-institutes/poverty-inequality/; Isabella C.
Restrepo, "Pathologizing Latinas: Racialized Girlhood, Behavioral Diagnosis,
and California's Foster Care System," *Girlhood Studies* 12, no. 3 (Winter 2019): 9,
https://doi.org/10.3167/ghs.2019.120303.

34. "What Happened to You?: Talking Child and Family Trauma with Bruce
Perry," *The Imprint Weekly Podcast*, July 25, 2021, https://imprintnews.org/podcast
/child-family-trauma-bruce-perry?; Lundy Braun, *Breathing Race into the Machine:
The Surprising Career of the Spirometer from Plantation to Genetics* (Minneapolis: University of Minnesota Press, 2021).

35. Saada Saar et al., *The Sexual Abuse to Prison Pipeline*, 18, 24; Jerry Flores et
al., "Crossover Youth and Gender: What Are the Challenges of Girls Involved in
Both the Foster Care and Juvenile Justice Systems," *Children and Youth Services Review* 91, no. 3 (2018): 149–155, https://doi.org/10.1016/j.childyouth.2018.05.031;

Knowledge Brief, *Is There a Link Between Child Welfare and Disproportionate Minority Contact in Juvenile Justice?* (Chicago: Models for Change Research Initiative, 2011), 3, www.modelsforchange.net/publications/317.

36. Annie E. Casey Foundation, "What Are Status Offenses and Why Do They Matter?," April 6, 2019, www.aecf.org/blog/what-are-status-offenses-and -why-do-they-matter/; Patton, "The Foster Care System"; Michael Fitzgerald, "New York State Court Bars Child Welfare Systems from Pursuing Arrest Warrants for Runaway Foster Kids," *The Imprint*, May 8, 2019, https://imprintnews .org/child-welfare-2/new-york-state-court-bars-child-welfare-systems-from -pursuing-arrest-warrants-for-runaway-foster-kids/34913; Ali Watkins, "She Ran Away from Foster Care. She Ended Up in Handcuffs and Leg Irons," *New York Times*, December 6, 2018; Nina Shapiro, "Washington Handles Runaway Foster Kids with Handcuffs, Shackles and Jail. Is There a Better Way?," *Seattle Times*, February 17, 2019, updated October 25, 2019; Charlotte West, "When Running Away from Home Means Getting Locked Up," The Appeal, March 19, 2019, https:// theappeal.org/when-running-away-status-offenses-washington-state/.

37. Martin Guggenheim, Jessica Bryar Memorial Plenary Address, ABA Center on Children and the Law, July 20, 2021, video, www.youtube.com/watch ?v=v2V9CZ2I83Y; Council on Foster Care, Adoption, and Kinship Care and Committee on Early Childhood, American Academy of Pediatrics, "Health Care of Youth Aging Out of Foster Care," *Pediatrics* 130, no. 6 (2012): 1171, https:// pediatrics.aappublications.org/content/130/6/1170; Elizabeth Ahmaan, "Supporting Youth Aging Out of Foster Care," *Pediatric Nursing*, 43, no. 1 (2017): 43–48; Patrick J. Fowler et al., "Homelessness and Aging Out of Foster Care: A National Comparison of Child Welfare-Involved Adolescents," *Children and Youth Services Review* 77 (2017): 2–3, www.ncbi.nlm.nih.gov/pmc/articles/PMC5644395/pdf /nihms868116.pdf.

38. Adrienne L. Fernandes-Alcantara, *Youth Transitioning from Foster Care: Background and Federal Programs* (Washington, DC: Congressional Research Service, May 29, 2019), 3; Lindsay Schnell, "Foster Care Teen's Death Draws Scrutiny to Group Home Outbreaks: Who Is Looking Out for These Children?," *USA Today*, May 15, 2020, www.usatoday.com/story/news/nation/2020 /05/15/coronavirus-foster-care-death-draws-scrutiny-group-home-outbreaks /5196297002/.

39. Sara Tiano and Karen de Sá, "California Extended Foster Care to 21. Was It Enough?," *The Imprint*, June 14, 2020, https://imprintnews.org/foster-care /california-extended-foster-care-to-21-was-it-enough/44351; Courtney et al., *Midwest Evaluation*, 85; Elizabeth Amon, "California Approves First State-Guaranteed Income for Foster Youth," *The Imprint*, July 16, 2021, https://imprintnews.org /foster-care/california-approves-first-state-guaranteed-income-for-foster-youth /56957/.

40. Tiano and de Sá, "California Extended Foster Care to 21."

41. Noel Anaya, "After 20 Years, Young Man Leaves Foster Care on His Own Terms," *All Things Considered*, NPR, January 11, 2017, www.npr.org/2017 /01/11/508608745/after-20-years-young-man-leaves-foster-care-on-his-own -terms/.

42. Courtney, et al., *Midwest Evaluation*, 16–18; Fowler, "Homelessness and Aging Out of Foster Care," 36.

43. Courtney et al., *Midwest Evaluation*, 85–86.

44. Rachel P. Berger, Erin Dalton, and Kristine Campbell, "Understanding the Intergenerational Cycle of Child Protective Service Involvement," *Pediatrics* 141, no. 1 (2018); Lovie Foster, Blair Beadnell, and Peter J. Pecora, "Intergenerational Pathways Leading to Foster Care Placement of Foster Care Alumni's Children," *Child and Family Social Work* 72 (2015); Mark Echols, "Addressing Multi-Generational Dysfunction in Foster Care," *Huffington Post*, February 25, 2017, www.huffpost.com/entry/addressing-multigeneratio_b_9322696; Mikkel Mertz and Signe Hald Andersen, "The Hidden Cost of Foster-Care: New Evidence of Inter-generational Transmission of Foster-Care Experiences," *British Journal of Social Work* 47 (2017).

45. Emma Ketteringham, Sarah Cremer, and Caitlin Becker, "Healthy Mothers, Healthy Babies: A Reproductive Justice Response to the 'Womb-to-Foster-Care Pipeline,'" *CUNY Law Review* 20 (2016): 77–125, www.cunylawreview.org/wp-content/uploads/2017/03/04-Ketteringham.pdf; Tricia Stephens and Elizabeth M. Aparicio, "'It's Just Broken Branches': Child Welfare-Affected Mothers' Dual Experiences of Insecurity and Striving for Resilience in the Aftermath of Complex Trauma and Familial Substance Abuse," *Children and Youth Services Review* 73 (2017), 248–256, https://doi.org/10.1016/j.childyouth.2016.11.035.

46. Charles Blow, "Memories of the Tulsa Massacre," CBS News, May 30, 2021 (emphasis added), www.cbsnews.com/news/memories-of-the-1921-tulsa-massacre-charles-m-blow/.

CHAPTER 11: CARE IN PLACE OF TERROR

1. Megan Conn, "Pressure Builds to Reduce Racial Disproportionality in New York's Child Welfare System," *The Imprint*, January 19, 2021, https://imprintnews.org/child-welfare-2/new-york-calls-grow-address-racism-child-welfare/51073; *Rise Magazine*, "Black Families Matter: Parents Rally on MLK Day to Abolish ACS," January 21, 2021, www.risemagazine.org/2021/01/parents-rally-on-mlk-day-to-abolish-acs/.

2. Chris Gottlieb, "Black Families Are Outraged About Family Separation Within the U.S. It's Time to Listen to Them," *Time*, March 17, 2021, https://time.com/5946929/child-welfare-black-families/; Yasmeen Khan, "'It Is a Racist System': NYC Advocates, Lawmakers Demand Greater Oversight at Child Welfare Agency," *Gothamist*, September 30, 2019, https://gothamist.com/news/it-racist-system-nyc-advocates-lawmakers-demand-greater-oversight-child-welfare-agency.

3. Author's interview of Joyce McMillan, April 14, 2021. All quotes by McMillan in the chapter are from this interview unless otherwise attributed.

4. Home page of JMacForFamilies website, accessed July 6, 2021, www.jmacforfamilies.com/; David Tobis, *From Pariahs to Partners: How Parents and Their Allies Changed New York City's Child Welfare System* (New York: Oxford University Press, 2013).

5. Movement for Family Power, "Our Vision and Values," accessed July 6, 2021, www.movementforfamilypower.org/indexa; California Families Rise, "About Us," accessed August 25, 2021, https://californiafamiliesrise.com/about-us; UpEND, "About Us," accessed June 15, 2021, https://upendmovement.org/about/.

6. *Rise Magazine*, "About *Rise*," accessed July 11, 2021, www.risemagazine.org/about/; *Rise Magazine*, "Announcing *Rise*'s New Leadership: Co-Directors Jeanette Vega and Bianca Shaw," April 9, 2021, www.risemagazine.org/2021/04/announcing-rises-new-co-directors/; Think of Us, "About Think of Us," accessed August 25, 2021, www.thinkof-us.org/about/about-us; Tymber Hudson, "Meet Tymber," accessed August 7, 2021, https://thomashhudson.wordpress.com/about/; "upEnding the Child Welfare System: The Road to Abolition," remarks of Tymber Hudson, Center for the Study of Social Policy and University of Houston Graduate College of Social Work, October 20, 2020, video, 1:52:02 to 2:52:30, www.youtube.com/watch?v=xOcIMtYahUA.

7. Child Welfare Information Gateway, "Reform Based on Litigation," accessed July 11, 2021, www.childwelfare.gov/topics/management/reform/litigation/; Casey Family Programs, "Can You Share a Summary of Child Welfare Consent Decrees?," July 10, 2019, www.casey.org/consent-decree-summary/; Roxanna Asgarian, "Judge Holds Texas Child Welfare in Contempt . . . Again," *The Imprint*, September 4, 2020, https://imprintnews.org/foster-care/judge-holds-texas-child-welfare-in-contempt-again/47218.

8. Geo Maher, *A World Without Police: How Strong Communities Make Cops Obsolete* (New York: Verso Books, 2021), 74.

9. Mariame Kaba, *We Do This 'til We Free Us: Abolitionist Organizing and Transforming Justice* (Chicago: Haymarket Books, 2021), 2–25; Maher, *A World Without Police*, 71–96; Dylan Rodríguez, "Abolition as Praxis of Human Being: A Foreword," *Harvard Law Review* 132 (April 2019): 1601.

10. Emily Palmer, "Trial of 6-Year-Old's Killer Exposes Lapses in City's Child Welfare System," *New York Times*, January 15, 2020, www.nytimes.com/2020/01/15/nyregion/zymere-perkins-rysheim-smith-trial.html; Sarah Maslin Nir, "A Dozen Calls to Child Abuse Hotline Did Not Save 8-Year-Old Boy," *New York Times*, February 2, 2020, updated February 23, 2020, www.nytimes.com/2020/02/02/nyregion/nypd-cop-autistic-son.html; Ashley Southall, "A Young Father Was Investigated 4 Times. Then His Newborn Died," *New York Times*, February 7, 2020, www.nytimes.com/2020/02/07/nyregion/kaseem-watkins-murdered-father.html.

11. Palmer, "Trial of 6-Year-Old's Killer Exposes Lapses in City's Child Welfare System."

12. Juliet F. Gainsborough, "Scandals, Lawsuits, and Politics: Child Welfare Policy in the U.S. States," *State Politics and Policy Quarterly* 9, no. 3 (Fall 2009): 325–355; Richard Wexler, "Shrinking Size of Haystack Key to Preventing Child Abuse: Child Safety and Family Preservation Are Not Opposites," *CommonWealth*, November 28, 2020, https://commonwealthmagazine.org/opinion/shrinking-size-of-haystack-key-to-preventing-child-abuse/; Richard Wexler, *Foster Care Panics*, Issue Paper 2, National Coalition for Child Protection Reform, 2019; Tina Lee,

Catching a Case: Inequality and Fear in New York City's Child Welfare System (New York: Rutgers University Press, 2016), 54–55.

13. Palmer, "Trial of 6-Year-Old's Killer Exposes Lapses in City's Child Welfare System"; Southall, "A Young Father Was Investigated 4 Times. Then His Newborn Died."

14. Vivek Sankaran and Christopher Church, "Rethinking Foster Care: Why Our Current Approach to Child Welfare Has Failed," *SMU Law Review Forum* 73, no. 12 (April 2020): 123–139; Jane Burstain, *Child Abuse and Neglect Deaths in Texas*, Center for Public Policy Priorities, December 16, 2009, 7, http://library .cppp.org/files/4/427_Child_Deaths.pdf.

15. Areeba Haider, *The Basic Facts About Children in Poverty* (Washington, DC: Center for American Progress, January 12, 2021), 1–5, www.americanprogress .org/issues/poverty/reports/2021/01/12/494506/basic-facts-children-poverty/; Children's Defense Fund, "The State of America's Children 2021: Child Poverty," accessed September 2, 2021, www.childrensdefense.org/state-of-americas -children/soac-2021-child-poverty/; Jeff Madrick, *Invisible Americans: The Tragic Cost of Child Poverty* (New York: Alfred Knopf, 2020).

16. National Academies of Sciences, Engineering, and Medicine, *A Roadmap to Reducing Child Poverty*, ed. Greg Duncan and Suzanne Le Menestrel (Washington, DC: National Academies Press, 2019), ix, 3, 11, www.ncbi.nlm.nih.gov /books/NBK547361/.

17. Angela Y. Davis, *Abolition Democracy: Beyond Empire, Prisons, and Torture* (New York: Seven Stories Press, 2005), 73–74.

18. Kaba, *We Do This 'til We Free Us*, 2; Charlene Carruthers, *Unapologetic: A Black, Queer, and Feminist Mandate for Radical Movements* (Boston: Beacon Press, 2018), x; Alexander Lee, "Prickly Coalitions: Moving Prison Abolitionism Forward," in *Abolition Now! Ten Years of Strategy and Struggle Against the Prison Industrial Complex*, ed. CR10 Publications Collective (Chico, CA: AK Press, 2008), 111.; Robin D. G. Kelley, "What Abolition Looks Like, from the Panthers to the People," *Level*, October 26, 2020, https://level.medium.com/what -abolition-looks-like-from-the-panthers-to-the-people-6c2e537eac71.

19. Anna Arons, "An Unintended Abolition: Family Regulation During the COVID-19 Crisis," *Columbia Journal of Race and Law* (last revised June 25, 2021): 1, 10, https://ssrn.com/abstract=3815217; Kendra Hurley, "How the Pandemic Became an Unplanned Experiment in Abolishing the Child Welfare System," *New Republic*, August 18, 2021, https://newrepublic.com/article/163281 /pandemic-became-unplanned-experiment-abolishing-child-welfare-system; Eli Hager, "Is Child Abuse Really Rising During the Pandemic?," Marshall Project and *Daily Beast*, June 15, 2020, www.themarshallproject.org/2020/06/15 /is-child-abuse-really-rising-during-the-pandemic; Garret Therolf, Daniel Lempres, and Aksaule Alzhan, "They're Children at Risk of Abuse, and Their Caseworkers Are Stuck Home," *New York Times*, August 7, 2020, www.nytimes .com/2020/08/07/us/virus-child-abuse.html.

20. Arons, "An Unintended Abolition," 18.

21. Mutual aid groups sprang into action in other cities, as well as New York, to meet community needs during the COVID pandemic. See, e.g., Zoie

Matthew, "'Solidarity Not Charity': How L.A.'s 'Mutual Aid' Groups Are Creating Community During a Crisis," *Los Angeles Magazine*, April 3, 2020, www.lamag.com/citythinkblog/mutual-aid-covid/.

22. Arons, "An Unintended Abolition," 3.

23. Kaba, *We Do This 'til We Free Us*, 99.

24. Darlene Clark Hine, *Hine Sight: Black Women and the Re-Construction of American History*, (Brooklyn: Carlson Publishing, 1994), 109–128; Dorothy Salem, *To Better Our World: Black Women in Organizing Reform, 1890–1920* (Brooklyn: Carlson Publishing, 1990), 82–84; Dorothy E. Roberts, "Black Club Women and Child Welfare: Lessons for Modern Reform," *Florida State University Law Review* 32, no. 3 (2005), 957–972.

25. Mary Church Terrell, "The Duty of the National Association of Colored Women to the Race," *AME Church Review* (January 1900): 340, 353, reprinted in Beverly Washington Jones, *Quest for Equality: The Life and Writings of Mary Eliza Church Terrell, 1863–1954*, eds. Darlene Clark Hine et al. (Brooklyn: Carlson Publishing, 1990), 139, 149.

26. Alondra Nelson, *Body and Soul: The Black Panther Party and the Fight Against Medical Discrimination* (Minneapolis: University of Minnesota Press, 2011); Diane Pien, "Black Panther Party's Free Breakfast Program (1969–1980)," *Black Past*, February 11, 2010, www.blackpast.org/african-american-history/black-panther-partys-free-breakfast-program-1969-1980/; Cassandra Pintro, "How Chanel Porchia-Albert, Doula and Mother of Six, Is Advocating for Black Maternal Health," *Vogue*, June 18, 2021, www.vogue.com/article/ancient-song-doula-services.

27. Ryan Johnson, *Disrupt Disparities: Kinship Care in Crisis* (Washington, DC: AARP, 2021), https://aarp-states.brightspotcdn.com/80/58/66bd55214a8b9581fae55af253b6/disrupt-disparities-kinship-care-in-crisis-3-21.pdf; Patricia Hill Collins, *Black Feminist Thought: Knowledge, Consciousness, and the Politics of Empowerment* (Oxfordshire, UK: Rutledge 1991), 119–123; Robert Hill, *Informal Adoption Among Black Families* (Washington, DC: National Urban League, Research Department, 1977); Andrew Billingsley, *Climbing Jacob's Ladder: The Enduring Legacy of African-American Families* (New York: Simon and Schuster, 1992); Carol B. Stack, *All Our Kin* (New York: Basic Books, 1997); Elmer P. Martin and Joanne Mitchell Martin, *The Black Extended Family* (Chicago: University of Chicago Press, 1978); Rob Geen, "In the Interest of Children: Rethinking Federal and State Policies Affecting Kinship Care," *Policy and Practice of Human Services* 58, no. 1 (2000): 19, 21.

28. Heidi Redlich Epstein, "Kinship Care Is Better for Children and Families," *ABA Child Law Practice Today* 36, no. 4 (July/August 2017), www.grandfamilies.org/Portals/0/CLP%20full%20kinship%20edition%20-%20julyaug2017.pdf.

29. Dorothy Roberts, *Shattered Bonds: The Color of Child Welfare* (New York: Basic Civitas Books, 2001), 266.

30. Kaba, *We Do This 'til We Free Us*, 93–101; Dan Berger, Mariame Kaba, and David Stein, "What Abolitionists Do," *Jacobin*, August 24, 2017, www.jacobinmag.com/2017/08/prison-abolition-reform-mass-incarceration; Ruth Wilson Gilmore, *Golden Gulag: Prisons, Surplus, Crisis, and Opposition in Globalizing California*

(Berkeley: University of California Press, 2007), 242; Dorothy E. Roberts, "Foreword: Abolition Constitutionalism," *Harvard Law Review* 133, no. 1 (2019): 114–117, https://harvardlawreview.org/wp-content/uploads/2019/11/1-122_Online.pdf; Amna A. Akbar, "Demands for a Democratic Political Economy," *Harvard Law Review Forum* 134 (2020): 90–118, https://harvardlawreview.org/wp-content/uploads/2020/12/134-Harv.-L.-Rev.-F.-90.pdf.

31. Home page of JMacForFamilies website.

32. Vivek Sankaran, "With Child Welfare, Racism Is Hiding in the Discretion," *The Imprint*, June 21, 2020, https://imprintnews.org/child-welfare-2/with-child-welfare-racism-is-hiding-in-the-discretion/44616.

33. Kathleen Creamer, "Family Surveillance: A Future Without Foster Care," video remarks, University of Pennsylvania Carey Law School, February 18, 2021, www.youtube.com/watch?app=desktop&list=PLR5Q3wC5nyVlQtVsgjCPInPzsLUFEddX2&v=HjrDythN4bo&feature=youtu.be; John Kelly and Michael Fitzgerald, "New York's Parent Defender Model Lowers Reliance on Foster Care, Study Finds," *The Imprint*, May 6, 2019, https://imprintnews.org/child-welfare-2/in-new-york-parent-defender-model-means-less-days-in-foster-care/34832; Jaya Sundaresh, "New York Child Welfare Advocates Want Parents to Have Representation When Their Children Removed," *Youth Today*, June 5, 2019, https://youthtoday.org/2019/06/new-york-child-welfare-advocates-want-parents-to-have-representation-when-their-children-removed/.

34. Maher, *A World Without Police*, 94; Cynthia Godsoe and Steven Dean, "It's Time for An Antiracist Welfare Policy," *The Imprint*, March 15, 2021, https://imprintnews.org/child-welfare-2/time-for-an-antiracist-welfare-policy-america/52691; UpEND, *How We endUP: A Future Without Family Policing,* last updated June 18, 2021, 12, http://upendmovement.org/wp-content/uploads/2021/06/How-We-endUP-6.18.21.pdf. For studies demonstrating that antipoverty policies reduce child maltreatment, see Lawrence M. Berger et al., "Income and Child Maltreatment in Unmarried Families: Evidence from the Earned Income Tax Credit," *Review of Economics of the Household* 15, no. 4 (2017): 1345–1372; Maria Cancian, Mi-Young Yang, and Kristen Shook Slack, "The Effect of Additional Child Support Income on the Risk of Child Maltreatment," *Social Science Review*, 87, no. 3 (2012): 417–438; Kerri Raissian and Lindsey Bullinger, "Money Matters: Does the Minimum Wage Affect Child Maltreatment Rates?," *Child and Youth Services Review* 70 (2017): 60–70; Mi-Young Yang et al., "Child Care Subsidy and Child Maltreatment," *Child and Family Social Work* 24, no. 4 (2019): 547–554.

35. Angela Olivia Burton and Angeline Montauban, "Toward Community Control of Child Welfare Funding: Repeal the Child Abuse Prevention and Treatment Act and Delink Child Protection from Family Well-Being," *Columbia Journal of Race and Law* 11, no. 3: 639–680 (2021), https://doi.org/10.52214/cjrl.v11i3.8747; Miriam Mack, "The White Supremacy Hydra: How the Family First Prevention Services Act Reifies Pathology, Control, and Punishment in the Family Regulation System," *Columbia Journal of Race and Law* 11, no. 3: 767–810 (2021), https://doi.org/10.52214/cjrl.v11i3.8751.

36. Thomas Kaplan and Jason DeParle, "Tax Credits for Children, $1,400 Direct Payments and More. Here's What's Included in the Stimulus Plan," *New York Times*, March 8, 2021, www.nytimes.com/live/2021/03/08/us/joe-biden -news/tax-credits-for-children-1400-direct-payments-and-more-heres-whats -included-in-the-stimulus-plan; Kendra Hurley, "The American Rescue Plan Provides a Blueprint for Keeping Kids Safe and Reducing Reliance on the Foster Care System," *Early Learning Nation*, April 13, 2021, http://earlylearningnation .com/2021/04/the-american-rescue-plan-provides-a-blueprint-for-keeping -kids-safe-and-reducing-reliance-on-the-foster-care-system/; H. Luke Shae-fer and Kathryn J. Edin, "A Simple Approach to Ending Extreme Poverty," *The Atlantic*, May 2, 2021, www.theatlantic.com/magazine/archive/2021/06/how-to -end-extreme-child-poverty/618720/.

37. Dean Spade, *Mutual Aid: Building Solidarity During This Crisis (And the Next)* (New York: Verso Books, 2020), 1–8; Tierney Sheree Peprah, *Fostering False Identity: The Child Welfare System's Design of Social Control of the Black Family* (independently published, 2021), 218–224.

38. Author's interview of Carolyn Hill and Phoebe Jones, DHS Give Us Back Our Children, June 3, 2021; Every Mother Is a Working Mother Network, "Philly DHS/DCFS: Give Us Back Our Children!," accessed July 11, 2021, www.everymothernetwork.net/philly/; Welfare Warriors, "Our Mission," accessed July 11, 2021, www.welfarewarriors.org/mission.htm.

39. Tracy Serdjenian and Nora McCarthy, *Rise Insights: Someone to Turn To: A Vision for Creating Networks of Parent Peer Care* (New York: *Rise Magazine*, 2021), 5, www.risemagazine.org/wp-content/uploads/2021/05/Rise_PeerCareInsights 2021_Final.pdf; Jeanette Vega and Bianca Shaw, "Expand Support for Families, but Not Inside the Child Welfare System," *The Imprint*, June 4, 2021, https:// imprintnews.org/opinion/expand-support-for-families-but-not-inside-the-child -welfare-system/55650; Hurley, "How the Pandemic Became an Unplanned Experiment in Abolishing the Child Welfare System."

40. Philadelphia Housing Action, "Release: Philadelphia Housing Action Claims Victory After 6 Month Direct Action Campaign Forces City to Relinquish 50 Vacant Homes to Community Land Trust," September 26, 2020, https://philadelphiahousingaction.info/release-philadelphia-housing-action -claims-victory-after-6-month-direct-action-campaign-forces-city-to-relinquish -50-vacant-homes-to-community-land-trust/; Ximena Conde, "Philly Encampment Organizers Say They've Reached a Tentative Deal with the City," WHYY, September 27, 2020, https://whyy.org/articles/philly-is-open-to-giving-50 -homes-to-encampment-protesters/.

41. Pintro, "How Chanel Porchia-Albert, Doula and Mother of Six, Is Advocating for Black Maternal Health"; Loretta J. Ross and Rickie Solinger, *Reproductive Justice: An Introduction* (Berkeley: University of California Press, 2017), 9; Julia Oparah and Alicia Bonaparte, *Birthing Justice: Black Women, Pregnancy, and Childbirth* (New York: Routledge, 2016); Asteir Bey et al., *Advancing Birth Justice: Community-Based Doula Models as a Standard of Care for Ending Racial Disparities* (Ancient Song Doula Services, Village Birth International, Every Mother Counts,

2019), https://blackmamasmatter.org/wp-content/uploads/2019/03/Advancing -Birth-Justice-CBD-Models-as-Std-of-Care-3-25-19.pdf.

42. Kaba, *We Do This 'til We Free Us*, 59–60; Isabel Cristo, "Policing Doesn't Protect Women," *New Republic*, July 6, 2020, https://newrepublic.com/article /158365/policing-doesnt-protect-women; Aishah Shahidah Simmons, ed., *Love with Accountability: Digging Up the Roots of Child Sexual Abuse* (Chico, CA: AK Press, 2019); Ejeris Dixon and Leah Lakshmi Piepzna-Samarasinha, eds., *Beyond Survival: Strategies and Stories from the Transformative Justice Movement* (Chico, CA: AK Press, 2020); generationFIVE, *Ending Child Sexual Abuse: A Transformative Justice Handbook* (2017), www.generationfive.org/wp-content/uploads/2017/06 /Transformative-Justice-Handbook.pdf.

43. Elena Gormley et al., *Alternatives to Calling DCFS* (Shriver Center on Poverty Law, December 2020), www.povertylaw.org/wp-content/uploads/2020 /12/Before-you-call-DCFS_FINAL-2.pdf.

44. Elize Manoukian, Ellen Moynihan, and Dave Goldiner, "Black Parents March to Demand Racial Justice in NYC Child-Welfare System," *New York Daily News*, June 20, 2020, www.nydailynews.com/news/politics/ny -protest-black-lives-matter-20200620-sqiyn27g45fn7jyuynwrmyd7la-story .html; "To Los Angeles County Board of Supervisors: #ReimagineChildSafety: Get Cops Out of Child Protective Services," Campaign by Chris Martin, accessed July 11, 2021, https://campaigns.organizefor.org/petitions/reimaginechildsafety-get -cops-out-of-child-protective-services.

Index

DOROTHY ROBERTS is the George A. Weiss University Professor of Law and Sociology and the Raymond Pace & Sadie Tanner Mossell Alexander Professor of Civil Rights at the University of Pennsylvania, where she directs the Penn Program on Race, Science, and Society. The author of four books, including *Killing the Black Body*, she lives in Philadelphia, Pennsylvania.